Good Vibrations

TRACKING POP

SERIES EDITORS: JOCELYN NEAL, JOHN COVACH, AND ALBIN ZAK

Listening to Popular Music: Or, How I Learned to Stop Worrying
and Love Led Zeppelin
by Theodore Gracyk

Sounding Out Pop: Analytical Essays in Popular Music
edited by Mark Spicer and John Covach

I Don't Sound Like Nobody: Remaking Music in 1950s America
by Albin J. Zak III

Soul Music: Tracking the Spiritual Roots of Pop from Plato
to Motown
by Joel Rudinow

Are We Not New Wave? Modern Pop at the Turn of the 1980s
by Theo Cateforis

Bytes and Backbeats: Repurposing Music in the Digital Age
by Steve Savage

Powerful Voices: The Musical and Social World of Collegiate A Cappella
by Joshua S. Duchan

Rhymin' and Stealin': Musical Borrowing in Hip-Hop
by Justin A. Williams

Sounds of the Underground: A Cultural, Political and Aesthetic
Mapping of Underground and Fringe Music
by Stephen Graham

Krautrock: German Music in the Seventies
by Ulrich Adelt

Good Vibrations: Brian Wilson and the Beach Boys in
Critical Perspective
edited by Philip Lambert

Good Vibrations

Brian Wilson and the Beach Boys in Critical Perspective

Edited by
Philip Lambert

University of Michigan Press • *Ann Arbor*

Published in the United States of America by
The University of Michigan Press
Manufactured in the United States of America
⊗ Printed on acid-free paper

2019   2018   2017   2016   4   3   2   1

A CIP catalog record for this book is available from the British Library.

ISBN 978-0-472-11995-0 (hardcover : alk. paper)

ISBN 978-0-472-12227-1 (e-book)

Preface

IN 2012, to celebrate fifty years since their music first hit
the airwaves, the surviving members of the Beach Boys set aside decades
of litigious acrimony and reunited for a months-long international tour
and the group's first album of all-new material in twenty years. Huge
crowds danced and cheered, oblivious to a sea of incongruities: septua-
genarians calling themselves "Boys," song lyrics seemingly aimed at the
sensibilities of their grandchildren, and striking differences between the
youthful voices on their familiar hit records and the more mature vocal-
isms of creative mastermind Brian Wilson, his cousin, lead singer Mike
Love, and lifelong friend Al Jardine. But the shows were a success for the
same reason that the band has always been a concert draw: soaring vocal harmonies, infectious themes capturing the pristine innocence of an
idealized era, and a danceable blend of classic rock 'n' roll with elements
of doo-wop and jazz. In seventeen top-ten singles and thirteen hit albums
of the group's first four years, and seventeen more albums of new music
in the ensuing decades, the Beach Boys amassed a repertory that would
still be influencing the shape of popular music generations later, from
the 1990s indie collective Elephant 6 to millennial alternative rock bands
such as Animal Collective and Fleet Foxes. Other fiftieth anniversaries
soon followed: Brian Wilson's first number-one single as coauthor (Jan
and Dean's "Surf City," which topped the *Billboard* Hot 100 in July 1963);
the Beach Boys' first number-one single ("I Get Around," July 1964); the
Beach Boys' first number-one album and first gold album (*Beach Boys'
Concert*, in the top spot in December 1964, certified gold in February
1965); the pinnacles of Brian Wilson's artistic ambitions, in album format (*Pet Sounds*, released in May 1966), in 45 rpm ("Good Vibrations,"
number one and gold in December 1966), and in rock mythology (the
unfinished *Smile*, 1966–67).

The history of the Beach Boys began as an apt reflection of their times. Their sun-soaked pop songs of the early sixties were just catchy and distinctive enough to share airtime with the British invaders. Later in the decade, influenced in part by a friendly rivalry with the Beatles, they evolved toward more ambitious album projects and immersion in the drug culture. Then, as Brian Wilson withdrew as exclusive leader, the band flirted with variable absorptions in pop styles of the seventies and eighties, all while releasing chart-topping greatest hits albums and continuing to thrive as a touring band. Since the late eighties, when Brian Wilson began to record as a solo artist, the band has been splintered but never out of the public eye. What has stayed constant throughout this half-century is a core belief in the warmth and immediacy of blended vocal harmony and in the myth of the California lifestyle, rich with possibility and opportunity. The Beach Boys can still sing about it because, in their lyrics at least, they still believe in it.

Good Vibrations: Brian Wilson and the Beach Boys in Critical Perspective helps mark a milestone in this history by exploring the band's legacy and place in American culture. The book brings together scholars of diverse specialties, hailing from four countries over three continents. The essays gathered here take on the full fifty-year range of the Beach Boys' music, from the perspectives of music historians, music theorists, and cultural critics. Together these new scholarly examinations will refresh our understanding of some of the familiar tropes in the group's history, including the Beach Boys' musical contributions to 1960s culture and the California myth; the style of their music, indebted in variable proportions to pop and rock traditions; and the legend of *Smile*, one of popular music's most notorious unfinished albums. The book places special focus on the individual whose creative vision brought the whole enterprise to life, Brian Wilson, without minimizing contributions made by others, such as frequent lyricist Mike Love. This focus helps to advance our understanding of Brian Wilson's gifts, first displayed in well-crafted songs of the early Beach Boys albums, equally evident in the group's multipart vocal arrangements, and eventually expanding to include innovations in the recording studio.

Fifty years of biographies and rock criticism have elevated Brian Wilson to his rightful place in the pantheon of American record-makers. After early spurts of revelatory journalism by the likes of Jules Siegel ("The Religious Conversion of Brian Wilson: Goodbye Surfing, Hello God," *Cheetah*, October 1967) and Tom Nolan ("The Beach Boys: A California Saga," *Rolling Stone*, October 28 and November 11, 1971), serious commentary on the Beach Boys and their creative leader began in 1978 with

David Leaf's *The Beach Boys and the California Myth* (New York: Grosset and Dunlap). In 1994, Timothy White's *The Nearest Faraway Place* gave the group a deeper historical context (New York: Henry Holt), and in 2006, Peter Ames Carlin's biography *Catch a Wave* sharpened the focus on Brian Wilson and his personal triumphs and struggles (Emmaus, Penn.: Rodale). Other authors have offered richer accounts of watershed moments in Brian Wilson's creative evolution, notably Charles L. Granata's *Wouldn't It Be Nice* of 2003, a study of the circumstances surrounding the making of *Pet Sounds* (Chicago: Chicago Review Press), and Domenic Priore's investigation of the *Smile* story in 2005 (London: Sanctuary). Serious scrutiny of music and lyrics began with Daniel Harrison's essay "After Sundown" in 1997 (in *Understanding Rock*, ed. Covach and Boone, New York: Oxford University Press) and continued with my book *Inside the Music of Brian Wilson* in 2007 (New York: Continuum) and Kirk Curnutt's *Brian Wilson* in 2012 (Bristol, Conn.: Equinox).

These latter three authors begin the collection of essays presented here. First, Kirk Curnutt explores the various critical responses to Beach Boys songs, in light of common perceptions of Brian Wilson and his authorial sensibilities. Curnutt lends a rich, personal perspective to the entire corpus of Brian Wilson's work to date, offering valuable insights into the nature of celebrity and the limitations of biography. Daniel Harrison then focuses very specifically on an element of Beach Boys songs that many admirers probably haven't thought much about: extramusical enhancements provided by scene-setting spoken words or sound effects. Readers of Harrison's essay will find serious, enlightening discussion of cuts from Beach Boys albums that don't usually attract much attention, such as "Drive-In" (from *All Summer Long*, 1964) and "Bull Session with 'Big Daddy'" (*The Beach Boys Today!*, 1965). Concluding the opening trio of musical commentaries, my essay about the harmony of Brian Wilson songs highlights favorite chords and progressions in music spanning the songwriter's entire career, encompassing Beach Boys albums, solo work, and collaborations with other artists. It demonstrates one way of probing a basic question: What makes a Brian Wilson song sound like a Brian Wilson song?

The middle portion of the book is a quartet of essays focused on particular moments in Beach Boys history. Keir Keightley first brings us out of the formative years of rock 'n' roll and into the early 1960s, examining the Beach Boys as contributors to, and definers of, a new culture of popular music. Bringing special focus to the Beach Boys' *All Summer Long* album (1964), Keightley situates the group within American society and the changing face of popular music in a pivotal decade. Jadey O'Regan then surveys trends and developments in nine of the early Beach Boys albums, bringing the historical focus up to 1966 and *Pet Sounds*. O'Regan provides rich detail for the evolution of the group's song forms, lyrical themes, and vocal styles during this crucial time period. After that, Dale Carter takes us into the volatile politics and drug culture of the decade's middle years, offering a thoughtful perspective on an influential cultural milieu. Carter's synthesis lends valuable context to what are Brian Wilson's most ambitious musical aspirations in album format—the thoughtful craftsmanship and studio innovations of *Pet Sounds* (1966) and *Smile* (1967). My essay that follows then explores his most important achievement in the genre of the hit single: "Good Vibrations" (1966). I focus especially on the song's evolution after its initial release: how it changed in live performance, and how it has been reimagined by countless cover artists in the fifty-odd years since its first release.

The book concludes with a duet of essays about one of pop-rock's most infamous musical sagas: the *Smile* project, filled with artistic promise but tragically abandoned in 1967, only to be rejuvenated by the Brian Wilson Band in 2004. Andrew Flory first considers what happened to the *Smile* tapes—and to the *Smile* myth—in the decades since Brian Wilson walked away from them. Flory asks thoughtful questions about the nature of an amorphous masterpiece, and about the role of ardent fans in shaping the music's legacy. Finally, Larry Starr reflects on the entirety of the *Smile* legend, from initial recording sessions through occasional releases of *Smile* material on subsequent Beach Boys albums, up to the 2004 "premiere." Starr's personal response to a compelling, convoluted tale enriches the experience of the music for all of us.

What next for Brian Wilson and the Beach Boys? Brian was back on tour with his band in 2013, double-billed with Jeff Beck and sharing the stage with Al Jardine and onetime Beach Boy David Marks. In 2015, he released a new solo album (*No Pier Pressure*). Mike Love and Bruce Johnston continued playing state fairs and casinos as the "Beach Boys." Longtime fans danced along, a little more slowly than they once did, while new generations of audiences had first encounters with the effervescence of a jazzy vocal harmony, the exuberance of a falsetto wail. After a half-century, the good vibrations were still resonating.

Note: Source references for all of the essays are listed together at the end of the book.

Contents

PART 1 | Musical Commentaries

ONE | "Brian Comes Alive"

Celebrity, Performance, and the
Limitations of Biography in Lyric Reading

KIRK CURNUTT

IN 1976, the summer I was eleven, two things were prevalent on my suburban Michigan street: pot and Peter Frampton. I par-
took of neither. My squeaky-clean coming of age never resembled the
recreational stoner culture nostalgically celebrated in such 1990s films
as Richard Linklater's *Dazed and Confused,* James Melkonian's *The Stoned
Age,* and Adam Rifkin's *Detroit Rock City.* Instead, my idea of adolescent
adventure involved riding my ten-speed bike around the neighborhood with a Panasonic tape recorder belted to the handlebars in hopes
of impressing girls known to wear lip gloss and satin shorts. As for the
guitar wiz famous for his squawking "talk box" effects pedal, Frampton
did nothing but salt my impatience. Shortly to be named "Album of
the Year," the double LP *Frampton Comes Alive!* annoyed me not simply
because it was ubiquitous, pouring out of every open window. Clocking
in at seventy-eight minutes, it also felt damned interminable—as endless as the drought that withered our green lawns to a crackling dead
brown. At the time I considered myself a connoisseur of bubblegum
music. I liked my songs done and gone in 2'20" or less, which was why
even Wings' frothy "Silly Love Songs," at a whopping 5'53" on the 45
rpm, pressed its luck. For going on two years my favorite album (another double platter) had been the Beach Boys' *Endless Summer.* Exactly
one song on that album broke the three-minute barrier, and the majority landed closer to two, so each of the twenty cuts felt like an intense

3

flash as opposed to a long, drawn-out endurance test. Be it silly joy or pristine sorrow, the emotion in those songs packed such a sonic flare I couldn't imagine them lasting a second longer than they did. Their bliss would have incinerated me.

Of the many *Frampton Comes Alive!* devotees I knew that summer, I really only remember one. His name was Jerry, he had just graduated high school, and he was forever offering me the mouthpiece of what looked like a glass hookah bubbling with aromatic smoke. When we were not shooting baskets we hung out in his parents' basement with several other kids of mixed ages, arguing over music. I was rather alone in my position that the Hues Corporation was better than Led Zeppelin. As my ardent advocacy of Hamilton, Joe Frank, and Reynolds and the Andrea True Connection excited guffaws, I would sneer at the leaden, joyless cock rock of Bad Company and Nazareth. Then, one night that August, somewhere around minute 11 of "Do You Feel Like We Do" on side 4 of *Comes Alive!*, I played my trump card and explained why *Endless Summer* elevated me to such a state of ecstasy: "It's fun," I philosophized. "The Beach Boys—they're fun."

Jerry's succinct reply was, "They're not fun—they're weird." And to prove it, he pointed to a stack of *People Weekly* magazines topped by a cover photo of the band, then in the thick of their ursine bearded years. As the rest of the basement imitated ad infinitum the strangely distorted *Do you feel . . . do you feels* of their cherubic, curly-headed guitar hero's voice, I pulled up a beanbag chair and devoured an article whose headline declared BRIAN WILSON'S BACK FROM HIS CRACK-UP.

And I never experienced Beach Boys music the same way again.

As silly or melodramatic as it sounds to credit *People Weekly* with altering my personal relationship to art, the blame lay not so much with the periodical as with the type of discourse the article represented. The catalyst for my shift could have easily been *Rolling Stone*'s November 4 cover story ("The Healing of Brother Brian"), or the contemporaneous coverage in *Newsweek*, *Creem*, or *Oui*, among countless others. It could have even been the August 5, 1976, NBC-TV special produced by *Saturday Night Live*'s Lorne Michaels that famously featured Brian dragged to the ocean and forced to surf by comedians Dan Akroyd and John Belushi.[1] As Beach Boys fans well know, the talking points of that summer's poignantly premature "Brian is back" campaign were pretty much the same no matter what the venue. As *People* told it, "Big Brother Brian Wilson, formative genius of the group," had suffered an "imaginative flipout" after writing and producing some of the 1960s' most essential pop music, becoming a rock-'n'-roll hermit by "spend[ing] three and a half years in bed" (*sic*). Now, "after an absence of 11 harrowing years, the sensitive, withdrawn oldest brother" was sufficiently "on his way to recovery" to "ventur[e] out again" into music-making, albeit with the demeanor of "an amiable child . . . trying to relearn the simple social graces" ("The Beach Boys Hang 15" 1976, 33–34).

As I would later learn, with minor variations in details, the storyline of this "flipout" dated back even further, to Jules Siegel's classic 1967 essay "Goodbye Surfing, Hello God!," the definitive chronicle of the conception and abandonment of the doomed *Smile* album. The basic outline would be reiterated as well for upwards of forty years, as Brian Wilson embarked on a series of consecutive comebacks in 1988, 1995, 1998, 1999–2000, 2004, and all the way up to 2012's fiftieth anniversary reunion tour with surviving members of the Beach Boys.

Before that issue of *People*, I neither knew nor cared about Brian's life. His music was simply available for my appropriation, and whether "Surfin' USA," "I Get Around," or my favorite recent song in 1976, "It's OK," I used it to channel my own feelings, desires, and fantasies. As my fandom grew and steepened, however, the story of Brian Wilson began to dominate my appreciation of his songbook. My reading about the Beach Boys taught me that their music was the expression of a deeply troubled, tragic figure, and I began to believe that the significance of the songs was tied exclusively to their creator's personality, or what in literary studies goes by the somewhat discredited term "sensibility." Two years later in 1978, after reading the first full-length book devoted to the Brian Wilson story—David Leaf's *The Beach Boys and the California Myth*—I was even conditioned to assume that the importance of a particular track or album was measurable by the degree to which it allowed me to understand the man. To put it another way, Brian's best music was his most personal music, the songs in which he grappled with his traumas and poured out his feelings. I might identify with that personality and perhaps even define myself through it to some degree, but my primary task as a listener was to interpret Brian Wilson, not myself.

This shift in my consumption aesthetic marked my immersion in a popular culture in which celebrities—whether rock stars, movie stars, sports heroes, or those merely famous for being famous—are as much commodities as their art. As Ellis Cashmore writes, "Instead of just being devices for marketing films, music, or the consumer products they endorse . . . celebrities have become products themselves. They are now commodities in the sense that they've become articles of trade that can be bought and sold in the marketplace. Obviously, you can't buy *them*, but you can buy their representations, the sounds and the products with which they're associated" (Cashmore 2006, 3). What fans specifically pay for is the illusion of "presence," a sense of familiarity or even intimacy with a performer that fulfills individual needs and aims that can be as varied as human desire itself. Some celebrities function as "articles of trade" by embodying standards of glamor or rebellion that we emulate. Others serve as ambassadors of authenticity by helping us define norms of what we consider real or genuine. Still others represent the savvy craft of bricolage, the determined appropriation if not outright subversion of received marketplace meanings that allows us to imagine ourselves as proactive instead of passive consumers.

Whatever particular moral or value celebrities may emblematize, the discourse that inculcates us in their meanings is extratextual, a supplement to their actual art. As an interpretive tool, this discourse may take the form of standard biographies such as Leaf's aforementioned volume, or they may be personal appreciations that celebrate a corpus's contribution to the development of a genre or medium, such as Jim Fusilli's 2005 tribute to *Pet Sounds* or Mark Dillon's *Fifty Sides of the Beach Boys* (2012). To date, Beach Boys completists have nearly three dozen volumes crowding their bookshelves, and despite their diversity, these texts all reinforce certain narrative plot points that are key to constructing Brian's sensibility: his abusive upbringing at the hands of father Murry Wilson; his decision after his December 1964 nervous breakdown not to tour with his band but to immerse himself in the recording studio; his reported battles with bandmate Mike Love over the increasingly avant-garde direction of Beach Boys' music in the *Pet Sounds / Smile* era; his withdrawal after shelving *Smile* and the onset of mental illness and drug abuse that for decades rendered him "the Orson Welles of rock" (his "crack-up" or "imaginative flipout"); the numerous efforts on the part of record companies, managers, and handlers to return him, Humpty Dumpty–like, to the productivity of his peak 1962–67 years; his troubling exploitation at the hands of psychologist Dr. Eugene E. Landy in the 1980s and early 1990s; and his return to steady recording and touring since the mid-1990s, despite minor brain damage and a schizoaffective disorder that causes him to suffer auditory hallucinations. Brianistas can recite these narrative threads as easily as they can recite personal data, for the story lines are reiterated incessantly to create the image of the Beach Boys' founder as a rock-'n'-roll Icarus, an innate musical talent who flew too close to the sun and has been trying to take renewed flight ever since his precipitous plunge.

As influential as biographies and full-length critical appreciations are, however, they are by no means the only extratextual sources for shaping perceptions of Brian Wilson's sensibility. Because they are cast in the durable form of books, major retellings of the Beach Boys' story tend to overshadow more transitory if not disposable media such as periodicals and newspapers. Reviews are the most obvious site of sensibility articulation, for they are as definitional as they are evaluative—they not only tell us whether a particular song or album is "good" but contribute to the construction of the artist's public image. Interviews are another popular medium that allow the performer to speak with a minimum of editorial intrusion. A less celebrated journalistic form that arguably provides more immediate information for the consumption of celebrities is the personality profile. This narrative genre dates back to the late nineteenth century, as the press fed the public appetite for human interest by publishing biographies that in miniature accounted for accomplished men's success in business, politics, and civic leadership (Ponce de Leon 2002, 51–57). By the 1920s, with the emergence of movies as popular entertainment, profiles stoked consumer curiosity about whether actors and actresses bore any resemblance in their private life to the public images they projected on the screen—thus the profusion of "stars at home" stories in which the likes of Douglas Fairbanks or Gloria Swanson invited fans to view them "off camera" to ensure their audience they were not manipulating silver-screen magic to deceive (Shield 2013, 18).

By the mid-1960s, when rock-music reporting emerged as a distinct journalistic niche thanks to *Crawdaddy!*, *Rolling Stone*, *Creem*, and other magazines, the personality profile helped validate the music's aspirations to be recognized as more than just popular entertainment—to be revered as Art with a capital A, in other words. Profiles allowed music reporters to disseminate the values that rock music was supposed to embody, from transgression to innovation to the high seriousness of aesthetic and sociopolitical intent (Keightley 2001, 109). Siegel's "Goodbye Surfing, Hello God!" is a perfect example of the institutionalization of these ideals. Although not the first to tout Brian Wilson as a musical "genius"—that honor belongs to the numerous articles either written or commissioned by publicist Derek Taylor in 1966—it was certainly the most instrumental in establishing the image of Brian as mercurial in the broader senses of that term: as an eccentric and erratic artist perilously pursuing the muse instead of blithely serving the masses. In *Brian Wilson,* my 2012 contribution to Equinox Publishing's Icons of Pop Music series, I argue that this "genius" narrative defining Brian reflects rock criticism's investment in auteur theory, the school of criticism that locates meaning in personal vision. What I did not explore there is how personality profiles remain eminently suitable for instilling this aesthetic in readers for a simple reason: the founding idea of auteurship is the singularity of sensibility, the insistence that the greatest voices are the most unique.[2] As a result, this particular genre of celebrity discourse and the content of auteur criticism function in perfect alignment, for both foreground the centrality of personality, emphasizing it as the primary interpretive context for understanding the music.

As an adult, I can look back to my adolescence and recognize how the fan devotion to Brian Wilson I expressed by reading and collecting personality-oriented discourse narrowed my overall listening tastes. Simply put, once initiated in Brian's story, I found myself drawn to artists celebrated as auteurs. What I lost in the Banana Splits and the Bay City Rollers I gained in Bob Dylan, John Lennon, Pete Townshend, and others defined by their sensibility. Only in recent years have I begun to appreciate what a wealth of music I missed out on enjoying. Well into my middle age I was geared toward contempt for disco, country, and pop stars who did not write their own songs, and even one-hit wonders who lacked the charisma to maintain a career. Peter Frampton is a good example of my indifference for performers who did not meet auteur criteria. I could recite factoids I knew about him—the disastrous *Sgt. Pepper's Lonely Hearts Club Band* movie in 1978 costarring the Bee Gees, something about a career-careening automobile wreck in the late 1970s, his fall into "has been" status, the self-deprecatingly good humor of his recent Geico auto insurance commercial, where he pokes fun at his "talk box" guitar celebrity—but nothing of substance. I could not begin to explain why *Frampton Comes Alive!* caught the public fancy in 1976; egregiously, I presumed the question was not important enough to ponder.[3]

More importantly, I also recognize how the prejudices inherent in auteur criticism narrowed my ability to appreciate Brian Wilson and the Beach Boys. As I previously suggested, my taste, in the most basic of ways, leaned toward songs whose lyrics could be read as autobiographical (all of *Pet Sounds*, 1971's "'Til I Die") as opposed to efforts that seemed to offer no interpretive context whatsoever, not even one related to the band's early subcultural identification with surfing and hot rods (say, 1967's "Wild Honey"). My only consolation is that I have not been alone. Surveying Brian Wilson / Beach Boys criticism, one discovers a consistent tendency to "read" songs as latest chapters in the biographical narrative in order to make them meaningful. A recent case in point is "Summer's Gone," the closing track of the Beach Boys' 2012 album, *That's Why God Made the Radio.* Throughout reviews and profiles of the band during its short-lived reunion, commentators pointed to this lilting, autumnal ballad as a meditation on the group's own lion-in-winter senescence as its members entered their seventies. Indeed, with a closing line about life's inevitable decline and the temptation to look back to the past ("We laugh, we cry / We live, we die / And dream about our yesterday"), many suggested the song was a worthy finale to a phenomenal body of work, an appropriately wistful note upon which to end the Beach Boys' recording career. To be sure, the seed for this interpretation was planted by the album's coproducer, Joe Thomas, who in an interview with the *Daily Beast's* Andrew Romano described how a skeletal version of the song had floated in limbo since 1998 until the time was right for the band to reunite: "Basically what Brian always wanted to do was make that the last song on the last Beach Boys record." In the early stages of recording, the symbolic import of "Summer's Gone" was intended to be emphasized by entitling the whole album after it—at least until Brian hedged on whether this would indeed be the final Beach Boys recording ever: "He wanted the original title of the album to be *Summer's Gone.* But he had so much fun with Mike and the guys that he scratched that about halfway through the recording process and insisted on changing the title to *That's Why God Made the Radio,* because he really didn't in a lot of ways want this to be the last Beach Boys record. Or he didn't want that stigma that it had to be" (Romano 2012b).[4] Despite Brian's change of heart, many fans could not help but hear the song as an epitaph. My point is that celebrity discourse (in this case, an interview) provides a context for understanding what the song is "about." The fact that Thomas both offers and then retracts that meaning does not negate the possibility of that meaning—if anything, the album's name change fuels the debate and maintains fan interest by keeping the drama of the Beach Boys ongoing, unresolved.[5] Discussing the shift in the song's biographical relevance, a fan blogger known as "Arkhonia" makes my exact point about how Thomas's revelations function extratextually:

> So it is perception and context that have given "Summer's Gone" its meaning—once Brian decided not to close the door on The Beach Boys, the song stopped being "the last song on the last Beach Boys record," and instead, "it just means summer's over." Far as I can tell

from all of this though, the song itself, as originally conceived, didn't change—but what it was meant to signify did. (Arkhonia 2012)

In what follows, I want to do three things concerning how songs are "meant to signify." First, I want to explore ways in which "perception and context" can limit what Brian Wilson songs mean when interpretation is restricted to the context of authorial sensibility. Second, I want to examine relatively rare instances when cultural significance has been wrought from Brian's music outside of his "star image."[6] Finally, I want to return to the constraints of the celebrity narrative for which Brian is known, to explore how reviews of his live performances invoke biography to compensate for his inscrutable stage presence. Doing so, critics effectively project drama onto a rendition that might otherwise seem passive and detached, the very antithesis of charismatic. As I hope to show, Brian is said to "come alive" in concert at moments when he confronts his complex and legendary legacy, as if even for the man himself, performing music becomes an inevitable reenactment of the celebrity story line that has defined his career and shaped evaluation of his art.

Making Sense of Sensibility

To explore how biography allows listeners to interpret lyrics, we begin with what should seem the unlikely example of a surf song, the genre through which the Beach Boys first came to fame and one that, on the surface, would seem as irrelevant to auteur theory as any category of novelty music can be. As the closing track on *All Summer Long* (1964), "Don't Back Down" is perhaps best known for being the group's final golden-era tribute to the coastal sport it had helped bring to national attention in 1962–63.[7] In addition to its subject matter, "Don't Back Down" is musically notable for what Philip Lambert describes as its "sense of urgency and forward momentum." Although nominally built upon a standard blues progression, the song's structure is given an "interesting," off-kilter jolt thanks to a half-step key shift up from A♭ to A in the eleventh measure of the verses, a highly unusual place for such a change (Lambert 2007, 155). The resulting jumpiness in the "surging arrangement" has inspired some commentators to detect a corresponding "undercurrent of lyrical anxiety" that is atypical of "the self-assurance of the Beach Boys' earlier surf numbers" (Schinder 2008, 110). With its admonitions against fear and incitements to "go a little nuts" by "show[ing] 'em now who's got guts," the text not only exposes a vulnerability not heard in the bonhomie confidence of "Surfin'" or "Surfin' Safari"; it also lacks the invitation-to-join-the-surf-nation quality of "Surfin' USA" and "Catch a Wave" that was in no small part responsible for the Beach Boys' early popularity.

What could possibly account for this newfound anxiety? In *The Beach Boys and the California Myth,* David Leaf thought he discovered an answer when he detected Brian alluding to the lyrics when explaining the pressures that led to his post-1967 withdrawal from the music industry:

> As Brian sang it, you just "Grit your teeth / They don't back down." Was Brian singing the song to himself? This excerpt from a 1977 interview indicates that it was at least a possibility: "There was a compulsion involved [in pouring out singles]. We did it out of a compulsive drive. You see so many pressures happening at once, and you grit your teeth, and you more or less flip-out." . . . Before the pressure forced a cave-in, Brian thinks it put him "in a state of creative panic, where you begin to use your creativity to give to people. Something was lacking. I felt the creativity but something was lacking; something was wrong somewhere." (Leaf 1985, 57)

Since Leaf's biography, it has become de rigueur to read "Don't Back Down" as a plot point in the story of Brian's crack-up. The lyrics serve as evidence of the competitive pressures he felt at the mid-1964 height of Beatlemania; of the exhausting demands for product placed upon him by Capitol Records; of his burgeoning desire to make more personal, challenging music rather than "give to people" the teenage content expected of him. To be sure, such readings are almost decreed by the eerie coincidence of a misprint on the first pressing of the *All Summer Long* jacket that identified the song as "Don't *Break* Down"—a typo invariably described as "prophetic" (Leaf 1985, 57). Brian's most recent biographer, Peter Ames Carlin, even adds a Freudian twist to this interpretation. Seizing upon what Leaf calls the song's "parental tone" ("Not my boys"), he suggests the lyrical anxiety reflects how Murry Wilson's hectoring lessons about striving for success, fueled by his own disappointments and failures, left the Wilson brothers "splayed between hope and fear":

> "Kick ass! Kick ass!" their father liked to roar at them. And they already knew whose ass would be kicked if [Murry] began to suspect they weren't getting the message. . . . [In the *guts* line of "Don't Back Down"], did [Brian] realize he was echoing his father lecturing about

fighting for success? Perhaps not, but what seems clear is that, at least in some respects, the California paradise he'd imagined was already fading before his eyes. But now that Brian's talents had proven powerful enough to allow him and his family to finally complete their journey across the continent, they had nowhere to go. "Kick ass! Kick ass!" Murry kept commanding. So Brian paddled out into the darkness, humming a song to himself.

Don't back down from that wave! (Carlin 2006, 51–52)

Both Leaf and Carlin rather cagily stage their autobiographical readings as speculation by employing the rhetorical question ("Was Brian singing . . . to himself?"; "did [Brian] realize . . . ?"). Nevertheless, a formalist critic might accuse them of committing that dreaded interpretive sin of the intentional fallacy by presuming the lyric reflects its author's personal issues at this juncture of the biography. The objection has merit because in the case of "Don't Back Down" (and many other Brian Wilson songs) we are not just dealing with *one* author but *two*: the composition is cocredited to Mike Love, albeit only since 1994, when Love successfully sued to have his name added to this and three dozen other Beach Boys songs for which he claimed he had been denied both authorship and royalties. As Mike angrily told *Goldmine* in 1992, "'Don't Back Down.' It's very well-known that Brian Wilson did not surf. I wrote 'Catch a Wave' and 'Don't Back Down.' He's credited 100 percent. He didn't give me any credit" (Sharp 1992, 14). For Mike Love, suffice it to say, "Don't Back Down" is not "about" Brian Wilson even at a metaphorical level. If its place in the Beach Boys' fiftieth anniversary set list is any indication, it is "just" a surfing song that fits seamlessly among "Do It Again," "Hawaii," "Catch a Wave," and "Surfin' Safari." I do not make this distinction to invoke the oft-discussed "two Beach Boys" argument, the idea that Brian Wilson's "art" and Mike Love's "mass entertainment" are frequently at odds with each other. I make it to ask whether there is any substantive evidence of this biographical valence beyond Leaf's and Carlin's hypothetical staging of the possibility. To my knowledge, Brian has never spoken of "Don't Back Down" as particularly autobiographical in the way that he has "In My Room" or "Please Let Me Wonder" (although it does appear among a list of "personal" songs in the now-disowned Landy-era memoir *Wouldn't It Be Nice: My Own Story*, written by Todd Gold supposedly with little participation from its subject [Wilson 1991, 90]). Nor do all critics agree that the text belies an "undercurrent of lyrical anxiety." Lambert, for one, views "Don't Back Down" as a departure from the "confession

of fear and need for female reassurance" overtly voiced in contemporaneous hits such as "Don't Worry, Baby," favoring "boastful masculine
bravado" over sensitive vulnerability (Lambert 2007, 155). To claim the
song somehow *reflects* Brian's mind-set in 1964 is to fail to acknowledge
that biography gives those interpreters who want it enough information
to *project* meaning onto the words—and, in the process, to make the lyric
meaningful enough to validate the narrative we are constructing.

   While one can question how the biographical interpretation of
"Don't Back Down" is construed, dismissing the reading as erroneous is
not quite fair. Indeed, as Lee Marshall writes, arguing against biography
as an "arbiter of a meaning of a song" may be even more "intuitively
wrong" than presuming authorial intent. In his study of Bob Dylan's celebrity, Marshall argues that formalist readings of lyrics that deny the
author's significance "make use of a literary perspective" that "overlooks
the critical way that stardom itself generates meaning." Simply stated, unlike a written text, lyrics are delivered through a voice that draws listener
attention to the physical presence of the performer. "The meaning of
Dylan's songs is not 'in the words' but 'in the voice,'" Marshall insists.
"While we could conceivably remove the authorial figure from our understanding of the songs, we cannot remove the star. . . . Ultimately, it is
the star that shapes the meaning of the song, not the words" (Marshall
2007, 25). Celebrity does not affect all listeners uniformly, of course, and
an image may change over time so songs acquire multiple meanings.
Yet to some degree stardom "always impinges on musical meaning";
Marshall is adamant that "songs can never be innocent." Dismissing biographical interpretations of songs is therefore naive. "What we need to
consider," he concludes, is "how a particular star-image (of which biography is a part) works to give a song meaning" (Marshall 2007, 26).

   To this listener, the most interesting trademark of original Beach
Boys recordings responsible for "giv[ing] a song meaning" is the texture
of the voices, an integral feature of the band's "star-image" and, in Brian
Wilson's case in particular, one responsible for shaping perceptions of
his sensibility.[8] In essence, knowing the disharmony the band suffered
throughout its career imbues its vocal harmonies with poignancy: whether in a fast romp such as "Surfers Rule" or in a gorgeously lachrymose
ballad like "The Warmth of the Sun," the vocal blend evokes not just
youth and innocence but to post-1960s ears, *lost* youth and *irrecoverable*
innocence. The losses may be the Beach Boys' in general (the group's
decline from pop innovators to nostalgia act), or they may evoke the
generational mythology of baby boomers' fall from sixties idealism to

seventies disillusionment; either way, the gravitas of these narrative associations heightens the affective power of the music, giving listeners cognizant of this background an additional aura of pathos that we do not perceive—or have not been taught to perceive—in equally excellent and enjoyable "classics" by, say, the Four Seasons or Little Anthony and the Imperials. Brian's clarion falsetto, meanwhile, is the device that explains how such a long, agonizing history of abuse and exploitation could befall someone so creative and innovative at his musical peak: the high, expressive voice projects the sensitivity and vulnerability of a soul too guileless and frail to protect itself from personal excess and music-industry avarice. The oft-noted vocal weaknesses Brian has exhibited since the midseventies—pitch problems, poor enunciation, a general aura of detachment and disengagement—in turn reinscribe the sorrowfulness of this story line in latter-day performances: they are further proof of lost genius and suffering.

I spend so much time summarizing how the meaning of a Beach Boys song can be found "not 'in the words' but 'in the voice,'" as Marshall writes, for a very simple reason: a "star-image" can also cause us to misread a song, or at least cause us to presume facts about it that historical evidence may very well contradict. Here is one example. In *Song Means: Analyzing and Interpreting Recorded Popular Song*, Allan F. Moore compares the classic 1966 recording of "Good Vibrations" to the 2004 remake that concludes *Brian Wilson Presents Smile*. Two elements in particular make the latter distinctly different from its predecessor: different lyrics and the quality of Brian's sexagenarian voice. In the case of the former, instead of a youthful appreciation of feminine vivacity, the verses present a more mature celebration of the mutuality of relationships, signaled by the new line, "I wonder what she's picking up from me." As Moore casually suggests, "the lyrics of the first verse have been rewritten" because Brian's aged voice cannot convey the naïveté of nineteen-year-old Carl Wilson's delivery four decades earlier. Yet, in fact, the lyrics to this new "Good Vibrations" are not "rewritten" at all. In rerecording the song Brian retrieved lyrics by *Pet Sounds* collaborator Tony Asher written *before* Mike Love scripted the final, familiar version. In other words, the words to the 2004 version are the original lyrics, and the classic version the revision; Asher's words were simply set aside for forty years until Brian (or his collaborators) decided *Smile* needed a distinct take on the song instead of a faithful rerecording. (Thus, *Brian Wilson Presents Smile* also tweaks the compositional structure by including musical passages first attempted in 1966 but not included in the classic version).

What would lead a musicologist as astute as Moore to presume the lyrics were rewritten in 2004? Listeners with even a cursory knowledge of Beach Boys history would likely recognize Asher's name from credits to *Pet Sounds*. It is also widely known that the collaboration was short-lived, with Brian soon moving on to Van Dyke Parks as lyricist for *Smile*. (Brian and Asher did write a few new songs together in 1996.) Moreover, a great deal of the press *Brian Wilson Presents Smile* generated in 2004 noted that Brian and his team chose to revive Asher's original lyrics, presumably (so the speculation ran) to spite Mike Love and minimize his claim that he came up with the song's infectious "I'm picking up good vibrations" hook. Something of an answer to the question appears in an odd sentence that shows up almost as an aside in Moore's analysis of Brian's late-in-life voice: "With our knowledge of Brian Wilson's personal history, it is hard not to hear in this voice the scars of that history" (Moore 2012, 276–77). To his credit, Moore does not literally project the "scars of that history" onto his reading of Asher's "new" lyrics. He does not, in other words, read the text as an allegory of Brian's biography. Nevertheless, his knowledge of Brian's "personal history" does account for why he hears in the voice more than just the infirmities of advancing age and eroded skills. His knowledge of the Brian Wilson story demands a 2004 "Good Vibrations" that somehow speaks to that tragedy. As a result, the "new" lyrics must convey a more wizened and poignant perspective than the giddy original. From a formalist perspective, if read separately from Brian's performance, Asher's text is no more adult or mature than Love's—the differences between the two sets of lyrics are actually very minimal. The significance of the minor verse variations rests entirely on the qualities Brian's contemporary voice projects. And for Moore, those qualities are inexorably tied to Brian's history.

Despite Moore's mistake, I would not reject his assessment of *Brian Wilson Presents Smile*'s "Good Vibrations." The reason is that his "knowledge of Brian Wilson's personal history" does not shape a detrimental reading of the song; nowhere in his analysis does Moore betray bias against the star image that unjustly diminishes the composition's spirit or message. Where I take issue with interpretations is when sensibility is evoked to *depreciate* Brian Wilson songs, many of which have wholly different meanings than detractors presume if we decline to inflect biographical connotations into them. Consider "In My Room," which invariably inspires comments like this from *Mojo*'s Mat Snow in 2008: "Hearing the music of Brian Wilson [evokes] the decades of breakdown, withdrawal and desolation even in his most carefree music before his mind crashed in 1967; how tragic with foreboding does 'In My Room' sound when you recall the recluse he was to become?" Rarely do we speak of "In My Room" as reflecting the adolescent propensity for withdrawal or even what in 1963 was for many American teenagers the first-generation luxury of having a bedroom or basement of one's own to retreat to. Instead, the song is always about Brian's hermitic reputation.

The downside of that exclusive focus can be illustrated through a Beatles comparison. Many rock critics argue that the intense introspection of "In My Room" parallels the Fab Four's "There's a Place," recorded six months before "Room," in which John Lennon sings of escaping to another sanctuary, only this time "it's my mind" where "there's no time" for sorrow. Beatleologist Tim Riley insists that "Place" is "a much better song than its American cousin" because it celebrates a quality completely foreign to Brian: confidence. To make his case, he cites the venerable Robert Christgau, whose comparison of the two lyrics gives the advantage to "Place" because it is an "avowal of self-sufficiency" that manages "to transcend the isolation [the protagonist] dreads" instead of wallowing in it, as Brian's narrator seems to. As Christgau bluntly states, "Lennon has better places to go but his room, and better ways to get there than Brian Wilson."[9]

But do Riley's and Christgau's interpretation of "In My Room" as a hermitic ode accurately reflect its message? Does the song really advocate isolation from the world? Not to all readers. In a study called *The Lyrics of Civility: Biblical Images and Popular Music Lyrics in American Culture*, Kenneth G. Bielen argues that by retreating to his room the narrator creates a sanctuary for prayer or meditation that allows him to cope with his fears, as the third verse explicitly states ("Now it's dark / And I'm alone / But I won't be afraid"). Interestingly, appreciating this character growth for Bielen requires disassociating the song from its author, of *not* reading it as "a first glimpse into Brian Wilson's reclusive side":

> Without ignoring the biographical elements of the song, it can be argued that the lyrics go beyond the idea of closing the door on reality, or discovering a protective musical cocoon. . . . In revealing his secrets [the narrator] is not talking to himself. He recognizes the idea of a sacred order, though as is the usual case, there is no specific reference to God. There is someone outside the room who aids in bringing about the peace he finds in his quiet refuge, so he is empowered to "laugh at yesterday." (Bielen 1999, 54)

Armed with Bielen's reading, we can return to Riley's and Christgau's to appreciate how their interpretation of the differences between "In My Room" and "There's a Place" is influenced as much by Brian Wilson's and John Lennon's respective public images as the actual text. Lennon is privileged as utilizing "better ways" because the brand of dreaming associated with him celebrates imagination as a transformative device that betters the world, whereas Brian's is stereotyped as escaping from it (those "better places" to get to "than Brian Wilson"). In essence, we have here the difference between "Imagine" and "Your Imagination," between sociopolitical engagement and living in one's own reality, Walter Mitty–like. Remove the meaning supplied by star images, however, and the difference between the lyrics virtually evaporates, for both are "about" coping. "Place" may do it by discounting sorrow ("there's no time") while "Room" embraces sadness to overcome it, but the net result is that both narrators persevere. Ultimately, "In My Room" may sound more melancholy than its counterpart, but that is a product of melody, harmony, tempo, and production, not the literal level of the words.

To differing degrees, these examples reveal how thoroughly perceptions of Brian Wilson saturate perceptions of Brian Wilson songs. They reflect how we rely upon authorial sensibility and biography to create meaning, whether explicitly associating it with a life story (as Leaf and Carlin do) or more unconsciously allowing the star image to influence an interpretation (as in the case of Moore, Riley, and Christgau). Admittedly, I do not address here how pop stars encourage author-centered readings by explicitly invoking their own biography. In Brian's case, such songs may range from the ethereal (2008's "Southern California") to the bathetic (1990's unreleased "Brian," from the doomed, Landy-contrived fiasco *Sweet Insanity*). However they differ in quality, such songs share an autobiographical specificity that distinguishes them from those generally considered personal statements, though at a more figural level. Works as varied as "'Til I Die," "Still I Dream of It," "Happy Days," and "Midnight's Another Day" are interpreted either as postcards from the thick of Brian's private despair or retellings of his recovery. Either way, the "I" in these songs is not scripted to refer exclusively to Brian Wilson; one can follow the lyrics and ply them to one's own life as easily as Brian's, which is not the case with "Southern California" or "Brian." Obviously then, one element affecting the degree to which listeners allow stardom to mediate their reception of popular music is the degree to which a song requires that reaction.[10] That said, I would argue that Brian Wilson criticism, because of its investment in the auteur aesthetic, has not even begun to broach the question Stephen Scobie posed of Dylan scholarship nearly a quarter-century ago: "What purpose has been served by determining a biographical reference? Does it really contribute anything worthwhile to our critical understanding and appreciation of the songs themselves?" (Scobie 2003, 88). By way of encouraging that question, I turn now to interpretations of Brian Wilson songs that do not rely on their author to make sense of lyrics.

Beyond Sensibility

According to Marshall, songs accrue meaning apart from their author's life through usage over time: "The meaning of the text changes because of its social circulation, because of how we as listeners [create] meaning" (Marshall 2007, 20). For critics, appreciating this "social circulation" requires reception or reader-response analysis as opposed to creator-oriented interpretation. Marshall's central example of the process is the Bob Dylan line "Even the president of the United States sometimes must have to stand naked" from "It's Alright, Ma (I'm Only Bleeding)." As he notes, this line was written in 1964 but did not really gain valence until a decade later during the Watergate era. Its sudden relevance to Richard Nixon is captured on the live album *Before the Flood* (1974), where Dylan's delivery of it is greeted with a combustive crowd cheer that all but stops the song in its tracks. The reaction became such an iconic moment in rock music that to this day crowds reenact the outburst when Dylan performs "It's Alright, Ma" live, although the line's meaning perforce changes depending on the context of the current presidency. While it may be hard to imagine "Little Deuce Coupe" or "Help Me, Rhonda" sparking such a sociopolitically powerful moment, in at least two instances Brian Wilson songs have prompted significant cultural commentary that has nothing whatsoever to do with their author's celebrity story line.

Interestingly, both examples involve *Pet Sounds*, which is not only celebrated as Brian's masterwork—*finished* masterwork, anyway—but also his most intensely personal collection of songs. Twenty-four years after its original 1966 vinyl release, the album's first-ever appearance on CD was celebrated in a five-strip story-arc in the syndicated political cartoon *Doonesbury* by Garry Trudeau. The context of celebration was very different from the auteur discourse within which *Pet Sounds* is usually heralded, however. The character obsessing over the music was Andy Lippincott, who first identified himself as gay in a 1976 appearance and who since

1989 had been suffering a terminal battle against AIDS. Predictably, the treatment of Andy's illness proved controversial, with a handful of newspapers refusing to publish the installments. Commentary on the censorship was overshadowed, however, by Brian's unexpected invocation in the climactic installments. The Beach Boys had never before been identified with gay audiences; nor were they were among the celebrities and performers who in the late 1980s and early 1990s protested homophobic misunderstandings of AIDS. For a gay man to profess his love for *Pet Sounds* during his dying days thus challenged perceptions both of Beach Boys fans (usually depicted as middle-aged heterosexual white men in Hawaiian shirts) and of gay listening tastes (usually stereotyped as preferring dance music and female vocalists of the "diva" variety).

Trudeau's handling of the story line also proved refreshing in the way it avoided the melodrama that mars many AIDS narratives of the era, including the Jonathan Demme film *Philadelphia* (1993). Most obviously, the five strips proved surprisingly funny for a tragedy of such personal and political import. As Andy listens to the barking dogs coda of "Caroline, No," for example, he speaks of being overwhelmed by the memories that the album's finale evokes. "Of your first love?" his friend Joanie Caucus asks. "No," Andy replies. "My first dog" (Trudeau 2010, 318). In the sequence's most famous panel, Andy dies while listening to "Wouldn't It Be Nice," the opening song on *Pet Sounds.* To this day, the image of his body curled on its side in bed as the song plays remains one of the most iconic in *Doonesbury*'s forty-three-year history, often crediting with helping humanize AIDS victims when both gay and straight sufferers were severely stigmatized. As a sign of the story's importance, Andy Lippincott remains the only fictional character represented among the 48,000-plus panels on the NAMES Project AIDS Memorial Quilt commemorating the pandemic's victims.

What strikes me as particularly useful about this example is the moving way it dramatizes the effect of the Beach Boys' music. With some qualification, it can be seen as celebrating the emotional power of *Pet Sounds* without simply asserting Brian's genius or the personal motivations behind the album. I say "some qualification" because Andy's last words, found scribbled on a notepad at his deathbed, are "Brian Wilson is God." ("Hmm," his doctor decides. "He must have gotten hold of the *Pet Sounds* CD" [Trudeau 2010, 318].) At first glance, this wry appropriation of the famous 1960s "Clapton is God" graffiti from London's Islington Tube Station would seem as auteur-centric a celebration of a rock legend as possible. Yet in the context of mortality itself the phrase conveys appreciation for the comfort that music in general provides in moments of human suffering, functioning less as an assertion of Brian's brilliance than of Andy's choice to die to a soundtrack of uplift. In other words, the strip provides a graceful, poignant modeling of the optimism with which one may confront mortality, with "Wouldn't It Be Nice" serving as the vehicle for inspiring that acceptance. Blogger Jeff Price's open letter to Andy on the eighteenth anniversary of his death captures what I attempt to articulate here:

> Eighteen years ago your death filled me full of sadness. . . . I cried. I had followed the last tragic weeks of your life as AIDS overwhelmed your ability to resist the inevitable. Every time you fought back it just got stronger and still you faced it all with a stoicism I couldn't understand. If I had been you I would have been so angry. I would have spat out my frustration and railed against the world. Instead you checked out listening to the Beach Boys playing "Wouldn't It Be Nice." (Price 2008)

As this example suggests, within the world of the AIDS crisis, the power of Andy's death rests in the attitude exhibited by the song selection, not the song itself. "Brian Wilson is God" may celebrate the ability of *Pet Sounds* to evoke that poignancy—and "Wouldn't It Be Nice" is a song often described as unbearably poignant—yet the sensibility *Doonesbury* is interested in isn't Brian's but Andy's. Indeed, among writers and artists celebrating positive representations of gay men in popular culture, it is not at all uncommon to find sentiments like these from Batman and Spiderman cartoonist Ty Templeton: "I will say this, the song from *Pet Sounds*, 'Wouldn't It Be Nice?' [*sic*], made me sob like a baby for years because of Andy's relationship to that song. It no longer belongs to Brian Wilson and the Beach Boys. . . . It's Andy's" (Templeton 2010). It may overstate the case to describe "Wouldn't It Be Nice" as a gay anthem, but the comfort Andy derives from *Pet Sounds* provides an opportunity to talk about the consolations of Beach Boys music by focusing on its affective power instead of reverting to valedictories of genius.[11]

Another, far less serious example of how songs accrue meaning outside of biographical context centers on another *Pet Sounds* cut. For many years, critics counted "I Just Wasn't Made for These Times" among *the* most personal of Brian Wilson songs, said to capture Brian's resentments toward band and family members who did not support the more sophisticated musical direction he plotted for the Beach Boys in 1966. Its significance in the biographical narrative is captured in this passage from Leaf's biography: "In the midst of his masterpiece, Brian was already coming to an awareness that if he wanted to pursue his artistic muse, there were going to be major changes in his life. What these changes would have been won't ever be known, because Brian abandoned his art rather than break from his life as it was" (Leaf 1985, 80). Because Leaf's thesis is that the Beach Boys (or at least Mike Love) were partly responsible for derailing Brian's ambitions at the peak of his experimentation, "I Just Wasn't Made for These Times" has proved essential to constructing the tragedy of the auteur's fall. In 1995, producer Don Was borrowed the title for his documentary on Brian's career, despite not including the actual song in the movie or on the soundtrack. So identified is this song with Brian's personal feelings in 1966 that one struggles to find commentary on it before 2012 that is not biographical. If liner notes to the 1990 *Pet Sounds* CD, the 1993 Beach Boys box set *Good Vibrations*, or the 1996 box set *The Pet Sounds Sessions* are any indication, the song only makes sense as a personal artistic statement.

That impasse broke on April 22, 2012, however, with the unexpected use of "I Just Wasn't Made for These Times" as the score for an iconic scene of the AMC-TV series *Mad Men* (in an episode entitled "Far Away Places"). The specific sequence did not involve an alienated adolescent or artist as the lyrics might lend themselves to illustrating. Instead, the scene centered upon an LSD trip undertaken by the show's World War II veteran / gray fox, Roger Sterling, who, one hazards to guess, would not have been either a Brian Wilson or a *Pet Sounds* enthusiast in the midsixties. Several aspects of the relationship between song and plotline render the relevance of the former downright confounding for Beach Boys fans. For starters, the song's playing is a scripted action in the scene, with the wife of the psychotherapist administering the LSD cueing it up on a reel-to-reel tape player. Because of its musical sophistication and introspective lyrics, *Pet Sounds* has the reputation as a quintessential "headphones album," a listening experience best enjoyed privately, between one's own ears, so to speak. Fictional or not, the premise that a nonadolescent audience in 1966 would consider "I Just Wasn't Made for These Times" appropriate music for a party—never mind an acid party—jarringly removes the record from the context with which fans are most accustomed to associating it, thereby challenging our conceptions of its meaning. Moreover, Sterling's acid trip is depicted as a slapstick moment, his hallucinations played for laughs, generating further interpretive dissonance from the somber, introspective music. Finally, the scene's closing moments are overlaid with a second, prerock generation song Sterling seems to hear in his own head, Connie Conway's "I Should Not Be Seeing You" (1954), calling attention to the generation gap the character feels between himself and his much-younger wife, Jane, and raising questions about whether he is even aware that *Pet Sounds*' eleventh track is playing.

Because of these ambiguities, *Mad Men*'s use of "I Just Wasn't Made for These Times" ignited Internet debate. Some commentators complained that the lyrics were too literal in underscoring Sterling's alienation from the social changes of the 1960s; others appreciated the fact that producers had not selected a song notorious for its LSD connotations (such as the Beatles' "Tomorrow Never Knows," which appeared in a subsequent episode in a nondrug context). Either way, the song's appearance accomplished unexpected things. It popularized "I Just Wasn't Made for These Times" to the point that the Beach Boys themselves added it to their fiftieth anniversary set list in the weeks after the episode's broadcast. More importantly, it popularized this heretofore cult classic entirely outside the context of the Brian Wilson story line, giving it new and surprising relevance that is no longer simply biographical but cultural, as a reflection of the 1960s itself. Given how much discourse *Mad Men* has generated since its 2007 debut, one suspects that the name Roger Sterling will arise alongside Brian Wilson's in many future references to the song.

Such idiosyncratic uses of Beach Boys songs remain relatively rare, but they are invigorating. They remind us that the band can evoke more than surfing and summer (as important and fun as those experiences are) and that Brian Wilson himself can stand for more than the tragedy of the auteur (as compelling as that narrative is). The past twenty years have witnessed an increasing tendency to recontextualize Brian and his band outside of their chosen iconography and narrative associations. One thinks of the use of "Sloop John B." as a Vietnam allegory in *Forrest Gump* (1994), or the playful weirdness *Fabulous Mr. Fox* (2009) achieves with a montage scored to "Heroes and Villains" (whose cartoon images can finally breathe once freed from the shelving-of-*Smile* story line) and its use of the unreleased 1968 a cappella spin on "Ol' Man River." Despite this variety, however, sensibility and the star image have proved inescapable in rock discourse. For the final section of this chapter, I want to show how the biography has been essential to encoding Brian Wilson's in-concert demeanor in order to illustrate the connection between performance and celebrity.

Brian Comes Alive: Sensibility in Action

An enduring mystery from that summer of 1976 when Peter Frampton was all the rage: what did it mean to "come alive," as his album title insisted he was doing? Why not just call the record *Frampton Live* or *Frampton in Concert?* According to Fred Goodman, the star and his management wanted the double album to stand out in a marketplace saturated with live albums using those generic designations, many of them perfunctory contractual obligations by this point in rock history. Because *Comes Alive!* was the culmination of a five-year plan to make Peter Frampton a star in the United States through constant touring, the record needed to announce itself to the audience as a career breakthrough (Goodman 1997, 312–13). Even so, most commentators agree that the name has a certain pompous ring to it, its pretention underscored by the fact that it has been parodied and spoofed more than any other live-album title in rock history.[12]

Outside of Frampton and as simple slang, to "come alive" is an expressive act, the performative moment the star most fully inhabits a song, whether musically (as in an "on fire" guitar solo), lyrically (by sincerely conveying the drama of the words), or through gesture (by physically rendering the song's mood through a dance move or an impassioned motion such as an airborne scissor-kick). As many critics have argued, live performance for rock stars is a credential of authenticity. By "coming alive," they demonstrate their innate talents and virtuoso skills to distinguish themselves from "mediated" stars who require devices of extrinsic spectacle to sell a song. Live performance is also the truest test of charisma, for commanding audience attention requires creating a sense of engagement and connection that can break down the barrier between stage and seat. In simplified terms, "coming alive" is an apotheosis of presence.

As with most values invoked to define rock authenticity, "coming alive" is also a construct. In reality, a rock star's stage moves are rarely spontaneous, tending rather to be a carefully cultivated repertoire of tics and maneuvers that audiences are groomed to expect and cheer as if on command. Nor is the performer's engagement with a song objectively assessable, for we have no clue as to what truly passes through his or her mind during a performance. Despite the fact that we cannot peer behind the facade of exhibition, the idea of "coming alive" remains entrenched in the critical vocabulary. For reviewers, it often provides a

dramatic trope for assessing the structure and flow of a concert experience. Audiences look for moments when the performer "comes alive" to
decide whether the star is merely a proficient entertainer or a transcendent artist.

What is interesting about the concept of "coming alive" in regards
to Brian Wilson is how, at first glance, it seems an utterly inapplicable
measure. Few musicians from the rock generation are more famous for
not igniting the stage than Brian. Aversion to live performance is an integral part of his legend, from his 1965 retirement from touring to his
remote detachment a decade later when he was coerced into rejoining
the Beach Boys' road show. Even since striking out as a solo draw since
1999, Brian has been a notoriously aloof stage presence, often described
as downright gnomic in his impassivity. Perched behind a keyboard that
he only randomly touches, reading lyrics off a teleprompter, occasionally
snapping his fingers or making motions that can seem the dictionary
definition of the word "stilted," he remains as awkward and unnatural a
marquee attraction as pop music has ever produced.

Yet despite Brian's dispassionate, even disinterested, demeanor, the
"comes alive" motif is prevalent throughout reviews of his live appearances. Typically the idea plays out along the lines of Andrew Romano's
assessment of the early fiftieth anniversary shows, where a competent but
uninspired appearance with the reunited Beach Boys at the New Orleans
JazzFest was followed by an unexpectedly engaged show at New York's
Beacon Theater. "I'm not sure what I'm expecting," Romano writes as
the curtain goes up at the Beacon. "Not much, at this point. The same
cardboard nostalgia [the Beach Boys] conveyed at JazzFest; the same sad
void where Brian Wilson should be. I'm quickly proven wrong." Without
warning, Brian's voice in the middle-eight of "Surfer Girl" sounds ach-
ingly emotive, leading to deliveries of "Please Let Me Wonder," "When
I Grow Up (to Be a Man)," and others that are "each lovelier and more
alive than the last." The high point for Romano is "I Just Wasn't Made for
These Times," where the technical imperfections of Brian's present-day
voice (his pitch problems and propensity for slurring) invest the song
with enough pathos to transform its meaning into something wholly distinct from that of the studio original:

> When Brian wrote the song in 1966, it was about his budding ambi-
> tion ("to look for places where new things might be found") and
> his fear of letting himself down ("each time things start to happen
> again . . . what goes wrong?") But now, forty-six years later, "Times"

sounds more ragged than before, and in its fragile beauty, it seems to be saying something new, something that every grown-up eventually discovers: that even when things go wrong—when your youthful ambitions don't pan out—you can still find your way back. The applause begins before the last note fades away. "Thank you," Wilson says, laughing. "Thank you. That's enough!"

Time and time again in commentary on live appearances, one finds reviewers like Romano fixating on this moment when Brian's performance unexpectedly rises to the soulfulness of his prebreakdown years. This happens not by Brian recapturing the purity of his trademark falsetto and tenor, but by virtue of his "raggedy," aged timber, which, not unlike Moore's reading of the voice, now conveys the heartbreak and tragedy suffered since the Beach Boys' youth. Romano ends his essay wondering what accounts for the difference between a "faithful rendition" of a song and a powerfully "moving" and "alive" one. His answers seem perfunctory at best, though, suggesting Brian's need for emotional support will inspire him on a good night to come out of his onstage shell ("Maybe it was seeing his wife, Melinda, in the audience").

A more intriguing answer is implicit in the critic's interpretation of how this weathered, imperfect performance of "I Just Wasn't Made for These Times" turns the song into "something new." For Romano, the message changes from capturing the fear of failing one's ambitions to a survivor's acceptance of failure, the idea that when "youthful ambitions don't pan out . . . you can still find your way back." This perceived change is not a product of rewriting or revision; the lyrics are not updated to reflect Brian's current circumstance. Rather, the new meaning is purely the result of interpretation, the "something new" arrived at by Romano's reading the lyrics in the context of its composer's biography. What, after all, is this narrative of "finding one's way back" after thwarted ambitions other than a concise recapitulation of Brian's perpetual comeback after his post-*Smile* fall? What we have here, in other words, is another example of how the star image is projected upon a performance in order to generate meaning.[13] The ultimate significance of that meaning may be universally applicable according to Romano ("something that every grown-up eventually discovers"), but the "finding one's way back" story line is very much Brian Wilson's. It is the same "recovery-after-the-imaginative-flipout" plot that *People* introduced me to way back in 1976.

As many reviews will testify, since the late 1990s there have been concerts when Brian *never* came alive. There are also inevitable instances when his sudden engagement with the music he performs has no logical biographical relevance. When I attended the Atlanta stop of fiftieth anniversary reunion tour, for example, Brian's most animated moment occurred during the cover version of the Mamas and Papas' "California Dreamin'," when he stepped in for Carl Wilson's lead on the second verse ("Stopped into a church . . .") with a surprisingly soulful approximation of his late brother's delivery.[14] Responding to a crowd cheer, Brian spun toward the audience as he hit the words "and I began to pray" to cap his "coming alive" with a large-hearted thumbs-up. The moment was endearing in its spontaneity, but it bore no relevance whatsoever to the legend of Brian Wilson. If anything, it seemed an opportunity for the performer to inhabit somebody else's music without the burden of having to be himself. Nevertheless, surveying assessments of Brian's shows, the "comes alive" moment seems to occur disproportionately during songs with autobiographical relevance such as "Break Away" or "Sail on, Sailor" rather than amid "Drive-In," "Girl Don't Tell Me," or "Fun, Fun, Fun." This in itself should be telling: it should call attention to our desire as critics and reviewers to find performative instances rich in narrative significance. The problem for Brian Wilson criticism is that the auteur story line of his fall and rehabilitation seems the only significance we can ever find.

When the Beach Boys released *That's Why God Made the Radio*, the track that most captivated me was not "Summer's Gone" but "From There to Back Again." Here finally was everything that for decades I had been wanting in a new Brian Wilson / Beach Boys' song: lush chords and harmonies, tumbling bass lines and reverb-laden guitar figures, a segmented structure that takes the listener to unexpected places, and a whistling coda that captures the wistful quintessence of sunshine pop, all of which somehow sounds evocative rather than derivative, capturing the promise of an *adult* Beach Boys in a way that Brian either with or without the band has only sporadically attempted since his heyday ("The Night Was So Young," "Still I Dream of It," the live version of "Love and Mercy"). What cemented my fixation was the lack of even a subtextual hint of Brian's story. Unlike "Summer's Gone" or earlier solo efforts credited with living up to the *Pet Sounds* legacy (again, "Midnight's Another Day"), the lyrics did not rely on biographical references to bolster their sense of poignancy and serious import. On its own, the text seems elliptical if not unremarkable, the words serving the musical emotion rather than calling attention to any extratextual significance (or any poetic pretense, for that matter). For that reason alone, I found "From There to Back Again" freeing. It enabled me to enjoy the listening experience without relating it to Brian's sensibility, something that had happened only intermittently in the past forty years.

The legend of Brian Wilson is certainly not going away anytime soon. Between the time this article was written and this book's publication, a major Hollywood biopic entitled *Love and Mercy* (named after the first single from Brian's 1988 solo album) was released to positive reviews and several award nominations. Director Bill Pohlad and screenwriter Oren Moverman were congratulated for the film's unconventional structure, which contrasts the buildup to Brian's 1967 breakdown to his efforts in the late 1980s to free himself from Eugene Landy's perfidious clutches. The divide between Brian's rise and fall and his subsequent redemption through his marriage to Melinda Ledbetter was made vivid by the unusual choice to employ two different actors who look nothing alike to portray the icon in his twenties and in his forties (Paul Dano and John Cusack, respectively). Critics also praised the script's emphasis on the creative aspects of art to refresh the stale "great man" approach to the biopic genre: in several scenes, Brian's compositional and recording innovations are painstakingly recreated so general audiences can appreciate why *Pet Sounds* and *Smile* are considered such musical milestones. Yet while the movie is refreshing in its aversion to sensationalism, the emphasis on its subject's genius reinforces Brian's star image by encouraging biographical analysis instead of challenging or complicating our attraction to it as consumers of popular culture. In other words, *Love and Mercy* makes it all the harder for listeners to ignore the specter of Brian Wilson's celebrity while enjoying his music. For scholar/fans, the challenge is to understand how that stardom contributes to song meanings without letting those meanings obscure others that may accrue through social usage. As the examples of *Doonesbury* and *Mad Men* demonstrate, familiar music can gain meaning in surprising ways outside the auteur aesthetic. Exploring these usages allows us to appreciate just what breadth of beauty, love, and pleasure a Brian Wilson / Beach Boys song can add to our day.

NOTES FOR CHAPTER 1

1. After years of circulating on the black market, this special is finally available in an authorized format as *Good Vibrations Tour*, released by Eagle Rock Entertainment.

2. Rock historians generally credit Jon Landau, Bruce Springsteen's eventual manager, with establishing auteur theory as the critical norm in rock journalism in the late 1960s and early 1970s. One formative comment in particular is cited pervasively: "The criterion of art in rock is the capacity of the musician to create a personal, almost private, universe and express it fully." Quoted in Marshall 2007, 102.

3. The most thorough examination of Frampton's rise and fall is Goodman's, but it remains a dissatisfying assessment. Goodman makes no effort to account for the popularity of *Frampton Comes Alive!* with audiences, asserting instead that its massive sales were simply engineered through "years of touring [that] provided Frampton with a following and produced the explosive sales" (Goodman 1997, 312). In assessing how the relentless tour schedule ultimately derailed Frampton's career through oversaturation and inferior follow-up product, Goodman also fails to acknowledge that since the 1990s the guitarist has enjoyed a lucrative if not spectacular career on the nostalgia circuit, where he often performs *Frampton Comes Alive!* in its entirety.

4. "The Beach Boys' Crazy Summer" is Romano's "official" article on the reunion. "The Joe Thomas Interview" is a transcript of a Q & A held during research for the piece that Romano published on his *Tumblr* account.

5. As it turns out, "Summer's Gone" may prove the Beach Boys' final song after all. As the fiftieth anniversary tour wrapped up, Mike Love's plan to return to touring under the band's name without Brian or Alan Jardine was interpreted as him "firing" his bandmates. Most of the reports misrepresented the incident, failing to appreciate that Mike was simply doing what he had planned all along after the anniversary wrapped. The controversy inspired competing editorials by Mike and Brian in the *Los Angeles Times* (or by their representatives) that in turn made the possibility of further collaboration unlikely—at least for the time being. Of course, Beach Boys' fans long ago learned never to say never. In the meantime, Brian began an unexpected collaboration with British guitar legend Jeff Beck, including a short fall 2013 coheadlining tour and an impending album.

6. I intentionally use simplified terms such as "sensibility" here to avoid the jargon that renders much academic criticism on celebrity painful to read. By "sensibility" I refer to what theorists often call a celebrity's "star image." As Greco explains, "The star image of a celebrity refers to an interaction between various aspects of a celebrity. These elements include the discourse that might surround a celebrity away from, or in conjunction with, his or her performance. This includes the biography of the performer, as known publicly and as constructed in narrative form. Also, these elements include the roles with which a performer is associated, which have certain continuities and discontinuities between them. Finally, the celebrity can be thought of as a performer as part of a certain kind of tradition, which he or she embodies or transforms. It is in the interaction of these different parts of celebrity that a star image takes form" (Greco 2011, 95).

7. "Do It Again" would reestablish the Beach Boys' connection to surfing a mere four years later, but by 1968 they could only evoke beach life nostalgically instead of as a contemporary fad.

8. See also my *Brian Wilson*, where I explore the sensibility conveyed by Brian's classic falsetto and tenor (Curnutt 2012, 68–75).

9. Christgau 1998, 108; Riley 1988, 56. The Christgau essay Riley cites originally appeared in *The Ballad of John and Yoko* (1982), a *Rolling Stone* collection compiled in the wake of the Beatle's 1980 murder. The essay is usually cocredited to John Piccarella. Because *Ballad* is out of print, I cite the piece from its republication in a more recent collection of Christgau's work.

10. One issue I do not have space here to address is the fact that many of these "autobiographical" lyrics are authored by collaborators speaking for Brian in the first person, sometimes at his insistence (as in *Pet Sounds*), sometimes with only his most ambivalent participation ("Brian"). In my book I explore how *That Lucky Old Sun* lyricist Scott Bennett specifically evoked Brian's breakdown in "Midnight's Another Day" in order to bring gravitas to that 2008 project (Curnutt 2012, 129–31). Bennett's most peculiar addition to a Brian Wilson song may be the confession interjected into *Sun*'s otherwise lightweight album closer "Going Home," where the "flipout and recovery" narrative is once again reiterated: "At 25 I turned out the light / Cause I couldn't handle the glare in my tired eyes / But now I'm back, drawing shades of kind blue skies."

11. Or maybe it is becoming one. In recent years "Wouldn't It Be Nice" has been performed at numerous rallies against anti-gay marriage legislation, with the line "Wouldn't it be nice to live together / In the kind of world where we belong" proving a LGBT rallying cry.

12. The only other live title that comes close to inspiring as many spoofs is *At Budokan*, inspired by 1978's *Cheap Trick at Budokan* and 1979's *Bob Dylan at Budokan*.

13. The star image is not always invoked to describe such uplifting in-concert moments. Reviewing a 2006 London rendition of "Break Away," for example, *Mojo* critic Peter Doggett notes how the autobiographical relevance of the second verse's casual reference to hearing "voices in my head" became uncomfortably vivid as Brian seemed to grapple with its implication: "As Brian reached [the line], his hands dropped abruptly to his side, and blind panic crossed his face. For a moment, the mood changed from celebration to freakshow. It was impossible to forget that this is a man who frequently hears voices in his head, threatening to kill him" (Doggett 2007, 54).

14. The Beach Boys first recorded "California Dreamin'" in the early 1980s with a nasally first-verse vocal by Mike Love. Produced by future "Kokomo" cowriter and producer Terry Melcher, it appeared on an obscure album called *Rock and Roll City* that was sold only at the electronics retailer Radio Shack in 1983. Three years later, the band released an altered version showcasing Alan Jardine. (Both versions feature Carl Wilson's soulful lead on the second verse.) The 1986 version appeared on the otherwise perfunctory compilation *Made in the USA* with the guilty pleasure "Rock 'n' Roll to the Rescue" and charted as a single, reaching number fifty-seven on Billboard. A music video was released to both MTV and VH-1 to promote the song; depending on one's affection for the Hawaiian shirt-laden "Kokomo," which also features clips from the Tom Cruise movie *Cocktail* (1988), "California Dreamin'" has the distinction of being the

best Beach Boys' music video—mainly because, unlike videos for "Getcha Back" (1985) or "That's Why God Made the Radio" (2012), the imagery does not exploit Beach Boys nostalgia. The Beach Boys' rendition of "California Dreamin'" became an amusing source of trivia in 1988 when the punk band Dead Milkmen namechecked it in their classic single "Punk Rock Girl" ("We went to the Philly Pizza Company. . . . Someone played a Beach Boys song / On the jukebox / It was 'California Dreamin'' / So we started screamin' / 'On such a winter's day'"); many listeners, unaware of the Beach Boys' cover version, assumed the Milkmen mistakenly thought the original "California Dreamin'" was by the Boys, not the Mamas and the Papas.

TWO | Pet Sound Effects

DANIEL HARRISON

IN THE MID-1950S, as rock 'n' roll began to dominate sales charts, popular-music recordings increasingly played with the boundaries of "song" and "sound effect." Spoken interludes, as in Mickey and Sylvia's "Love Is Strange" (1957), had singers briefly enacting a dramatic scene. New types of radio presenters (DJs) brought their broadcast shtick to the recording studio, introducing songs with affected speech and Foley effects familiar from radio shows (e.g., the Big Bopper's "Chantilly Lace," 1958). The "hootin' and hollerin'" of amped-up blues infiltrated other genres, including instrumental ones (Duane Eddy's "Rebel Rouser," 1958). Finally, "novelty" numbers of the era could show off recent advances in recording arts and science with a heavy application of production effects (viz., "The Flying Saucer," 1956).

By the time the Beach Boys recorded their second single, "409" (first recording, according to Badman 2004: April 1962), Brian Wilson and cowriter Gary Usher were familiar with all of these developments.[1] And while starting a track with the sound of a revving engine may not have been original with them, that they showed an interest in "sound effects" in only their second release shows noteworthy flexibility about what might be put on a record besides music. This flexibility has characterized the music of Brian Wilson and the Beach Boys ever since, well after car songs were faddish and their topical repertory fresh.

Readers who are curious, but not (yet!) fans will be introduced in this chapter to songs that have rarely been anthologized throughout the fascinating history of Beach Boys' compilation albums; familiar standards, like "409," will be refreshed. Some of the "new" songs will likely come off as immature, weird, strangely hooked, unpolished, unfinished, psychedelically sketchy. Some were filler tracks on the pre–*Pet Sounds* albums and aren't really songs in the traditional sense (and have never been anthologized). Yet none fail to show off something characteristically interesting if not admirable about the Beach Boys. If curiosity is piqued by the foregoing description, readers might avail themselves of a Spotify playlist I've prepared of the songs referenced here and check out the unfamiliar ones before continuing.[2] Fears that you are in for a Gidget-movie hell of surf guitar, woodies, and deuce coupes will be quickly dispelled. But you've been warned.

For the fan who knows the catalog well, this chapter will pull together songs from various depths and eras, and it will bring to mind, if not point out, the large range and varied types of sound effects. It will also juxtapose well-known and thought-about songs in (I hope) interesting ways. It will make the case that the revving engine, chanting cheerleaders, and affected surfing and hot-rod lingo is of a piece with the crashing waves in "Diamond Head," the fabulist of "Mt. Vernon and Fairway," and the copper's cry in the cantina of "Heroes and Villains." And this is not even to mention production and postproduction effects layered on in the studio, of which Brian was an industry-leading master in the mid-1960s. The reverb of the surf guitar is of a piece with the thrumming cello of "Good Vibrations." An interest in "effect through sound" is a red thread throughout the Beach Boys catalog as well as in Brian's solo work. For present purposes, I want this chapter to demonstrate a mutuality of the "song" and "nonsong" sounds. It can't help but to be appreciative of it as a significant achievement in popular musique concrète.

As I developed these ideas and appreciations, I revisited ideas about the title of the Beach Boys' most widely acclaimed album: *Pet Sounds*. What makes the second word of the title so apt? Why not *Pet Songs* or *Pet Music*? What about the first word: *Favorite Sounds*? *Special Sounds*? (The cover art famously didn't rule out *Mammalian Sounds*!) The out-of-focus title seems to describe a feature of a certain kind of sonic life, one blessed with curious ears and talent for imitation and innovation, and one also characterized by a playful and innocent disposition. In the end, I concluded that, with Brian Wilson and the Beach Boys, there is no sound that can't be a pet sound. And I put that insight into the title of this chapter.

The analytic approach taken here is primarily hermeneutic, in that the sound effects are presumed to be meaningful and open to interpretation. Some effects are rather specific and authorial intention easily inferred, either from the context of the song or—insofar as known—

from contexts surrounding the composition of the song or from Brian Wilson's general songwriting habits. In these cases, the interpretation is largely exegetical, drawing out items that can be overlooked, dismissed, or (mistakenly) believed to be self-explanatory. Other effects are enigmatic and admit multiple interpretations; these are tried out in connection with the more definite elements of the song structure, and the results analyzed for their contributions to understanding and appreciation. In both cases, the work is to listen to all the sonic elements of the song with the same attention that can be given to notes, chords, rhythms, forms, and so forth, which comprise the usual network of musical structure. Ultimately, interpretation moves between evidence provided by the artwork and piecing together this evidence into a narrative whole. The results are, of course, reducible to my own critical readings of the songs discussed in the remainder of the chapter. If these readings are interesting, then I've done well; if they prompt new ways of listening to these and other songs, then all the better.

Scene

The revving engine of "409" sets *scene*; listeners are placed somewhere definite—in this case, very near the front of a late-model Chevy Impala Super Sport with the titular superhot motor, circa 1963. But much is left unaccounted for. The color of the car, where it's located (e.g., at a racetrack), the weather, time of day, and so on, are all unspecified. Even so, there is—or would be, if we bothered to test for it—broad intersubjective agreement about these details. Many of these rely on certain unmarked, generic defaults that, if not indicated explicitly by the effect itself, can nonetheless still be suggested, implied, or at least not disallowed. Exploring these is interesting and (I hope) rewarding work in elementary "sound studies." So, in the case of "409," asking more "journalist's questions" of the scene elicits the following:

- Location: stationary at the beginning, so possibly a garage but really anywhere. In the middle of the song, the engine is heard again, but is audibly in motion, as in a drive-by at a race. So: drag strip or even a straight stretch of highway (for illegal street racing). (Note a few things now being ruled out: windy, curvy mountain road; congested city street; inclement weather; parking lot.)
- Time of day: When asked, most people I've put this question to imagine daylight, sunny and warm. The Beach Boys' surf songs also

take place then, and many listeners unconsciously assume that the
car songs do as well.

• Color of car? Undetermined.

One way to appreciate the role of the imagination in interpreting
scene effects is to compare this description with the actual production
methods. It turns out that the sound effects in "409" were recorded at
night and on a residential street. The Wilsons' neighbors feared illegal
street racing and called the police. (The boys apparently shut it down before the cops showed up, and no one got into trouble.) And for readers
interested in automotive technology, the car recorded did not actually
have a 409 motor but rather the predecessor, a 348.[3] Analysis like this
is one of the royal roads into appreciation and interpretation of scene
effects in songs: what's unspecified can be imagined variously and in different contexts, with lyrics then read from those vantage points.

In "409," we discover that the scene effect is powerful enough to dis-
allow a setting perfectly supported by the lyrics. These, as Philip Lambert
points out, focus on possession of and admiration for an object clearly
likened to a girl (Lambert 2007, 39). Without the revving engine to suggest otherwise, the car the lyrics describes might as well be parked in the
driveway for public approval if not under a protective tarp in a garage.
Though they do touch upon racing, they are without immediacy, describing past or future achievements. (The telling line is "*When* I take
her to the track . . .") The question of when the scene takes place comes
up: is the racing going on right now? Or are we hearing memories, flash-
backs, or some kind of soundtrack of a sports-highlights show?

It's instructive to compare this tension between lyrics and scene effect
with another song Brian cowrote with Roger Christian and Jan Berry,
"Drag City," recorded by Jan and Dean (October 1963). This song also
opens with a revving-engine effect very similar to "409" but extended to
include a powerful acceleration off a starting line. (The stereo mix locates this on the listener's left; as the car accelerates, it moves quickly to
the right channel, giving further detail to the scene.) We are thus placed,
more specifically than in "409," as spectating a drag race some ways down
a strip at the titular location. The lyrics suggest that the scene effect is
about both vivid memory and powerful anticipation; the singer is "*going*
to Drag City" rather than already there. (He actually is still at or near
the garage where he had "just tuned" his car, and is about to go pick up
his girlfriend before heading out.) The vivid description of race day at a
track coupled with the scene effect of actual racing integrates the entire

story. The effect here is clearly marked as imagined and anticipatory; removing it doesn't change the "Drag City" setting, while removing it in "409" makes that song an up-tempo version of "Cherry, Cherry Coupe," where the verses set a tone of (stationary) bodywork description. (Even when the second verse barely slips in a reference to satisfactory racing credentials, it comes off as a shutdown to suspicions that the car might be a "No-Go Showboat.")

Speech

Talking during a song is a marked effect, and the Beach Boys continued the tradition modeled in late-1950s songs, added their own material, used it consistently in post–*Pet Sounds* albums leading up to *Holland* (1973), and kept using it, more modestly, even after tastes about it had changed in the mid-1970s. Among the conventions of the times, using speech at seams in the song structure is especially effective, as in the transition from verse to chorus in "Custom Machine" (September 1963). The entire song has exhilaratingly high harmonic velocity thanks to the complex chord changes (Lambert 2007, 113–14). So harmonic g-forces are relieved for a spell when the lyric line introducing the chorus ("When I step on the gas she goes . . .") is taken out of the melody and put into speech. This predication boosts the entrance accent of the chorus, a thrilling, onomatopoeic rendition of a high-revving engine, followed by more rapid, energetic chord changes.[4] It's a well-portrayed moment of anticipatory windup, congruent with excitement just before a race, when contestants are staged in the gates and waiting for a starting signal. Once the chorus is greenlighted, it takes off with a high-revving whine.

The speech effect here is delivered as part of the song lyrics—in rhythm, in conventional contours, a kind of *Sprechstimme*, in other words. Introductory or concluding speech has more intriguing effects. These events usually happen just once, not rotationally, and interpretive antennas usually can pick up strong semantic signals as a result. A particularly clear example is the amazingly lewd "Pom Pom Play Girl" (February 1964). The narrator, a spectator at a football game, gazes with a bit of contemptuous desire at the head cheerleader (whose given name is suppressed by the titular moniker). She is quickly attributed with top-clique stereotypes of beauty, self-absorption, and indifference to social inferiors—including, presumably, the narrator. (A comedic reading would costume him as a "nerd," exaggerating his unattractiveness.) As Lambert points out, periodic statements of the hook are accompanied by drum booms "worthy of a burlesque routine" (Lambert 2007, 134). That's indeed where they end up, but they start out as scene effects of a high-school cheerleading routine as seen from the sidelines of a football game. It's only in the outro that the leering turns lewd. There, the hook is repeated to fade, but rapidly upshifting stepwise through four iterations, starting from the key of A♭, before settling on the key of B, with "burlesque" drum booms for each iteration. This is all but tumescent in import. During the upshift, drum booms are preceded by "woo!"—styled feminine, as if a cheerleader is heard doing a routine. After settling, a horny teenager's interior monologue emerges deep in the mix, too loud not to be noticed but too soft to shock: "Shake it! [pause] Wave those pom poms *all* around!" This is the brilliantly speech-effective sound of teenaged sexuality escaping 1950s-era repression.

To show range in atmosphere and mix placement, the intimate, spoken "I love you" in "Please Let Me Wonder" (January 1965) makes a good comparison. In this lushly arranged ballad, the singer waits, hopes, and fantasizes hearing these very words from his beloved. The first opportunity the beloved has to respond is at the end of the final verse-chorus pair, before the coda-outro of repeating choruses signals imminent end of song. The words are indeed spoken there—not gently gushed, but hurried and almost blurted; still intimate, and maybe even a little embarrassed. It has been a point of interest that it's not the voice of the lead singer (Mike Love) that's heard, but rather that of a chorus member (a closely miked Carl Wilson), since it gives rise to a number of interesting scenarios. A sweet and innocent reading has Carl voicing the subconscious of Mike's narrator, which begs the question that Mike's subconscious should have a different voice. (Recall that the narrator and speaker in "Pom Pom Play Girl" are the same.) Even so, there is richness to this reading, which stages a one-sided conversation from the narrator's point of view. But there are tantalizing alternatives. One is a kind of figure/ground reversal, understanding the music as a soundtrack to a movie scene, an involved couple wordlessly enjoying each other's company, and Carl Wilson's character saying the only line of dialogue. Though not likely envisioned in the original poietic process, a gay or alternately gendered scenario can be part of contemporary aesthetics with this text, which allows the voice of the beloved indeed to be heard in the song.

While the punctuating speeches of "Custom Machine" recur in the course of rotation through the song structures, coda speeches, like that in "Pom Pom Play Girl" happen just once, giving them unique import. A charming effect combining these two features is in "Busy Doin' Nothin'"

(March 1968). The song has two strophes, each in two halves, with the first half narrating aspects of Brian's morning experiences, and the second focusing in vivid detail on some episode of the day. A relaxed and loping Latin-style groove, sweetly orchestrated with woodwinds, supports a "loungey" melody in the first half and singsong recitation in the second. In the first strophe, the vivid episode is about giving driving directions to Brian's house (famously accurate—as long as one knew the starting place). In the second, after he sings about an old friend he'd like to see more of, Brian breaks into speech and announces, "I think I'll make a call," as if interrupting the recording session and threatening to act on pure impulse. As in "Custom Machine," the speech effect prefaces, marks, and accents an important seam in the song structure. But here it happens once and seems initially "not of the lyrics." It thus focuses attention on the second vivid episode, which details an unsuccessful telephone call, circa 1968. This episode is an extraordinary feat of sustained narrative pressure given the already intense stream-of-consciousness lyrical atmosphere. Jim Miller esteems the song as "one of Brian's most subtle lyrical conquests" (1992, 196).

Interestingly, Brian and the Beach Boys allowed more extended speech into their albums from time to time, with *Holland* (1971) as the extreme case. That album's "California Saga" intersperses song between recitations from Robinson Jeffers's poem "Beaks of Eagles." But this is only a foretaste of the elaborate twenty-minute, multipart "fairy tale," "Mt. Vernon and Fairway," which has all the accouterments of an old-style radio show: narration, music, scene, and other special effects.[5] For various reasons, not least of which is that it likely couldn't fit on the LP with the rest of the songs, "Mt. Vernon and Fairway" was a separate seven-inch EP, which contributes to a generic divorce between the "songs" on the LP and the "fairy tale" on the EP. In the latter, music is the special effect upon narration. Finally, given that the narrated interludes in Brian's *That Lucky Old Sun* (2008) are credited to Van Dyke Parks (e.g., "Narrative: Between Pictures"), one can imagine that integrating spoken narrative with song was a tantalizing prospect for *Smile*.

Character

Brian Wilson and the Beach Boys have a taste for the low-comedy arts of mimicry, camp, and cartoon (see cover art for *Smile*). It was certainly acquired when they were juveniles, and it persisted long into adulthood. It is legible in their choice of cover versions, especially early on, when they were still learning style and repertory. It is a taste for novelty numbers like Bobby "Boris" Pickett's "Monster Mash" (1962), which the Beach Boys played often in concert, as preserved on their first live album in 1964. Over a doo-wop groove and backing, the lead vocal is delivered in *Sprechstimme* as a hammy impression of Boris Karloff (the star of "Frankenstein" movies from the 1930s). Mike Love, showing off his own abilities as a ham, thus practices a full-blown *character effect*—the (lead) singer taking on a role as if acting a part, portraying a marked character rather than the default persona of "honest singer/narrator."[6] Character effects are the sound of the singer putting on a mask, or switching to handle a different puppet.

There's an instructive case to be made that the entire catalog of surf and car songs is generalized character effect. The Beach Boys were "acting" as surfers and hot-rodders in their songs, since Dennis Wilson and Mike Love seemed to have been the only band members who had a clue about surfing, and since no one knew anything special about cars (which explains the role of coauthors Gary Usher and Roger Christian, both of whom were quite knowledgeable and who provided the necessary vocabulary). Capitol Records publicity tried to reinforce this pretense. Photos of the band carrying surfboards (borrowed) or admiring hot rods (rented) all have a heavily staged affect even given the sheen of a corporate-funded photo-shoot. They look at cars somewhat quizzically, carry surfboards a bit awkwardly, and generally seem to be taking direction dutifully.[7] Granting this curious artistic position, in analyzing individual songs we still want to make distinctions between generic expressions—no matter if these are "inauthentic"—and ostentatiously acting a part. The innocent yet surely imagined exhilaration acted out in "Catch a Wave" is different from the knowing donning of a Frankenstein mask in "Monster Mash."

Also covered on the 1964 live album was "Papa-Oom-Mow-Mow." A faithful rendition of the Rivingtons' original (though faster), it gave Mike Love a chance to play a gravelly voiced "wild man" spouting the titular nonsense, while Brian—cast against type—was able to indulge in theatrical, out-of-tune, near howling in the outro. The band chose to record it again in *The Beach Boys Party!* of 1965 along with another novelty song, "Alley Oop," about a comic-strip caveman, originally recorded by a group of Los Angeles session players. Love's rendition is faithful to the affected character of the original while layering in other affectations: "Boris" from "Monster Mash" is heard at 1:45 (the line "great big monsters"); later (2:30), a mincing "sissy" shows up.

The *Party* album is a fund of character effects. Like other live albums, it is also heavily marked by speech effects—chatter, instructions to musicians, and the background hum of a well-attended studio party. Leaving aside the pretense that it was recorded live rather than over several days in a studio (and thus having the Beach Boys assume the character of "partygoers" throughout), the band's background chatter is characterized by many role-playing moments—for example, preparing to play "Devoted to You," Brian, sounding somewhat like his father, Murry, calls for order with mock sternness: "If you don't know it, then *shut up and go home!*"

The general atmosphere in *Party* is the same as found in certain album filler-tracks from the early 1960s. In "Bull Session with 'Big Daddy'" (January 1965), the genial mugging, horseplay, and dumb jokery on display at mealtime is familiar to anyone who has dealt with kids of that age. (I can hear Carl's "Get outta here" at 1:41 as accompanying a swat to someone's hand, preventing a playful grab at the french fries.) The only adult in the room is Earl Leaf, from the Capitol Records publicity department, who gets to pitch a few softball questions into the buzzing group of hungry kids. Two lines from the transcript are worth noting. In light of subsequent events, soon to unravel around *Smile*, it's chilling to hear Brian confidently say, "I still haven't made a mistake my whole career," and have Mike respond nonchalantly, "We keep waiting for you to make a mistake, Brian" (1:00–06). Finally, a potential inside joke. At 1:32, during a loose discussion about the Beach Boys' recently completed European tour, Brian takes the lead to announce with (mock?) solemnity: "You know who was a great help was Dick Rising, Capitol Records representative over there—one of the greatest guys I've ever met in my life." The way this testimonial is staged, produced, and delivered suggests that risen dicks were another great part of that tour.

"Bull Session with 'Big Daddy'" shows the kind of characters the Beach Boys were (when happy and being fed). "'Cassius' Love vs. 'Sonny' Wilson" (February 1964) shows how those characters could be scripted and exaggerated. Again, in light of subsequent events, staging a heated, emotional argument between Mike and Brian, each making fun of the other's voice, is all but prophetic. Similar to a novelty number like Buchanan and Goodman's "Flying Saucer" of 1956 (which interspersed "radio news" speech effects between short clips of hit tunes), the Love-versus-Wilson contest has short clips of Beach Boys' songs—but rendered grotesquely, in parody. The most clever effect is letting "Farmer's Daughter" get a sincere first verse before having a weak, out-of-tune falsetto gradually break through the mix in the second. This track and "Our Favorite Recording Sessions" show a rare talent for self-mockery in the way the group treated their own songs. This is nowhere better exemplified than the "doofus" mask put on the narrator of "I Get Around" during *Party*, who sings an appropriate contrafactum (sample: "We always take my car / although it's a heap").[8] This is a revealing act: on one hand, the Beach Boys don't take themselves too seriously to perform self-parody, but on the other, it suggests that the original isn't serious, genuine, or developed from deep feeling—in other words, that it supports the generalized character effect of the "surf and hot rod" songs. It's not so much putting on a mask, but replacing one mask with another.

Production and Arrangement

So far, work from as early as "409" and as recent as *That Lucky Old Sun* has been sampled for certain characteristic effects. Scene, speech, and character are well marked, foregrounded, and discrete. The same can be said for certain *production* effects, recognizable because they estrange natural acoustic sound. The processing applied to the snare drum opening of "Do It Again" (June 1968) and which continues variously for the rest of the song is a clear instance. Another is the momentary vocal double-tracking, with a dose of ambience, in "Busy Doin' Nothin'" at the line "Slowly, it came to me" (2:02), marking a welcome remembering of a telephone number. Pitch-height processing in "She's Going Bald" (July 1967) is another. Production effects can also be recognized in the background of Beach Boys' songs, as in the twangy reverb of the surf guitar, or the ambience that flatters the well-sung choral lines Brian heard in the Four Freshmen, the Lettermen, and the like. Finally, some aspire to the illegibility of the deep background, such as Murry Wilson's advice to speed up playback to make the singers sound younger, an effect that shows up when the song is in a "weird" key or otherwise not tuned at A = 440. Indeed, most production effects are baked in at an early stage and lose markedness—reverb, mic distance, mix, and so forth. When Brian took over as record producer, more and more of these came to characterize Beach Boys' recordings, and his mastery of them was acknowledged throughout the music and recording industry in the mid-1960s. Production effects—whether fore- or background—pervade the Beach Boys recording catalog.

If there's a genius to these sounds, it's encountered in the musical arranger, the figure who maps the trail from "demo" and piano-backed frameworks to a fully worked-out, effects-laden recording. The arranger chooses sonic details for the musicians, selecting instruments and players, deciding on special instruments, voicing the choral parts for the band, and establishing the general atmosphere and groove of the song. When the arranger is also the producer, sonic details for both musicians and engineers can be coordinated, to great effect. One can't help but hear Brian Wilson's impressive growth in mastering production effects as accompanying equally impressive growth in sophisticated arranging. His imaginative use of the electro-theremin, for example, should be cited in orchestration textbooks. Beautifully reverbed harp at the beginning of "Wouldn't It Be Nice" is also a distinct instrumental choice. So is the thrumming cello of "Good Vibrations." And the overdubbing of his group's already tight vocal ensemble enabled trademarked choral densities no other rock group tried to imitate.[9] In Brian's mid-1960s productions, the variety of sonic experience on offer is extraordinary.

Arranging, producing, and songwriting together comprise the compositional act in this music. Brian Wilson did, coordinated, and collaborated on all three. He got his start as a youngster, doing admirable ear-training work transcribing Four Freshmen songs on the piano, by all accounts with near obsessive interest (Leaf 1985, 18). This activity—as anyone who's gone to a good music school can attest—makes for a fine "musical ear," an easy familiarity with song, and an enduring interest in many kinds of sounds. Arrangers need all these as a matter of course. As he had a close-knit group of good singers nearby who already knew the style, his abilities to teach dense Four Freshmen chord changes by rote grew stronger. His own chord changes started acquiring exhilarating modulatory hookiness (think of the beginnings of "Custom Machine" and "I Get Around," among many others). Eventually, he had a group of first-rate session instrumentalists whom he could trust to work out certain details (the same with recording engineers), and a small number of specially chosen recording studios where he felt his professional best. He had his hand in everything in those years: songwriting, arranging, producing, and rehearsing, and he was singularly inventive with it all.

Comparisons and Contrasts

Having analyzed a few specific scene, speech, and character effects, as well as brought them under the umbrella of production effects, and finally identifying arrangement as the coordinating art above all, we now turn to analytic vignettes of individual songs gathered into thematic pairs.[10] Each song in the pair has multiple effects, but also shares a central effect with the other—scene, arrangement, production, speech—though shown from a different aspect. The hope is that previous description and discussion of effects have prepared the way for focused analyses of them, while also widening the range of exposure to hooky, interesting, and surprising songs in the Beach Boys' extensive catalog. Taken together, these songs (along with those mentioned so far) are a remarkable collection of pet sounds, a well-stocked menagerie of Brian Wilson's musical imagination.

Versions: "Help Me, R(h)onda" and "Wonderful"

Two versions of "Help Me, Rhonda" are sometimes characterized by fans as "Ronda" and "Rhonda"—the version without the "h" referring to the album track on *Today!* (as spelled on the record label) and the version with the "h" referring to a remake released as a single (with this spelling) only a few months later. Casual listeners might distinguish between the "weird one" and the "sing-along one." The reader can take an inventory of the notable and interesting differences between the two—and should focus particularly on the second half of the song.

"Ronda" ostentatiously plays with fade-out, the reasons for which aren't immediately clear from the lyrics. And this is dangerous play, since "fade to finish" is the strongest signal of musical closure record production can generate. Feigning a finishing fade is a serious breach of convention. The effect begins in the chorus following the instrumental bridge (ca. 2:24), where mm. 5–6 are unexpectedly soft (*subito piano,* as musicians put it). The next pair of measures returns to regular pressure, but then even softer in mm. 9–10. Is the song concluding or not? Apparently not, since the chorus concludes at normal levels. But then Brian begins a fourth chorus (ca. 2:49) and applies the effect again until the song does indeed fade to close after the fourth measure, making the song well over three minutes long, a standard for length that would not be exceeded until *Pet Sounds.*

While I can imagine analyses that unify the lyric and production effect, they seem to need a good deal of force and detail to be convincing. And the existence of a "hit" single version that doesn't use this effect complicates if not undermines this effort. Further, the play with fade in "Ronda" is best appreciated with headphones, which flies in the face of standard wisdom about Brian's productions being designed for a low-fidelity, single-speaker car radio. In that noisy and distracting environment, the fade effect could prompt a listener to think something might be wrong with the sound equipment. Given all this, I prefer not to push through with hermeneutics, turning instead to uncharacteristic infelicities in the background vocal arrangement, which is lower and thicker than Brian's usual practice. A focused hearing of the beginning of the chorus will confirm the observation. The voices are pitched low in the third octave, deployed in a "muddy" close position, and frequently sing a difficult "aww" vowel (the "o" in Ronda). It's a strange sound the voices make there, especially in comparison to the beautifully arranged background vocals of the prechorus ("Ronda, you look so fine . . .").[11] The singers are also miked noticeably closer than Brian's usual practice for background vocals, while the lead-vocal pair seems farther away. Moving toward the close of the chorus, mm. 9–16, Brian removes the background to emphasize the high point of the line: "Help me, Ronda, *yeah!*," delivered by single instead of a paired lead vocal. Though a powerful moment, it seems not to be arranged most effectively.

In "Rhonda," the single version, Brian made a number of adjustments to the vocal and instrumental mix. He does not play fade games, which eliminates the need for two outro choruses (the first with feigning fade and the second with actual fade). Thirteen seconds are thereby saved.[12] His other changes work to dampen the background low chords and bring up the lead singing—in essence, reversing the decision made in mixing the album version. Since that decision was about *making the mix itself an effect*, the reversal makes a pop-music hit out of what had been a catchy but weird (as well as long and chorus-heavy) album number. These changes required slight adjustments in the arrangement (e.g., to coda after the third chorus). More significant changes not only fix the heavy choral background in the chorus, but layer in new voices that have become "sing-along" lines at Beach Boys concerts ever since—in effect, ratifying Brian's instincts for tuneful hooks. The clearest addition is toward the end of the chorus, as the chord changes work toward accenting the final word of the line: "Help me, Rhonda, *yeah!*" Here, a sudden falsetto flies in and lands squarely on "*yeah!*"—a beautifully conceived contrapuntal emphasis and the proper telos of harmonic tension, which then drains out in stop time with the final line, "get her out of my heart." A no less noticeable addition is in the bass—the vocally delivered "walking bass" line every four measures of the chorus: "bow bow bow bow bow." Interestingly, Brian recorded another version in which a falsetto line is present throughout the chorus and partly doubles the "walking bass" line.[13] Compared to the released version, which saves the falsetto

line for a climactic moment, the continuous version seems a bit over-
done, though it proves Brian's interest in the basic arranging idea in the
single, which was to open up the "top" register to counteract the low
background vocals.[14]

A different balance of production and arrangement effects can be observed in the two versions of "Wonderful," written by Brian and Van
Dyke Parks. One was released on *Smiley Smile* (July 1967). The other
was known originally from bootlegs from the *Smile* recording sessions
(August 1966–January 1967), later released on the *Good Vibrations* boxed
set (1993) and *Smile Sessions* (2011). Like "R(h)onda," casual listeners
would readily distinguish between the "weird" version and (in this case)
a "pretty" version. Fans distinguish between *Smiley Smile* and *Smile* versions. Those familiar with pop-music genres can distinguish between the
"bridged" and "strophic" versions, which reflect significant differences
in arrangement with attendant changes in production.

  Example 2.1 represents the song structure using hierarchically stacked
rectangles that enclose formal units. (Timings for section boundaries
are shown underneath the rectangles.) The large rectangles denote
verses, which have two endings. Ending A is relatively conclusive (and
contains the title lyric), while ending B is progressive. The small rectangles enclose musical phrases, with those in the B verses easily heard
as four measures each while the A phrases sound an asymmetrical 5 + 3
measures. The strophic version in example 2.1a, from the *Smile* sessions
of late 1966, is very much a vehicle for the five verses of Van Dyke Parks's
rich and dense lyrics. A number of features suggest that this version was
unfinished both in songwriting (an abrupt ending) and in production
(an uncharacteristically thin backing).[15] As mentioned above, it was only
known through bootlegs until released as part of a boxed set in 1993.
Judging from even less finished versions released in 2011 (*Smile Sessions*),
it is further along and evinces a developmental plan—starting from a
bare harpsichord in the first verse, adding bass and a lightly strummed
tenor ukulele in the second, and folding in background vocals in the
third. (The fourth and fifth verses repeat the arrangement scheme of
the second and third.) Yet the background vocals are tentative rather
than polished, as if they were guide tracks for an upcoming backing vocal session. Other sessions document work on a "tag" or "insert" that
was (probably?) meant for an outro, as well as restless experimentation
with the keyboard instrument (using a "lute" stop on the harpsichord,
for example, or using the piano), and including some drum-kit work as

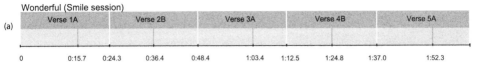

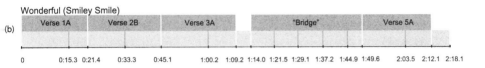

Example 2.1: Structural representations of "Wonderful"
(a) Strophic version (*Smile*); (b) Bridged version (*Smiley Smile*)

well. In any case, the "best" session version, while beautiful, seems to promise an even more beautiful finished product. Yet when *Brian Wilson Presents Smile* was released in 2004, this version was lovingly reproduced (covered) rather than finished, though the ending was artfully patched with new Van Dyke Parks lyrics that linked to the next track, "Song for Children."

The version of "Wonderful" the Beach Boys recorded for *Smiley Smile* is diagrammed in example 2.1b. It is a very different arrangement that suppresses the fourth verse in favor of a "bridge" based on the "Bicycle Rider" theme heard elsewhere in *Smile*, introduced by a short linking tag in an unrelated key. (This is the small, singleton box after verse 3A.) The tag appears again at the end, but without consequent—that is, linking to nowhere, making the song very open-ended and "purposefully" unfinished. The scare quotes around "bridge" denote that while the section is located in its usual spot (i.e., halfway through the song) and fulfills the usual functions of digression, departure, and deviation, it is musically unrelated to the strophes, being set in a different key and style, with clearly marked, conventional chord changes and lightly intoned doo-wop nonsense syllables. Both of these features, however, sit on a remarkable foundation of speech-effect "party noise." As I have noted elsewhere, some of the party sounds subtly alight upon members of the underlying chords, giving the section a delicately wrought cohesion (Harrison 1997, 48–49). Compared to the atmosphere of the verses—hushed, very close, even more thinly arranged than the strophic version—the "party" bridge is a riot of music and speech effects. Further, it takes the place of the fourth verse, which, while not advancing the plot of the lyrics, nonetheless nudges it suggestively. Further, the fourth verse in the strophic version has a B ending, and removing it makes the second verse's B something of an orphan and no longer a part of a coherent ABABA design.

The arrangement differences between the two versions are obvious, striking, radical, and need no further clarification. While the strophic version may indeed have been wanting some kind of bridge or outro, the *Smiley Smile* version seems to have been arranged with the "party" bridge as a starting point, its unconventional atmosphere requiring equally unconventional atmosphere for the verses. Strange production effects are heard throughout: "helium voiced" background singing in the ending of verse 1, subtle premonitions of the "party" scene during the ending of verses 2 and 3, and a soft but discordant harmonica at the end of verse 3. Whereas in "R(h)onda" a change in production concept necessitated alterations in the arrangement, in "Wonderful" the situation is reversed: a completely new arrangement concept called for reinforcing production effects.

Silence: "Drive-In" and "The Little Girl I Once Knew"

The "grand" or "general" pause (GP) is a familiar bit of arranging rhetoric. The music winds up to a climax, *crescendo e ritardando* to a big, dissonant chord that cuts off into silence (reverb optional but recommended). The resolution chord is lit up like a target for a big accent on the next appropriate downbeat. It is most satisfying when that mark is hit as expected—a resolution chord starting an important part of a song, typically the chorus.[16] A clear example in the Beach Boys' catalog is in "Good Vibrations": the three-beated silence following the massive E♭-over-F-bass chord at 2:54, followed by expected high-energy discharge on the opening of the chorus and its hook. This schematic association with the GP makes experimenting with it quite tricky. For the three-beated silence alone, moving it to the center of a large bridge and repeating it three times is a signature effect in Brian Eno's "Needle in the Camel's Eye," starting at 1:42.

Changing the length of the GP can be even more startling, as "Drive-In" shows. This high-energy, imaginatively arranged rocker is diagrammed in example 2.2. The large boxes show the four sections of the song, which express the common scheme of "Statement–Restatement–Departure–Conclusion" (Everett 2009, 140). The verses are themselves quartered, in four-measure units, according to the same scheme, as the diagram shows. The darker D-quarter box indicates that lyrics there are spoken, with song gratifyingly restored in the final C-quarter. Faster har-

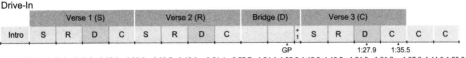

Example 2.2: Structural representation of "Drive-In"

monic rhythm, begun at the end of D, continues into C and creates a strong pull towards cadential closure in the tonic key. The coordination of effects here makes ending of the verse particularly fulfilling.

The departure function of the bridge is conveyed in conventional ways. Vocals are tacet, making it a purely instrumental section, and it is ostensibly in a different key (B♭, though barely). But the unexpected extension of the GP (1:08) is a notable deviation. The graphic shows the onset of the GP with an arrowhead, after the downbeat of m. 8. A return to the verse material is targeted for the next downbeat, but an extra measure of rest intervenes—shown as a small sliver of a box in the diagram—and disrupts the regularity of phrase length observed from the beginning of the song.

Example 2.3, in its bottom system, shows the effect embedded in more structural and musical detail and offers two "normalizations," which attempt to locate the underlying regular structure overwritten by the extended GP. Version (a) is a conventional finish, with harmonic acceleration from the secondary dominant to the primary and then into the tonic of the restored verse music (e.g., "Fun, Fun, Fun," among others). In "Drive-In," this possibility is anticipated but can't materialize once the downbeat of m. 8 sounds and the G chord hasn't made the anticipated move to the C chord. This event prompts version (b), which assumes that a consistent harmonic rhythm is intended by staying on G and reserves a two-measure span for C—of which only one appears before the verse returns. The GP here is either too long or too short, and the last-heard chord before it is highly tensed toward a resolution that never materializes. Overall, it's an unnerving effect. But it does provide the returning verse music with notable emphasis, and the speech effect in the D phrase is boosted by an amusing character effect: "Smokey Bear" makes an appearance to give his standard warning ("Remember, only *you* can prevent forest fires"; see the middle arrow in example 2.2).[17]

Though it would take some work to explain why the extended GP is appropriate to a song about an outdoor venue for cinema, the arrangement of other elements in the song suggest that "silence as missingness"

○ = 1 measure

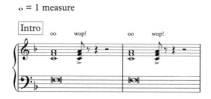

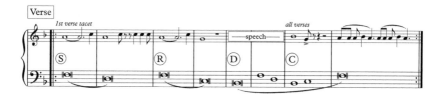

Example 2.3: "Drive-In" rhythmic reduction, capsuling some tonal, melodic, and rhythmic features. Bass staff shows the fundamental bass (i.e., chord roots) one octave lower than written. Treble notes in the verse system show uppermost notes of background vocals.

is a central theme. Even before the GP, the bridge is curiously empty of any solo instrumental effort, sounding like a backing track for a missing solo on a guitar, organ, or saxophone. This initially inchoate impression is remembered and noted when a lead guitar finally enters the texture— but so late that it coincides with the beginning of the outro (marked by the rightmost arrowhead in example 2.2, at ca. 1:35 in a 1:50 song). So, there *is* a lead guitar part, but it's missing until the end of the song.

Example 2.3 also makes clear that the same kind of downbeated accent announcing the GP in the bridge is foreshadowed in the introduction, which features supporting vocals without any activity in the second and fourth measures, making them as empty as those in the bridge. When background vocals enter again, in the C phrase of verse 1, they reprise this figure before delivering a tag. While conventional arranging practice, "unmuting" the background vocals in the second verse is especially effective in "Drive-In." Activity in the second measure of the figure is also particularly welcome and underscores that it had been missing in the previous verse. However, there is no corresponding activity in the fourth measure, a rhetorical deflation that makes the following two measures of speech especially effective.

If the GP in "Drive-In" is startling, it is truly disorienting in "The Little Girl I Once Knew" (October 1965). A common myth is that the song failed to "hit" on the charts because DJs thought the GP would make listeners wonder whether the station went off the air and switch stations (the morbid fear of "dead air"). Hence, they didn't put it into frequent broadcast rotation. What makes a hit is as mysterious as what doesn't, but the GP is indeed unusually built here, and it's easy to see how it could attract concern and criticism. Example 2.4 represents the (complex!) structure in now familiar nested boxes. The largest boxes enclose the two main verse/chorus rotations. These have three parts, a form that was increasingly popular by 1965. The middle section is normally reserved for a prechorus—a passage contrived to somehow magnetize the chorus hook and thereby increase the impact of its arrival. (See Summach 2011.) Brian's composition here reverses the conventional polarity, for the middle part of "The Little Girl I Once Knew" drains energy out of the rotations, letting them spin down completely into a GP. It's not so much dead air that is at issue here, but a palpable sense of air actually *dying* during the prechorus spot—in exactly the place where it normally would be pressurizing toward release.

In the first rotation, the middle section is labeled "FX" (effects) in example 2.4. It has two phrases: (1) a speech effect ("Look out, babe") over a rapidly thinning instrumental background, highlighted by the dark rectangle; and (2) an extended GP, with only a dying, soft vibraphone F♯ to cue that it is *not* a moment of dead air. It's rather a moment of great expectancy and uncertainty. Because the chorus enters on the downbeat, the GP here is longer by one beat than the corresponding effect in "Drive-In," which was broken by pickup notes for the chorus, three eighth notes before the downbeat. The one extra beat makes the effect seem longer than it is. The chorus entrance is powerful on B major, and at full volume to boot. Its second half feels like a new beginning in a different key, D, but subsides back toward the key level of the verse. (See example 2.4 for relevant labels.) The second rotation is like the first—except that the speech module is one measure longer, spinning down more slowly and somehow more portentously. It is as if Brian has

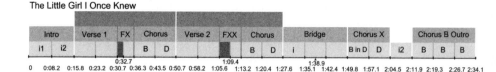

The Little Girl I Once Knew

Intro		Verse 1	FX	Chorus	Verse 2	FXX	Chorus	Bridge	Chorus X	Chorus B Outro
i1	i2			B	D			B	D	i		B in D	D	i2	B	B	B

0:32.7   1:09.4   1:38.9
0   0:08.2   0:15.8   0:23.2   0:30.7   0:36.3   0:43.5   0:50.7   0:58.2   1:05.6   1:13.2   1:20.4   1:27.6   1:35.1   1:42.4   1:49.8   1:57.1   2:04.5   2:11.9   2:19.3   2:26.7   2:34.1

Example 2.4: Structural representation of "The Little Girl I Once Knew"

doubled down on his idea for an "anti-prechorus." (This difference is marked "FXX" in example 2.4.)

Example 2.5 explains the harmonic situation. Whereas the GP in "Drive-In" left the progression very much in the air, tensed toward resolution, filling the moment with anticipation, the one here emerges from a low-energy and dissipating state. The chord-root motion from verse to chorus is analyzed into three layers. The F♯ layer fits comfortably into the first part of the verse as a repeated ii–V motion. The transposition of this motion in the second part, while possible to work into F♯, brings with it an option to modulate and open a second layer in C♯. At the beginning of FX, chords themselves stop, but their roots continue as shown. Without upper structures, the roots cannot denote (energized) seventh chords, defaulting to triads instead. In the F♯ layer, the opening chord of FX is nominally a dominant and thus potentially energized toward resolution. Without a seventh, however, it's the motion in the C♯ layer, ii^7-V^7-I, that describes the situation better. Yet motion continues onward into the downbeated F♯ of the second measure, announcing the GP with another potentially conclusive motion in this key (all the more sure in the second rotation, thanks to the longer spin down). Thus, FX is all resolution and no buildup. After the chorus begins, a weak V–I connection through the GP can be recognized in retrospect, but this relationship is more inferred subsequently than experienced live.

Unlike "Drive-In," the GP in "The Little Girl I Once Knew" is part of the verse structure and thus rotates through more than once during the course of the song. Yet as example 2.4 shows, the verse/chorus blocks take up only the first half of the song, and the GP thus happens but twice. The second half of the song has a bridge and concluding choruses. The choruses are adjusted, however, so that they don't fully agree with those in the first half. "Chorus X," after the Bridge, starts with a B-style chorus but in the key of D; no modulation occurs in the second half as a result. In the outro, D-style chorus modules disappear, leaving only B to cycle into the fade-out. This structural division of the song into

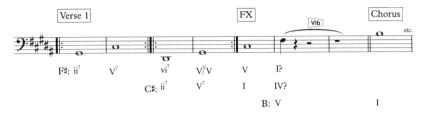

Example 2.5: Chord progression from verse 1 to chorus in "The Little Girl I Once Knew"

halves is underscored by a recall of introduction music at the beginning of the bridge, and by an actual reprise of the second module of the Intro after Chorus X. Just as the D module seemed to mark a new beginning in the Chorus, so the double re-use of introductory music signals new beginnings in the entire song structure.

"The Little Girl I Once Knew" is the last single Brian composed before turning all his attention to *Pet Sounds*. It is also the last plausibly written in an adolescent voice; Tony Asher and Van Dyke Parks wrote lyrics for young adults, not high-school kids. For these reasons it's a fitting cap to the Beach Boys' first rush of success as Capitol Records artists—a beautifully written, arranged, and produced love song of considerable musical and formal complexity. It is an ambitious work, reaching for effect. That it perhaps overreached, in the estimation of the record-buying public, is a portent of near-future troubles Brian would have reconciling commercial need for product and "live air" with his artistic interests and development as a composer.

Final Scene: "Do It Again" and "Caroline, No"

Scene effects at the beginning of a song set the stage for subsequent action; such effects at the end, while reflecting on completed action, seem also to show a result, final outcome, or next stage. They don't, in other words, seem to reveal a previously hidden scene as much as bring the lights up on the next one. As we discovered at the beginning of this chapter, a revving engine at the beginning of "409" sets up a song about a car, whereas one at the end would serve a reading that the car is ready for racing now that the song about it is over.

"Do It Again" (May 1968) begins with a production effect of the estranging kind: "running a series of press rolls on a snare drum through a tape-delay system" (White 1994, 282–83). It's an arresting "call to attention" gesture that introduces a simple verse-chorus number with contrasting bridge, artfully constructed to increase intensity subtly yet consistently throughout the song, which then concludes with a scene effect taken from the *Smile* sessions of eighteen months earlier: the sounds of hammering by a crew of carpenters. On bootlegs, it was called "workshop" or "woodshop," and Brian did incorporate it into his 2004 *Smile* version, but its first release was as the very fitting concluding scene effect of "Do It Again."

By simple verse-chorus, I mean that the chorus has the same chord progression as the verse: four measures of I followed by one measure each of IV and V and concluding with two measures of I—among the most unambiguous affirmations of tonal center as can be composed. In this, it is markedly different from Brian's signature harmonic style, with its unexpected chord changes and thrilling turns of musical phrase. (It is not hard to read this as pointing to Brian's earliest up-tempo hits, modeled on equally simple blues structures. This is among the things he is doing again in this song.) It is common arranging practice with simple verse-chorus songs to add musical elements at each large-scale repetition—background vocals, instruments, and so on—in an effort to maintain listener interest. It is an unavoidably teleological scheme; since each repetition is stronger than the previous, the last is thus the strongest. Here's how Brian manages the scene:

- Verse 1 continues the processed drum groove under Mike Love's lead vocal, which is delivered in a notably nasal way reminiscent of his singing five years previously; it easily brings to mind Brian's parody of it in "'Cassius' Love vs. 'Sonny' Wilson." After the opening four-measure E♭ (= I) harmony, the A♭ (= IV) chord enters, but the bass remains on E♭, providing the most immobile and static support possible.

- At the beginning of verse 2 (0:24), middle-distance, on-beat handclaps are added to the percussion groove. After two measures, sustained, mellow, background chords rise gently in the mix (ca. 0:30). After two more measures, the bass does indeed move to A♭ to support the IV chord, feeding subtle supporting energy into the verse. When the final E♭ tonic chord is reached, the background chords have raised a short ascending line from stable tonic (doh) to the active third scale degree (mi). At the end, another subtle touch. Just before the chorus begins (0:40), a bent, bluesy guitar note sounds as an announcement—the first instrumental sound that hasn't been pure chordal structure.

- The chorus (starting at 0:41) is a significant jump in musical density. Trademarked Beach Boy vocal sound explodes into the mix—tightly tuned from bass all the way up to falsetto, but easy with the groove, contrapuntal without affecting learnedness, and—all the more by being a wordless doo-wop—performed with assured comfort and evident fun. High-end spectrum is also activated with the addition of a tambourine to the percussion mix.
- The bridge (0:57) departs from the groove completely, setting up an effective contrasting section and thus resetting the bar for the subsequent verse-chorus rotation. Lambert aptly describes the first two phrases (8 mm.) as "a kind of moonlit dream sequence" (Lambert 2007, 301). Once the harmony locks on B♭ (= V), the original groove returns (processed snare drum) for one measure, followed by another four that build the groove all the way back up, topping the chord off with an urgent seventh.
- The bridge discharges into an untexted verse (1:16), featuring a bluesy electric guitar solo supported by layers of doo-wop background vocals different from those found in the chorus.
- The resetting effect of the bridge and untexted verse allows Brian to make another run at a powerful chorus entrance. The beginning of verse 3 (1:40) not only resumes lyrics, but adds an unprocessed, "natural" drum kit at the front of the mix, effectively effacing the processed drum sound of the opening. As in verse 2, adjustments to the mellow background chords are made after two measures (ca. 1:43), but here they are dialed back down, as if setting the composition into a crouch before springing into the final chorus. Also as in verse 2, the "bent bluesy note" returns, but here sung by the background vocals as a chord. The supremely heartfelt, easygoing, and perfectly tuned delivery makes this a great moment in the Beach Boys recorded catalog, where one can appreciate the value of having turned down the mellow background in order to make the "bent bluesy chord" pop out of the texture.
- The second, and final, chorus (1:56) is even denser than the first. The foregrounded drum kit continues, and the "different" layer of background doo-wop vocals from the bridge is mixed in with the previous chorus vocals—softly at first, but by halfway through (2:04), they emerge clearly before joining in the general fade-out; last to appear and last to go.
- By the time that fade-out is apparent, the attractions of the arrangement and production have been amply displayed: to lyrics that are an open call to "return to roots," a very simple verse-chorus form

supports Mike's old-school delivery. The estrangement of the opening production effect on the drum kit, coupled with the static bass line and (retrospectively) spare backing gives way, ultimately, to a virtuosic display of Beach Boys' layered backing vocals supported by a "real" drum kit and prefaced by a seemingly tossed-off yet perfectly executed bluesy chord. The composition is the perfect soundtrack for a "Yeah, we're back, and as good as ever" scene.

The end of "Do It Again" is a call to fundamental renewal. The fundamentals are communicated with directness. The lyrics reference all the themes of past hits: beach, surfing, girls, warmth, California, and so forth. But then the chorus shows what is truly loved: the wordless beauty of harmony singing by relatives and close friends—a powerful enactment of the *Biedermeier* vision of domestic uplift through music. While the joyful doo-wop syllables that take the place of lyrics are not sounds of the early nineteenth century, they are nonetheless sounds of a comfortable contemporary family.

As "Do It Again" fades out, a scene effect fades in that focuses the emotional outcome of the song. Many hammers (= many hands, many actors) are heard working on various pieces (wood, metal). A busy construction site is suggested, but the variety of materials being worked suggests a small manufactory or woodshop, where craftsmen work on individual pieces of a larger object. (The miking of the scene also suggests close quarters of the shop rather than the larger expanse of construction site.) One subtle but telling character effect is heard amid the shop noise: just before fade-out, someone "on the scene" exclaims "Ow!," presumably because of a misplaced hammer blow. There is a genial, good-naturedness to this shout that paints the workshop in the kindly colors of artisanal, social, and voluntary effort—something like a barn-raising or workday at the community center—this, rather than the site of some Fordist regime of mass production, where a smashed finger would likely elicit more profane oaths, colorfully extended. Given the general bonhomie and domesticity of the lyrics, the purposeful buzz of construction activity makes even clearer what the wordless chorus suggest, that getting back to fundamentals means rebuilding the Beach Boys from their starting point in love for making music together, especially vocal harmony. It's good-natured fun, portable to a variety of music-making settings and themes, and immensely rewarding, as anyone who has sung in harmony can attest. "Build the Beach Boys Again" is one way to concretize the "it" of the song's title as the workshop scene concludes.

"Do It Again" is the first song on the *20/20* album, and it thus seems to promise subsequent songs that show off the new construction. This promise itself is founded on the scene-setting powers of the workshop effect, themselves fueled by extremely explicit and lyrical joy in making something (= music) together. "Caroline, No," in contrast, is the last song on *Pet Sounds*; its concluding scene effect trails off and leaves listeners alone with their thoughts.

Pet Sounds is a beautiful collection of songs, fully deserving the *Liederkreis* honor bestowed on the album from its release in 1966. Among the many levels at which the album coheres, the way it uses purely instrumental tracks to preface the last song on each side is pertinent here. These give those final tracks particular emphasis. On the A-side, the instrumental track is the breezy "Let's Go Away for Awhile"; the final track on that side, in contrast, famously describes "the worst trip I've ever been on," styled with top-notch Brian Wilson choral writing on a happy Caribbean theme. "Sloop John B." is, in the context of the album, an unexpected "downer" ending—composed though it is with hopeful joy and happy affect. This interpretation is fully underwritten by the preceding, travel-themed song.

The A-side begins happy, with the groovy "Wouldn't It Be Nice," but it ends strangely with perhaps the best happy-affect song about a series of bad travel experiences composed to date. Side B begins with the evergreen "God Only Knows," a widely admired gem of twentieth-century American songwriting. The prefacing instrumental track near the end of that side is titled "Pet Sounds," but may be better recalled as a spec piece for a James Bond movie soundtrack. The low, lazy, twangy lead guitar brings to mind the bright days of rock instrumental groups like the Ventures and, of course, the surf guitarists that the Beach Boys heard around Southern California. A powerful, slow groove supports a bluesy lead guitar line that's in no hurry. It's a piece that could proceed directly from the guitar riff that opens all (official) James Bond movies. It may also be the thickest wall of background sound that Brian ever produced, richly orchestrated and reveling in reverb. If this track started as a musical introduction to Sean Connery's James Bond—confident, classy, suave, sexy, cool, and so forth—it is rendered brilliantly.

"Caroline, No" follows, an exquisite song of aching nostalgia, sung by Brian alone, and introduced by a memorable arranging effect: a haunting series of drum strokes on a upside-down and empty water jug, followed by an oscillating harpsichord background supporting his lead vocal. (This is the same harpsichord idea as in strophic "Wonderful.") The self-assuredness of Bond is completely undercut by this lonesome wail of a song. Somehow, the "Pet Sounds" instrumental track turned into an even worse "trip" than the one on the previous side, and the downer result is here magnified rather than dissipated by the musical arrangement.

And further: after the song fades (and not cross-faded as in "Do It Again"), a scene effect is heard, full of signifiers that all but paint an Edward Hopper scene of loneliness, isolation, and alienation—*Nighthawks* in sound. Characteristically for the Beach Boys, a bit of love, affection, loyalty, and companionship is also mixed in. Example 2.6 zooms in on the effect, using a bow instead of rectangles to note symbolically its gradual emergence and disappearance. It's useful to note that the initial fade-in is not dialed up from the control booth, but by the dynamics of the scene itself, which includes powerfully suggestive Doppler effect. The timepoints and associated arrowheads are an initial inventory of events in the scene:

- 0:00 in the diagram begins at 2:17 in the song; the scene effect begins with crossing bells and train horn.
- At 3.6 seconds, a pair of medium-sized dogs begin to bark.
- At 10.5 seconds, the train horn sounds a second time, louder than before; dogs stop barking.
- At 13 seconds, the train horn sounds a third time (short).
- From 16.8 through 19.2, the train horns sounds the last time, and the locomotive passes.
- At 22.0, train cars are passing by.
- Between 22 and 26, the dogs begin barking again.
- At 26, the last car passes by, and the dogs continue barking into fade-out.

This inventory of the scene has a train approaching a crossing, and some nearby dogs. A second inventory accounts for more detail. Clanging bells, of the type still used at railroad crossings, raise the curtain on one set (at least) of long, straight railroad tracks interrupted by a road, possibly unpaved. We surmise this because the high speed of the approaching train (judged by Doppler effect at 19.2, ca. 80 mph) precludes tight curves and complex track junctions (i.e., trainyard). It is also a setting far beyond the most recent station stop, with far yet to go to the next. It cannot be an urban setting, but a rural one. Dogs suggest nearby inhabitation—a station house, perhaps a small village, maybe a

Caroline No, scene effect

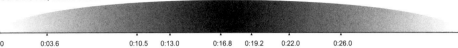

0   0:03.6   0:10.5   0:13.0   0:16.8 0:19.2 0:22.0   0:26.0

Example 2.6: Timeline of scene effect in "Caroline, No"

solitary farmstead. The train is pulled by a modern (for 1965) diesel-electric locomotive, not an old-fashioned steam engine. (The air horn instead of a steam whistle is the clue.) This is an interesting distinction, as it refuses to project the profound nostalgia of the lyrics (for an earlier, younger lover) onto an emerging public symbol of nostalgia (i.e., for the great age of American industrial output). In truth, the diesel horn is actually the sound of American railroading at the beginning of an age of spectacular decline. It's the sound of a present less optimistic than the past. There's no little irony that this effect was put on record by a group noted for their songs about cars.

The train horn sounds the proper warning signal as it approaches the crossing: two longs, a short, and a long. The last coincides with the locomotive reaching and passing the crossing, when the Doppler effect shifts the horn's $B\flat^7$ trichord to G^7. After the locomotive and horn recede and their sounds diminish, passenger cars are heard passing by—no more than a dozen, judging from the time intervals between "clacks" of the wheels on a nearby rail joint (intervals that are too wide for freight cars, given the speed). All train sound-clues suggest an intercity passenger train, possibly with sleeping and lounge cars.[18]

I'm pretty sure I've described accurately the recorded setting of the scene effect—that is, a recording technician set up equipment at a railroad crossing that had high-speed passenger service and captured the sonic scene. Unlike the workshop in "Do It Again," which was created in studio for a specific project (though, as we've seen, repurposed successfully for another), the train scene in "Caroline, No" likely was part of a library of sounds available to broadcast and recording studios. Thus, Brian would have had his choice among various railroad effects (e.g., "steam engine starting," "slow freight," etc.) once he had narrowed his interests there. The choice of speeding passenger train was intentional.

His dogs, Banana and Louie, were recorded later and mixed into the train scene. Their bark gives away their medium-small size, if nothing else. The barks themselves are of the "aroused and actively noticing" kind rather than those prefacing a dogfight or facing down a threat. It's fully reasonable to expect that the dogs have been aroused by the train. Agreeing to this subtly shifts ownership of the animals. If the dogs were a stationmaster's, say, or working dogs on the farm, such barking would not long be tolerated by their master. (We know the train line is active with both passenger and freight because of the expense of maintaining crossing signals and 80 mph speeds.) The dogs might now belong to a transient observer of the scene, waiting at the crossing for the train to pass before proceeding. At this point, we can easily finish a painting of a single pickup truck at a dusty railroad crossing, two dogs roaming around back in the truck bed, as a speeding locomotive is whisking away people with a destination and purpose, people on a journey that's on track and proceeding apace, people maybe even enjoying the conviviality of a lounge car. And the pickup driver's circumstances? The same as ours after the intense loneliness of the song: down, emotionally spent, stunned stationary while anonymous others speed by unheeding. The two dogs, our only comfort.

Two final scene details might be teased out. While long straights of rural rail can be found all over the country, the original train recording—as well as Brian's own imaginary setting for it—was likely in arid Southern California, in a valley or even desert. The landscape is open, big, and not heavily forested. This bigger, "empty" stage intensifies the puniness of the "pickup truck driver's" observing perspective—a small isolate amid a vast expanse. Finally, all the preceding makes perfectly plausible and likely a setting of this scene in the deep night, perhaps moonless, though nothing prevents lighting the scene with blazing sun at midday. But the bleakness of the song suggests a blackness for the scene.

Before closing the book on pet sound effects, we should note how much they are creatures of the recording. Scene effects in particular can be removed without challenging the unity of a song, and indeed live versions usually omit them altogether—which is to say that the Beach Boys don't start with a revving engine when they perform "409" in concert. Speech and character effects transfer, but not all production and arranging effects. In this light, one can appreciate how getting rid of "Ronda's" feigning fade made "Rhonda" better for live performance. To my knowledge, "Drive-In" and "The Little Girl I Once Knew" have rarely if ever been on the live set list, but concert audiences abhor silence even more than radio DJs, and so these songs remain best on record. The "finished bootleg" that is strophic "Wonderful" has been performed live, while the bridged version (again, to my knowledge) has never been attempted;

the problems in re-creating the "party scene" for the bridge are per-haps not worth the effort. As for "Do It Again," the subtle arrangement detailed some pages ago cannot be conveyed well in live performance. Their most recent concert arrangement (for the fiftieth anniversary tour) mostly dispenses with background manipulation, leaves the bent bluesy note to the discretion of the lead guitarist (David Marks), and doesn't bother with bringing in the unprocessed snare for the final verse. Instead of the easy and nearly effortless buildup of the recording, the live arrangement, in its treatment of the bluesy chord, overinflates what had originally been the most effective sung moment on the track. Stop time arrests the instrumentals, opening a bit of silence to introduce the chord, delivered forcefully and with conceivably even more bend than the original. No longer a gesture of easy mastery, it is a demonstration of raw power. All this goes to show that effects are products of the arrang-er's imagination. Any that are indispensable to a song are kept (or the song isn't given any subsequent arrangement without them), and those that are ornamental, as it were, don't need to be transferred to other ar-rangements. Nevertheless, this chapter has argued that they are valuable artifacts for interpreting the songs, that they document an extremely inventive and imaginative arranger who knew his musicians as family, relatives, and friends, and who wrote for the admirable effects he knew he could achieve with them.

Finally, an envoi and a performance-practice recommendation. One of the earliest ingredients the arranger/producer mixes into the final confection is mono/stereo. Stereo background effects are extraordinary compared to mono, which can be appreciated perfectly with headphones plugged into a receiver with a mono-out switch. Toggling between the two modes is an ear-opening exercise. Stereo spreads sound horizontally between the ears, while mono concentrates it vertically, as if in a column bisecting that same between-the-ear space. Stereo-specific foreground ef-fects can be extraordinary as well, including all those that descend from the bouncing ping-pong ball demonstrations used to sell early models of home stereophonic equipment. But Brian had only one good ear (the other disabled in childhood; circumstances unclear) and so couldn't hear in stereo. He continued to mix down in mono. One might worry that Brian would be "lapped" by stereo-abled young producer/arrangers who had gone to school on his records, and who aspired to an audience with expensive stereos who listened to LPs on headphones. (Pink Floyd would make a strong play for this group.) As noted previously, Brian's mono style was perfectly suited for the single speaker of the car radio picking up a local Top 40 AM station. It is an underappreciated statement of demotic appeal.

There's another venue besides the car where mono sounds better than stereo. Parties, rock concerts, clubs (really, all versions of the same thing) are crowds of people buzzing, mingling, moving, laughing, dancing. They aren't an ideal formation for stereo effects, which is to say standing in single file, a bisector to the line between the stereo speaker-array, or wearing headphones. So those who end up in front of one side of a stereo output will hear a distorted mix, as will those on the opposite. In these venues and conditions, it's better to use mono and pump equal sound mix from both sides. It is true that stereo remixes of Beach Boys records have been issued in order to keep them consonant with modern production norms. They are tastefully done and show off Brian's original arrangements beautifully. They sound great on headphones. But if you find yourself putting on some Beach Boys tunes for a group, whether for friends, colleagues, students, please use the mono version. (Even the later, all-stereo tracks benefit from mono output!) In other words, the Beach Boys are generally best heard while in a crowd, or at least a group, and maybe best at a party. They make music you want to sing along to, and in parts, too. And it's music, thanks to its remarkable deployment of effects, that stays fresh and compelling.

NOTES FOR CHAPTER 2

1. Starting the song with the distinctive sound of a powerful car motor was not, in fact, an idea original to the Beach Boys, but an emerging norm of writing "car songs" for the Southern California pop music market, as in The Duals' "Stick Shift" (1961). The revving engine at the beginning, screeching tires in the middle, and police siren at the end recall similar sounds from driver's ed films or moralizing radio dramas. According to The Duals' producer, Ron Barrett, the idea for using an engine sound came to him after he remembered Vernon Green's imitation of car sound-effects in The Medallions' "Buick 59" (1954), http://www.starrevue.com/TheDuals.htm. The Duals reused the engine opening for a follow-up single, "The Big Race," which did not chart. Interestingly, this song is about a 409 (which ultimately loses after leading for most of the race). The resemblance in vocal delivery between this song and the Beach Boys' "409" is uncannily close.

2. The URL is http://open.spotify.com/user/1210513370/playlist/5ivKqKJ HzUKK0J4QqO47Zf.

3. Timothy White describes both Gary Usher's *desire* to upgrade his current street rod to a 409 and the setting for the effects recording in the Wilson's neighborhood (White 1994, 153–56). Jon Stebbins, apparently drawing from memo-

ries of early Beach Boy David Marks, affirmatively states that Usher's car was a 348, not a 409 (Stebbins 2007, 40).

4. Cf. "Drag City," where backing chorus in second and subsequent verses sing "whine, whine, whine," the same onomatopoeia as in "Custom Machine."

5. For added effect, listeners were exhorted, via a notice on the record label, to listen in the dark.

6. In the case of Brian Wilson in particular, this identification is an important part of his latter-day image and an active site of critical interpretation. See Curnutt 2012. To be sure, the narrating persona of a song need not be closely identified with the person of the songwriter, though in some genres this is encouraged and seen as a mark of sincerity. But, in general, songs are heard as appropriate to their singers, even if written by another, and the best, most versatile singers can maintain this connection through remarkable range.

7. The highest tension in this staging of the Beach Boys' career is the unquestionably queasy-looking cover photo for the overinsistently titled album *Summer Days (and Summer Nights!!)*.

8. See Harrison 1997, 41, for further transcription.

9. I think a comparison with the Association or with the Four Seasons is appropriate here. The Beach Boys choral technique was built off the beautifully led vocal lines in Four Freshmen ballads, which the boys learned by rote at an early age with close family members, surely peerless ensemble training. Moreover, Brian had an effective falsetto, which put a strong high cap on their chord voicings. This foundation, enhanced by production effects, made for an extraordinarily tight and luxurious choral sound, among the most distinctive in the recorded history of American popular music.

10. The songs are limited to those recorded between 1964 and 1968 for various reasons (not least of which is space), but mostly to showcase the vigor and youth of the band's voices during that time.

11. Harmonists should also note the dissonant 6/4 effects the background vocals create in mm. 9–12 of the chorus.

12. Another seven seconds are shaved in the single version by dispensing with the instrumental introduction.

13. This version was officially released on the *Endless Harmony* compilation (1998).

14. A final word about "R(h)onda." A bootleg of a drunk Wilson paterfamilias, Murry, disrupting a recording session for the single version has been known to fans since the 1990s. (Excerpts are transcribed in White 1994, 230–33, and Carlin 2006, 53–58.) A psychotherapist who heard the bootleg found it an extraordinary document of family dysfunction, with Murry berating the band for not "singing from their hearts," and for having let success go to their heads. Other cutting, angry, and even vicious remarks punctuate these themes. While Murry was no longer involved in day-to-day management of the Beach Boys by this time and thus wasn't the presence he had once been, the enduring power of formative family dynamics is on display. That Murry's criticisms about what was going on in the session were leveled at a future number-one hit song is sadly ironic and shows how out of touch he had become with Brian's compositional abilities.

15. Brad Elliot claims that the song was indeed finished (Priore 1995, 147).

Questions remain as to why the Beach Boys didn't use it in *Smiley Smile* or patch it up for later release, as they did with "Surf's Up," "Our Prayer," and "Cabinessence."

16. Everett discusses a similar effect as "stop time," though many of his examples have some kind of fill—drum, vocal, or solo instrumental—and are thus more like cadenzas than grand pauses (Everett 2009, 311–13).

17. This public-service announcement was widely broadcast in fire-prone Western states, and was also likely shown in movie previews.

18. Already in evident decline in 1965, such trains threatened to disappear completely by 1968, and in 1971, Amtrak was formed to run a vastly reduced system.

THREE | Brian Wilson's Harmonic Language

PHILIP LAMBERT

WHAT ARE THE DEFINING features of a Brian Wilson song? The sound of male voices singing three-or-more-part harmony—typically involving a ringing falsetto at the top, possibly a doo-wop-inspired bass line underneath—stands out above all else. The voices might move together in block chords ("Surfer Girl," "Wendy") or interrelate in some sort of dialogue ("Fun, Fun, Fun," "I Get Around") or in counterpoint (the layered endings of "Wouldn't It Be Nice" and "God Only Knows"). The sound ingeniously blends the style of classic jazz vocal groups, such as the Four Freshmen and the Hi-Lo's, with 1950s doo-wop and rhythm and blues, and the rhythms and temperaments of rock 'n' roll.

But that's the vocal arrangement. What about the song itself, insofar as it can be separated from its manner of presentation? This chapter explores the underlying chord progressions of a Brian Wilson song—not the "vocal harmonies" but the basic harmonic language, expressed by both voices and instruments. It's a topic that has begun to receive more attention in recent years, starting with Daniel Harrison's (1997) essay on "experimental" tendencies in the chord structures and key relations of Beach Boys songs. My writings on this subject (2007, 2008) have highlighted selected harmonic aspects in a general song-by-song discussion of the Brian Wilson song catalog, and in a close study of his magnum opus, the Beach Boys' *Pet Sounds*. Most recently, Kirk Curnutt (2012) likewise considers chord types and progressions as distinctive elements of the Brian Wilson style. By exploring a core element in the craft of songwriting, we can learn more about his tastes and tendencies as a songwriter, as well as his musical models and influences.

63

More broadly, this chapter joins a surge in recent scholarly interest toward a deeper, categorical understanding of pop-rock harmony. Walter Everett (2009) stands at the forefront of this trend, building on his earlier work (2004, 2008) to examine intricate details of some sixty-five hundred recordings made between 1955 and 1969. Other valuable commentaries on the realms of pitch and harmony in this music include studies of harmonic patterns by Allan F. Moore (1992, 2001), harmony as a style element in an overview by Ken Stephenson (2002), and an examination of harmonic tendencies in one hundred top-rated songs from the 1950s through the 1990s by Trevor de Clercq and David Temperley (2011). Such studies bring us closer to defining a "common practice" of popular harmony for the second half of the twentieth century, both reflecting and absorbing the work of Brian Wilson and his generation of songwriters.

The entire corpus of available Brian Wilson songs includes not only cuts from Beach Boys albums but also recordings by other artists for whom he wrote, such as Jan and Dean and the Honeys in the 1960s, and his work as a solo artist since the late 1980s. The music considered for this chapter therefore includes all the original songs in the chronological listing in Lambert 2007 (334–68), plus tracks from Brian's more recent solo album *That Lucky Old Sun* (2008) and from the even newer album by the surviving, reunited Beach Boys, *That's Why God Made the Radio* (2012). The Brian Wilson songs singled out for discussion here are listed, with background and source information, in appendix 3.1.[1] Appendix 3.2 summarizes the chapter's methods of chord classification and identification, which are adapted from Everett (2009).

Origins and Influences

Brian Wilson has always built his songs from the ground up. "It starts with chords," he told an interviewer in 2011. "Then I come to the melody. The chords inspire the melody, and the melody inspires the lyrics" (Ghomeshi 2011). In the final product, his melodies hardly come across as afterthoughts, yet a strong harmonic foundation is one of his trademarks. As his collaborator Joe Thomas observed recently, "What Brian likes is chords" (Romano 2012b). His harmonic language ranges from staples of rock harmony to progressions rarely heard in the genre. And like other piano-based songwriters of his era, such as Carole King, Elton John, and Billy Joel, he draws expressivity and nuance from voicings, juxtapositions, and inversions.

Chord progressions in most of Brian's early songs reflect one, or at least one, of his three main musical influences: rock 'n' roll, doo-wop, and vocal jazz. Foremost among his acquisitions from rock 'n' roll, and its subgenre surf music, is the blues progression, both standard and modified. Straight twelve-bar blues progressions appear in the early surf instrumentals "Karate" (aka "Beach Boy Stomp," 1962), "Surf Jam" (1963), "Stoked" (1963), "Boogie Woodie" (1963), and "Carl's Big Chance" (1964), and in the early songs "Judy" (1962), "409" (1962), "The Baker Man" (1963), "Our Car Club" (1963), "Hide Go Seek" (1963), and "Little Honda" (1964). After the mid-1960s Brian essentially abandoned the blues progression in his songwriting, finally returning to it four decades later, for musical reminiscences of a Southern California childhood in three songs on *That Lucky Old Sun* (2008): "Morning Beat," "California Role," and "Going Home."

Some of the blues variants in early Brian Wilson songs arise from simple chord substitutions: ♭III in place of V in bar 9 of an otherwise standard blues progression in "Punchline" (1963); ♭VI in place of IV in bar 10 of a blues progression in a surf instrumental credited to Carl Wilson, "Shut Down, Part II" (1964). Other harmonic variants result when he replaces the third phrase of a blues progression (the last four bars) with a four-bar hook that doesn't conform to the blues chord pattern. Brian surely knew many earlier songs with two- or four-bar hooks inserted as the last two or four bars of blues progressions—Little Richard's "Tutti Frutti" (1956), Jerry Lee Lewis's "Whole Lotta Shakin' Goin' On" (1957), Elvis Presley's "Stuck on You" (1960), and The Vibrations' "Peanut Butter" (1961), among others—but in those cases the harmony of the hook conforms precisely to the standard harmonic structure of V–IV–I–I for bars 9–12 (one chord per bar). The typical Brian Wilson hook involves non-standard harmonies, more like Elvis Presley's "Don't Be Cruel" (1956), whose blues progression ends with ii–V–I–I ("Don't be [ii] cruel [V] to a heart that's [I] true"). In the Beach Boys' "Shut Down" (1963), for example, the third phrase of a blues progression restates the hook first heard in the song's introduction, which begins on II and moves through iv to V ("[II] Tach it up, Tach it up, [iv] buddy gonna [V] shut you [I] down"). A short time later the Beach Boys recorded "Little Deuce Coupe" (1963), whose hook moves back and forth between V and ii within bars 9 and 10 of a blues progression (0:21 "She's my [V] little deuce [ii] coupe, [V] you don't [ii] know what [V] I [I] got").

Actually, the first two times Brian inserted a hook in place of the final phrase of a blues progression, he also stretched its length. In the first Beach Boys single, "Surfin'" (1961), a six-bar hook ("Surfin' is the only life") expands a blues progression to fourteen bars (see Lambert 2007, 22–24). As Walter Everett (2009, 139) observes, that happens in this song because of an inner repetition of the V–IV in bars 9 and 10 of the blues progression, just as in fourteen-bar blues progressions in later recordings such as Jackie Wilson's "Baby Workout" (1963) and Mongo Santamaria's "Watermelon Man" (1963). A few months after "Surfin'," the Beach Boys recorded a derivative, "Surfin' Safari" (1962), that does something similar with a five-bar hook ("[V] Let's go surfin' now, [IV] everybody's learning how, [II] come on a safari with [V] me"), yielding a thirteen-bar progression (see Lambert 2007, 25–26). These two songs are typical of other examples of elongated blues progressions Everett describes in music of that period (Everett 2009, 139–40).

From Brian's second main influence, doo-wop, he inherited the I–vi–<IV or ii>–V chord pattern. He was not alone: the doo-wop progression represented, in Everett's words, "perhaps the single most constant element in early sixties pop music" (Everett 2009, 219). Brian's lifelong devotion to this progression began with one of his earliest songs, "Surfer Girl" (0:14 "[I] Little [vi] surfer, [IV] little [V] one") and recurs throughout Beach Boys albums and other projects of the 1960s (e.g., 1964's "Keep an Eye on Summer," 0:14 "[I] We said good- [vi] -bye last Sep- [ii^7] -tember [V]"). In the decades to come, his treatment of this single progression follows his own personal development and history. The chord pattern appears, for example, when he needs to establish centricity quickly in one of his tonally peripatetic songs of the late sixties, "This Whole World" (0:12 "[I] Lots of [vi] different [ii^7] people [V] every . . ."). In the midseventies, when he was reembracing the simplicity and directness of some of his earlier work, the progression makes several prominent appearances in *The Beach Boys Love You* (1977), including the choruses of "I Wanna Pick You Up" (0:54 "[I] I [vi^7] want to [ii^7] pick you [V^7] up") and "Johnny Carson" (2:12 "[I] Who's the [vi] man that [IV] we ad- [V] -mire?"), and looped underneath a repeating melodic phrase throughout "Mona" (0:00 "[I] Mona, come-a come-a come-a come [vi^7] to me, give me give me give me some [ii^7] lovin', tell me tell me tell me you [V] want it"). A retro aesthetic was again on display in the next decade, when Brian emerged from a low period in his personal life to make substantial contributions to *The Beach Boys* (1985), featuring doo-wop progressions in the choruses of "I'm So Lonely" (1:00 "[I] I've [vi^7] wished, [ii^7] since you went a- [V^7] -way"), "It's Just a Matter of Time" (0:00 "[I] Darlin', [vi^7–ii^7] I'm [V^7] lost without [I] you"), and "Male

Ego" (0:26 "[I] Male [vi⁷] ego is a [ii⁷] worldwide [V⁷] game"). And the decade after that, one of the highlights of Brian's second solo album, *Imagination* (1998), is the song he often sings in concerts as a tribute to his brother Carl, "Lay Down Burden," which uses a doo-wop progression to assist the reminiscence (first heard in the introduction, then again in the main verse at 0:52, "[I] So many years spent [vi⁹] runnin' away, [IV⁷] how many times I [V⁷] wished I could stay"). Most recently, recollections of the good old days in *That Lucky Old Sun* (2008) include a doo-wop pattern in the bridge of "Forever She'll Be My Surfer Girl" (1:31 "[I] Now there's all kinds of music [vi⁷] And don't you know the truth is [ii⁷] You were my special lover [I/5̂ V⁷]"). Fittingly, "Summer's Gone," the final track on *That's Why God Made the Radio* (2012)—thus perhaps the last new Brian Wilson song on a Beach Boys album—is a mellow, continuous loop of this same progression, as the voices reflect wistfully on days gone by (0:25 "[I⁹] Summer's gone, summer's gone away [vi⁹] Gone away with [IV⁹] yesterday [V]").

Among Brian's early doo-wop variants is "The Warmth of the Sun" (1964), whose initial I–vi descent is echoed a tritone below, ♭III–i♭⁷, before the familiar pattern gets back on track (0:13 "What [I] good is the [vi] dawn [♭III] that [i♭⁷] grows into [ii⁷] day? [V⁵⁺♯⁵]"). Later variants include basic chord alterations, such as the minor subdominant in "Baby Let Your Hair Grow Long" from the 1988 solo album (0:20 "[I] In my [vi♭⁷] mind [iv♭⁷] I can [V⁷] see"), and a surprising iii intruding between IV and V in a doo-wop throwback phrase of "Good Kind of Love" from the recent *That Lucky Old Sun* (0:31 "[I] Just him and [vi] her, [IV] there so close to- [iii] -geth- [V] -er").

Musical evidence of Brian's third primary influence, vocal jazz, can be as specific as the Beach Boys' literal re-creations of Four Freshmen songs "Their Hearts Were Full of Spring" (1962), which was retexted by Mike Love as "A Young Man Is Gone" (1963), and "Graduation Day" (1964). Brian also directly imitated Four Freshmen style in his arrangements of "The Lord's Prayer" (1963), "Auld Lang Syne" (1964), and "Baa Baa Black Sheep" ("Twinkle Twinkle") as "And Your Dream Comes True" (1965), and in brief passages from original songs such as 1963's "Ballad of Ole' Betsy" (in the ending, starting at 1:58) and "Being with the One You Love" from his first (1988) solo album (at 1:31, "in our private space"). But the Four Freshmen influence is equally, if less overtly, evident as one component of the Beach Boys sound itself, in songs like "Surfer Girl" (1962), "In My Room" (1963), "Ballad of Ole' Betsy" (1963), "The Warmth of the Sun" (1964), "Keep an Eye on Summer"

(1964), "Girls on the Beach" (1964), and many others. The general style and harmonic progressions in these songs are adapted from Top 40 radio, but their rich vocal harmonies, declaimed by voices moving rhythmically together, were directly inspired by Brian's close study of Four Freshmen records during his teenage years, up through about 1961 (see Lambert 2007, 4–11).

Further, as his songwriting matured, he also began to borrow more liberally from jazz harmony. "Your Summer Dream" (1963), for example, bears no imprints of Four Freshmen–style vocals at all—indeed, it is sung entirely by Brian Wilson alone, without vocal backing of any kind—and yet the seventh and ninth chords in its harmonic vocabulary, and many of the progressions that relate them, come from older jazz tunes that Brian knew well from Four Freshmen albums, not from current hits. Jazzy chord types and relations appear throughout Beach Boys albums of the mid-1960s, in songs such as "We'll Run Away" (1964), "When I Grow Up" (1964), "Kiss Me, Baby" (1965), "Let Him Run Wild" (1965), and "Please Let Me Wonder" (1965). The overall style of these songs is consistent with popular norms, but the jazz infusions add sophistication and artistry.

So too does the harmonic mobility of many early Brian Wilson songs recall Four Freshmen arrangements. From Freshmen recordings such as "Guilty" (1956) and "Time Was (Duerme)" (1958), he found inspiration to move the key upward by thirds in a song's bridge followed by a return to the original tonic for the returning main melody, in songs such as "Surfer Moon" (1963) and "Keep an Eye on Summer" (1964). In Freshmen recordings such as "I Remember You" (1956) and "I'll Remember April" (1958), he found models for modulating temporarily to the submediant major in the bridge, as in Beach Boys songs "Your Summer Dream" (1963) and "Wouldn't It Be Nice" (1965). Other instances of key variety within his music may not so specifically reflect Four Freshmen precedents, but likely came about from his intense familiarity with their recordings.

On the other hand, key changes within verse-chorus forms—usually exemplifying Christopher Doll's "expressive modulation" (Doll 2011)—may be equally indebted to other influences, because instances of this form in Four Freshmen albums are rare. The Beach Boys recorded "Finders Keepers," for example, whose choruses are a whole step higher than its verses, in February 1963, shortly after the Four Seasons' "Walk Like a Man," which has choruses in the subdominant, hit the charts (Lambert 2007, 71–73). Earlier verse-chorus key shifts that Brian had undoubtedly heard on the radio include Guy Mitchell's "Ninety-Nine Years" (1956) and the Ames Brothers' "Pussy Cat" (1958). In his songwriting the following year, 1964, the trend continued, in the shifts up by whole step for the choruses of "Don't Worry, Baby"; this is one of the few things this song does that Phil Spector's "Be My Baby" does *not* do. Around that same time Brian also shifted up by half step for the choruses of "Pom Pom Play Girl" and "Don't Back Down," and down by major third for the choruses of "All Dressed Up for School."

Key changes up by half or whole step without returning, Everett's "truck driver's modulation" (Everett 2009, 283–84), are equally common in all of Brian Wilson's influences. When he shifts up a half step for the final quatrain of "Surfer Girl" (1962), this seems a direct echo of the Four Freshmen's "Their Hearts Were Full of Spring" (1961) and many other Freshmen recordings, but has many other precedents as well, including recordings released as far back as the midforties and fifties, such as the Dick Haymes–Helen Forrest duet "It Had to Be You" (1944), the Frank Sinatra–Dinah Shore duet "It's All Up to You" (1946), Frank Loesser's "A Bushel and a Peck" from *Guys and Dolls* (1950), the Mills Brothers' "The Glow-Worm" (1952), Joan Weber's "Let Me Go, Lover" (1954), the McGuire Sisters' "Sincerely" (1955), the Four Coins' "Shangri-La" (1957), the Four Lads' "There's Only One of You" (1958), and Chubby Checker's very proto–Beach Boys "The Hucklebuck" (1960). In the Brian Wilson catalog, half-step ascents before a lyric is finished are common, as in "The Warmth of the Sun" (1964), "I Get Around" (1964), "Goin' On" (1979), "California Calling" (1984), and "Midnight's Another Day" (2008). Just as frequent are half-step shifts after a lyric is finished, only for a final restatement or ending, as in the single release of "Be True to Your School" (1963), "Keep an Eye on Summer" (1964), "When I Grow Up (to Be a Man)" (1964), "Don't Let Her Know She's an Angel" (1985), "Your Imagination" (1997), and "That's Why God Made the Radio" (1999).

Standard Practices

In the six-year period from 1961, when Brian Wilson began to develop his songwriting skills in earnest, to 1967, when he turned twenty-five, he wrote songs for eleven Beach Boys albums, including music of remarkable sophistication in *Pet Sounds* (1966) and *Smile* (1967), along with material for various friends and collaborators. The decades that followed have seen high and low periods, personally and musically, but have included songs for seventeen more Beach Boys albums since 1967 and, starting in 1988, material for a string of albums as a solo artist—five that were completed and released and several others that were not. His music since the midsixties has occasionally rekindled the spirit of innovation from his prodigious youth but more often searched for new possibilities in familiar resources.

Along with the early instances of blues progressions and the constancy of doo-wop and Four Freshmen–style harmonies, Brian's mature harmonic language features techniques that are broadly typical of popular music of his era. As Everett observes, "There is a great body of pop music . . . featuring only three chords" (Everett 2009, 223). Brian Wilson's devotion to the I, IV, and V chords begins with his earliest Beach Boys songs, "Surfin'" (1961) and "Surfin' Safari" (1962), and persists throughout his career. This includes not only blues progressions but also songs that unfold the three basic harmonic functions in a very orderly manner: I–IV–V–I, one chord per bar (as in the first example cited by Everett 2009, 223, Joni James's "You Are My Love" of 1955). In the verse from "Noble Surfer," on the second Beach Boys album (1963), the directness and simplicity of this pattern underscores the nobility of the protagonist (0:06 "[I] The surfers call him noble and that's [IV] just what he is, he's [V] dedicated to the mighty [I] sea"). The following year, however, he used the same progression for less noble purposes, in the lascivious "All Dressed Up for School" (0:11 "[I] Well, she first caught my eye runnin' [IV] 'round in shorts, but she [V] never bothered with her [I] hair"), later sanitized as "I Just Got My Pay" (1970). A few years later, this progression was just out for a "Good Time" (0:43 "[I] Maybe it won't last, but [IV] what do we care? My [V] baby and I just want a [I] good time"). In two later songs, "He Couldn't Get His Poor Old Body to Move" (1988) and "The Private Life of Bill and Sue" (2012), it underlies both verse and chorus. But there are also many examples from throughout his music of I–IV–V–I in unequal proportions, notably "Do It Again" (1968), which uses the three-chord pattern as a musical reminiscence of the old days, starting with four bars of tonic before moving more rapidly through the IV and V and returning I (0:08 "[I] It's automatic when I talk with old friends, the conversation turns to girls we knew, and their [IV] hair was soft and [V] long and the beach was the [I] place to go").

Another common ordering of the three chords begins with the neighboring I–IV–I before moving to the dominant, like the beginning succession of a blues progression but in different, roughly equal proportions, usually one chord per bar. Brian and his collaborators used this pattern in Jan and Dean's "She's My Summer Girl" (1963), in both verse (0:17 "Well, I [I] met her at the grad night [IV] party this year, day [I] dun dun dun dun, day [V] dun dun dun") and chorus (0:32 "And now [I] she's my [IV] summer girl, [I] you know we're havin' [V] fun"). In the verse of Brian's "Back Home," written in 1963 but not recorded by the Beach Boys until 1976, the progression adopts an air of nostalgia (0:08 "[I] Well I'm goin' back this summer to O- [IV] -hio, I'm gonna [I] seek out all my friends I've always [V] known"), perpetuated by I–IV–V–I in the chorus (0:39 "Back [I] home, I spent my [IV] summer, [V] back home, Back [I] home"). And the immediacy of the I–IV–I–V pattern is the perfect complement for a joyride in "Fun, Fun, Fun" (0:18 "Well, she [I] got her daddy's car and she cruised through the hamburger [IV] stand now, Seems she for- [I] -got all about the library like she told her old [V] man now"). For the Honeys' "He's a Doll" (1964), Brian's venture into the girl-group medium with his future wife and her sister, the I–IV–I–V pattern is a direct imitation of one of Phil Spector's girl-group recordings, the Crystals' "Da Doo Ron Ron (When He Walked Me Home)" of the previous year: the Honeys' verse (0:06 "[I] Well, he's not very tall but he's not too short, he's just all [IV] right now, And with his [I] sandy blonde hair and his great big smile, oh what a [V] sight now") remakes the Crystals' chorus (0:20 "[I] Yes, my [IV] heart stood still, [I] Yes, his [V] name was Bill"). (The Crystals' verse is an equally proportioned I–IV–V–I.) Finally, the I–IV–I–V in "With Me Tonight" offers a perfect window into the simplicity of *Smiley Smile*, the first Beach Boys album just after the *Smile* project ran aground in 1967. First, a basic doo-wop phrase, "On and on, she go dum be do dah, On and on, she go dum be do" reappears transposed to IV (0:09), back to I (0:18), then to V (0:27). After that the lyric proper begins ("With me tonight . . .") and develops and decorates the same transpositional relations (I [0:36]– IV [0:44]–I [0:53]–V [1:03]).

In another song on *Smiley Smile*, "Gettin' Hungry," the chorus progression repeats the first two chords in the I–IV–I–V pattern before completing it, accentuating the ornamenting function of the IV in relation to tonic and the desperation of a fruitless search for companionship (0:39 "Gettin' [I] hungry, hungry for [IV] my kind of woman, I'm gettin' [I] hungry, soon I gotta [IV] find me a woman, I'm gettin' [I] hungry, searchin' for a [V] pretty girl"). Indeed, almost two decades later, in "I'm So Lonely" (1985), that same ornamenting repetition communicates the same sort of emotional longing (0:20 "[I] I'm so [IV] lonely, [I] really really so [IV] lonely, [I] I wish that [V] you could comfort [vi⁷] me, oh-

oh- [V] -oh"). But still another decade after that, in "South American" (1997), the I–IV alternation supports a more positive message, surrounding the relaxed pace of a subtropical getaway, first in the verse (0:24 "Got a [IV] letter from a long lost [I] cousin of mine, who wants a [IV] little piece of heaven in the [I] Argentine, It's a [IV] different planet, it's a [I] different place, because it's [V] out of this world without travelin' to space"), then in the chorus (0:57 "South A- [I] -merican, well you [IV] know I would, South A- [I] -merican, if I [IV] only could, [I] I wanna be, [IV] I wanna be [V] where it's at").

Other instances of I–IV alternations simply ornament tonic without moving so readily to other harmonic functions. I and IV exclusively dominate the instrumental break, with wordless vocals, near the end of the Beach Boys' "The Little Girl I Once Knew" (1:27–1:49). The I–IV interplay emerges as a harmonic motif in the *Smile* songs "Cabin Essence," "Wind Chimes," and "Mrs. O'Leary's Cow" (as discussed in Lambert 2007, 281–83). Around that same time, "Friends" (1968), a collaboration among all three Wilson brothers and Al Jardine, used the I–IV combination with a harmonic shift (0:00 "[DM: I] We've been [IV] friends now for [I] so many [IV] years, [E♭M: I] We've been to- [IV] -gether through the [I] good times and the [IV] tears"); a few years later, the refrain from "Marcella" (1971) did something similar without the key change. In recent years the I–IV alternation has become Brian's go-to progression for evoking relaxed, happy times, as in "South American" (see above), also the verse of "It's OK" (0:00 "Fun is [I] in, it's no sin, it's that time again, To shed your [IV] load, hit the road, on the run again, Summer [I] skies in our eyes and a warmer sun, It's one for [IV] all, all for one, all for all-out fun"), and in verse and chorus of "Beaches in Mind" (2012), highlighting the pattern's reggae associations. When repeated as a plagal ending, however, the I–IV alternation sounds even mellower, almost submissive, helping a song to "Melt Away" (1987).

Examples of other ornamentations of tonic are equally abundant in Brian Wilson efforts. He wrote only one song, "Child of Winter" (1974), of pure I–vi alternations—unavoidably evoking the Isley Brothers' iconic "Shout" (1959)—and used a vi–I pairing in the chorus of "Help Me, Rhonda" (1965), just before the hook, to delay an anticipated return to I from IV (0:42 "[IV] Help me, Rhonda, help help me, Rhonda, [vi⁷] Help me, Rhonda, [I] help help me, Rhonda"). More commonly, however, interplay between I and vi precedes a move to the dominant. In "Run-Around Lover" (1963) the vi moves directly to V (0:07 "[I] I've heard lately of the [vi] lover's fool, [V] And how he treated all his [I] girls so cruel"), while in "Drive-In" (1963) the vi returns to I before progressing to V (0:06 "[I] Every time I have a date there's only one place to go, that's to the [vi] drive-in, It's such a [I] groovy place to talk and maybe watch a show, down at the [V] drive-in"). Brian used the same technique in another recreational song the following year, "Amusement Parks USA" (0:07 "[I] At Palisades and Salisbury parks, the rolly coasters are [vi] flyin', At Euclid [I] beach on the flyin' turns I bet you can't keep from [V] smilin'"). Some later songs extend the I–vi alternation before arriving at the dominant: the verse of "Some of Your Love" (1972) repeats the interplay along with a text repetition (0:14 "[I] Some, some, some of your [vi] love, won't you give me some, [I] some of your [vi] love, [I] Some, some, some of your [vi] love, doot doo, [V] oh"), while "Crack at Your Love" (1984) uses a wordless I–vi alternation (starting at 0:23) that extends into the verse (0:32 "[I] I been keepin' my [vi] eyes on you, [I] I finally found the nerve to [vi] talk to you, [V] There's somethin' that you [vi] oughta know, [V] don't you know that I [I] love you so").

A I–vi alternation leading to a pre-dominant (IV or ii) can resemble an elaborated doo-wop progression, as in the verse of "Heads You Win, Tails I Lose" from the Beach Boys' first album in 1962 (0:11 "[I] Why do we have to gamble just to [vi] see who's right, Why [I] can't we arbitrarily re- [vi] -solve a fight, But [IV] with your style of gamblin' there's no [V] chance to win, That's [IV] how it is and that's the way it's [V] always been"), and in a song recorded the next day, "Land Ahoy," that was later retexted as "Cherry, Cherry Coupe" and released on the Beach Boys' fourth album (1963). In later years Brian added twists to this idea, such as a minor subdominant in "I'll Bet He's Nice" (1976) from the *Beach Boys Love You* album (0:27 "[I] You, pretty [vi] darlin', [I] You, my pretty [vi] darlin', [I] You, pretty darlin', [iv] You, my pretty [V] darlin'"), and a stepwise approach to the dominant in a song with vocals recorded by his brother Carl in the midnineties but posthumously supplemented by the Brian Wilson band a decade later, "Soul Searchin'": first at the end of the verse (0:35 "While my [ii] tears keep [iii] fallin' down [IV–V]"), then again in the chorus (0:38 "[I] Soul [vi] searchin', [I] soul [vi] searchin', I'm [I] soul [vi] searchin', [ii] how could I [iii] say good- [IV] -bye? [V]"), and in longer durations at the end of the bridge (2:12 "I keep [ii^9] walkin' and I'm [iii^7] wonderin' and I'm [IV^7] lookin' for a [V] sign"). In 2012 Brian was still exploring this pattern's possibilities, in the latter-day Beach Boys' "Isn't It Time," with a I–vi alternation leading to a ii–V alternation (0:00 "After it's [I] all been said, [vi] The music spinnin' [I] in our head, [vi] Can't forget the [ii^7] feelin' of, [V] The magic of that [ii⁷] summer love [V]"). This progression dominates the chorus of that song as well.

The ii–V alternation seen here and earlier in "Little Deuce Coupe" (1963) is a Brian Wilson favorite. Frank Zappa was also an advocate: the return of V to ii in the "Little Deuce Coupe" hook, wrote Zappa, was "an important step forward by going backward" (Zappa 1989, 187). Brian's awareness of this technique may have begun with the Four Freshmen recording of "Day by Day" (1955), which starts with two cycles of ii–V before arriving at tonic ("[ii⁹] Day by [V⁹] day, I'm falling [ii⁹] more in love with [V⁹] you, And [I⁹] day by day . . ."). In the verse of the Beach Boys' "I Get Around" (1964), the ii–V alternation is implied by a forceful solitary guitar figure (0:19 "I'm gettin' [ii] bugged drivin' [V] up and down this [ii] same old [V] strip, I gotta [ii] find a new [V] place where the [ii] kids are [V] hip"), building anticipation for the arrival of tonic in the later chorus (0:36 "I get a- [I] -round"). And in the chorus of "I Just Wasn't Made for These Times" from *Pet Sounds* (1966), the refusal of tonic to fulfill the promise of the repeating pre-dominant and dominant accentuates the singer's existential despair (0:43 "[ii⁷] Sometimes, I feel [V⁷] very sad, [ii⁷] Sometimes, I feel [V⁷] very sad, [ii⁷] Sometimes, I feel [V⁷] very sad"). Sunnier skies dawned on the progression a few years later, however, in "All I Wanna Do" (1969) from the Beach Boys' *Sunflower* (0:11 "[ii] All I wanna [V] do, is [ii] always bring good to [V] you, to [ii] give you all the love I [V] can, and [ii] help you in whatever you [V] do").

In "Don't Worry, Baby" (1964), the ii–V connection is repeated up a whole step to shift the key up at the end of the verse, as if intensifying the emotional message. The first V is reinterpreted as IV to pivot between the two keys:

```
0:34   But she looks in my eyes,   and makes me realize when she says...
E:     ii⁷            V
F♯:                   IV        ii⁷              V                    I
```

When Brian reminisced about his formative years more than four decades later, in "Southern California" (2008), he also recalled these same ii–V alternations and whole-step shifts:

```
0:31   Down the Pacific coast,   Surfin' on the A. M.,   heard those voices again
G:     I ⁷                       iii⁷
A:                               ii⁷        V        ii⁷             V

       Southern California,   dreams wake up for you,   And when you wake up here,   you wake up everywhere
G:                            ii⁷          V            ii⁷            V
A:     I      IV⁷      I      IV⁷          ♭⁷
```

Some of Brian's ii–V alternations are modeled very specifically on "He's So Fine," a hit for the Chiffons in early 1963, which uses this pattern in two long a phrases, alternating with extended tonics in two long b phrases:

(a1) He's so [ii] fine, [V] wish he were [ii] mine, [V] that handsome [ii] boy over there, [V] the one with the [ii] wavy hair [V]
(b1) I don't know how I'm gonna [I] do it, but I'm gonna make him mine, be the envy of all the girls, it's just a matter of time
(a2) He's a soft-spoken [ii] guy, [V] also [ii] seems kinda shy, [V] makes me [ii] wonder if I [V] should even [ii] give him a try [V]
(b2) But then again he can't [I] shy, he can't shy away forever, and I'm gonna make him mine, if it takes me forever

The Beach Boys' "Little Saint Nick," recorded later that year for a Christmas release, adopts the same harmonic pattern and four-part phrase structure, although with shorter phrases:

(a1) Well, a- [ii] -way up [V] north where the [ii] air gets [V] cold
(b1) There's a [I] tale about Christmas that you've all been told
(a2) And a [ii] real famous [V] cat all dressed [ii] up in [V] red
(b2) And he [I] spends the whole year workin' out on his sled

The following year Brian used the scheme again as the basis for "Thinkin' 'bout You Baby," a song he wrote and produced for a friend of Mike Love's, Sharon Marie, that later became the basis for the verse of "Darlin'" (1967). He added a I–vi alternation in the b phrase (as did George Harrison in "My Sweet Lord" a few years later), and moved directly into the chorus after the second a phrase:

(a1) I lie a- [ii] -wake in bed, [V] as thoughts go [ii] through my head, [V]
(b)   Thinking of [I] what I'll do [vi] to make you [I] love me too [vi]
(a1) I hardly [ii] sleep a wink, [V] just lie a- [ii] -wake and think [V]
(c)   I'll do any- [I] -thing, babe... [begins chorus]

Brian's devotion to this same harmonic pattern and phrase structure continued unabated in 2008, with yet another nod to earlier days, in the bridge (0:49) of "California Role":

(a1) [ii] Every [V] girl's the next [ii] Mari- [V] -lyn
(b2) [I] Every guy, Errol Flynn
(a2) [ii] Sometime's you've [V] got to [ii] edit your [V] dreams
(b2) [I] And find the spotlight behind the scenes

These songs starting with ii–V alternations are also among the best examples in Brian Wilson's work of the off-tonic opening, or *auxiliary cadence*. He has also explored other ways of delaying a song's first tonic. One reason "Let Him Run Wild" (1965) works as a tribute to Burt Bacharach is the harmonic resemblance of its off-tonic opening ("[iii⁷/ĝ] When I [vi⁷] watched you walk with him, [iii⁷/ĝ] tears filled my [vi⁷] eyes") to Bacharach songs with off-tonic openings such as "Wives and Lovers" (1963), "Anyone Who Had a Heart" (1963), or "Walk On By" (1964). Less harmonically disorienting are Brian Wilson songs beginning on the dominant but finding their tonics soon enough, including "A Thing or Two" (1967), "Roller Skating Child" (1976), and "Baby Let Your Hair Grow Long" (1988). In Everett's words, the eventual arrival of tonic in such cases brings "a rush of familiarity that often seems like the dissipation of clouds" (Everett 2009, 215). The effect is particularly pronounced when a song starts on vi and thus stakes a reasonable claim as a minor tonic, before eventually giving way to the true tonic I—as Everett describes in the Beatles' "She Loves You" (1963). Brian's "My Diane" (1976) begins on vi ("[vi] Now that I have lost my [IV] Diane . . .") and delays the first I throughout the verse, as the lyric mourns the loss of a lover, revealing the true tonic only at the beginning of the chorus, which tries to reduce the heartbreak to its essence (0:27 "[I] Everything is [IV] old and [V] nothing is [I] new"). "Let's Go to Heaven in My Car" (1986) starts on vi but finally finds its first tonic within the verse (0:22 "[vi⁷] "So many times I've had that helpless [iii⁷] feelin, But [ii⁷] no one or any kind of [V] medicine worked at [I] all").

The role of the iii in "Let's Go to Heaven in My Car," and in other songs discussed earlier ("Good Kind of Love," "Let Him Run Wild," "Soul Searchin'," "Southern California"), begs for individual attention, as a window into other aspects of Brian's basic harmonic practice. As Everett points out, because the iii shares two tones with both tonic and dominant, it has somewhat of a "conflicted identity," often appearing "when a special sort of sensitivity is desired" (Everett 2009, 218). The iii–vi interplay in "Baby Let Your Hair Grow Long" and "Let Him Run Wild" (above) is typical. In "Girl Don't Tell Me" (1965) that interplay helps avoid tonic at the end of the verse (0:23 "You didn't [vi] answer my [iii] letters so I [vi] figured it was [iii] just a [II] lie [IV]"), then continues to serve that purpose in the chorus (1:01 "[ii] Girl don't [iii] tell me you'll [vi] write [iii]"). "Funky Pretty" (1972) begins with a key-defining I–V alternation, but then the second section uses V–I's minor analogue, iii–vi, to avoid tonic until the stanza is complete (0:37 "But [iii⁷] where's my spark in the [vi⁷] dark, [iii⁷] Glow, glow, glow, c'mon [vi⁷] glow, The funky [iii⁷] pretty flame in my [vi⁷] heart, Me and my [iii⁷] Pisces lady [V/2̂] are a- [I] -part"). In other songs the iii simply becomes a tonic partner with I, as in the verse of "I'll Bet He's Nice" (0:00 "I'll bet he's [I] nice, [iii] I'll bet he's [I] nice [iii]"), or participates in a standard stepwise bass descent from I to vi, as in "Good Timin'" (1974), both chorus (0:00 "[I] Good, good [iii/7̂] timin', [vi⁷] good, good timin'") and verse (0:20 "[I] All us [iii/7̂] people [vi⁷]"). Other instances of bass lines stepping down from I to vi don't use the iii to harmonize 7̂ but just leave it dissonant against the held-over I (e.g., first section of "TM Song," bridge of "Baby Let Your Hair Grow Long," chorus of "Fantasy Is Reality," beginning of "Christmasey").

One consequence of an oft-mentioned watershed moment in Brian Wilson's life and work, the release of Phil Spector's production of the Ronettes' "Be My Baby" in August 1963, was a more intense interest in root movement by fifth, as in the chain of secondary dominants at the end of the verse of that song (0:22 "[III] So won't you say you love me, [VI] I'll make you so proud of me, [II] We'll make 'em turn their heads, [V] Every place we go"). It was under this song's influence that Brian recorded a cluster of songs the following year with progressions by fifths starting on iii, including the bridge of "We'll Run Away" (1:06 "If our [iii⁷] love is that much [vi⁷] stronger, it will [ii⁷] last that much [V] lon-ger"), the bridge of "Girls on the Beach" (1:14 "The [iii⁷] sun in her [vi⁷] hair, the [iii⁷] warmth of the [vi⁷] air, On a [II⁷] summer [ii⁷] day [V]"), and the end of the main section of "The Man with All the Toys" (0:23 "A [IV] big man in a [iv] chair, and [iii] little tiny men every- [vi] -where, he's the [II] man with all the [ii] toys [V]"). Brian has returned to the fifths progression starting on iii often in the years since, including a song begun in 1969, "Soulful Old Man Sunshine" (0:35 "[I] She looks so [IV] fresh and sweet, [I] Keeps herself [IV] soft and tender, [iii] No wonder that [vi] I can sing a [ii] song about my [V] baby"), the passage just after the I–iii alternation mentioned above in "I'll Bet He's Nice" (0:19 "[iii⁷] Please don't tell me [vi⁷] if it's true, Be- [ii⁷] -cause I'm still in [V] love with [I] you"), and a song from the mideighties eventually recorded for the 2004 solo album, "Don't Let Her Know She's an Angel" (0:37 "[iii⁷] Don't let her [vi⁷] know that she's [ii⁷] touchin' me, I'm [V] scared that she'll want to go [I] free"). By adding two other chords, rooted on 4̂ and 7̂, to these progressions, the diatonic circle of fifths can be completed, as Brian Wilson did in two songs in minor keys: the wordless, a cappella "One for the Boys" (1988) from his first solo album, and "Cry" (1997), a highlight of his second solo album (0:35 "[i] You broke my [iv] heart, [♭VII] broke it in [♭III] two, how [♭VI] could I have [iv] left you a- [ii⁰⁷] -lone [V]").

In a number of instances Brian has used the iii–vi–ii–V(–I) pattern as a starting point or framework for ornamentation or variation. In one variation he moves the first two chords in the sequence later, after the dominant, thus hinting at a tonality shift toward the relative minor, with the iii implying a minor dominant of vi. This happens at the end of the verse of "When I Grow Up (to Be a Man)" (1964), just before the hook (0:18 "Will I joke a- [ii⁷] -round, [V] and still dig those [iii⁷] sounds [vi⁷]"), and again in the chorus of "Shelter" from the recent reunited Beach Boys album (0:44 "I'll give you shelter [ii⁷] from the storm, [V] And a house to [iii⁷] keep you warm [vi⁷]"). Another variation simply reverses positions of the iii and vi within the fifths progression, as in two songs from the midseventies, "Hey Little Tomboy" (0:31 "[vi⁷] Hey little, hey little, hey little tom- [iii⁷] -boy, [ii] time to turn [V] into a [I] girl") and "Still I Dream of It" (0:45 "And it [vi] haunts me so, like a [iii] dream that's somehow linked to all the [ii] stars above [V]").

The iii chord leads even more commonly to the pre-dominant IV and then V, what Everett calls a "single coherent, goal-directed gesture" (Everett 2009, 224). I–iii–IV–V appears often in early Brian Wilson songs, perhaps imitating older songs he knew well, not on Four Freshmen albums but in popular hits such as the Platters' "Heaven on Earth" (1956), the Fleetwoods' "Mr. Blue" (1959), and Jan and Dean's "It's Such a Good Night for Dreaming" (1960). Brian used this progression underneath the voice-over in "The Lonely Sea" (1962) on the second Beach Boys album (starting at 1:31); supporting the main melody of "Ballad of Ole' Betsy" (1963) on the fourth Beach Boys album (0:13 "She was [I] born in [iii] '32, and [IV] was she ever [V] pretty"); in the chorus of "I Do" (1963), written for the Castells (0:19 "And that's I [I] do, take [iii] you, for my [IV] wife, for the rest of my [V] life"); in the refrain of a song written for television star Paul Petersen, "She Rides with Me" (1964), tacked on to the end of a blues progression (0:28 "[iii] All the guys try but I [IV] know she'll pass 'em [V] by, she rides with [I] me"); and in the refrain of "Keep an Eye on Summer" (1964) on the fifth Beach Boys album (0:27 "[I] Keep an [iii] eye on [IV] summer, [ii–V] this [I] year"). Any progression with step-related roots, as in the iii–IV–V in these songs, invites artful contrary motion between melody and bass line (see Everett 2009, 224–25), and while many early Brian Wilson examples display a variety of relationships between melody and bass, another song from the same era,

"Fun, Fun, Fun" (1964), moves the melody of its hook deftly downward against the rising bass (0:36 "And she'll have [I] fun, fun, [iii] fun 'til her [IV] daddy takes the [V] T-bird a- [I] -way"). Later examples of the I–iii–IV–V may involve slight modifications, such as a detour from IV to ii, expanding the pre-dominant, in the bridge of "I'll Bet He's Nice" (1:18 "[I] Baby, [iii] don't you ever tell me that your [IV] leaving, [ii] now that you [V] got me to [I] believe in"); a detour from iii to vi, recalling the iii–vi alternations, in the bridge of "Everything I Need" (1:48 "[I] Everyone I [iii] ever knew, is [vi] looking for a [iii] someone who, can [IV] fit into the [V] spaces in their [I] dreams"); an insertion of vi on the way from I to iii in the chorus of "Lay Down Burden" (1:31 "[I] Down, lay me [vi⁷] down, lay me [iii] down, [IV] lay down [V] burden"); and several diversions in "Live Let Live" (0:07 "I've got a notion we come from the ocean and [I] God [iii] all [vi] might- [I] -y [IV] passed his [ii] hand on the [I/$\hat{5}$] waters [V]").

Although I–iii–IV–V progressions are rare in Four Freshmen recordings, fully stepwise ascents from tonic are common, as they are in old standards generally. Indeed, when called upon to demonstrate Four Freshmen harmonies at the piano in a video interview (on the *I Just Wasn't Made for These Times* DVD, 1996), a stepwise ascent, I–ii–iii–IV, is the progression Brian played, from the beginning of the Freshmen recording of "I'll Remember April" (1958). He was also certainly familiar with fully stepwise progressions in the Freshmen recordings of "I Heard You Cried Last Night (and So Did I)" (1958) and "My Funny Valentine" (1961). A complete diatonic rise from I to V appears in his own music in "Merry Christmas, Baby," on the 1964 *Beach Boys Christmas* album (0:11 "[I] She's gonna leave me, and she don't believe me, but [ii] I'll [iii] be [IV] true [V] now"), but in general he is more likely to alter or decorate the progression, as in "From There to Back Again" (1999), which starts up the ladder but then reverses course (0:43 "You've been [I⁷] thinking 'bout some things we [ii⁷] used to do, [iii⁷] Thinking 'bout when life was still in [IV⁷] front of you, [iii⁷] Back where you belong, our [ii⁷] favorite song, Won't you [V¹¹] listen"), and the beginning of the chorus of "Fairy Tale" (1990), which jumps up to vi before getting back on track (1:05 "[I] Your heart's my [ii⁷] hope, my [I/$\hat{3}$] kingdom [vi⁷] and my [ii⁷] destiny [iii⁷–IV–V–I]"). In his duet with his first wife, Marilyn, "Let's Put Our Hearts Together" (1976) on the *Beach Boys Love You*, her first phrase is supported by a stepwise progression making it from I up to IV but then backtracking to iii and stabilizing, using a secondary dominant, on vi, as she questions his devotion (0:24 "[I] I know you've [ii⁷] had so much ex- [I/3̂] -perience that [IV] you don't need a- [III⁷] -nother person in your [vi⁷] life"). Brian's subsequent reassuring response takes a cue from Marilyn's III–vi and continues the progression as a series of fifth-relations (0:36 "[vi⁷/2̂] I know it [II⁷] may sound funny, [vi⁷/2̂] but you're the [II⁷] kind of woman [V] who'd make a [ii⁷] very sweet [V⁷] wife").

Stepwise progressions that are missing the initial tonic usually just elaborate the pre-dominant function, as in the example from "Soul Searchin'" cited above, also the end of the chorus of "Let's Stick Together," a song written for one of several abandoned solo projects in the late 1980s (0:57 "[ii⁷] Let's stick to- [iii⁷] -gether and [IV] always to- [V] -gether"). In "Sweet Mountain" (1972), written for Marilyn and her sister to record as American Spring, the stepwise dominant preparation is more fragmented (0:28 "[IV] Stand- [iii⁷] -in' [ii⁷] there, [IV] Stand- [iii⁷] -in' [ii⁷] there, [IV⁷] When [iii⁹] will I [ii⁹] see [V¹¹] him").

A Brian Wilson bass line often carries weight and prominence—a by-product, perhaps, of his own experience as the Beach Boys' bassist in the early years. "Melodic bass lines" in his music were one object of ad-miration for his contemporary Paul McCartney in 1993 (in the booklet accompanying the *Good Vibrations* CD set, page 36). But it is not just a bass line's tunefulness that drew McCartney's praise; he also singled out Brian's use of chord inversion, or in McCartney's words, "using notes that weren't the obvious notes to use." Elton John has highlighted this same facet in Brian's work as a particular influence on his own songwrit-ing (in an interview included as a special feature on the *All-Star Tribute to Brian Wilson* DVD, 2001, among other places). We've seen examples of chord inversion already, much earlier in "Let Him Run Wild" (iii⁷/7̂) and "Funky Pretty" (V/2̂), and just above in two of the songs with step-wise ascents, "Fairy Tale" and "Let's Put Our Hearts Together," which use I/3̂ in place of iii.

One frequent instance of inversion in Brian's music is the cadential 6/4, notated here as I/5̂ preceding a dominant ("cadential I/5̂"). It was a cadence formula he knew well, not from Mozart but from Four Freshmen records (e.g., the "learned" passage in "Now You Know," 1951) and from pop songs such as Rick Nelson's "Travelin' Man" (1961), Elvis Presley's "Can't Help Falling in Love" (1962), and Chuck Jackson's re-cording of Burt Bacharach's "Any Day Now" (1962). And he often used it quite traditionally: as part of a music history lesson in "That Same Song" (0:45 "[IV] We're [iii⁷] singin' that [vi⁷] same [iii⁷] song, that [IV] same [I/5̂] song, that [V] same [I] song"); expressing a mournful good-bye in "She Says That She Needs Me" (1:00 "[I/5̂] Sorry, baby, it's

[V¹¹] time we said good- [I] -bye"). He used the cadential I/5̂ in the title song of *That Lucky Old Sun* (2008), not only at cadence points but within phrases as well (0:09 "[I/5̂] Up in the mornin', [I⁷] out on the job, [I/3̂] work so [IV] hard for my [I/5̂] pay, [V] But that [vi] lucky old [I/5̂] sun's got [I/3̂] nothin' to [IV] do [♯iv°⁷] But [I/5̂] roll around [V⁷] heaven all [I] day"). Later in that album we hear the cadential I/5̂ again in the examples cited above from "Forever She'll Be My Surfer Girl" and "Live Let Live."

One aspect of the harmonic invention in *Pet Sounds* (1966) is the embellishment and variation of cadential I/5̂s. In one of the most expressive songs of the cycle, "Don't Talk (Put Your Head on My Shoulder)," an intricate chromatic elaboration enriches an instrumental meditation (see Lambert 2008, 124–25, example 7). The entire chorus of "I Know There's an Answer" is essentially a cadential I/5̂ elaborated with diversions to vi and ii (0:46 "[I/5̂] I know there's an [vi] answer, [I/5̂] I know now, but [vi] I had to find it [ii⁷] by myself [V¹¹]"). Later Beach Boys albums bring more of the same, including "Meant for You" (1968) from *Friends* (0:00 "[I/5̂] As I [I] sit and close my eyes, there's [vi] peace in my mind, and I'm [I/5̂] hopin' that you'll find it [IV] too, [♯iv°⁷] and these [I/5̂] feelings in my heart I know are meant for [ii⁷] you, meant for [V] you [I/5̂-V]") and "All I Wanna Do" (1970) from *Sunflower*, just after the ii–V alternation mentioned earlier (0:31 "[vi⁷] Sure as the [IV⁷] sun will come around again to [I/5̂] start off another [III⁷] day, [vi⁷] You can be [IV⁷] sure that in my heart and soul I'll [I/5̂] love you in every [V] way"). In 2012, displaying an enduring spirit of innovation at age seventy, he ended the chorus of the title song on *That's Why God Made the Radio* with a big buildup to a I/5̂ in F♯ major, resolving via a stepwise bass ascent to the dominant in C major, a tritone away:

0:48	He waved his hand, gave us rock and roll, the soundtrack of falling in
F♯:	I I⁷ I♭⁷ IV ♭VI
	love, falling in love, falling in—That's why God made the radio
F♯:	I/5̂ V⁹ I/5̂ V⁹
	C: ii⁹ I/3̂ IV⁷ Vsus4 V

Noncadential I/5̂ chords in Brian Wilson songs serve typical passing functions between vi and IV in descending bass lines, as in the chorus of "Time to Get Alone" (1968) from the Beach Boys' *20/20* album (0:23 "[I] Time to get a- [I/7̂] -lone, to get a- [vi⁷] -lone and [I/5̂] just be to- [IV] -gether"). "Your Imagination" (1997), on Brian's second solo album, includes the I/5̂ in a full octave descent in both verse and chorus. The chorus progression (0:53 "[I] Your im- [V/$\hat{7}$] -agin- [vi] -ation [I/$\hat{5}$] runnin' [IV] wild [I/$\hat{3}$–ii–V–I]") updates the bass descent from the chorus of "Love and Mercy" (1987) on his first solo album, which uses iii/$\hat{5}$ rather than I/$\hat{5}$ (0:18 "[I] Love and [V/$\hat{7}$] mercy, that's [vi] what you [iii/$\hat{5}$] need to- [IV] -night [I/$\hat{3}$–ii–V–I]"). (His brother Dennis's earlier song "Forever," on the Beach Boys' *Sunflower*, also uses the iii/$\hat{5}$ within a full-octave bass descent.) Brian returned to this progression again in 2008, in the verse and chorus of "Oxygen to the Brain" (0:00 "[I] Open up, [I/$\hat{7}$] open up, [vi^7] open your [I/$\hat{5}$] eyes, [IV] Time, it's [IV/$\hat{3}$] time, it's [ii^7] time to [V] rise").

Some Brian Wilson songs give special treatment to noncadential second-inversion chords, savoring their duplicitous blend of sonic familiarity and functional ambiguity. "Wonderful" (1966) from *Smile* begins with a rising triadic melody above a stepwise descending bass involving two second-inversion chords, the second providing a moment of tentative repose (0:00 "[D♭] She be- [D♭/C♭–B♭m^7] -longs [D♭/A♭] there, [C♭/G♭] left with her [A♭m^7] liberty"). Ambiguity itself can be a central goal of Brian's harmonic choices, even reaching back to some Beach Boys songs of the first half of the sixties such as "Custom Machine," "She Knows Me Too Well," and "In the Back of My Mind." By the time he wrote songs for *Pet Sounds* (1966) and *Smile* (1967), he was drawing on all sorts of ambiguous root movements, unexpected chord inversions, and artful counterpoint to foment tonal disorientation in listeners' ears. The centerpiece of *Pet Sounds*, "God Only Knows" (1966), for example, begins with an instrumental introduction that seems to be in A, except for the D♯ in the French horn, which wants to pull the key to E. Then the verse begins and offers no clarifications, using a variety of chord types and inversions:

[D/A] I may not [G♯^{ø7}/B] always love you, [F♯m] but long as there [B^7/A] are stars above you, [E/B] you never [F♯^{o7}/C] need to doubt it, [E/B] I'll make you so [A♯^{ø7}] sure about it, [A] God only [E/G♯] knows what I'd be with- [F♯m^7] -out you.

"Caroline No," the final cut on *Pet Sounds*, begins with the notoriously ambiguous m^7/M^{add6} chord (Fm^7/A♭ = A♭ ^{add6}), which alternates with E♭m^7/D♭ throughout the first two phrases to imply no key whatsoever, before finally stabilizing in G♭ major:

[Fm^7/A♭] Where did your [E♭m^7/D♭] long hair go?
[Fm^7/A♭] Where is the girl I [E♭m^7/D♭] used to know?
[Fm^7/A♭] How could you [A♭m^7] lose that [A♭m^7/D♭] happy [D♭^{add6}] glow?
Oh, Caroline [G♭maj^9] no

"Surf's Up," a highlight of Brian's collaboration with Van Dyke Parks for *Smile*, begins with an ambiguous alternation between an inverted Gm^7 chord and an F/G chord, then seems to be gravitating toward the key of F with the arrival of the F/C, suggesting I/$\hat{5}$ in F that is immediately followed by F:V^7, but eventually settles on a second-inversion D chord:

[Gm^7/D] A diamond necklace played the pawn. Hand in hand, some drummed along
[Dm^7/G] to a handsome mannered baton.
[Gm^7/D] A blind class aristocracy, back through the op'ra glass you see
[Dm^7/G] the pit and the pendulum drawn.
[B♭maj⁹] Colum- [Gm^7] -nated ruins [F/C] dom- [C^7] -i- [D^7/C] -no.
[G/D] Canvas the town and brush the [A^7/G] back drop.
Are you [D/A] sleeping?

The Wilson-Parks songs for *Smile* also include "Wonderful," which simply refuses to settle in, or even offer strong hints toward, a key at any point:

[D♭] She be- [B♭m^7] -longs [D♭/A♭] there, [C♭/G♭] left with her [A♭m^7] liberty,
[D♭⁷/F] Never [D♭m^7] known as a [F♯m^7] non-be- [B^7] -liever,
She [A♭m^7] laughs and [D♭m^7] stays in her [A♭/E♭] one, [D♭/F] one, one,
[A♭/E♭] Wonderful. [D♭/F - A♭/E♭ - D♭/F]

Although later work occasionally recalls such harmonic novelty—"Solar System" (1976) from *The Beach Boys Love You*, for example, features chord inversions and tonal transience—*Pet Sounds* and *Smile* represent pinnacles of harmonic ingenuity that he has never surpassed.

Chromatic Harmony

Diminished seventh chords such as those in progressions mentioned above are common in the Brian Wilson catalog, passing between IV and I/$\hat{5}$ in "Meant for You," or neighboring what sounds ephemerally like EM:I/$\hat{5}$ in "God Only Knows" ("[E/B] You never [F♯°⁷/C] need to doubt it [E/B]"). He had heard passing diminished sevenths in virtually every Four Freshmen arrangement, and often found ways to imbue them with special expressive impact. "Still I Dream of It" (1976), a remnant of the *Adult Child* solo project of the mid-1970s, is rich with lush harmonies and diminished sevenths throughout, culminating in a bass line rising chromatically from î to $\hat{4}$ through passing chords in the bridge (1:42 "[$I^{♭7}$] When I was younger, my mother told me Jesus [♯î°⁷] loved the world, [ii^7]

And if that's true then, why hasn't He helped me to [♯ii°⁷] find a girl, and [I/3̂] find my world? [III+] 'Til [IV] then . . ."). "This Isn't Love" (1997), a later collaboration with *Pet Sounds* lyricist Tony Asher, dramaticizes the word "love" with a diminished seventh chord that essentially becomes an incomplete neighbor to the subsequent ii (0:08 "[I] This isn't [i°⁷/♭3̂] love, this is [ii⁷] ecstasy [V]").

Although Brian has never shifted between major and minor modes from verse to chorus, as in Del Shannon's "Runaway" (1961) or the Crystals' "Uptown" (1962), he has often slipped out of major into minor for one phrase or subphrase, recalling a Four Freshmen arrangement such as "Come Rain or Come Shine" (1959), or a pop tune such as the Fleetwoods' "Out My Window" (1960). The ♭III–i succession expanding a doo-wop progression in "The Warmth of the Sun" mentioned earlier hints at this, but the idea is more extensively explored in "No-Go Showboat" (1963), with an entire phrase of parallel minor interrupting a major blues progression (0:20 "[i] White wall slicks with [iv] racing mags, [i] It's just for looks, man, [iv] not for drags"), and in "Kiss Me, Baby" (1964), with a wistful reflective sentiment evoking the parallel minor (0:39 "[iv] Late, late last [♭III] night, we [ii] said it was [I⁷] over"). A restless back-and-forth between major and parallel minor comes to symbolize dissatisfaction and unfulfilled dreams in "Still I Dream of It" (1976), first resulting from chromatic movement in the verse (0:10 "[I] Time for supper now, day's been [I⁷] hard and I'm so tired I feel like [i♭⁷] eating now"), finally summarized in the ending (2:56 "I'll find my [I⁷] world, [i♭⁷] I'll find my [I⁷] world, [i♭⁷] someday I'll find my [I⁷] world").

The single nondiatonic chord that most often intrudes on major modality in Brian Wilson's songs is ♭VII—not surprisingly, given the prevalence of this chord in Four Freshmen arrangements and in popular music in general (Everett 2009, 264; de Clercq and Temperley 2011, 60). Of course, Brian was well schooled in I–♭VII–I barre chords and surf music, and included a cover of a surf tune permeated with I–♭VII–I, the Gamblers' "Moon Dawg" (1959), on the first Beach Boys album in 1962. (And "Moon Dawg" echoed the I–♭VII–I heard frequently on the airwaves since the previous year, in the Champs' "Tequila," Link Wray & The Wraymen's "Rumble," and Dale Hawkins's "La-Do-Dada.") Brian used I–♭VII alternations above tonic pedals in "Guess I'm Dumb," a song he wrote in 1964 for Glen Campbell (0:09 "[I] The way I [♭VII/î] act don't seem like [I] me, [♭VII/î–I] I'm not on [♭VII/î] top like I used to [IV] be"); in the instrumental introduction to "California Girls" (1965); and decades later in the verse of "Gettin' in over My Head" (0:20 "[I]

I [♭VII/î] couldn't believe the sensation when you kissed my [I] face, The [♭VII/î] look in your eyes and the feelin' of your em- [I] -brace"). He used the I→♭VII–I without an underlying pedal in "Add Some Music to Your Day" (1969), demonstrating a close neighboring of tonic just after an initial phrase that neighbors tonic with the IV (0:00 "[I] The Sunday mornin' gospel goes good with a song, There's [IV] blues, folk, and country, and rock like a rolling [I] stone, The [♭VII] world could come together as [I] one, if [♭VII] everybody under the [I] sun . . .").

The neighboring ♭VII is also commonly preceded not by a I but by a subdominant, hinting at the ♭VII as dominant surrogate—the "backdoor progression." This is common in Four Freshmen arrangements, as in "It's a Blue World" (1952), one of the group's first singles (0:46 "[IV⁷] My days and nights that [♭VII] once were filled with [I] heaven"). Brian Wilson used the ♭VII this way in the 1965 song "Sandy," which eventually became "She Says That She Needs Me" (1998) on his second solo album (0:28 "[IV] Baby if you [♭VII] don't stop [I] cryin' I'll just [ii⁷] wanna [I/ĝ] die"), and in "Aren't You Glad" (1967) from the Beach Boys' *Wild Honey* (0:36 "[IV] I got a [♭VII] heart that just won't stop [I] beatin' for you"). In the introduction to the Beach Boys' "Keep an Eye on Summer" (1964), the ♭VII arrives from the minor subdominant (0:00 "[I] Keep an [vi] eye on [iv] sum- [♭VII] -er [I]").

In "In My Room" (1963) a I→♭VII–I neighboring leads to a doo-wop progression that is interrupted by another typical use of ♭VII, as an embellishment of V (0:08 "[I] There's a world where I can go and tell my [♭VII⁷] secrets [I] to, [vi] in my [ii⁷] room [♭VII–V] in my [I] room"). "Car Crazy Cutie" (1963), a retexting of "Pamela Jean" (1963), does something similar but with IV instead of ii, thus isolating the ♭VII–V third relation from the two falling thirds I–vi and vi–IV that precede it (0:14 "Well, my [I] steady little doll is a real-live beauty, And [vi] everybody knows she's a car crazy cutie, She's [IV] hip to everything, man, from customs to rails, And [♭VII] axle grease embedded 'neath her [V] fingernails"). These two patterns merge as one long chain of third-related roots in "Surf City" (1963), a collaboration with Jan Berry of Jan and Dean (0:16 "[I] Surf City, [vi] here we come! Well it [IV] ain't got a back seat or a [ii] rear window, [♭VII] But it still gets me where I [V] want to go"). And an analogous long thirds chain in "She Knows Me Too Well" (1964) begins with VI and IV in the opening hook, reaching completion, including a backtrack to ii, in the verse (0:08 "Some- [ii⁷] -times I have a weird way of [♭VII] showing my love, And I [ii⁷] always expect her to [V] know what I'm thinking").

In other songs Brian underscores the whole-step relationship between ♭VII and I by tacking on an additional whole-step-related root
at the front, ♭VI–♭VII–I. This progression carries the hook of "Sail on,
Sailor" (1972) from *Holland* (0:26 "[♭VI] Sail on, [♭VII] sail on, [I] sail-
or") and shows up in many other songs (e.g., "Roller Skating Child"
at 2:08, "Happy Days" at 3:30). The chorus of a Beach Boys anthem,
"California Girls" (1965), recalling the whole-step root relations in the
introduction mentioned earlier, first encircles tonic with a whole step
above and below, then lands on a minor tonic before reaching down to
♭VI and stepping back up to tonic via a minor triad on ♭7̂ (0:59 "I [I] wish
they all could [ii⁷] be California [♭VII] girls [i⁷], I [♭VI] wish they all could
[♭vii⁷] be California [I] girls").

Of course, whole-step root movement also commonly travels in the
downward direction, in the time-honored tradition of the "lament" bass,
well known to Brian Wilson from earlier songs like Jimmie Rodgers's
"Make Me a Miracle" (1958), Donnie Brooks's "Mission Bell" (1960),
and the Ventures' "Walk—Don't Run" (1961). This progression appears
often in Brian's early songs, heard in the introduction to "Heads You
Win, Tails I Lose" (1962) on the Beach Boys' first album (0:00 "[I] Every
time [♭VII] we have a fight [♭VI] we flip a coin [V] to see who's right"),
and in "Lonely Sea" (1962) on their second (0:14 "[I] The lonely sea,
[♭VII] the [♭VI] lonely sea, [V]"). Two years later, in the chorus of "Don't
Hurt My Little Sister," the whole-step descent provides the backbone of
a descending-fifths sequence moving away from tonic (0:41 "[I] Don't
hurt my [IV] little sister, [♭VII] don't hurt my [♭III] little sister, [♭VI] don't
hurt my [♭II] little sister [V]"). By the time of his masterstroke in 45 rpm,
"Good Vibrations" (1966), he was starting the pattern on a minor tonic
(which eventually relates as vi in the key of the chorus) and adding sixths
to the middle two chords (0:00 "[i] I, I love the colorful [♭VII^add6] clothes
she wears, and the [♭VI^add6] way the sunlight plays upon her [V] hair").

It's common to find any of these nondiatonic chords as pivots in
modulations in a Brian Wilson song. The shift down a whole step for the
instrumental break in the Beach Boys' "No-Go Showboat" (1963), for
example, first uses the IV as pivot, reinterpreted as V, but to return to the
main key at the end of the section, the I is reinterpreted as ♭VII, which
then moves to its dominant partner:

	0:58	1:00	1:03	1:06	1:09
D♭:	IV			♭VII	V
C♭:	V	I	IV	I	

A modulation by rising half step in "Girls on the Beach" (1964) first re-interprets iv as iii; the return just shifts from EM:ii^7 to E♭M:V^{13}, without a pivot:

0:20 In the sun and salty air, The girls on the beach are all within reach, if you know what to do.
E♭: I VI^7 ii^7 iv   V^{13}
          E: iii   I^7 vi^7 I^7 vi^7 ii^7

And in "She Says That She Needs Me," a I–IV neighboring throughout the bridge eventually lands on a IV that is reinterpreted as ♭VI to return to the main key, down a minor third:

1:51 Sorry, baby, I just can't stand it, It didn't work out the way we planned it,
G: I   IV/î   I   IV/î

        I don't know whether we're gonna be together, Sorry, baby, it's time we said goodbye.
G: I   IV
          E: ♭VI   I/ŝ   V^7 I

Key mobility was a particular fascination of Brian Wilson's in the late 1960s, in songs such as his collaboration with brother Carl, "I Went to Sleep" (1968), which starts and ends in A major but tonicizes G major (pivoting on ii = iii) and B minor (pivoting on V = ♭III):

0:06 I took a walk and sat down in a park, The gardener walked out and the sprinklers went on
A: I   VI^9 ii^7 VI^7 ii^7/î
                                       G: iii^7/2̂   V$^{9(\#7)}$ I$^{9(\#7)}$ V$^{9(\#7)}$

        They watered the lawn and I went to sleep
G: I$^{9(\#7)}$ V$^{9(\#7)}$
              B: ♭III^9 ii^7 V$^{\#5}$ i
                                        A: ii   V

The Beach Boys' "This Whole World" (1969) takes tonal transience to its upper limits. First, a C-major phrase ends on IV, which becomes ♭VI in A, and then an A-major phrase ends on iii, which becomes a new i in C♯. This new phrase then moves through a diatonic bass descent from î to ŝ, eventually arriving at the key of B♭ using the same pivot relationship heard earlier between C and A (IV = ♭VI). Finally, the phrase in B♭ con-cludes on V, which is reinterpreted as IV to return to C major:

0:05   Late at night I think about the love of this whole world. Lots of different people every-
    C: I   IV   iii⁷   V   vi   IV
                                  A: ♭VI   I   vi   ii   V

    -where.   And when I go anywhere, I see love, I see love, I see love.
    A: iii
    C♯:   i   I   I/7̂   IV/6̂   V   vi   IV
                                    B♭:   ♭VI

    When girls get mad at boys and go, many times they're just puttin' on a show
    B♭:   I   IV⁷

    But when they leave, you wait alone.
    B♭:   I   V
    C: IV   V

Nondiatonic chords also stand out in one of Brian Wilson's early signatures, the hook flavored with chromaticism and modal mixture, even
in songs that are otherwise unapologetically faithful to a single key and
modality. We saw this earlier, in the hook for "Shut Down," used as the
third phrase of a blues progression. Recorded the same year, 1963, are
five other songs with harmonically adventurous hooks:

"Surf City" (0:00 "[♭III] Two girls for [♭VI] every [V] boy")
"Catch a Wave" (0:00 "[V] Catch a [♭III] wave and you're [IV] sit-
    tin' on [V] top of the [I] world")
"Surfers Rule" (0:00 "It's a [♭VI] genuine [iv♭⁷] fact that the [ii°⁷]
    surfers [V] rule")
"Custom Machine" (0:00 "[♭VI] Check my [♭VII] custom ma- [V]
    -chine" or 0:14 "[♭VII] Check my [V] custom ma- [I] -chine")
"Drag City" (0:10 "[♭VII] Burn up that [♭VI] quarter [V] mile")

In each case, the presence of chords from outside the main key connotes
adventure, or conquest: if we're willing to use chords like this, they seem
to say, then we're willing to try anything, able to conquer any wave or
hot rod. The habit of adventurous hooks endured in many later Brian
Wilson songs, even for lyrics that don't suggest such bravado—or perhaps, when the song displays its own harmonic bravado. The harmony
throughout "You Still Believe in Me" (1965) on *Pet Sounds* is mostly a
repeating I–ii⁷–V⁷–I, but the incantation of the song title is another thing
entirely (0:44 "You [vi⁷/2̂] still be- [ii⁷/î] -lieve [vi⁷/5̂] in [♭VI] me"). The
Beach Boys' "'Til I Die" (1969) harmonically wanders, searching for its
tonal moorings just as the despondent lyric searches for answers to philo-

sophical questions, until the ending, which includes the ♭III and ♭VI but eventually provides long-sought tonal stability (1:41 "[I] These things I'll [♭III] be un- [♭VI⁷] -til [V] I [I] die"). "It's Over Now" (1976), another survivor of the *Adult Child* solo project, is quite chromatic throughout, but the hook/refrain takes it up a notch, with a diminished-seventh-chord-enriched chromatic bass descent from $\hat6$ down to $\hat4$ leading to the dominant substitute ♭II for the final cadence (0:39 "It's [II/$\hat6$] over now, [P°⁷/♭$\hat6$] It's [I/$\hat5$] over now, [P°⁷/♭$\hat5$–IV⁷] shades of blue and [♭II⁷] purple haunt me [I⁷]").

Another Wilsonesque implementation of chromatic harmonies is the sudden moment of a cappella singing, what I have called the "interrupting celestial choir," a legacy of the Four Freshmen influence (Lambert 2007, 132, 215). Although not all such passages involve unusual harmonies—the sudden absence of accompanying instruments is surprising enough on its own—some bring harmonic surprises akin to those in adventurous hooks. Near the end of "Salt Lake City" (1965), a final, out-of-rhythm choral declamation includes the iv and ii° evoking the parallel minor (1:38 "[iv♭⁷/♭$\hat6$] We'll [ii°/$\hat4$] be [V¹¹] com- [V⁷] -in' [I] soon"). The suddenly a cappella conclusion of the bridge of "Being with the One You Love" (1988) harmonizes a chromatic bass descent from $\hat3$ to $\hat1$ (1:31 "[iii⁷] In [i/♭$\hat3$] our [ii⁷] pri- [♭vii/♭$\hat2$] -vate [I⁷] space"). And a harmonically fairly routine choral introduction of "How Could We Still Be Dancin'" (2004) suddenly veers into an a cappella harmonic excursion involving the ♭III–i relation reminiscent of "The Warmth of the Sun" (0:16 "Dancin' my [IV] love [ii⁷–♭III⁷–i♭⁷–Vˢᵘˢ⁴]").

The high point of Brian Wilson's choral artistry is the invocation to *Smile*, "Our Prayer" (1966), where the celestial choir doesn't interrupt but occupies a musical space all its own (see Lambert 2007, 270–71). Within the phrases of the wordless chorale are every technique of chromatic harmony he had ever heard or imagined. It begins with two short phrases starting in E♭ (numbered 1 and 2 below), the first ending on i/$\hat5$, the second on I/$\hat5$, approached with progressions that mix ♭III and IV in the first, v and V in the second. A third, longer phrase follows (3), controlled by a rising bass line arriving on v via ♯iv°⁷:

phrase:	1	2	3
starts at:	0:00	0:08	0:15
E♭:	i ♭III/$\hat{2}$ IV/♭$\hat{3}$ IV i/$\hat{5}$	♭III P v V/$\hat{4}$ I/$\hat{5}$	IV V I/♭$\hat{7}$ IV/$\hat{6}$ V/♮$\hat{7}$ I ♭VII/$\hat{2}$ P ii/$\hat{4}$ #iv°⁷ v⁴⁻³

	4	5	6
	0:26	0:34	0:43
E♭:	i ♭III/$\hat{2}$ IV/♭$\hat{3}$ IV i/$\hat{5}$ i♭⁷	v I♭⁷/$\hat{3}$ IV P V⁴⁻³ V/$\hat{7}$ i	IV V I/♭$\hat{7}$ IV/$\hat{6}$ V/♮$\hat{7}$ I ♭VII/$\hat{2}$ P ii/$\hat{4}$ #iv°⁷ i/$\hat{5}$ v
			B♭: i

	7	8
	0:54	1:04
B♭:	i♭⁷ IV⁷/$\hat{1}$ vii°⁷ iii°⁷/♭$\hat{7}$ #iv°⁷/$\hat{6}$ ♭VI#⁶ ii°⁷/♭$\hat{6}$ V⁷/$\hat{2}$ i	i♭⁷/$\hat{5}$ ♭VI i♭⁷/♭$\hat{7}$ iv/$\hat{1}$ I ... I

Phrase 4 repeats phrase 1, except for a final i♭⁷ that signals a new direction for phrase 5, which moves through a secondary dominant of IV before eventually cadencing on the only root-position tonic harmony since the initial chords of phrases 1 and 4. Then phrase 6 repeats phrase 3, except for a tiny variation in the ending, and its final v is reinterpreted as i in B♭ for the last two phrases. Phrase 7 establishes the new B♭ centricity over a chromatically descending bass, including a German +6 chord (the ♭VI#⁶) that doesn't move directly to V. The final brief phrase (8) is an elaborated plagal cadence, a still wordless "amen."

The chromatic bass descent in phrase 7 of "Our Prayer" draws attention again to the stepwise bass. Bass descents involving some sort of chromaticism became a thematic element in the songs of *Pet Sounds* (see Lambert 2008) and remained a focus for decades after, although never approaching the sophistication of "Our Prayer." In descents from $\hat{1}$ down to $\hat{5}$, Brian usually skips $\hat{7}$, favoring the I♭⁷ harmonizing ♭$\hat{7}$ and acting as a secondary dominant to the subsequent IV/$\hat{6}$. When the final destination is V ("Pet Sounds," "Here Today"), he prepares the dominant with ii° (°⁷) harmonizing ♭$\hat{6}$, but when the destination is I/$\hat{5}$ ("Our Sweet Love," "Baby Let Your Hair Grow Long"), he has used both iv and ♭VII to harmonize ♭$\hat{6}$:

Bass scale degree:	$\hat{1}$	$\hat{7}$	♭$\hat{7}$	$\hat{6}$	♭$\hat{6}$	$\hat{5}$
"Pet Sounds" (1965) (0:13)	I(add 9)	-	♭VIIadd6+9	IV	ii°⁷	V¹¹
"Here Today" (1966) chorus (0:39)	I	-	I♭⁷	IV	ii°	V¹³
"I Just Wasn't..." (1966) verse (0:00)	I⁹	-	♭VII⁹(#11)	vi¹¹	-	Vadd6
"Our Sweet Love" (1969) verse (0:00)	I	V	I♭⁷	IV	iv	I
"Our Sweet Love" chorus (0:17)	I	-	I♭⁷	IV	♭VII⁷	I
"I'm So Lonely" (1984) bridge (1:20)	I	-	I♭⁷	IV	iv	-
"Baby . . . Long" (1988) verse (0:30)	I	-	I♭⁷	IV	iv	I

For an all-half-step descent from $\hat{1}$ to $\hat{4}$ in the second part of the *Pet Sounds* instrumental "Let's Go Away for Awhile" (1966), he used mostly these same basic harmonies except for ♭III alternating with iii° above the ♭$\hat{7}$:

(1:02) $\hat{1}$ $\hat{7}$ ♭$\hat{7}$ ♭$\hat{7}$ $\hat{6}$ ♭$\hat{6}$ $\hat{5}$ ♭$\hat{5}$ $\hat{4}$
      I   V   ♭III$^{♭7}$ iii^{o7} IV   iv   I   P^{ø7} IV^7

The passing half-diminished seventh harmonizing ♭$\hat{5}$ here, filling in the whole step from $\hat{5}$ down to $\hat{4}$, is a Brian Wilson signature. It's also a staple of jazz harmony that he had heard in Four Freshmen arrangements, such as their recording of Frank Loesser's "I Wish I Didn't Love You So" ("But when I **try**, something in my heart says no"), and perhaps in old standards not recorded by the Freshmen during the early days, such as Cole Porter's "Night and Day" ("In the **roaring traffic's** boom") and "Just One of Those Things" ("We'd have been aware that our **love af**-fair was too hot not to cool down"). Songwriters in the 1960s used the passing half-diminished chord when repeating a minor triad above a descending bass line, as when vi combines with a bass ♭$\hat{5}$ in Classic IV's "Traces" ("[vi] Traces of [vi/$\hat{5}$] love long a- [**vi**/♭$\hat{5}$] -go, that [ii/$\hat{4}$] didn't work out"). In a minor key, the chord is often formed from the repeating tonic triad over a bass descent from $\hat{1}$, combining the notes of i with the sixth degree of the parallel major, as in the Lovin' Spoonful's "Summer in the City" ("[i] Hot town, [i/♭$\hat{7}$] summer in the city, [i/$\hat{6}$] Back of my neck gettin' [♭VI] dirty and [V] gritty"). Essentially the same thing happens in the third measure of the Crucifixus from J. S. Bach's B Minor Mass.

When the P^{ø7} makes an appearance in a Brian Wilson song, it is almost always at a dramatic moment, drawing attention to an important word or phrase. Besides "Let's Go Away for Awhile," the chord appears in two other songs on *Pet Sounds*, "Don't Talk (Put Your Head on My Shoulder)" (0:08 "And I can see so much in your **eyes**"), and "God Only Knows" (0:29 "I'll make you so **sure about it**"; 0:54 "So what good would **livin' do me**?"). For solo projects of the 1980s, Brian used it in the verse of "Walkin' the Line" (0:23 "If I don't get my way this time I'll **die**"), in the chorus of "Let's Go to Heaven in My Car" (1:06 "Huggin' the curves and I'm out of control, Goin' eye to eye with the **radio**"), and in the hook of "Meet Me in My Dreams Tonight" (0:48 "Meet me in my **dreams** to-night"), among others. More recently we hear it in "A Friend Like You," his duet with Paul McCartney on his 2004 solo album (0:32 "You're the one who **helps me make it** through"; 0:47 "None of my wishes **ever**

came through"), in "Christmasey," a collaboration with Jimmy Webb on the 2005 Christmas album (0:35 "Put up the lights, So we can **see**"), and in the dramatic apex of the verse of "Good Kind of Love" on the 2008 solo album (0:52 "Run to him, run to him, right to his **arms**"). The 2012 Beach Boys album begins with a mellow, wordless vocal meditation, "Think About the Days," that features the $P^{ø7}$ within a repeating progression (i–$V^{+5}/\hat{7}$–i$^{b7}/b\hat{7}$–$P^{ø7}/\hat{6}$↓VI^{7}↓VII), and thereby anticipates yet another appearance of the chord in the album's penultimate track, "Pacific Coast Highway" (0:48 "Sunlight's fading and there's not much left to **say**"). Brian Wilson didn't invent the $P^{ø7}$, but he has probably used it more frequently and more expressively than any other songwriter.

Because the outer minor seventh in the $P^{ø7}$ can be respelled as an augmented sixth, and because Billy Joel, who is often identified with Levittown, New York, used it in his song "Everybody Loves You Now" (1971), Walter Everett has named this chord the "Levittown sixth" (Everett 2000, 112). To view it is an augmented-sixth chord, however, implies a specific voice-leading pattern in its resolution, which often isn't applicable in popular idioms. In any case, the role of the augmented-sixth chord in Brian Wilson's music is an entirely separate issue. He did use them quite traditionally, first, and most conspicuously, in the wordless introduction to the Beach Boys' "All Dressed Up for School" (1964)—recycled later in "Goin' On" (1979)—where melody and bass wedge outward, preceding I/$\hat{5}$ with a correctly resolving German^{+6}:

melody:	$\hat{1}$	$\hat{3}$	$\hat{4}$	$\#\hat{4}$	$\hat{5}$	$\#\hat{5}$	$\hat{6}$	$\hat{7}$	$\hat{1}$
	I	Ib7	IV/6	bVI$^{\#6}$	I/$\hat{5}$	bVI	IV	V	I

The instrumental bridge of "Passing By" (1968) on *Friends* forms the same chord when the bass repeats $b\hat{6}$ (starting at 0:54) while the melody rises, eventually to $\#\hat{4}$ (at 1:00) just at the end of the section, resolving to I/$\hat{5}$ when the main theme returns (at 1:03). And a prolonged E dominant seventh chord in the verse of "Wake the World" (1968), also on the *Friends* album, eventually resolves as a German^{+6} when the chorus arrives (at 0:35) in the key of Ab major: E–G$\#$–B–D is reinterpreted as bVI$^{\sharp6}$ in Ab, or Fb–Ab–Cb–D. The verse melody rises to the upper note of the augmented sixth (D) on its last syllable ("The sky goes brighter every minute of the sun-**rise**"), melting into the emergence of the sun just at the moment of harmonic enlightenment ("Wake the world").

Of course, what helps elevate such moments are the sounds that surround them. The German^{+6} resolution in "Wake the World" is followed by a conspicuously ordinary I–IV–V–I chorus, in a wash of vocal harmony anchored by a strikingly melodic tuba line. In "Passing By" the climactic German^{+6} becomes the retransition back to the disarmingly simple wordless vocal melody. After that song is over, the next cut on the *Friends* album, "Anna Lee, the Healer," brings back multipart vocals while hardly straying from E-major diatonicism, most overtly in the "Louie, Louie"-inspired I–IV–V–IV verse. Within a song or from track to track in an album, the harmonic aspect may recede into the backdrop, yielding the spotlight to a catchy melody, or a dazzling vocal arrangement. A collection of Brian Wilson songs earns distinction from its diverse appeals to individual tastes, from the variety of its musical imprints. His skills as a harmonist, melodist, arranger, and producer are equally refined.

His harmonic language, considered separately, represents a mastery and expansion of the British-American pop idiom of the 1960s. Brian Wilson songs include progressions that have been used by songwriters many times before, and since, and progressions that are rarer and more distinctive, that open new windows into the harmonic spectrum for popular songs. Their range of harmonic imagination represents a distinguished contribution to music in the second half of the twentieth century and beyond, balancing the achievements of his artistic forebears, such as his avowed hero George Gershwin, in the first half. And in a perfect marriage of idea and execution, these resources are never so captivating as when carried through the air by a brotherly vocal blend.

NOTES FOR CHAPTER 3

1. Recordings of the songs appear in the Spotify playlist "Harmonic Language," http://open.spotify.com/user/lambertessay/playlist/5Du8hb6EqF uM1ZkFsAz3na.

APPENDIX 3.1: SONGS DISCUSSED IN CHAPTER 3

KEY TO ABBREVIATIONS

AJ Al Jardine	JB Jan Berry
BW Brian Wilson	JT Joe Thomas
BB Beach Boys	ML Mike Love
CW Carl Wilson	RC Roger Christian
DW Dennis Wilson	SB Scott Bennett
EL Eugene Landy	TA Tony Asher
GU Gary Usher	VDP Van Dyke Parks
J&D Jan & Dean	

Song Title	Year Begun	Credit	Source Used Here	Artist(s)
409	1962	BW, GU, ML	*Surfin' Safari* (1962)	BB
A Friend Like You	2004	BW, Kalinich	*Gettin' in over My Head* (2004)	BW
A Thing or Two	1967	BW, ML	*Wild Honey* (1967)	BB
A Young Man Is Gone	1963	Troup, ML	*Little Deuce Coupe* (1963)	BB
Add Some Music to Your Day	1969	BW, Knott, ML	*Sunflower* (1970)	BB
All Dressed Up for School	1964	BW (+RC?)	*LDC/ASL* bonus track (1990)	BB
All I Wanna Do	1969	BW, ML	*Sunflower* (1970)	BB
Amusement Parks USA	1965	BW, ML	*Summer Days* (1965)	BB
And Your Dream Comes True	1965	BW, ML	*Summer Days* (1965)	BB
Anna Lee, the Healer	1968	BW, ML	*Friends* (1968)	BB
Aren't You Glad	1967	BW, ML	*Wild Honey* (1967)	BB
Auld Lang Syne	1964	trad. arr. BW	*Christmas Album* (1964)	BB
Baby Let Your Hair Grow Long	1988	BW	*Brian Wilson* (1988)	BW
Back Home	1963	BW	*15 Big Ones* (1976)	BB
The Baker Man	1963	BW	*SS/SUSA* bonus track (1990)	BB
Ballad of Ole' Betsy	1963	BW, RC	*Little Deuce Coupe* (1963)	BB
Be True to Your School (single version)	1963	BW, ML	*Good Vibrations* (1993)	BB
Beaches in Mind	2012	BW, ML, JT	*That's Why God Made the Radio* (2012)	BB
Being With the One You Love	1988	BW	*Brian Wilson* remix bonus track (2000)	BW
Boogie Woodie	1963	Rimsky-Korsakov arr. BW	*Surfer Girl* (1963)	BB
Cabin Essence	1966	BW, VDP	*Smile Sessions* (2011)	BB
California Calling	1984	AJ, BW	*The Beach Boys* (1985)	BB
California Girls	1965	BW, ML	*Summer Days* (1965)	BB
California Role	2008	BW, SB	*That Lucky Old Sun* (2008)	BW
Car Crazy Cutie	1963	BW, RC	*Little Deuce Coupe* (1963)	BB
Carl's Big Chance	1964	BW, CW	*All Summer Long* (1964)	BB
Caroline, No	1966	BW, TA	*Pet Sounds* (1966)	BB
Catch a Wave	1963	BW, ML	*Surfer Girl* (1963)	BB
Cherry, Cherry Coupe	1963	BW, RC	*Little Deuce Coupe* (1963)	BB
Child of Winter	1974	BW, Kalinich	*Ultimate Christmas* (1998)	BB
Christmas Day	1964	BW	*Christmas Album* (1964)	BB
Christmasey	2005	BW, Webb	*What I Really Want for Christmas* (2005)	BW
Crack at Your Love	1984	BW, AJ, EL	*The Beach Boys* (1985)	BB
Cry	1997	BW	*Imagination* (1998)	BW
Custom Machine	1963	BW	*Little Deuce Coupe* (1963)	BB
Darlin'	1967	BW, ML	*Wild Honey* (1967)	BB
Denny's Drums	1964	DW	*Shut Down, Vol. 2* (1964)	BB
Do It Again	1968	BW, ML	*20/20* (1969)	BB
Don't Back Down	1964	BW, ML	*All Summer Long* (1964)	BB
Don't Hurt My Little Sister	1964	BW, ML	*Today!* (1965)	BB

Song Title	Year Begun	Credit	Source Used Here	Artist(s)
Don't Let Her Know She's an Angel	1985	BW	*Gettin' in over My Head* (2004)	BW
Don't Talk (Put Your Head on My Shoulder)	1965	BW, TA	*Pet Sounds* (1966)	BB
Don't Worry, Baby	1964	BW, RC	*Shut Down, Vol. 2* (1964)	BB
Drag City	1963	JB, RC, BW	*Drag City* (1963)	J&D
Drive-In	1963	BW	*All Summer Long* (1964)	BB
Everything I Need	1997	BW, TA	*The Wilsons* (1997)	The Wilsons
Fairy Tale [originally Save the Day]	1990	BW, Foster	*Gettin' in over My Head* (2004)	BW
Fantasy is Reality / Bells of Madness	1993	Phillips, BW, Wasserman	*Trios* (1994)	Carnie W., BW
Finders Keepers	1963	BW, ML	*Surfin' USA* (1963)	BB
Forever She'll Be My Surfer Girl	2008	BW, SB	*That Lucky Old Sun* (2008)	BW
Friends	1968	BW, DW, CW, AJ	*Friends* (1968)	BB
From There to Back Again	1999	BW, JT	*That's Why God Made the Radio* (2012)	BB
Fun, Fun, Fun	1964	BW, ML	*Shut Down, Vol. 2* (1964)	BB
Funky Pretty	1972	BW, ML, Rieley	*Holland* (1973)	BB
Gettin' Hungry	1967	BW, ML	*Smiley Smile* (1967)	BB
Gettin' in Over my Head	1994	BW, Paley	*Gettin' in over My Head* (2004)	BW
Girl Don't Tell Me	1965	BW	*Summer Days* (1965)	BB
Girls on the Beach	1964	BW	*All Summer Long* (1964)	BB
God Only Knows	1966	BW, TA	*Pet Sounds* (1966)	BB
Going Home	2008	BW, SB	*That Lucky Old Sun* (2008)	BW
Goin' On	1979	BW, ML	*Keepin' the Summer Alive* (2008)	BB
Good Kind of Love	2008	BW	*That Lucky Old Sun* (2008)	BW
Good Time	1970	BW, AJ	*Love You* (1977)	BB
Good Timin'	1974	BW, CW	*L.A. (Light Album)* (1979)	BB
Good Vibrations	1966	BW, TA	*Good Vibrations* (1993)	BB
Graduation Day	1964	J. Sherman, N. Sherman	*Today!/SD* bonus track (1990)	BB
Guess I'm Dumb	1964	BW, Titelman	*Pet Projects: The BW Productions* (2003)	Glen Campbell
Happy Days	1997	BW	*Imagination* (1998)	BW
He Couldn't Get His Poor Old Body to Move	1988	BW, Buckingham	*Brian Wilson* (1988)	BW
He's A Doll	1964	BW	*Pet Projects: The BW Productions* (2003)	Honeys
Heads You Win, Tails I Lose	1962	BW, GU	*Surfin' Safari* (1962)	BB
Help Me, Rhonda	1965	BW, ML	*Summer Days* (1965)	BB
Here Today	1966	BW, TA	*Pet Sounds* (1966)	BB
Hey Little Tomboy	1976	BW	*M.I.U. Album* (1978)	BB
Hide Go Seek	1963	BW, Venet	*Pet Projects: The BW Productions* (2003)	Honeys
Honky Tonk	1963	Doggett et al.	*Surfin' USA* (1963)	BB
How Could We Still Be Dancin'	2004	BW, JT	*Gettin' in over My Head* (2004)	BW, Elton John

Song Title	Year Begun	Credit	Source Used Here	Artist(s)
I Do	1963	BW, RC	*SG/SD2* bonus track (1990)	BB
I Get Around	1964	BW, ML	*All Summer Long* (1964)	BB
I Just Got My Pay	1970	BW, ML	*Good Vibrations* (1993)	BB
I Just Wasn't Made for These Times	1966	BW, TA	*Pet Sounds* (1966)	BB
I Know There's an Answer	1966	BW, Sachen, ML	*Pet Sounds* (1966)	BB
I Wanna Pick You Up	1976	BW	*Love You* (1977)	BB
I Went to Sleep	1968	BW, CW	*20/20* (1969)	BB
I'll Bet He's Nice	1976	BW	*Love You* (1977)	BB
I'm So Lonely	1984	BW, EL	*The Beach Boys* (1985)	BB
I'm Waiting for the Day	1966	BW, ML	*Pet Sounds* (1966)	BB
In My Room	1963	BW, GU	*Surfer Girl* (1963)	BB
In the Back of My Mind	1965	BW, ML	*Today!* (1965)	BB
Isn't It Time	2012	BW, ML, Peterik, Millas, JT	*That's Why God Made the Radio* (2012)	BB
It's Just a Matter of Time	1984	BW, EL	*The Beach Boys* (1985)	BB
It's OK	1974	BW, ML	*15 Big Ones* (1976)	BB
It's Over Now	1976	BW	*Good Vibrations* (1993)	BW
Johnny B. Goode	1964	C. Berry	*Concert* (1964)	BB
Johnny Carson	1976	BW	*Love You* (1977)	BB
Judy	1962	BW	*Surfin'* (2000)	BB
Karate [a. k. a. Beach Boy Stomp]	1962	CW	*Surfin'* (2000)	BB
Keep an Eye on Summer	1964	BW, Norberg, ML	*Shut Down, Vol. 2* (1964)	BB
Kiss Me, Baby	1964	BW, ML	*Today!* (1965)	BB
Land Ahoy	1962	BW	*SS/SUSA* bonus track (1990)	BB
Lay Down Burden	1997	BW, JT	*Imagination* (1998)	BW
Let Him Run Wild	1965	BW, ML	*Summer Days* (1965)	BB
Let's Go Away for Awhile	1966	BW	*Pet Sounds* (1966)	studio orch.
Let's Go to Heaven in My Car	1986	BW, GU	*Brian Wilson* remix bonus track (2000)	BW
Let's Go Trippin'	1963	Dale	*Surfin' USA* (1963)	BB
Let's Put Our Hearts Together	1976	BW	*Love You* (1977)	BW, Marilyn W.
Let's Stick [Get] Together	1989	BW, EL	*Sweet Insanity* [bootleg]	BW
Little Deuce Coupe	1963	BW, RC	*Surfer Girl* (1963)	BB
The Little Girl I Once Knew	1965	BW	*Good Vibrations* (1993)	BB
Little Honda	1964	BW, ML	*All Summer Long* (1964)	BB
Little Saint Nick	1963	BW, ML	*Christmas Album* (1964)	BB
Live Let Live	2008	BW, VDP	*That Lucky Old Sun* (2008)	BW
Lonely Sea	1962	BW, GU	*Surfin' USA* (1963)	BB
The Lord's Prayer	1963	Malotte	*Hawthorne, CA* (2001)	BB
Love and Mercy	1987	BW	*Brian Wilson* (1988)	BW
Make a Wish	1989	BW	*Gettin' in over My Head* (2004)	BW
Male Ego	1984	BW, ML, EL	*The Beach Boys* (1985)	BB
The Man with All the Toys	1964	BW, ML	*Christmas Album* (1964)	BB
Marcella	1971	BW, Almer, Rieley	*Carl & the Passions* (1972)	BB
Meant for You	1968	BW, ML	*Friends* (1968)	BB

Song Title	Year Begun	Credit	Source Used Here	Artist(s)
Meet Me in My Dreams Tonight	1988	BW, Paley, Dean	*Brian Wilson* (1988)	BW
Melt Away	1987	BW	*Brian Wilson* (1988)	BW
Merry Christmas, Baby	1964	BW, ML	*Christmas Album* (1964)	BB
Midnight's Another Day	2008	BW, SB	*That Lucky Old Sun* (2008)	BW
Misirlou	1963	Roubanis, Wise, Leeds, Russell	*Surfin' USA* (1963)	BB
Mona	1976	BW	*Love You* (1977)	BB
Moon Dawg	1962	Weaver	*Surfin' Safari* (1962)	BB
Morning Beat	2008	BW, SB	*That Lucky Old Sun* (2008)	BW
Mrs. O'Leary's Cow [The Elements: Fire]	1966	BW	*Smile Sessions* (2011)	studio orch.
My Diane	1976	BW	*M.I.U. Album* (1978)	BB
No-Go Showboat	1963	BW, RC	*Little Deuce Coupe* (1963)	BB
Noble Surfer	1963	BW, ML	*Surfin' USA* (1963)	BB
One for the Boys	1988	BW	*Brian Wilson* (1988)	BW
Our Car Club	1963	BW, ML	*Surfer Girl* (1963)	BB
Our Prayer	1966	BW	*Brian Wilson Presents Smile* (2004)	BW band
Our Sweet Love	1969	BW, CW, AJ	*Sunflower* (1970)	BB
Oxygen to the Brain	2008	BW, SB	*That Lucky Old Sun* (2008)	BW
Pacific Coast Highway	2012	BW, JT	*That's Why God Made the Radio* (2012)	BB
Pamela Jean	1963	BW	*Pet Projects: The BW Productions* (2003)	The Survivors
Passing By	1968	BW	*Friends* (1968)	BB
Pet Sounds	1965	BW	*Pet Sounds* (1966)	studio orch.
Please Let Me Wonder	1965	BW. ML	*Today!* (1965)	BB
Pom Pom Play Girl	1964	BW, GU	*Shut Down, Vol. 2* (1964)	BB
The Private Life of Bill and Sue	2012	BW, JT	*That's Why God Made the Radio* (2012)	BB
Punchline	1963	BW	*Good Vibrations* (1993)	BB
The Rocking Surfer	1963	Trad. arr. BW	*Surfer Girl* (1963)	BB
Roller Skating Child	1976	BW	*Love You* (1977)	BB
Run-Around Lover	1963	BW, ML	*Pet Projects: The BW Productions* (2003)	Sharon Marie
Sail on, Sailor	1972	BW, Almer, Rieley, Kennedy, VDP	*Holland* (1973)	BB
Salt Lake City	1965	BW, ML	*Summer Days* (1965)	BB
She Knows Me Too Well	1964	BW, ML	*Today!* (1965)	BB
She Rides With Me	1964	BW, RC	*More Teenage Triangle* (1964)	Paul Petersen
She Says That She Needs Me	1965	BW, Titelman, Sager	*Imagination* (1998)	BW
She's My Summer Girl	1963	Altfield, JB, BW	*Ride the Wild Surf* (1964)	J&D
Shelter	2012	BW, JT	*That's Why God Made the Radio* (2012)	BB
Shut Down	1963	BW, RC	*Little Deuce Coupe* (1963)	BB
Shut Down, Part II	1964	CW	*Shut Down, Vol. 2* (1964)	BB
Solar System	1976	BW	*Love You* (1977)	BW

Song Title	Year Begun	Credit	Source Used Here	Artist(s)
Some of Your Love	1972	BW, ML	*Keepin' the Summer Alive* (1980)	BB
Soul Searchin'	1994	BW, Paley	*Gettin' in over My Head* (2004)	CW, BW
Soulful Old Man Sunshine	1969	BW, Henn	*Endless Harmony* (1998)	BB
South American	1997	BW, JT, Buffett	*Imagination* (1998)	BW
Southern California	2008	BW, SB	*That Lucky Old Sun* (2008)	BW
Still I Dream of It	1976	BW	*Good Vibrations* (1993)	BW
Stoked	1963	BW	*Surfin' USA* (1963)	BB
Summer's Gone	1999	BW, Bon Jovi, JT	*That's Why God Made the Radio* (2012)	BB
Surf City	1963	JB, BW	*Surf City* (1963)	J&D
Surf Jam	1963	CW	*Surfin' USA* (1963)	BB
Surf's Up	1966	BW, VDP	*Smile Sessions* (2011)	BB
Surfer Girl	1962	BW	*Surfer Girl* (1963)	BB
The Surfer Moon	1962	BW	*Surfer Girl* (1963)	BB
Surfers Rule	1963	BW, ML	*Surfer Girl* (1963)	BB
Surfin'	1961	BW, ML	*Surfin' Safari* (1962)	BB
Surfin' Safari	1962	BW, ML	*Surfin' Safari* (1962)	BB
Sweet Mountain	1972	BW, Sandler	*Spring* (1972)	Spring
That Lucky Old Sun	2008	Gillespie, Smith	*That Lucky Old Sun* (2008)	BW
That Same Song	1976	BW, ML	*15 Big Ones* (1976)	BB
That's Why God Made the Radio	1999	BW, Peterik, Millas, JT	*That's Why God Made the Radio* (2012)	BB
Their Hearts Were Full of Spring	1962	Troup	*Hawthorne, CA* (2001)	BB
Think About the Days	2012	BW, JT	*That's Why God Made the Radio* (2012)	BB
Thinkin' 'bout You Baby	1964	BW, ML	*Pet Projects: The BW Productions* (2003)	Sharon Marie
This Isn't Love	1997	BW, TA	*Live at the Roxy* (2000)	BW
This Whole World	1969	BW	*Sunflower* (1970)	BB
'Til I Die	1969	BW	*Surf's Up* (1971)	BB
Time to Get Alone	1968	BW	*20/20* (1969)	BB
TM Song	1976	BW	*15 Big Ones* (1976)	BB
Wake the World	1968	BW, AJ	*Friends* (1968)	BB
Walkin' the Line	1986	BW, Laird-Clowes	*Brian Wilson* (1988)	BW
The Warmth of the Sun	1964	BW, ML	*Shut Down, Vol. 2* (1964)	BB
We'll Run Away	1964	BW, GU	*All Summer Long* (1964)	BB
When I Grow Up (To Be a Man)	1964	BW, ML	*Today!* (1965)	BB
Wind Chimes	1966	BW	*Smile Sessions* (2011)	BB
With Me Tonight	1967	BW	*Smiley Smile* (1967)	BB
Wonderful	1966	BW, VDP	*Smile Sessions* (2011)	BB
Wouldn't It Be Nice	1966	BW, TA, ML	*Pet Sounds* (1966)	BB
You Still Believe in Me	1965	BW, TA	*Pet Sounds* (1966)	BB
Your Imagination	1997	BW, JT, Dahl	*Imagination* (1998)	BW
Your Summer Dream	1963	BW, Norberg	*Surfer Girl* (1963)	BB

Appendix 3.2: Chord Classification and Identification in Chapter 3

References to specific chords in this chapter adapt the classification system used by Walter Everett in his *Foundations of Rock* (2009), which is an amalgam of academic and popular conventions.

- For chords symbolized by Roman numerals, the major scale serves as the point of reference. Case indicates chord quality. Triads suggesting minor modalities may require a change in case and/or a flat sign preceding the Roman numeral, indicating a lowered root:

symbol	indicates	in C =	symbol	indicates	in C =
I	major triad on $\hat{1}$	C–E–G	i	minor triad on $\hat{1}$	C–E♭–G
ii	minor triad on $\hat{2}$	D–F–A	ii°	dim. triad on $\hat{2}$	D–F–A♭
iii	minor triad on $\hat{3}$	E–G–B	♭III	major triad on ♭$\hat{3}$	E♭–G–B♭
IV	major triad on $\hat{4}$	F–A–C	iv	minor triad on $\hat{4}$	F–A♭–C
V	major triad on $\hat{5}$	G–B–D	v	minor triad on $\hat{5}$	G–B♭–D
vi	minor triad on $\hat{6}$	A–C–E	♭VI	major triad on ♭$\hat{6}$	A♭–C–E♭
vii°	dim. triad on $\hat{7}$	B–D–F	♭VII	major triad on ♭$\hat{7}$	B♭–D–F

- The same principles apply to nondiatonic chords:

symbol	indicates	in C =
♭II	major triad on ♭$\hat{2}$	D♭–F–A♭
II	major triad on $\hat{2}$	D–F♯–A
III	major triad on $\hat{3}$	E–G♯–B
♯iv°	dim. triad on ♯$\hat{4}$	F♯–A–C
VI	major triad on $\hat{6}$	A–C♯–E
♭vii	minor triad on ♭$\hat{7}$	B♭–D♭–F
VII	major triad on $\hat{7}$	B–D♯–F♯

- Superscripts may indicate nondiatonic altered tones:

symbol	indicates	in C =
I$^{\sharp5}$	aug. triad on $\hat{1}$	C–E–G♯
III$^{\sharp5}$	aug. triad on $\hat{3}$	E–G♯–B♯
V$^{\sharp5}$	aug. triad on $\hat{5}$	G–B–D♯
♭VI$^{\sharp5}$	aug. triad on ♭$\hat{6}$	A♭–C–E

- For symbolizing added tones, such as sixths or sevenths, unaltered superscripts indicate notes from within the prevailing key, always using the major scale as the point of reference:

symbol	indicates	in C =
I^{add6}	major triad on $\hat{1}$ + added 6th	C–E–G–A
I^7	M^7 chord on $\hat{1}$	C–E–G–B
ii^7	m^7 chord on $\hat{2}$	D–F–A–C
$ii^{\emptyset7}$	half-diminished 7th chord on $\hat{2}$	D–F–A♭–C
II^7	dominant 7th chord on $\hat{2}$	D–F♯–A–C
$♭III^7$	M^7 chord on ♭$\hat{3}$	E♭–G–B♭–D
iii^7	m^7 chord on $\hat{3}$	E–G–B–D
III^7	dominant 7th chord on $\hat{3}$	E–G♯–B–D
IV^7	M^7 chord on $\hat{4}$	F–A–C–E
V^7	dominant 7th	G–B–D–F
V^9	dominant 9th	G–B–D–F–A
V^{11}	dominant 11th	G–B–D–F–A–C
$♭VI^7$	M^7 chord on ♭$\hat{6}$	A♭–C–E♭–G
vi^7	m^7 chord on $\hat{6}$	A–C–E–G
VI^7	dominant 7th chord on $\hat{6}$	A–C♯–E–G
$♭VII^7$	M7 chord on ♭$\hat{7}$	B♭–D–F–A
VII^7	dominant 7th chord on $\hat{7}$	B–D♯–F♯–A

• Added altered tones are indicated with an accidental:

symbol	indicates	in C =
$I^{♭7}$	dominant 7th chord on $\hat{1}$	C–E–G–B♭
$i^{♭7}$	m^7 chord on $\hat{1}$	C–E♭–G–B♭
$II^{♯7}$	M^7 chord on $\hat{2}$	D–F♯–A–C♯
$♭III^{♭7}$	dominant 7th chord on ♭$\hat{3}$	E♭–G–B♭–D♭
$IV^{♭7}$	dominant 7th chord on $\hat{4}$	F–A–C–E♭
$♯iv^{o7}$	fully diminished 7th chord on ♯$\hat{4}$	F♯–A–C–E♭
$V^{♭9}$	dominant 7th + ♭9	G–B–D–F–A♭
$V^{9(♯7)}$	M^9 on $\hat{5}$	G–B–D–F♯–A
$♭VI^{♯6}$	German augmented 6th chord on ♭$\hat{6}$	A♭–C–E♭–F♯
$♭VII^{♭7}$	dominant 7th chord on ♭$\hat{7}$	B♭–D–F–A♭

• When Roman numerals aren't called for, standard letter notation may be used:

symbol	indicates	spelling
C	C major triad	C–E–G
Dm	D minor triad	D–F–A
B°	B diminished triad	B–D–F
G+	G augmented triad	G–B–D♯
G^7	G dominant 7th chord	G–B–D–F
G^9	G dominant 9th chord	G–B–D–F–A
$G^{♭9}$	G dominant 7th chord + ♭9	G–B–D–F–A♭
Dm^7	D minor 7th chord	D–F–A–C
$Fmaj^7$	F major 7th chord	F–A–C–E
$B^{\emptyset7}$	B half-diminished 7th chord	B–D–F–A
$F♯^{o7}$	F♯ fully diminished 7th chord	F♯–A–C–E♭

- For Roman numerals or letter notation, symbols without slashes indicate root position. Symbols with slashes indicate inverted chords. The bass note is indicated after the slash, either as a degree in the major scale (for Roman numerals) or note name (for letter notation):

R.N.	letter notation	inversion	spelling	bass note
C: I	C	root position	C–E–G	C
C: I/$\hat{3}$	C/E	1st	C–E–G	E
C: I/$\hat{5}$	C/G	2nd	C–E–G	G
C: V^7	G^7	root position	G–B–D–F	G
C: V^7/$\hat{7}$	G^7/B	1st	G–B–D–F	B
C: V^7/$\hat{2}$	G^7/D	2nd	G–B–D–F	D
C: V^7/$\hat{4}$	G^7/F	3rd	G–B–D–F	F

The slash notation may also indicate a bass note that is not included in the chord above (e.g., C:♭VII/$\hat{1}$ = B♭/C = B♭–D–F over a C bass note).

PART 2 | Historical Inquiries

FOUR | Summer of '64

KEIR KEIGHTLEY

A sociologist might say I am trying to generate a feeling of social
superiority.
—Brian Wilson, liner notes to *All Summer Long* (1964)

BRIAN WILSON'S STATUS as one of the architects of rock has
rested on arguments about his superior musical achievements—his compositional innovations, his brilliance as an arranger, his groundbreaking use of the studio, the haunting beauty of his falsetto. This long-
germinating view of Brian has finally—and justly—propelled him to
the front ranks of a rock canon. Indeed, this volume itself attests to this
consecration as a rock composer. But classifying him as a rock composer
poses some historical problems.

There was no rock music culture in 1964. Certainly we can identify
many of the elements (sounds, attitudes, values) that would coalesce
to form a rock culture by around 1966–67. But like the components
of an as-yet-unassembled hi-fi kit—strewn across a suburban basement
floor, waiting to be wired together and turned up to "10"—rock was
more promise than reality in 1964. Teen pop, on the other hand, was
a smoothly humming machine reaching maximum velocity, and Brian
Wilson was among those driving its dominance. Circa 1964, the year of
the Beach Boys' first number-one single, first number-one LP, and first
million-seller, the work of Brian Wilson was rightly classified as teen pop,
as the front cover of their live LP, *Beach Boys Concert* (recorded August
1964), instructs us: "File Under: Beach Boys • Teen • Best Sellers."[1]

However, teen pop, especially as it became dominant around 1959–63, the so-called in-between years (Sten 1978) that separated Elvis and the Beatles, occupies a problematic place in rock culture, largely because of the enduring classificatory power of the notorious rock-versus-pop binary. In this essay, I explore Brian Wilson's implication in this opposition by focusing on his work circa 1964, particularly though not exclusively the album *All Summer Long*. In so doing, I want to revisit his place in the subsequent rise of rock culture as well as interrogate long-standing views of rock history and ideology. This will require recovering and resituating his role in the world of teen pop and its mass-mediated, mainstream, majority culture.

The liner notes for *All Summer Long* attributed to Brian address frequent inquiries about how he comes up with his song "ideas" (figure 4.1). He claims his "inspirations" are the "feelings" associated with common teen experiences (romance, school, "winning and losing in sports"). But he then makes an odd remark: "A sociologist might say I am trying to generate a feeling of social superiority." This seeming non sequitur is followed immediately by a more straightforward assertion: "I live with my piano and I love to make records that my friends like to hear." Here Brian's explicit linkage of "social superiority" and a "love" of creativity in an implicitly Romantic discourse ("feelings," "inspirations") points toward key tenets of an emergent rock community (Frith 2007, 31ff.): the amateur ("love") who lives and breathes music ("I live with my piano") is inspired by everyday experiences (school, sports) to create sound recordings that are then implicated in the creation and reproduction of group identity ("my friends")— but implicated also in the creation and reproduction of hierarchy and exclusion, so that some music (rock) may then be classified as "superior" to others (pop). Just as this volume of popular music studies research you are reading makes an implicit claim that Brian Wilson is more worthy than other popular artists who do not receive such scholarly attention, so too was the rise of rock culture driven by assertions about the "superiority" of this music over others. At some point, such distinctions were codified as the "rock-versus-pop binary." And exactly how and where Brian Wilson's work was—and is and ought to be—classified therein remain productive questions, particularly if we wish to explore and understand the stakes of a popular music culture

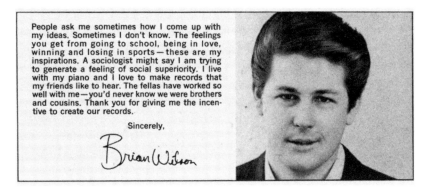

People ask me sometimes how I come up with my ideas. Sometimes I don't know. The feelings you get from going to school, being in love, winning and losing in sports — these are my inspirations. A sociologist might say I am trying to generate a feeling of social superiority. I live with my piano and I love to make records that my friends like to hear. The fellas have worked so well with me — you'd never know we were brothers and cousins. Thank you for giving me the incentive to create our records.

Sincerely,

Brian Wilson

Figure 4.1: Brian Wilson's liner notes on the back cover of *All Summer Long* (1964)

that simultaneously exhibits populist, capitalist, and elitist impulses. Acknowledging these various fault lines running through rock can also tell us something about the broader social, economic, and historical currents of modernity.

A Sociologist Might Say . . .

As I have argued elsewhere, the rock-versus-pop binary is a complex (and at times, contradictory) set of claims about popular musical value that have proven surprisingly resilient and yet historically underexamined (Keightley 2001, 2011). While it is clear that rock music culture was founded on taste distinctions made within mainstream music in the 1960s, precisely how those distinctions were made—and made to stick—remains somewhat obscure. One of the foundational texts of popular music studies from 1950, sociologist David Riesman's "Listening to Popular Music," offers some clues and thus merits some exposition. Writing well before the mid-1960s advent of rock culture, and several years prior to the emergence of rock 'n' roll, Riesman sketches out a sociology of popular music that distinguishes between two kinds of listener: what he calls the "majority listener" and the "minority listener." Riesman appears more interested in, and perhaps sympathetic to, the latter category, whose features presage those of the rock fan: minority listeners to popular music are "aware" (6), "active listeners" (9), most interested in "arrangement or technical virtuosity," insisting upon "rigorous standards of judgment and taste" (10), informed by knowledge gleaned from "trade journals" (9). They prefer "uncommercialized, unadvertised small bands rather than name bands," and express "a profound resentment of the commercialization of radio and musicians" (10). Minority listeners "resist certain conventional stereotypes" by "making a differential selection from what the adult media already provide" (8). Thus minority listeners constitute for Riesman a sort of politically unconscious "youth movement" (8), characterized by "dissident attitudes" (10) and "rebelliousness" (9) expressed through a taste for "hot jazz." It is noteworthy that they tend to be "highly articulate" men—according to Riesman, there are "very few hot jazz girls" (12), and moreover, "as the subordinate group with fewer other outlets, girls can less afford even a conventionalized resistance" (9). In Riesman's classification, majority listeners are uncritical female conformists with "undiscriminating tastes" who are "seldom even interested in the techniques of their exploitation or its extent" (8)—as good a capsule definition of the rock snob's stereotype of a pop fan as you will find (see also Frith and McRobbie 1978; Coates 1997).

Riesman's sociology of popular music approaches listeners in terms of binary classifications: "hot jazz" versus "name bands," marginal artists versus mainstream stars, and, most significantly, college-age men versus teenaged girls.[2] Gender is arguably the primal form of classification, the first social labeling ("It's a boy!"), and a divide that grows into a lifetime of possibilities and proscriptions. For the sociologist Riesman, minority listeners invest in popular music culture as a forum for acquiring and displaying what songwriter Brian Wilson would later call "social superiority." Thus the gendering of the minority/majority opposition shows how musical superiority is underpinned by, and contributes to, the maintenance of gendered power structures, despite the disingenuous labeling of the socially more powerful contingent as the "minority."

There is a further implication in the classification, "majority." As the reference to "commercialized" "name bands" suggests, mass-media popularity defines majority popular music culture. Riesman's minority/majority opposition suggests a difference in audience sizes that we might perhaps transcribe as niche/mainstream and map onto an older hierarchy that valued the rare or obscure or expensive over the plentiful or common or cheap.[3] So Brian Wilson's assertion of interest in "social superiority" on the back of a best-selling teen pop LP implicitly reconfigures these relationships, since he is proposing to "generate" something in a majority context that historically had been an exclusive property of the minority. The later 1960s rise of rock will involve scalar shifts that jumbled the historical relations between cultural hierarchy and audience size. Rock emerged as a mainstream that saw itself as a margin, a majority that identified with minorities, a dominant culture that felt subcultural. This is why I have called it "subdominant culture" (Keightley 2001), and why Robert Christgau (1970) addressed rock's paradoxes by classifying it as "semipopular music."[4] Returning to 1964, we find the songwriter offering the sociologist's majority listeners a set of songs that he hopes will "generate a feeling" of superior, minority taste—a historically innovative claim. Here we glimpse a nascent rock ideology as it is taking shape inside the very teen pop mainstream that rock will soon problematize and disavow.

So we might then ask, why did it take so long to fully recognize the groundbreaking aspects of Brian's work? The answer perhaps lies in what C. Wright Mills once called "the sociological imagination."[5] For minority listeners, as for rock fans, the social mapping functions of popular music are particularly crucial—popular music, its stars, genres, and values, offer images of the social world, of social groups and social others, as Riesman made clear in 1950:

> When [the teenager] listens to music, even if no one else is around, he listens in the context of imaginary "others"—his listening is indeed often an effort to connect with them. . . . It is the pressure of conformity with the group that invites and compels the individual to have recourse to the media both in order to learn from them what the group expects and to identify with the group by sharing a common focus for attention and talk. (Riesman 1950, 10)

Here yet another historical shift needs to be acknowledged in qualifying Riesman's important account. As noted above, Riesman understands "the adult media" (8) to be the source of the "exploitation" and "commercialization" of popular music. The rise of rock 'n' roll, but especially the expansion of "teen music" in the in-between years (1959–63), saw ever-younger professionals entering the music industry during a period popularly understood to witness a growing "generation gap." Brian Wilson (born in 1942) was nineteen years old when he made his first single, and turned twenty-two during the summer of 1964 (his band at this time contained two teenagers: Dennis, nineteen, and Carl, seventeen). The songs of teen life written and sung by the Beach Boys are undeniably the work of successful media professionals and may contain strong elements of fantasy, but they are also being created and performed by a group made up of teenagers and other members only a few years removed from adolescence. As lyricist Roger Christian told *Life* magazine in 1964, Brian Wilson's forte is his "grasp of the teenage mind" (quoted in Alexander 1964, 33). Riesman's claim for music's important role in both grasping and shaping social relations reminds us that the "feeling of social superiority" the songwriter hopes to communicate to his listeners likewise involved an admixture of documentary and fantasy elements.

Brian Wilson's assertion of "social superiority" needs also to be considered in light of Paul Williams's 1968 comment about the role of "class prejudice" in neglect of the Beach Boys' work. In one of the earliest defenses of the Beach Boys by a rock critic, they are characterized as "a group that class prejudice prevents many of us from appreciating."[6] Williams is not simply referring to social class, however. Like Riesman, he is interested in how classifications of music and listeners shape, and are shaped by, our senses of ourselves and of the social world. Writing as one of the founders of rock criticism, Williams had previously sketched out a growing divide within the mainstream music market of the late 1960s, contrasting a teenybop, transistor-AM-radio-listening segment against an older, more serious, rock-LP-listening segment—thereby articulating an emergent rock-versus-pop dichotomy. It's important to note here that Williams explicitly marks the pop fans in terms of gender and generation ("housewives" and "subteens"; Williams 1967, 23) yet leaves the rock fans unmarked—suggesting that they are white, male, college students like the author himself. But unlike many critics at the time, Williams immediately turns around and problematizes this foundational division, expressing concern about what is being lost as a result of the bifurcation: these classifications may help constitute rock culture, but they also may prevent rock fans from appreciating what he considers to be great music, such as that of Brian Wilson.

So, despite the shifting positions—Wilson's 1964 "feeling of social superiority" will be in 1968 employed and enjoyed by others who look down on his music—all claim value by making complex links between music and society.[7] The anti–Beach Boys position Williams criticizes is not only a rocker's knee-jerk disdain for pop, a classificatory "prejudice" that results in a kind of aesthetic deafness. Equally importantly, it is a classification and rejection of imagined social others. Where Riesman's majority listener experiences a kind of musical belonging to a desired social group, in Williams the distaste for the Beach Boys involves an imaginary distancing from the class of listeners who *do* indeed enjoy the Beach

Boys' music—and this distancing from Wilson's presumed pop serves to reinforce the in-group identity of the rock listener. Again, the categories of "rock" and "pop" are not simply musical descriptions but judgments evaluating the presumed links between musics and audiences. Acts of classification animate all of these discussions, and as Pierre Bourdieu has argued, classification struggles shape much more than aesthetic debate. For Bourdieu, taste is a crucial dimension of social stratification: aesthetic distinctions (this is ugly, this is beautiful) contribute to the complex maintenance and reproduction of social divisions, such as social class (Bourdieu 1984). In Williams's argument, class-as-classification can simultaneously render one deaf to beauty while working to divide audiences. (This division of the popular music audience is of great concern to the populist Williams.) In the newborn rock culture of 1967–68, the Beach Boys tended to be classified as pop, as old-fashioned, as out of touch, and as thus unworthy of the authentic rock fan's attention. But whatever shunning they experienced at the hands of rock snobs, this was also tied to the band's image as representatives of a white, suburban, majority culture that, by 1968, was widely understood to represent more than an aesthetic problem.

The use of music to draw lines of social division is long-standing, seen perhaps most spectacularly in the so-called classical/popular divide of the late nineteenth century, with its ties to the historical struggle between the forces of democracy and plutocracy, between the many and the few (Levine 1988; Van Der Merwe 1992, 18ff.). Sociological accounts approach popular music as involving a series of position-takings in social space, wherein liking ("My friends like to hear . . .") contributes both to group solidarity and to social division and, thereby, to a potential "feeling of social superiority." The long-standing and widespread perception of the Beach Boys as privileged, suburban whites who sound like members of a college fraternity is particularly germane here. Recall the band's origin myth and its nexus of cash, class, and parental permissiveness: they supposedly started their band by renting instruments with grocery money left behind by a vacationing Murry and Audree.[8] One of the ways rock asserted its social difference (and cultural superiority) was by affiliating with the musical practices of social inferiors—with marginalized groups whose parents tended not to provide financial support for a fledgling rock band. Rock's symbolic affiliations—with minorities, outsiders, underdogs, underclasses—here stand in contrast to the Beach Boys' celebrations of membership in the majority. Indeed, the subtle racial anxiety sometimes provoked by their frat-boy harmonies is, unsurprisingly, tied to the history of the racial majority's treatment of racial minorities in the United States. Thus those who hear excessive sonic whiteness in the band's massive pop success presume the Beach Boys to be antithetical to the interests of minority cultures, real or fantasized—whether to the faux underground of rock or to members of actual economic underclasses. This pushed them beyond the ken of rock cognoscenti in the 1960s, despite ample evidence of their role in the formation of rock culture.

Here we need to consider the relatively rapid transformation of the majority/teen pop mainstream into the rock mainstream in the space of a few years. Rock culture came into existence precisely *as* majority culture, inside the mainstream, fully mediated, industrialized, and best-selling—even as it questioned or misrecognized or disavowed these aspects, even as it pretended to minority listening protocols in asserting its self-proclaimed superior taste. If we take the Beatles as a definitive rock act, then it says everything that they were always already "mainstream" in the United States. Rock's later infusions by subcultural or crossover musics should not mislead us into thinking that rock arose in such fashion. Rock was actually a mutation of teen pop. However, this mutation not only refused to acknowledge its most immediate relative—rock aggressively classified teen pop as its antithesis. This negative definition (rock is the opposite of pop) also helped obscure rock's status as the new majority music by circa 1967–68.[9] Brian Wilson and the Beach Boys, however, remained marked by their prominence in the earlier majority music, and this contributed to their odd status in a newborn rock culture. In the following sections, I trace out several aspects of Brian Wilson's deep implication in the majority culture of teen pop. From there I shift to a discussion of some of his groundbreaking work circa 1964 and how it might have "generate[d] a feeling of social superiority," one appropriate to those in the avant-garde of teen pop just before it becomes rock (and before rock itself becomes the new majority culture).

Superiority

Consider the cover of *Shut Down, Volume 2*, released in the spring of 1964 and remaining on *Billboard*'s "Top LPs" chart all summer long: standing next to their custom machines, sporting perfect hair, perfect teeth, perfect harmonies, the band exudes affluence, confidence, solidarity—and perhaps even superiority. In colloquial terms they are "winners"—at racing, at music, at life. They represent the fantasy car club many longed to join, even as such a club necessarily rejected those who couldn't afford the Stingray or XKE included in the band's earlier "Our Car Club" (1963)—a club whose stated goals were to "show some class and style" and "wipe out the other clubs." The matching car-club windbreakers adorning the cover of *Shut Down, Volume 2* recall the famous red one worn by fellow hot-rodder James Dean in *Rebel Without a Cause* (1955). Most commentators emphasize that star's outsider status and the film's epoch-making representations of the postwar generation gap that so crucially contributed to the taste politics of rock (cf. Doherty 1988; Keightley 2001). Yet for a teenaged Geoffrey O'Brien (2004, 234), more than anything else *Rebel* depicted Southern California class privilege, a moving image of the world the Beach Boys would embody musically.

Minimizing the rebellious, conflictual aspects of the film, O'Brien contends it was less generation gap than generational privilege that *Rebel Without a Cause* celebrated. In O'Brien's reading, then, Brian Wilson rendered into music the remarkable affluence and freedom of the white, suburban, Los Angeles teenagers portrayed in the film. *Rebel*'s Cinemascoped teeth and hair and hot rods thus return in recorded form via the early hits of the Beach Boys, in ever-more-perfected and endlessly repeatable vinyl slices of teen utopia. While rock's countercultural politics of difference may have built on the generation gap of the 1950s, that gap was widely expressed and experienced via mainstream forms of consumption, with leisure commodities such as sound recordings at the forefront. This then means that majority consumer culture played a much more formative role in rock ideology than could be acknowledged at the time. But the Beach Boys more than acknowledged it—they reveled in it.

As singing billboards for a hyperconsumptive life of affluent leisure, the Beach Boys would become unsubtle reminders of an awkward truth: despite its countercultural accoutrements, the so-called rock revolution of the 1960s was a crucial contributor to a much larger consumer revolution, one that ultimately encouraged greater consumer conformity (Buxton 1983). Just as the band had initially wanted to be named after a brand of consumer goods (Pendleton shirts), their early national success purveyed a brand identity built on preexisting consumer-goods marketing (surfboards, hot rods, California produce). Their trademark, "The Beach Boys," was itself tightly tethered not only to athletics and seaside leisure but to Tin Pan Alley and minstrel predecessors.[10] For example, a 1931 radio listing in the *Los Angeles Times* features broadcasts by no less than *five* vocal groups called the "—— Boys": the Banjo Boys, the Alabama Boys, the Ranch Boys, Three Boys, and, most intriguingly, the

Canfield Beach Boys ("Radio Pictures Parade Today," 1931). Ancestors such as these will make it harder for Brian's band to play the emerging chameleon game of a modernist rock culture, one animated by dreams of antimaterialism and committed to a fantasy of historical rupture with the majority, parent culture. As Stephen Nugent puts it, "An implicit premise [of rock criticism] has been that the genre represents a radical break with its antecedents" (1986, 82). Yet it is clear that even as rock expanded the purview of consumer culture, it did so under a newer brand name, "rebellion." The Beach Boys, on the other hand, remained anachronistically anchored in the old majority mass culture of Madison Avenue, Hollywood, and Tin Pan Alley.

A key theme of this majority culture was "success." As Albert McLean explains in his study of the roots of U.S. mass culture, *American Vaudeville as Ritual*, "success" was the main message of every vaudeville show (McLean 1965; see also Horton and Wohl 1956). This is especially significant given the contrast between the Beach Boys' portrayal on the cover of *Shut Down, Volume 2* as "winners" and the post-*Smile* representations of Brian Wilson as some sort of "loser." His image as a disheveled, disoriented, dissolute hermit was crucial to his much later rehabilitation inside a popular music canon. Redemption is a grand narrative, and he first had to be a loser to become a winner. Yet this sad-sack portrait appears preposterous juxtaposed against the 1964 model-year Brian Wilson, the very embodiment of success.

In the summer of '64, Brian Wilson stood very tall indeed, the golden boy of a Golden State in a golden age of pop singles. At the peak of his power as a hit maker, creating more Top 40 hits than his erstwhile rival Phil Spector, innovating faster and moving farther than the Beatles of that year, Brian Wilson was a tireless industry overachiever.[11] Indeed, his massive success as a creator of "materialistic and happy" anthems (Goldstein 1966, 7) would later contribute to his problematic position in a burgeoning rock canon. If rock privileges the outsider, the nonconformist, the industry rebel, then circa 1964 Brian Wilson was almost an antithesis of rock—he was the ultimate *in*sider, working quickly and effectively, writing and producing hits for his band and for others, and happily contributing to the economic expansion of the teen market. He and the Beach Boys were emblems of "winning" at a moment in American history when winning seemed manifest destiny.[12] So, as *All Summer Long* hit record stores that July, Brian Wilson was driving a superior vehicle that had "never been beat" ("I Get Around") and thriving at the very center of the majority culture.[13]

Packaging

From the perspective of majority culture, *All Summer Long* indeed appears as the perfect packaging of a popular brand: a dozen songs retailing summer fun, all wrapped in the high-gloss sheen of state-of-the-art, multitrack recording, and ably advertised in advance by the number-one hit single "I Get Around" (included as track 1 of side 1, in case you might miss it). The album reached as high as number four, remained on the *Billboard* "Top LPs" chart for forty-nine weeks, and was certified "Gold" by the RIAA. It can thus be characterized as a hit, a commercial success. The album is filled with a variety of songs (seven up-tempo/dance numbers, three slow ballads, one midtempo ballad, one novelty sound collage) expounding experiences of the consumer good life, presumably as lived by affluent California teenagers like the Wilson brothers: car and motorbike racing ("I Get Around," "Little Honda"), teen romance ("Wendy," "Hushabye," "We'll Run Away"), the consumption of mass-media forms of entertainment ("Drive-In," "Do You Remember?"). As befitting the brand in question, there are songs about beach life and surfing ("Girls on the Beach," "Don't Back Down") and various other forms of summer fun ("All Summer Long"). The enumerations of the latter, title track (placed on side 1, track 2, immediately following "I Get Around") thematize the contents of the album as a whole. Quickly listing numerous summer activities, events, and feelings, the lyrics of "All Summer Long" take the form of a verbal collage that in turn serves as a synopsis or miniature version of the entirety of the LP itself. The album is rounded out by a surf guitar instrumental ("Carl's Big Chance") and what might be termed an audio novelty ("Our Favorite Recording Sessions") that consists of studio outtakes, sound effects, and dialogue collaged together via tape editing.

Like the collage structure of the tracks "All Summer Long" and "Our Favorite Recording Sessions," the cover of the album, with its collection of various photos and colored squares, can also be characterized as a collage. It will be productive to attend to its genealogy in some detail, particularly since the cover art, visually advertising the variety of audio pleasures to be found within, says much about Brian Wilson and the Beach Boys' position in the majority, mass culture of the time.

The rise of the twelve-inch, 33⅓ rpm long-play record was an economic boon to the postwar U.S. recording industry. Not only did it allow for the collation of multiple songs that could then be sold at a higher price (and higher profit margin) than individual 45 rpm singles—its packaging also created a new medium for marketing music (Keightley 2004). Indeed, LPs were known in trade slang as "packages," and this had two meanings. The first, as a container that allowed the bundling together of songs, was somewhat metaphorical. The second, however, was more literal, since the cardboard LP sleeve acted as a form of protective packaging that also permitted a new emphasis on the commodity's decoration with attractive images and text. The LP sleeve can be considered a new medium for marketing popular music. Its twelve-inch square cover offered a kind of minibillboard that could catch the eye of potential customers, an advertising medium that allowed (and indeed encouraged) new images and ideas to be attached to popular music. The design of LP covers became increasingly sophisticated in the mid-1950s, and by the early 1960s constituted an important space for the creation and dissemination of enhanced value and meaning for popular music.

All Summer Long's packaging draws on well-established traditions of mainstream design that position the band as products of the majority consumer culture relentlessly promoted by Madison Avenue, Tin Pan Alley, and Hollywood. Its basic composition—a series of snapshots of beach fun casually organized around variously colored geometric shapes—draws strongly on the work of Piet Mondrian, a key member of the modernist Establishment (e.g., *Composition with Large Red Plane, Yellow, Black, Gray, and Blue*, 1921). Mondrian's bright colors and quirky, yet controlled, geometric compositions contributed one of the dominant design tropes of 1950s mass culture (Hine 1986, 73). It was used for numerous film titles (e.g., Saul Bass's credit sequence for *The Seven Year Itch*, 1955), the design of furniture (e.g., Charles and Ray Eames), and clothing, posters, and dozens of album covers, such as the Four Lads' *Breezin' Along* (Columbia, 1958).[14] The attraction of commercial artists to the bright colors and right angles of what I will call the Fifties Mondrian style may have been a result of its combination of whimsical collage and geometric precision, its simultaneous connotations of freedom and organization.[15]

While seeming haphazard, Fifties Mondrian offered a precise formula to commercial designers required to work within rationalized spaces; after all, squares and rectangles are the most efficient means of covering rectangular spaces such as magazine pages or movie frames. At a time when the semiscientific claims of Madison Avenue motivational researchers attempted to tap the consumer's unconscious desires as a means of moving more goods, the seemingly casual, yet grid-like, nature of Fifties Mondrian permitted a subtle reconciliation of industrial rationalization

Figure 4.2: Detail from the cover of the Beach Boys' *All Summer Long* LP (1964); note Coke bottles in bottom right panel.

and irrational pleasure.[16] It also allowed graphic designers to carefully construct imaginary filmic montages of products involving some sort of action such as vacationing or drinking. Both are found in a 1963 ad campaign entitled "All Summer Long, Say Seagram's and Be Sure." These ads for Seagram's Canadian whisky were widely circulated in newspapers and magazines throughout the United States.[17] The print ads used a Mondrian-derived composition to portray "a world of pleasure" via a series of images reminiscent of snapshots of pleasant summertime fun, all enabled by the consumption of Seagram's rye.

I am not claiming here that the campaign's linkage of the catchphrase "all summer long," photos of the consumer good life, and Mondrian design constitutes some sort of direct "influence" or "source" for the cover of *All Summer Long*. Instead, it points up just how clearly the Beach Boys' cover was enmeshed in mainstream commercial design and majority advertising styles, and underlines their parallel promotion of a good life likewise defined by brand-name consumption: the songs of *All Summer Long* are filled with cars, surfboards, T-shirts, records, movies, popcorn, hot dogs, Coke, Honda scooters, and so forth. The album cover includes that apotheosis of twentieth-century packaging, a Coke bottle (held by Dennis). The product is mentioned in two songs: "Drive-In" ("A big buttered popcorn and an extra large Coke") and the title track ("'member when you spilled Coke all over your blouse"). "All Summer Long" also mentions Honda scooters ("miniature golf and Hondas in the heat"), a product that is itself the topic of an entire song on the LP ("Little Honda").[18] In other words, the album cover's deep imbrication in a world of consumer marketing assists its visualization of the songs' lyrical allusions to brand-name consumer goods that are in turn evidence of Brian Wilson's—and his audience's—deep immersion in the majority mass culture of U.S. consumer society.

Synergy

I will return presently to *All Summer Long*, but first I would like to identify several minor but revealing contributions of Brian Wilson and the Beach Boys to the majority culture of the period. Their work for the Walt Disney Corporation in the summer of 1964 places them in the very belly of Hollywood's industrial complex. They shared lead vocal duties with Annette Funicello on the title track of her film *The Monkey's Uncle*. From one perspective, it is definitely a Disney song (from the pens of *Mary Poppins* composers the Sherman brothers). But it is also, unmistakably, a

Beach Boys track, with Brian's trademark falsetto and a quite enjoyable groove. Indeed, when I was finally able to hear it, after years of searching, I was pleasantly shocked. I had expected a subpar track, something that had been buried out of musical embarrassment. On the contrary, it is close enough to typical Beach Boys work of the period that I would argue its suppression from their acknowledged body of work is as much an index of its perceived ideological awkwardness as of any intellectual property issues (the master was owned by Buena Vista Records, a Disney subsidiary). It is likely its status as a "Disney product" was believed to mark it as a painfully obvious reminder of just how deep into majority culture "America's Greatest Band" (as the subtitle of Badman's 2004 catalogue raisonné puts it) were willing to wade.

Less compelling is their recording of the theme song to an NBC sitcom that summer. The Beach Boys' performance of Jack Marshall and Bob Mosher's theme to *Karen* (fall 1964) marks the band as industry insiders complicit in the factory production of mediocre majority culture. The sitcom is about a sixteen-year-old girl living in Southern California.[19] The show's credit sequence is superimposed over the label of a spinning LP, and its theme opens with a quote from Dick Dale's recording of "Misirlou" (a fast downward slide and a repeated note on the guitar's open low E string). It features a lead vocal by Mike, who sings that "at a party she's a stomper and a rock-and-rollin' romper." At best, it sounds like a lazy throwback to the Beach Boys of early 1963 (it was covered by the Surfaris in 1964). The lyrics describe Karen as a "teen" and a "modern girl," noting sardonically that doing her hair is "her favorite indoor sport / and by the light of television she can even write a book report" (this insulting last line is backed by a musical allusion to Jan and Dean's "The Little Old Lady from Pasadena," whose lyricist was frequent Brian Wilson collaborator Roger Christian). Episodes sometimes concluded with a rapprochement between wise father and bubble-brained daughter over the generation gap. Notwithstanding the sexist Othering, "Karen" aligns the Beach Boys with the allegedly feminizing mass culture of television, dismissed at the time as "a vast wasteland" (Minow 1961; see also Keightley 2003). As with their soundtrack recording of the theme to a family-friendly Disney film, the Beach Boys are now as close to the center of majority mass media as is possible, and a review of their July 6 "Summer Safari" tour performance in Arizona hints at the perils of such associations when it characterizes the band as "homogenised" (1964 *Tucson Citizen* review cited by Badman 2004, 59).

Rock culture would adopt key elements of the modernist critique of mass culture, in which television was singled out as one of the most intellectually deadening, indeed homogenizing, forces in American society.[20] The rapid expansion of television in the 1950s, its reliance on formula and generic productions, and its domination by Madison Avenue made it an obvious target, even as the rise of television also assisted the development of AM radio formats that favored rock 'n' roll and teen music. (As radio networks turned their attention to their more profitable television networks, local stations began to have more programming autonomy.) At the same time, as the Disney and NBC examples suggest, the consolidation of Hollywood, television, Tin Pan Alley, and the sound-recording industry in the 1950s encouraged quests for synergy, for teen stars who could profitably cross media boundaries. This enabled media convergences through which television stars could become recording stars, like Rick(y) Nelson of *The Ozzie and Harriet Show*, an acme of the strategy. In 1964, this approach was evident when a minor teen star, Paul Petersen of *The Donna Reed Show*, released a single, "She Rides with Me," on the Colpix label. Colpix was a recording subsidiary of Columbia Pictures–Screen Gems, the producers of *The Donna Reed Show* (ABC, 1958–66), and they hired one of the top people in the business to write and produce the single—Brian Wilson. The single's promotion involved the seeking of cross-media synergies, with Petersen plugging it through performances on network television, and DJ spins plugging his TV show on AM radio—just as Brian Wilson was seeking to do with his film and television work. While "She Rides with Me" was not a hit, it is historically noteworthy for its pioneering use of a rotating Leslie speaker to treat the backing vocals—a technique that would become prominent in psychedelia a few years later.

Things We Did Last Summer

Other Colpix recordings tied in to the especially wholesome *Donna Reed Show* may offer further insight into Brian's industrial situation in the period. Shelley Fabares first gained attention via appearances on the show and, like Peterson, played a teenager.[21] Through plugging on the show, Fabares quickly became a recording star as well via her number-one hit, "Johnny Angel" (1962; backing vocals by Darlene Love and the Blossoms).[22] This might be taken to represent the worst of majority culture, of the power of "adult media" and its extensive "techniques of exploitation" to mechanically impose products on audiences. Indeed, for those seeking to assert social superiority via musical taste, the sweet sound of "Johnny Angel" might be adduced to reinforce claims about the supposedly too–Tin Pan Alley, too-teenybop, indeed too-*girly* quality of the in-between years (Sten 1978). This interpretation would highlight the song's powerful promotion via television as clear-cut evidence of the era's manufacture, rather than authentic earning, of musical popularity. The conjoining here of aesthetic elitism, anticommercialism, and misogyny is typical of modernist cultural politics more generally, as Huyssen (1986) shows.

In the fall of 1962 Fabares released her second LP, entitled *The Things We Did Last Summer*. Its cover art, like *All Summer Long*'s, features a series of what might be personal snapshots, seemingly glued haphazardly to the front of an LP album now reimagined as a photo album. Each has a "handwritten" caption commenting on the past event, reminding us that both photographs and phonograph records are forms of prosthetic memory. While the overall composition itself bears little relationship to the dominant Fifties Mondrian style, the use of a different color font for each word of the album title most definitely does, forming as it does a kind of concrete-poetry version of a Mondrian painting.[23] The nostalgic "things" in question include consumer goods, so two of the four images of Fabares on the cover of *The Things We Did Last Summer* feature her using the ultimate teen consumer good of the period, a sound recording.[24] This indexes an expanding "record consciousness" (Gracyk 1996) among listeners at the time—as I will contend, a phenomenon especially evident on *All Summer Long*.[25]

The music on Fabares's LP relies on the output of the so-called song factories of Tin Pan Alley, whether the older Styne-Cahn number, "The Things We Did Last Summer" (1946), or more recent emanations from the Alley's final outpost, the Brill Building (songs by Mann-Weill, Goffin-King, Sedaka-Greenfield).[26] As with "Johnny Angel," *The Things We Did Last Summer* could be criticized as just one more widget spit out by the pop assembly line, yet another teen pop product of the Madison Avenue approach that likewise produced the cover design for *All Summer Long*. In this context it is noteworthy that the lyrics of "All Summer Long" themselves owe such a strong debt to "The Things We Did Last Summer." The verses of both "The Things We Did Last Summer" and "All Summer Long" consist of lists of summer activities strung together so as to produce a sort of montage or collage effect. Both songs twice mention an important emblem of period romances, "our song." And the Styne-Cahn song features the refrain line "All winter long."

Composed by veteran Tin Pan Alleyites Jule Styne and Sammy Cahn,

"The Things We Did Last Summer" was a hit in the 1940s and widely recorded thereafter (Frank Sinatra, Jo Stafford, Vaughn Monroe, all 1946;
Four Lads, 1956; Helen Merrill, 1957; Dean Martin, 1959; Nancy Wilson
and George Shearing, 1961; Shelley Fabares, 1962). Adding to this long
list, the Beach Boys themselves cut it in 1963, about eight months before
they made "All Summer Long." Prerecorded for a guest appearance on
The Red Skelton Show (NBC, September 24, 1963), it features the Beach
Boys doing their best Four Freshmen imitation, heard especially in the
scoop on the word "we" in each refrain line.[27] The arrangement features brushes on the snare drum and muted brass and string sections,
resulting in a typical "easy listening" sound of the period. Since this
was their second song on the evening's show (the first had been the
upbeat "Surfin' USA"), it is likely that the Tin Pan Alley ballad was chosen to demonstrate their ability to reach television's mass audience of all
ages and tastes.[28] This majority appeal may also begin to explain Brian
Wilson's attraction to Styne and Cahn's enduring hit as a lyrical model
for his new composition.[29]

The sentiments and lyrics of "Things" have deep roots in several Tin
Pan Alley traditions, whether so-called list songs that enumerate elements
of a romance,[30] or seasonal songs both remembered ("In the Good Old
Summertime," 1902, or the Gershwins' "Summertime," 1935) and forgotten (Albert Gumble and Harry Williams's "In the Summertime,"
1911, whose protagonist Tilly likes to "hum a sentimental tune of winter
all ev'ning long"), or songs that are themselves about remembering.[31]
Indeed, "The Things We Did Last Summer" draws from the sentimental
well of nostalgia that was Tin Pan Alley's stock in trade (and the target
of many modernist critics). Much of Brian Wilson's songwriting likewise
could be characterized as sentimental (on *All Summer Long* alone, "We'll
Run Away" and "Girls on the Beach" easily fit that mold, and arguments
could be mounted for "Wendy" and "All Summer Long" as well). This
genealogy may partially account for the emotional complexity of "All
Summer Long," a surging song whose surface ebullience seems to mask
a deeper sadness or loss.[32] But it also suggests why Brian's work will fit so
uneasily into the harder modernisms of rock culture's emergent canon.

Selectivity

One index of a song's sentimental success is its selection by a couple as
"our song." Both "The Things We Did Last Summer" and "All Summer
Long" refer to "our song" as a key constituent of the summer experi-

ence. "The Things We Did Last Summer" comments on the enduring, mnemonic power of popular music and the sentimental price it can exact: "I've tried so to forget / At times I do and yet / The mem'ry of you lingers like our song / The things we did last summer / I'll remember all winter long."[33] This is the song's second reference to "our song" (the first being happier: "the way we danced and hummed our fav'rite song"). "All Summer Long" repeats the line "Ev'ry now and then we hear our song," making it the only nonrefrain line sung more than once. The phrase "now and then" returns to consciousness a sense of time passing ("won't be long 'til summertime is through") that the song otherwise claims to deny ("but not for us, now!"). It also suggests the couple may be experiencing the private meaning of "their song" through the public mass medium of radio airplay. Selecting a single song out of the mass of popular songs to stand as "our song" helps solidify a romantic union. It points once again to popular music's deep implication in social identity work, in creating a sense of "us" at a particular time and place (a sense that may then endure, even when forgetting is desired, as in "Things"). As a commodity totem of romantic intimacy, "our song" becomes a secret, yet public, sign of private, yet shared, emotions.

Pop music's capacity to overwhelm us with nostalgic feelings grows, in part, out of its ability to momentarily saturate the lived environment, whether at a dance, on a car radio, or in a cinema, and thereby to mark a moment in time. Seasonal songs frequently juxtapose summer against autumn or winter in order to highlight the ephemerality of nice weather and young love (likewise teen pop has historically been dismissed as impermanent and disposable). Yet the concept of "our song" resists the trivial or ephemeral by selecting one pop song to carry a deeper, enduring significance. "Our song" involves what Riesman might call a "differential selection" being made out of the mass of popular musical offerings, a choice that then acquires a special, perhaps transcendent, meaning—and it is just such an enduring meaning that makes "our song" so poignant as an object of loss and nostalgia (e.g., "Stardust," 1929). Popular music offers a commodity that can simultaneously be possessed by a listener (*"our* song") and possess the listener (the haunting, uncanny power of a song to return us involuntarily to a time, a place, a feeling). As transient sounds that sometimes last a lifetime, such special songs elevate popular music above the mundane.

It is therefore particularly significant that *All Summer Long* contains at least three tracks that self-consciously select specific works of popular music and single them out as more worthy than others, distinguishing them perhaps as "superior pop": "All Summer Long," "Our Favorite Recording Sessions," and "Do You Remember?"[34] The latter song pays homage to "the guys who gave us rock and roll" (Little Richard, Danny and the Juniors, Elvis Presley, Jerry Lee Lewis, Dick Clark, and Chuck Berry) and features a kind of sampling of Wilson's favorite records and early rock 'n' roll styles. (At one point, we hear an imitation of Lewis's trademark, "goodness gracious, great balls of fire," at another an allusion to Chuck Berry's lead-guitar style.) Berry is singled out as "the greatest thing that's come along" and praised for having written "the all-time greatest song" (which goes unnamed). A similar appraisal is seen in the title of the novelty sound collage of the band working in the studio, "Our Favorite Recording Sessions," which uses a locution resembling "our song" and echoes the ranking of sound recordings undertaken by all listeners. Most remarkably, this track contains samples of the other two tracks that praise popular music: we hear botched attempts to overdub vocals on both "All Summer Long" and "Do You Remember?" We hear a tape recorder rewinding at one point, we hear engineer Chuck Britz (who is addressed as "Charlie" by Brian at the end of the track) advising the band on the timing of the punch-in or overdub, and Mike Love offers an extremely early reference to "overdub" in the following dialogue: "Let's overdub a little fingerpoppin' . . . you put a little fingerpoppin' on that it's gonna be a million and two seller!"[35]

Whether or not the 1964 listener understood the precise technical details here, there is an implicitly pedagogical aspect to "Our Favorite Recording Sessions," an imparting of knowledge that also characterizes the popular music history lesson of "Do You Remember?"[36] Moreover, the self-reflexive nature of these tracks, and indeed the abymic quality of "Our Favorite's" embedding of one track inside another, suggest an unexpectedly modernist sensibility. "Our Favorite Recording Sessions" ends when Brian says, "Wait a minute, I forgot my note" and we hear footsteps as he walks to the piano to remind himself of the pitch.[37] The rhythm of the footsteps prefigures the rhythm of the solo kick drum heard at the opening of the next and final track of the LP, "Don't Back Down" (and thus the kick initially sounds like it is part of "Recording Sessions"). This constitutes a remarkably early linkage of LP tracks, tied to a self-reflexive exploration of the techniques and technology of the recording studio, appearing on a self-produced album addressing the concept of "summer" from multiple angles.

All Summer Long is an album named after a song; "All Summer Long" and "Do You Remember?" are songs that refer to other (unnamed) songs; "Our Favorite Recording Sessions" is a recording that includes other recordings. Such linkages and embeddings (of songs inside songs, recordings inside recordings, performances about performance) prefigure the artistic ambitiousness, the "taking popular music seriously" (Frith 2007), that will shortly constitute rock culture. Returning to the liner notes in this context, it seems that Brian was self-consciously working to generate a new form of "superior pop." For Gracyk (1996), the rise of rock involved yet another form of consciousness, the widespread awareness of sound recording as a distinct artistic medium that he calls "record consciousness." If we approach rock as a mass-distributed, populist articulation of modernist art sensibilities, then it is not surprising that various new forms of consciousness (self-, historical, record) achieved widespread dissemination via rock culture; what is perhaps unexpected is to find nascent instances of these on a teen pop commodity.[38]

Along with record consciousness, the historical recitation of "Do You Remember?" reveals a growing historical consciousness in the teen pop of the period. The lyrics contend that Elvis Presley "paved the way for the rock-and-roll stars," thereby situating *All Summer Long* in a very traditional rock-historical lineage. (Fitzgerald 1999 contends that "Wilson should be accorded more credit as the songwriter who was best able to create a logical development of 1950s rock.") The praise for Chuck Berry does likewise, and this is part of the burgeoning historical consensus about Berry's significance to the teen pop world of 1964. Appearing with the Beach Boys on *The T.A.M.I. Show* that year, Berry is singled out as a founding figure by hosts Jan and Dean, who introduce him as "the guy who started it all." The characterization of Berry as an originator by the hosts of the "Teen Age Music International" is part of teen pop's growing awareness of its own history.[39] The attribution of historical agency to the singer-songwriter Berry also underlines an increasing attention to authorship in claims of popular musical "superiority." Like his acolyte Brian Wilson, Chuck Berry was a dedicated chronicler of leisure consumption in the United States, and yet, unlike Wilson, Berry's celebrations of majority pleasures were qualified by his "minority" identities (as African American, his classification as R & B performer, and even his affiliation with an independent, rather than major, label).

Design

The self-conscious and historically conscious embeddings and linkages of *All Summer Long* can be taken as evidence of design—not simply graphic design or sound design, but of intent, of the deliberate planning and execution of a large-scale project, one that moves beyond conventional practices at the time.[40] There is contextual evidence that one of Brian Wilson's intentions was to create an album that would be something more than a container or package of hits. The dominant strategy within the industry at this time was to approach teen pop as primarily a singles market. Teen pop LPs were regularly recorded, released, and promoted, of course, but they were believed to be less likely to be bought in great numbers by teenagers.[41] Thus teen-oriented LPs became "value-added" or "premium" versions of a hit single or star, rather than free-standing entities conceived as ends in themselves. This encouraged the inclusion of so-called filler tracks to pad out "LP's created as the result of a hit single" ("WB-Reprise Target: Teen Mart" 1964, 8). The placement of the number-one single "I Get Around" as the LP's first track on side 1 is evidence of the persistence of this industrial understanding of the teen market as a 45 rpm market. It is significant, then, that the album is *not* entitled something like "The Beach Boys Sing 'I Get Around' and 11 Other Summer Hits." While "I Get Around" is given the first track, the album still has its theme song, "All Summer Long," on track 2. Although it was never released as a single in the United States in the 1960s, the very high quality of its writing, arranging, performance, and production point to a degree of design or care—perhaps a level of "love," to echo again Wilson's liner notes—that is particularly impressive given the existence of an already-proven quantity ("I Get Around") that would have sufficed for a "theme" song.[42]

Unlike many teen pop albums of the period, *All Summer Long* is not stuffed with covers or so-called filler tracks, but again shows evidence of careful design in the inclusion of songs that reveal a high level of consistency in writing, production, and performance.[43] Several either became hits for others ("Little Honda," which reached number nine as covered by the Hondells) or are believed to have been hits by many Beach Boys fans ("Wendy," "Girls on the Beach," "All Summer Long"), despite never making the Top Forty (and the latter three songs appear repeatedly on "Greatest Hits" compilations). This kind of "superior" quality control is new to teen pop at this time and will be a key factor in the rise of album-oriented rock. (Although it is worth noting that an adult-oriented performer such as Frank Sinatra had, at this point, already been pursuing a similar policy at Capitol and then Reprise for a decade, segregating his hit singles from his "theme" LPs). This consistency also applies to the ongoing thematic attention to the concept of "summer" across the span of the album.

The design of the LP can be attributed to the increasing creative control Brian Wilson was able to exercise as producer and arranger, and as sole songwriter on seven of the twelve tracks (along with his listing as a collaborator on four of the remaining five).[44] The integration of musical functions (songwriting, arranging, producing, performing) in a single figure contrasts strongly with the dominant division of labor in the U.S. industry at this time. It serves to differentiate Wilson from other teen pop stars and position him as something relatively foreign to teen pop, an "author." By addressing his creative "ideas" and "inspirations," the LP liner notes help constitute Brian as the "author" of the record, just as his songwriting tended to be singled out in the few extant interviews from that summer (e.g., Blackburn 1964; see note 13). The back cover of *All Summer Long* tells listeners that the LP was "Arranged and Produced by Brian Wilson," potentially contributing to conceptions of Wilson as an auteur (a term adapted from film criticism by early rock critics; see Frith 1983, 53; Frith 2007, 260). An undated *Teen Set* magazine (likely late 1964) highlights Wilson's authorship in an article entitled "Brian Births a New Song" that quotes actress Peggy Lipton on how Beatles "Paul and John are infatuated with the Beach Boy sound. . . . They played *All Summer Long* all night long and asked me many questions about them. Paul and John were fascinated by Brian's style of composing and arranging" (12). By March 1965, the front cover of *The Beach Boys Today!* will announce "great new songs written by Brian Wilson."

While the lyrics of Brian's songs (with and without collaborators) tend to attract less critical attention than the music, the consistency of their thematic attention to the California lifestyle is always noted. This thematic single-mindedness ought to have implications for his status as auteur. Yet because so much autobiographically driven criticism fixates on the artist's inner emotional life, such lyrics (documenting lifestyles, fashions, and language that will become central to rock culture) still tend to be overlooked or undervalued. Whereas the Beatles' lyrics circa 1964 tended to dwell, to the exclusion of almost all other topics, on love and romance, the Beach Boys' lyrics included far more sociological detail about everyday life. Though they had a notoriously "clean-cut" image, their first top-ten single, "Surfin' USA" (April 1963) had contained a prominent reference to the growing trend of long hair for men, alluding to the male surfers' "Bushy blonde hair-do[s]." Given California's historical status as an epicenter of countercultural style and thought, it should be unsurprising that their lyrics regularly invoked slang that captured and disseminated this new zeitgeist. Much of it draws from another subculture with a strong California presence, the Beat generation: "cruisin' ev'ry pad" ("Little St. Nick", 1963); "her old man" ("Fun, Fun, Fun" 1964); "I'm a real cool head" ("I Get Around"); "a groovy little motor bike" ("Little Honda"); "when you made it with another guy" ("Wendy"—last three songs from *All Summer Long*). "When I Grow Up to Be a Man," also from the summer of 1964, is filled with Beat argot as it becomes rockspeak, featuring such turns of phrase as "Will they think their old man's really a square?," "Will I dig those sounds?," and possibly the earliest appearance of the expression "turn on" in the U.S. Top 40: "Will I still like the things that turned me on as a kid?" These pioneering uses of slang in a teen pop context reveal how Brian Wilson and the Beach Boys helped construct the terms of a rock culture that would later classify them as anachronistic or square.

Auteurist aesthetics tend to privilege the individual artist's expression of a particular worldview.[45] As we know from the liner notes, Brian's songwriting was inspired by the everyday experiences of a teenaged social cohort ("The feelings you get from going to school, being in love, winning and losing at sports"). If we then read *All Summer Long* as a kind of amateur sociology of the affluent, white, suburban, California adolescent experience, it can be argued that this makes it an early form of socially conscious pop: it is music that sets out to articulate a set of identity politics and a worldview. While some observers may not like the values animating this particular consumerist/majority world, it still remains an instance of pop music self-consciously chronicling a social reality. Insofar as we, like O'Brien, hear it as sonic sociology, it is thus a form of knowledge—and here we need to return to Bourdieu, for whom knowledge is key to classification struggles.[46] It matters how we classify this music because the stakes are always more than musical—for Bourdieu, all debates about taste are aspects of larger struggles for social power, bids at domination via aesthetic discourse. Recall Riesman's emphasis on the minority listener's awareness and articulateness and "rigorous standards of judgment and taste"—all suggesting an ability to wield musical knowledge to gain advantage in social interaction. The expression "I Get Around" means "I know what's what" (including inside info like "where the kids are hip"), and this superior knowledge, albeit deployed as braggadocio, is part of the pleasure of this track. The "social superiority" potentially generated by *All Summer Long* is an aspect of wider struggles for domination, inspiring not only highly competitive teen pop auteurs like Brian Wilson, but also rock culture's later claims of superiority to pop— not to forget the efforts of popular music scholars to have their objects of study, and themselves, taken seriously.

O'Brien's account of the Beach Boys circa 1964 frames their artistic achievement in terms of individual listeners' knowledge as they navigate the musical mainstream:

> The Beatles, of course, belonged to everyone; that was their peculiarity. The Beach Boys by contrast suggested a more rarefied indulgence. To enter their domain fully involved an initiation. Not that they were hidden; they were rather, at the outset, the very emblem of obviousness. Our journey consisted in finding, in the heart of that obviousness, what was most secret. (O'Brien 2004, 233)

For O'Brien, this paradoxical conception of the Beach Boys as an "obvious secret" continues after 1964 and into the rock era, as dedicated listening to older songs slowly produces new knowledge, a new cognizance of "secret jokes planted in the fade-outs, tiny sub-layerings designed to test if you were paying attention" (O'Brien 2004, 237):

> This archaeology of Brian Wilson provided the strange sensation that at the very time everyone was moving forward, into new identities, new decibel ranges, new scales of Dionysiac self-abandonment, a hidden truth was to be found in what had already been tossed aside, the pop hits of five years ago. Perhaps the secret instructions were: Don't follow the noise, follow the trail of hidden silences. (O'Brien 2004, 240)

In Riesman's terms, the art of Brian Wilson involved secreting minority musical pleasures inside majority-appeal packages. The ensuing feeling, long felt by fans of Brian Wilson's music, is best expressed by O'Brien: "Under a patina of easy prettiness lay a hard beauty" (O'Brien 2004, 242). This music of "social superiority" contributes to a remarkable reconfiguration of minority/majority aesthetic relations that, once upon a time, mapped tightly onto the ancient aristocratic/plebian distinction—a distinction crucially reimagined and rearranged, if never fully overcome, in midcentury music.

Conclusion

So why not simply call Brian Wilson's 1964 work "rock"? This question brings us back to the implications of Wilson's canonization as "rock composer." There is more than a grain of historical truth in rock's early "class prejudice" against the Beach Boys, but it is misinterpreted if taken to mean that they were somehow insufficiently "rock." Instead, I would contend that the real point here has been that Brian Wilson and the Beach Boys were a pop band and, a fortiori, that rock has itself been a form of pop all along.

And if any doubt remains about whether these classifications matter, look at the contortions undergone in the symbolic extrication of "Brian Wilson" from "Mike Love's Beach Boys" as the preferred object of canonical attention—this, despite the fact that all of Wilson's canonical works are indeed recordings by (t)his band.[47] Segregating "Brian" from "Mike" (or from "the Beach Boys") relies on and thus reinscribes the classificatory logic of rock versus pop so that the privileging of "Brian Wilson" now becomes an implicit dismissal of pop. In the rock-versus-pop binary, "pop" served as a sort of cesspool for rock, a repository of uncomfortable truths (i.e., that rock is indeed industrialized music, is part of consumer capitalism, is often an engine of hyperindividualism or conformity or patriarchy or sexism or racism, and so forth). Such a view of pop helps "purify" rock, just as having "Mike" encapsulate all that is or was awkward or problematic in their oeuvre serves to "purify" Brian of his majority-culture tendencies. But what is worse, it also utterly mischaracterizes Brian's real historical specificity. The relatively recent critical rehabilitation of Brian Wilson (in no small part due to this bisection) means that future generations of popular music scholars may mistakenly believe his work was always central to the rock canon—and this would mean that some of his historical significance will be lost. So part of what I have been trying to do here is recover and reconsider aspects that contributed to the early critical ambivalence toward this work while honoring the historical truth of Brian Wilson and the Beach Boys as teen pop. And if Brian's superior pop helped create a new musical culture, then it equally stands as a shiny reminder of the majority status of the music we now classify as "rock."

NOTES FOR CHAPTER 4

1. "I Get Around" reached the top of the charts in July, *Beach Boys Concert* became number one in December, and that album and *All Summer Long* were

certified Gold the following February. "Million-seller" is Brian Wilson's own characterization in a late August 1964 television interview in Oklahoma (Blackburn 1964).

2. There are relevant problems with Riesman's methodology here: while he did ethnographic fieldwork in a Chicago inner-city neighborhood to acquire the "majority" data, his "minority" informants appear mostly to have been his University of Chicago students, thereby likely skewing classed, gendered, and raced distributions.

3. Pierre Bourdieu's (1993) distinction, in *The Field of Cultural Production*, between heteronomy and autonomy as differing principles of taste legitimation might be applied here as well.

4. In this light, we might consider how *Pet Sounds'* faster canonization was assisted by its supposed "unpopularity."

5. I am appropriating Mills's (1959) turn of phrase to synopsize something Bourdieu (1984, 253) describes more densely: "It would be . . . absurd to exclude from social reality the representation which [social] agents form of that reality. The reality of the social world is in fact partly determined by the struggles between agents over the representation of their position in the social world and, consequently, of that world."

6. Williams 1968, 6. The essay was written in December 1967 (as noted in its third paragraph) and reevaluates *Beach Boys Party!* (1965) in light of the emergence of rock culture in general and of Williams's own evolution as a listener in particular. Williams initially disliked the LP, describing his earlier rejection of it as "a pretty snotty attitude" underpinned by a view of Beach Boys fans as "stupid." After two years of listening to and thinking about rock, Williams claims to have acquired "an educated response" to an album he now praises alongside *Pet Sounds*, and he does so after defining rock as "good creative art . . . appreciated by huge numbers of people" (Williams 1968, 6–7).

7. Independent of the Beach Boys question, Robert Levin argued in 1971 for "rock's *superiority* over previous popular musical forms" as growing more out of the actions of listeners than of musicians (cited in Frith 1983, 54; emphasis added).

8. I am here repeating the widely circulated, rather that historically accurate, version. As Al Jardine notes, this "is a great story, really sounds great in print" despite the fact that his mother was the more likely source of the start-up money, lending the band $300 she borrowed from the bank (quoted in Murphy 2015, 95–96).

9. See Keightley 2008 on the periodization of midcentury popular musics.

10. The term "beach boy," describing a young habitué of ocean resorts, has roots in the late nineteenth century, e.g., the "youth" novel by James K. Orton, *Beach Boy Joe; or, Among the Life Savers* (New York: Street & Smith, 1902). Its postwar connotations include proficiency at swimming and/or surfing, and thus reinforce the band's association with "winning . . . at sports." It is symptomatic of rock's disavowal of majority culture that athleticism has generally been downplayed in rock culture. (One exception is the dissident punk tradition extending from Iggy Pop to Henry Rollins and Anthony Kiedis, but even these figures are less "jocks" than members of a bodybuilding subculture; see Reynolds 1989.) A further, disavowed connotation involves the historical (mis)usage of the classifi-

cation "boy" in acts of symbolic violence supporting a racist hierarchy (e.g., the influential vocal close harmony of the Mills Brothers was sometimes advertised as "Four Boys and A Guitar").

11. Spector produced twelve Top 40 hits circa 1963–64 (only three in 1964), whereas Brian wrote or produced seventeen Top 40 hits in the same two-year period (including Beach Boys, Jan and Dean, and Hondells singles).

12. It is against exactly this background that Michael Harrington's 1962 muck-raking exposé of poverty in the United States, *The Other America*, stirred such controversy—how could there be such destitution amid such success?

13. Brian Wilson's status as a "superior" industry-insider committed to "winning" is evident in an interview he gave to Oklahoma television reporter Ida B. Blackburn in late August 1964 (Blackburn 1964). After a brief discussion of his writing hits for Jan and Dean in which he attempts to disabuse Ms. Blackburn of the notion that he wrote "The Little Old Lady from Pasadena," she asks him, "When you write a song for yourself, or for your group, what gives you the incentive to write them?" His answer is framed in terms of an ongoing struggle to win a commercial game: "Well, it usually, just the fact that we're in the industry and there's a lot of groups competing with us and I feel that competition, you know, and also I just, I love music, and I get very inspired, just generally creative, anyway, you know, it's, [I] do it all the time [inaudible conclusion]." Brian's "inspiration" conjoins business and creativity, like the top pop professional he is. When asked how many of his records have been "million sellers," he provides an actuarial answer: "Well, actually, 'million sellers,' we've had one million seller and that's 'I Get Around.'" Likewise, when asked about the band's latest release, he corrects himself after momentarily veering into imprecision: "'When I Grow Up to Be a Man' and 'She Knows Me Too Well' are our latest hit, ah, records." When asked about lyrics in particular, Brian claims he writes for a specific, teen-aged audience: "We usually like to try to identify and associate with teenagers; we're, I'm not so far out of my teenage years, I'm only twenty-two . . . usually the lyrics are supposed to be aimed at the everyday lives of kids." The middle-aged Blackburn keeps returning to a song Wilson did not have a hand in, "The Little Old Lady From Pasadena," and his "superiority" and "competitiveness" surface again in his subtle annoyance at her ignorance—at one point he looks away from Blackburn, enacting physically a social superiority whose telos is indeed denial of the other's subjectivity.

14. The geometric style tends to be found on album covers of clean-cut, often college-oriented, male groups and less frequently on packaging of sophisticated torch singers or R & B groups of the period—yet another reminder of the raced nature of such "majority" culture.

15. The 1957 paperback cover of William Whyte Jr.'s best-selling sociological study, *The Organization Man*, features a pseudo-Mondrian grid constructed out of that key business prop of the period, graph paper.

16. Cf. Maud Lavin's (1992) interpretation of geometric forms and grid composition in Weimar graphic design. We might also ponder here rock culture's own reconciliations of industrial rationalization and irrational pleasure as part of a broader condition of modernity.

17. See for example, *Life* 31 May: 50-51, and *Milwaukee Journal* 23 May: 4.

18. There is no evidence this was a paid product placement, remunerated endorsement, or commissioned work. A later television performance by the band on *The Andy Williams Show* (circa 1966), however, excised the brand name and replaced it with "Little Cycle," reminding us of the more explicit political-economic constraints of that advertiser-sponsored medium.

19. Luis Sanchez's doctoral dissertation, "To Catch a Wave: The Beach Boys and Rock Historiography" (2011), discusses this show and situates the Beach Boys amid a panoply of teen products and teen marketing efforts in Southern California at this time.

20. For an opposing view that sees television as crucial to the rise of rock, see Coates 2013.

21. Both Petersen and Fabares previously worked as Disney "Mouseketeers" on television, and Fabares had briefly costarred with Annette Funicello in *Walt Disney Presents: Annette*, a segment of Disney's *The Mickey Mouse Club* (1957–58). One might mount an argument that these attempts during the in-between years to build Disney child television stars into major pop music stars were arrested by the rise of rock, and only later reach fruition with the superstardom of former Disney contract players Britney Spears, Christina Aguilera, and Justin Timberlake in the twenty-first century, in turn marking the end of what we might now call "the rock interregnum."

22. It is worth noting that Fabares was married to record executive Lou Adler and wrote the liner notes for his protégés Jan and Dean's soundtrack LP, *Ride the Wild Surf* (Liberty, 1964), a film that starred Fabares and whose title track was cowritten by Brian Wilson. This means Wilson and Fabares moved in somewhat overlapping social/professional circles.

23. The four colored panels of the beach ball held by Fabares are also Mondrianesque.

24. The chorus of Petersen's Colpix hit single, "She Can't Find Her Keys" (number nineteen, 1962), lists the innumerable consumer goods his girlfriend carries in her purse, including "Presley records."

25. I discuss this further in Keightley 2015.

26. It also includes a version of "Johnny Get Angry" by Joanie Sommers, whose 1963 LP, *Sommers' Seasons* (WB-1504) features a Mondrian-inspired LP cover reminiscent of *All Summer Long*'s. This cover features four asymmetrically placed rectangles depicting the vocalist in each season, including summer. And the cover design of Sommers's earlier EP, *Sommer's Hot, Sommer's Here* (1959, Warner Bros. Pro 107), includes a stylized, anthropomorphic sun that will reappear on the upper-left-hand corner of *All Summer Long*.

27. The recording was officially released on the *Good Vibrations* compilation (1993), disc 1, track 19. Videos of the television appearance, in which the group lip-synchs along with the studio recording, have been posted on YouTube (e.g., <http://www.youtube.com/watch?v=h9JwveKr_Rc>).

28. Given the fact that "Little Deuce Coupe" was their current single (albeit as a B-side), still climbing the charts at this moment, the choice of the older hit "Surfin' USA" (with dance choreography and a beach set) also suggests a longer-term strategy of building mass audience appeal with crowd pleasers rather than going for the immediate plug.

29. While there is little musical similarity, it is interesting that the basic chord change of the A section of "All Summer Long" ($I{-}\flat III{-}ii^7{-}V^{7\flat 5}$) might be interpreted as a variation growing out of a long tradition of Tin Pan Alley "turnarounds" (e.g., $I{-}vi{-}ii^7{-}V^7$; $I{-}\flat III^{o7}{-}ii^7{-}V^7$), of which "The Things We Did Last Summer" partakes in its A section ($I{-}\flat II^{o7}{-}ii^7{-}V^7$).

30. These songs pile up seemingly random yet ultimately significant details (e.g., "Thanks for the Memory," 1938). They can be broadly understood to parallel early twentieth-century innovations like stream-of-consciousness writing, cubist painting, or montage film editing, all influenced by the rise of modern consumer culture and its proliferating lists (catalogs, menus, theater programs, and so forth). "These Foolish Things (Remind Me of You)" (1936) or "Memories of You" (1930), for example, contrast remembered experiences from the past with random events in the present they seem to resemble and thereby recall, whether "A tinkling piano in the next apartment" or "Waking skies at sunrise." Thus these lyrics propose the quite modern epistemology of considering an experience or object from two perspectives simultaneously: the present (the random object) is made sense of via the past (the memory it triggers), just as the past infects the present (the implication in many of these songs is that the narrator is "carrying a torch" for a lost love).

31. In the mid-1950s, just as Brian Wilson became a teenager, Tin Pan Alley produced yet another cycle of hit songs that collaged fragments of memory and read the present through the past. They may help us understand some of the nuances of the temporally ambivalent "All Summer Long" refrain, "we've been having fun all summer long." "Moments to Remember" (Four Lads, number two, 1955) and "Memories Are Made of This" (Dean Martin, number one, 1956) list actions and events and then comment on how they will be remembered later, in the future. They thus project the present (or very recent past) into an imagined future moment of retrospection, in effect proposing an experience of the present as the past. "Moments to Remember," for example, approaches nostalgia as a medium for apprehending life as it is lived, perhaps as a way to grasp a complex, ephemeral, and fragmentary present. Likewise, "Graduation Day" (Rover Boys, Four Freshmen; both top twenty, 1956), a song recorded by the Beach Boys in 1964 and often performed in concert, juxtaposes recent fun and future nostalgia: "At the senior prom, we danced 'til three / And then you gave your heart to me / We'll remember always, always / Graduation Day." The refrain line conveys a faith in future reminiscences as permanent, indeed endless, memories ("always, always") whose anticipation intensifies life as it is lived, just as "All Summer Long" celebrates fun in the past perfect tense to further energize its protagonists' experience of the present.

32. See O'Brien (2004) on the "contradictory emotions" (238) and "paradoxes" (242) of Brian Wilson's greatest music.

33. These lines are added at the end of Frank Sinatra's 1946 recording, although they do not appear in other versions (including the Beach Boys').

34. "Hushabye," a cover of a 1959 hit and the sole non-Wilson composition on the LP, could be considered a fourth "favorite," as it is rearranged and performed with great love (see Lambert 2007 on Wilson's innovative restructuring of the Mystics' version).

35. Love's comment appears in the context of band members playing with the effects of the echo chamber on their voices and other sounds, suggesting a conception of the studio as an experimental space that parallels some high-modernist approaches (see Huyssen 1986).

36. We have but a single report of a 1964 listener's response to this track, and he may be atypical: upon first hearing "Our Favorite Recording Sessions," Paul McCartney allegedly "whooped and hollered in delight." He then immediately telephoned the rest of the Beatles to insist they listen to the track, according to "Needling the Wax" (*Teen Set*, probably Fall 1964, 5–7).

The track may have been inspired by a 1959 Warner LP, *Behind Closed Doors at a Recording Session*, whose subtitle, *Confidential recording secrets revealed for the first time*, proposes access to secret knowledge. The educational aspect of the album is reinforced by the inclusion of an elaborate booklet that contains an informative "glossary" of studio technical jargon.

37. "Remembering" is a key theme here; "All Summer Long" begins by asking the listener to "remember when," and the rewinding tape of "Our Favorite Recording Sessions" reminds us that sound recording is a technology of memory.

38. To what extent a nascent "race consciousness" among white teen listeners might also be at play here is unclear. The summer of 1964 was a "Freedom Summer" of widely publicized civil rights activism that saw government authorities beating and killing U.S. citizens, yet these issues remain below the surface of teen pop at the time.

39. Less than a year later, the debut issue of the new teen pop magazine, *Tiger Beat*, will run a feature on Berry that cites Paul McCartney's evaluation of his historical significance ("Without talent like Chuck Berry . . . it's likely that today's sound would never exist") and John Lennon's endorsement of art over commerce ("Whether he sells the most records or not isn't important"). "Tiger Salutes Chuck Berry" 1965, 54.

40. As Frith puts it, "Self-consciousness became the measure of a record's artistic status" by the 1970s (1983, 53); see also pp. 29ff. on the role of a folk-derived self-consciousness in differentiating rock from teen pop. See also Laing 2015, 30, for a discussion of the idea of "design" as it relates to popular musicians.

41. However, "WB-Reprise Target: Teen Mart" (1964) suggests this is changing. See also "Singles Hit Makers Crash LP Charts Often, Fade Fast" (1963) and "Teen-Beat Soars on LP Chart" (1964).

42. "All Summer Long" was released as a B-side (to "Do You Wanna Dance") in the UK in 1965; neither side charted.

43. Cf. Mark Burford's (2012) argument about critiques of "filler" on Sam Cooke LPs.

44. Despite Mike Love's later acquisition via litigation of coauthorship rights on songs like "I Get Around" and "All Summer Long," the fact that collaborators (including Love himself on "Little Honda") were indeed listed on this LP in 1964 should give us pause when we read the songwriting credits on post-1994 releases that may seek to rewrite history.

45. And see Kirk Curnutt's ruminations on similar themes in the first chapter of this book.

46. For a current articulation of this, see the remarkable, spleen-filled review of the Beach Boys' fiftieth anniversary tour, by a dedicated indie-rock fan who worships Brian, loathes "Mike Love's Beach Boys," and yet reserves especial fury for the apparent *lack of knowledge* in the audience (at one point, he exchanges taunts with them!). The intertwining of musical classification and social othering in the review illustrates almost every point in the sociology of music I have been outlining (Pinto 2012).

47. If we follow Gracyk's argument about "record consciousness" as a definitive feature of rock, the suspicion arises that overattention to "Brian Wilson" (rather than "Beach Boys records," say) may be a sly strategy for reinstating a composer-based canon.

FIVE | When I Grow Up

The Beach Boys' Early Music

JADEY O'REGAN

IN AUGUST 2012, I was sitting in my seat at the Allphones Arena in Sydney, Australia, waiting for the Beach Boys' fiftieth anniversary show to start. As the lights faded to black, the group was announced—"Here they are, the Beach Boys!"—and five men, most of them in their seventies, shuffled out to play an enormous fifty-song, career-spanning set. There was something quite ironic about a group of retirement-aged men still being referred to as "boys," and this was made most obvious when Mike Love sang the opening of "When I Grow Up (to Be a Man)," questioning what life might be like when he officially "grows up." Listening to their music that night, I thought about how the Beach Boys' music really did "grow up" during the early to mid-1960s, and wondered how to explore some of those changes. Could we *hear* the Beach Boys "grow up" through their music?

This essay focuses on the Beach Boys' nine major studio albums released between 1962 and 1966, the years when they did most of their musical "growing up."[1] This was also the period when the group achieved its greatest commercial success. Of their thirty-six U.S. Top 40 singles released between 1962 and 1988, twenty-two first appeared between 1962 and 1966. Three of the twenty-two reached number one: "I Get Around," "Help Me, Rhonda," and "Good Vibrations" (Whitburn 2004). In other words, about two-thirds of the Beach Boys' hits were released in the first five years of their now fifty-year career.

Further, it was during this time period that Brian Wilson assumed total creative control of the group, and was at his most competitive and creative. He, with the help of his lyricists (most often Mike Love), wrote all of their original musical material, arranged the vocal harmonies, and produced the tracks in the studio—an unprecedented level of creative control at the time for a pop musician on a major recording label. In the early 1960s, the measure of a single's success was its chart position, and Brian Wilson strove to produce as many hits of the highest quality as time would allow. Plus, starting in 1964, he was additionally spurred on by a healthy competition with the Beatles, whose music he both greatly admired and aimed to surpass.

John Covach has described the musical growth of the Beatles as a progression from "craft" to "art": in the "craft" period, the group honed their abilities as professional songwriters, which led to the "art" period, when they purposely tried to break the rules they had previously learned. Covach explains:

> *Craftsperson* refers to an approach that privileges repeatable structure; songs are written according to patterns that are in common use. When innovation occurs within this approach, there is no difficulty with the idea of duplicating this innovation in subsequent songs. Opposed in a loose way to this craftsperson approach is the *artist* approach. Here, the emphasis is on the nonrepeatability of innovations; the worst criticism that can be leveled against a creative individual according to this approach is that he or she is "rewriting the same song over and over again." (Covach 2006, 39)

The Beach Boys followed a similar path in the early to mid-1960s, evolving from craftsmen to artists. We should also recognize, however, the enormous amount of work involved in becoming a craftsman. As Howard Becker explains, "Most crafts are quite difficult, with many years required to master the physical skills and mental disciplines of a first-class practitioner" (1978, 865). While Brian Wilson's school friends were out having fun, he was at home studying Four Freshmen records, working out their individual vocal harmonies, and finding out how they fit together (Carlin 2006, 22). He taught himself instrumental arranging, with help from a do-it-yourself record, and experimented with his own two-track voice recorder, often teaching parts to other family members so that he could practice the layering of vocal harmonies (Leaf 1985, 19). The young Brian Wilson dedicated himself fully to the craft of arranging and writing his own music, inspired by the professional songwriters of Tin Pan Alley and the Brill Building.

In training to become a craftsman, Brian was essentially an *apprentice*, learning from the master craftsmen he admired. His apprentice period encompassed the first two Beach Boys albums, *Surfin' Safari* (1962) and *Surfin' USA* (1963), just after the group's formation in late 1961. (The Beatles, by contrast, had extensive performing experience as a group before they began recording in 1962.) During the group's apprentice period their songs are defined by basic musical elements, such as twelve-bar and simple verse forms, simple rhythmic feels, and basic vocal harmonies. Subsequently, in later 1963, as the group moved into its craftsmen phase, they began to develop a better sense of their own musical style while employing more sophisticated techniques of professional songwriters, such as AABA and verse-chorus forms, and a broadening of lyrical themes in songs about love and loss. Their craftsmen phase included the *Surfer Girl* (1963), *Little Deuce Coupe* (1963), *Shut Down, Volume 2* (1964), and *All Summer Long* (1964) albums. Finally, having mastered their craft, Brian Wilson and the Beach Boys then moved into their final phase as *artists* in 1965 and 1966, often breaking the rules they had worked hard to learn. This phase included the *Beach Boys Today!* (1965), *Summer Days (and Summer Nights!!)* (1965), and *Pet Sounds* (1966) albums, and is defined by unexpected structures and chordal movements, dense vocal harmonies, and a wide variety of orchestral textures not often heard in popular music of the time. Example 5.1 is an overview of the nine albums in the apprentice-craftsmen-artist progression between 1962 and 1966.

The categorizations have inevitable overlappings. Aspects of the craftsmen phase are heard in early 1963 on "Finders Keepers" from *Surfin' USA*, for example. "Amusement Parks USA" and other songs on the *Summer Days* album, in the middle of the artist period, seem to be holdovers from the craftsmen phase. In rare cases, elements of all three categories occur in one song: "Lonely Sea" from *Surfin' USA*, for example, combines a rudimentary instrumentation most common in the apprentice phase, a descending chord progression more commonly used in the craftsmen phase (as explored in Lambert's essay earlier in this volume), and an unusual song structure typical of the artist phase. And some musical elements develop at different paces than others. But in spite of any vagaries, the apprentice-craftsmen-artist model is accurate and flexible enough to provide a revealing account of the evolution of the Beach Boys' sound.

This chapter views the early musical development of Brian Wilson and the Beach Boys through the lens of the A-C-A model, focusing on three musical aspects: song structures, lyrical themes, and vocal harmonies.

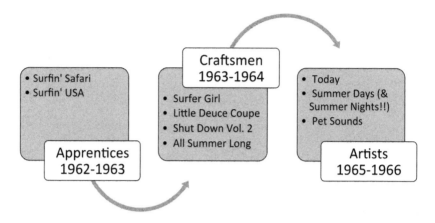

Craftsmen
1963-1964

• Surfer Girl
• Little Deuce Coupe
• Shut Down Vol. 2
• All Summer Long

• Surfin' Safari
• Surfin' USA

Apprentices
1962-1963

• Today
• Summer Days (&
  Summer Nights!!)
• Pet Sounds

Artists
1965-1966

Example 5.1: The apprentice-craft-art (A-C-A) model

Song Structures

In the early years of their careers, Brian Wilson and his ultimate British rivals, John Lennon and Paul McCartney, were intent on developing their songwriting abilities, following in the footsteps of the Tin Pan Alley and Brill Building songwriters they admired. They saw songwriting as a way to continue in the music business after their performing groups had fallen out of favor. Lennon commented in 1964, "You can be bigheaded and say we're going to last ten years, but as soon as you've said that, you think, I'll be lucky if we last three months." McCartney added in the same interview, "I think what John and I will do will be to write songs as we have been doing as sort of a sideline now. We'll probably develop that a bit more . . . we hope" (Godley, Smeaton, and Wonfor 1995). Similarly, in conversation with *Rolling Stone* founder Jann Wenner in 1973, Lennon commented, "Paul and I wanted to be the Goffin and King of England" (Lennon 2000, 47). While Brian Wilson's main musical focus was always the Beach Boys, once he succeeded in convincing Capitol Records to allow him to produce his own music, he began to branch out. The most successful of his side projects was Jan and Dean's number-one single "Surf City" (1963), but he also wrote and produced songs for the Honeys, Sharon Marie, and Glen Campbell, among others, during the early years. Early band member David Marks recalls: "Brian was writing songs with people off the street in the front of his house, disc jockeys, anyone. He had so much stuff flowing through him at once he could hardly handle

Surfin
Safari

Surfin'
USA

Surfer
Girl

Little
Deuce
Coupe

Shut
Down

All
Summer
Long

Today!

Summer
Days...

Pet
Sounds

Pattern Key						
AAB A	Verse - Chorus	12-Bar Blues	Complex	Simple Verse	Surf Rock	Spoken Word

Example 5.2: Visualization of song structures in the nine albums under consideration

it" (Carlin 2006, 38). This desire to hone his songwriting skill, through working with and learning from others, can be observed clearly in his use of different song structures and their progression over time in songs on Beach Boys albums, following the A-C-A model.

Beach Boys songs from 1962 to 1966 exemplify the five kinds of song structure commonly found in other popular music of the time: AABA, verse-chorus, twelve-bar blues, simple verse form (with or without refrain), and surf-rock form (two alternating sections, or AB). In a sixth category are "complex" structures that do not follow traditional norms. Example 5.2 is a visualization of all of these types in all nine albums under consideration. Each patterned block represents one of the structure types, ordered within each album (row) from most to least common.

Song Structures in the Apprentice Phase (1962–1963)

Blues structures. Songs based on blues structures are clustered in the first two albums. Appendix 5.1A lists only songs built entirely of blues progressions and does not include songs that use blues progressions in some sections but not in others (such as "Surfin' Safari," "Little Deuce Coupe," "Our Car Club," and "No-Go Showboat"). The list includes songs with traditional twelve-bar blues structures (e.g., "Stoked") and those with variants of other lengths (e.g., the sixteen-bar variant in "Surfin' USA"). Seven of the twelve are instrumentals, mostly in surf-rock style; the five that include vocals are "409," "Summertime Blues," "Surfin' USA," "Shut Down," and "Catch a Wave."

Of course, many of these songs are vehicles for improvisation. Carl Wilson, still a teenager when these early albums were recorded, is especially featured on lead guitar. On "The Rocking Surfer" and "Boogie Woodie" Brian Wilson improvises repeated phrases on the Hammond organ and piano respectively. After 1964, the blues structure appears only rarely in Beach Boys songs.

Surf-rock form. Surf-rock tunes that are not built from blues progressions often exemplify what has been called "surf-rock form" (appendix 5.1B). These structures alternate between two contrasting sections, a repeating AB design. Stephen J. McParland explains that the repeating alternation was a conscious effort to mimic the unpredictable movement of the ocean's waves (McParland 2006, 6). The inclusion of these songs on the early albums reminds us that the Beach Boys marketed themselves as a surf band at that time and often performed on the same gigs with surf bands such as Dick Dale and His Del-Tones, the Surfaris, and the Challengers. Although Dennis was the only Beach Boy who truly embraced the surfing subculture, the group did its best to appear authentic and ride a wave of popularity. The AB surf-rock structure appears on Beach Boys albums only three times through 1963, after which instrumental surf songs gave way to songs with broader musical material and more emotional themes.

Song Structures in the Craftsmen Phase (1963–1964)

AABA form. In the craftsmen phase we see an increase in the frequency of the AABA form (appendix 5.1C). About half of these are ballads (e.g., "Surfer Girl"), following the tradition of classic ballads of Tin Pan Alley. Using a structure popular in the 1940s and 1950s can give an AABA song a nostalgic quality that complements romantic or emotional themes in the lyrics.

The tight framework of the AABA form meant that many of the early to midperiod songs were quite short. "Little Deuce Coupe," for example, is over and done before the two-minute mark. It is an ideal structure for a time when the industry favored compact single releases over an entire album of "listening" music. From the same concerns arose AABA forms by the Beach Boys' contemporaries such as the Beatles ("Love Me Do" [1962], "This Boy" [1963]) and the Four Seasons ("Sherry" [1962]).

Simple verse form. The simple verse structure consists of a single musical section or "verse" that is repeated with different lyrics. Unlike AABA songs, there is no bridge or "B" section. Although some scholars categorize simple verse songs as a variation on the traditional verse-chorus structure, these two structures stem from different roots. Verse-chorus was relatively unused in popular music until the late 1950s to early 1960s, but simple verse has a long tradition in early folk and country music. Consequently, they have been separated into two distinct categories here.

Walter Everett (2009, 141) names several folk-inspired examples of simple verse form. With the exception of "Ten Little Indians," however, the Beach Boys' examples of this structure type do not musically stem from folk influences in the same way that, say, Bob Dylan's songs do. In Beach Boys' music, simple verse songs have more in common with recent hits like the Coasters' "Yakety Yak" (1958) or the Marvelettes' "Please Mister Postman" (1961). As shown in appendix 5.1D, simple verse forms demonstrate a modest increase in frequency during the craftsmen phase.

Verse-chorus form. The verse-chorus song structure is the most common song structure in the Beach Boys' music (appendix 5.1E). Many instances are straightforward verse-chorus alternations, although variants are not uncommon. Example 5.3 diagrams four illustrative songs. In "Noble Surfer" the verse-chorus structure is relatively unadorned, adding only a solo section played on toy piano and the introduction and outro featuring repetitions of the chorus. In "Car Crazy Cutie," "Good to My Baby," and "Help Me, Rhonda," the structure grows to include other sections, such as a bridge, prechorus, or instrumental break. The inclusion of these extra sections makes structures longer, leaving more room for experimentation. For example, each section could build on the one before it with the addition of more vocals, percussion, rhythmic instruments, and so forth, culminating in a climactic "final chorus" (e.g., "California Girls"). Or the verse and chorus could sound considerably different from each other (e.g., "Let Him Run Wild").

Longer and more flexible structures also allow for lyrical experimentation. The clearest example of this is the *Today* album, which features the most verse-chorus structures and also some of the most introspective

Noble Surfer (1963)	Car Crazy Cutie (1963)	Good To My Baby (1965)	Help Me, Rhonda (1965)
Intro/Chorus	Vocal Hook	Intro	Verse 1
Verse 1	Verse 1	Verse 1	Prechorus
Chorus	Chorus	Prechorus	Chorus
Verse 2	Verse 2	Chorus	Verse 2
Chorus	Chorus	Verse 2	Prechorus
Solo	Bridge	Prechorus	Chorus
Chorus	Verse 3	Chorus	Instrumental Break
Verse 3	Chorus	Instrumental Break	Chorus
Chorus/Outro	Reintro	Reintro	Outro
	Outro	Chorus	
	Chorus		

Example 5.3: Some examples of verse-chorus structures, 1963–1965

songs of the period. "When I Grow Up (to Be a Man)" poses some complex questions about life when one is no longer a teenager, ranging from "Will I dig the same things that turn me on as a kid?" to "Will I love my wife for the rest of my life?" "Please Let Me Wonder" explains the fear and self-consciousness in telling someone you love her—"Please forgive my shaking, can't you tell my heart is breaking? Can't make myself say what I plan to say." "Kiss Me, Baby" describes a fight between two lovers: "Can't remember what we fought about, late, late last night we said it was over, I remember when I got light we both had a broken heart," while harmonies that underpin the chorus repeat "Kiss a little bit, fight a little bit." These three examples show a maturing view of life and relationships that were underpinned by and reflected in the expandable and flexible verse-chorus form.

The verse-chorus structure provided Brian Wilson with increased structural flexibility and appears frequently on the early *Surfin' Safari* album, but returns fully developed on *Today* and *Summer Days*. In the later songs, sections are moved around in different ways. For example, "Please Let Me Wonder" features a more traditional verse-chorus structure, while "I Get Around" places the solo section right after the first full chorus. Both of these structures are verse-chorus, but their orders are moved around with greater flexibility.

Song Structures in the Artist Phase (1965–1966)

Complex structures. The progression toward nonstandard or "complex" musical frameworks in the latter part of the period coincided with a gravitation toward more complicated emotional themes, harmonies, instrumentation, rhythmic feels, and production styles (appendix 5.1F). This change marks a time when the Beach Boys moved their focus away from single releases to making experimental "album" music meant for dedicated listening. The change to complex forms on *Pet Sounds* supported the most musically and lyrically adventurous music of the Beach Boys repertoire and foreshadowed the modularities of "Good Vibrations" (1966) and *Smile* (1967).

Three of the five complex structures on *Pet Sounds*—"You Still Believe in Me," "Let's Go Away for Awhile," and "Pet Sounds"—use identical unconventional structures consisting of two contrasting sections. They do not alternate these sections, as in a surf-rock form, but simply divide into two main parts, the second contrasting with the first, ending with substantially different musical material than what they began with. "That's Not Me," however, does alternate two contrasting sections, like a surf-rock form but with additional developmental features. Similarly, "I'm Waiting for the Day" expands the simple verse form, repeating an initial section three times, with refrain, before ending with new, musically unrelated ideas.

Lyrical Themes

The trio of "surf, cars, and girls" has frequently been described in the lyrics of Beach Boys songs (e.g., Carter 2004, 393; Crowley 2011, 67; Curnutt 2012, 23; Dillon 2012, xi). It may be a cliché, but it is grounded in reality. At the same time, a complex swirl of emotions often lies underneath the surface. Brian Wilson and his lyrical collaborators explored these themes from a broad range of angles, from the simple pleasures of "Surfin' USA" to the sophisticated self-examination of *Pet Sounds*.

Appendix 5.2 categorizes the lyrics of the nine albums being studied using the traditional three themes plus a fourth category called "reflective," in which song lyrics explore more complicated emotions, such as those related to growing up and loss of innocence. Only thirteen songs from these albums (listed at the end of the table) do not belong in at least one category.[2] Some belong in more than one: "Surfer Girl," for example, is both a surfing song and a girl song.

Lyrical Themes in the Apprentice Phase (1962–1963)

Surfing songs. The Beach Boys' early music is defined by surfing songs. The album titles alone tell the story: *Surfin' Safari* and *Surfin' USA* in the apprentice phase, and *Surfer Girl* at the beginning of the craftsmen phase. And yet the image of the band as a contributor to surf culture comes from surprisingly few song lyrics: only two song lyrics celebrate surfing on their first album, and three on their second. Their surfer-dude image was completed by marketing, and by instrumentals that were either covers of well-known surf-band classics ("Misirlou" and "Let's Go Trippin'" on *Surfin' USA*) or originals conceived along similar lines ("Stoked" and "Surf Jam" on *Surfin' USA*).

The most common theme of a typical Beach Boys surf lyric is the "call to surf," touting the sport's fun and skill: "Come on a safari with me!" ("Surfin' Safari"); "Surfin' is the only life the only way for me" ("Surfin'"). These songs, along with "Surfin' USA," turned the idea of surfing, an established lifestyle experienced primarily on the West Coast, into a more accessible and inclusive preoccupation. Other lyrical angles include stories about individual surfers ("Noble Surfer") or groups of young surfers ("Surfers Rule"). In these songs, the confidence and bravery of the surfers, and the sense of community they share, are paramount: "All the boys are rough and ready to handle anything" ("South Bay Surfer"); "They grit their teeth, they won't back down" ("Don't Back Down"). Only one of these songs, "Surfer Girl," is both a surf song and a love song.

Although Brian Wilson and Mike Love had little actual experience with the surfing subculture, their surf songs aspire to authenticity by invoking surfing terms and slang. As Richard Hill observes, "The West Coast 'surfin'' phenomenon soon became 'Surfin' USA,' and by 1963 . . . use of surf slang terms like 'bitchin', 'twitchin', 'cowabunga', and 'dude' were nearly universal among youth of the surf faction, many of whom had never seen a beach" (Hill 1994, 324). Appendix 5.3 lists the various surf slang terms found in the Beach Boys surf songs, ranging from fashion (huarache sandals, baggies), to surfer cars (woodie), to surfing moves and waves (shooting the pier, walking the nose, body whop, raise, wiped out, twenty-footer), to special terms for surfer girls (honeys). Perhaps the most interesting of these surfing terms, in relation to the Beach Boys, is the term "hodad" or "hodaddy," defined by Stephen J. McParland as "the antithesis of the surfer" and "a brooding misfit with greased hair who generally hung out at a garage and listened to what was left of doo-wop and rockabilly music" (McParland 2006, 4). It is a fair description, in other words, of the Beach Boys themselves. They used terms like these with a self-aware wink, at the same time enhancing their image to advance their commercial interests. But this caused true surfers to

Example 5.4: Wordle diagram of the Beach Boys' surfing songs

recoil, feeling that the Beach Boys' "surf music" was making a gimmick out of their legitimate lifestyle (McParland 2006, 23).

Example 5.4 is a word-frequency diagram, or "Wordle," created from the lyrics of the Beach Boys' twelve early surfing songs. Drawing from the resources of Wordle.net, the diagram gives more prominent display to words in the data set with greater frequency. As noted by McNaught and Lam, the Wordle "allows viewers to have an overview of the main topics and the main themes in a text, and may illustrate the main standpoints held by the writer of the text." Further, "comparison of the word clouds generated from different texts should quickly reveal the differences between the ideas contained in these texts" (McNaught and Lam 2010, 630–31). Wordle diagrams have proved useful in studies of tertiary educational methods in writing and literature (Sorapure 2010; Huisman, Miller, and Trinoskey 2011), and in studies of research practices (McNaught and Lam 2010; Alencar, de Oliveira, and Paulovich 2012), among other contexts. With the collected lyrics of nine Beach Boys studio albums as their qualitative data, the Wordle can be similarly valuable here.

Of course, not "surfing" but "surfin'" occurs most frequently in the Wordle for the twelve surfing songs. G-dropping is the sort of pronunciation a parent or teacher might correct, and the Beach Boys' practice of dropping g's, not just in surf songs but in songs on other themes as well, gave their lyrics an underlying sense of "cool," an image the Beach Boys did not maintain for long (Holmes 2007, 348). Their G-dropping can be seen as a way of making their music exclusionary, drawing a boundary between teenagers and parents and marking their music as "for teenagers, by teenagers."

Not surprisingly, the diagram also gives prominence to "surfer," "surfers," "surf," "wave," and "beach." Naturally, "girl" and "girls" (and "baby") are conspicuously larger than "boys." One of Mike Love's favorite filler words, "now," also pops out ("Surfin' is the only life, the only way for me now"). But the frequency of "now" further reminds us of a common subtext of these early songs, valuing the youthful present over the irrelevant past. And the diagram highlights words that rouse and inspire, such as "go," "going," "come," and "coming." Notably smaller are words with negative messages such as "wait," "never," and "afraid."

Lyrical Themes in the Craftsmen Phase (1963–1964)

Car songs. As the Beach Boys progressed through their craftsmen period, their lyrical themes moved away from the beach and into the front seat of a hot rod (see appendix 5.2). Brian Wilson, along with his continuing lyricist Mike Love and new collaborator Roger Christian, found a variety of angles for their car songs, reflecting their growing craftsmanship and greater comfort with car culture.

The connection between cars and popular music has a long history stretching at least as far back as Jimmy Liggins's "Cadillac Boogie" (1946). Car-themed songs found a wide audience in the 1950s (McParland 2006, 127). In fact, the song often described as the first true rock-'n'-roll song, Jackie Brenston's "Rocket 88" (1951), is a car song: "A V8 motor baby; its modern design, black convertible top and the girls don't mind" (McParland 2006, 127). This and other songs, such as Chuck Berry's "Maybelline" (1955), formed a tradition that the Beach Boys eagerly joined when they began to move away from surf themes in 1963.

They did so at full throttle: *Little Deuce Coupe* (1963) includes only two songs that don't relate to hot-rod culture ("Be True to Your School" and "A Young Man Is Gone"). Four of the album's cuts are rereleases of car songs from earlier albums—"409," "Shut Down," "Little Deuce Coupe," and "Our Car Club"—and the remaining six are new songs celebrating car types ("Cherry, Cherry Coupe"), custom cars ("No-Go Showboat," "Custom Machine"), racing ("Spirit of America"), the personification of cars ("Ballad of Ole' Betsy"), and girls who love cars too ("Car Crazy Cutie"). Their next album, *Shut Down, Volume 2* (1964), was titled to evoke a drag race and boasted four new car-themed songs, two of which were successful singles ("Fun, Fun, Fun" and "Don't Worry, Baby").

The Beach Boys' car songs did not provoke the sort of backlash they had received to their earlier surf songs, perhaps because the sentiments were more sincere: members of the group were as interested in cars as any other American teenager or young adult. In fact, writes McParland, once the Beach Boys shifted from surfing songs to car songs, they were "much more readily accepted by the surfers," as the Beach Boys were "now communicating about their own world, a world they could convey with authority as their firsthand reality" (McParland 2006, 24–25). Cars represent freedom and independence. The sound of the revving engine at the beginning of "409" was taken from the 348 Chevy Impala of Brian's friend Gary Usher (Carlin 2006, 33). Brother Dennis was often seen "cruising" in his Stingray 85 (Preiss 1979, 26).

Car songs opened up a wider musical palette to Brian Wilson and his bandmates. Surf songs had required specific musical constraints, such as solid-body Fender guitars, Showman amplifiers, and heavy, flat-wound strings. But hot-rod music had no such musical signatures (Crowley 2011, 111–12). As a result, the lyrics to car songs carried greater weight in projecting themes and meanings. Brian Wilson and his collaborators embraced this freedom and expanded their range of angles and emphases. "Shut Down" boasts about a driver's cool-headedness in the face of a race, and the superior power of his vehicle. "Drive-In" celebrates a gathering place for teenagers in their cars, meeting girls and enjoying a sense of independence from their parents. Unlike the Beach Boys' surf songs, which were written primarily from the perspective of the guy, the car songs are more likely to involve both genders in themes of love and romance ("Fun, Fun, Fun," "In the Parkin' Lot"). In "Don't Worry, Baby" we witness a car-centered scenario laden with an early example of introspection and self-reflection.

Girl songs. As car songs began to fall out of favor in the middle part of the craftsmen period, the Beach Boys returned to girl songs, now with greater depth and maturity than earlier efforts such as "Heads You Win, Tails I Lose" and "The Shift" (see appendix 5.2). After a mixture of themes in *Shut Down, Volume 2* (1964) and *All Summer Long* (1964), the remaining three albums examined in this study are overwhelmingly focused on love and relationships. Brian Wilson explained: "We needed to grow. Up to this point we had milked every idea dry. We milked it fucking dry, we had done every possible angle about surfing and then we did the car routine. But we needed to grow artistically" (Badman 2004, 54).

In a study of 1960s song lyrics, Richard R. Cole segregates love songs according to the stage of the relationship being described: first crush,

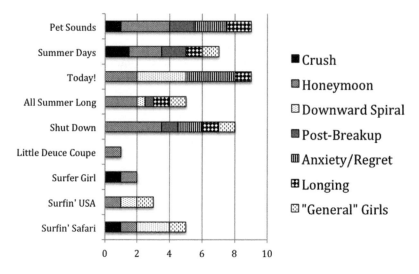

Example 5.5: Categories of the Beach Boys girl songs

honeymoon period, the "downward spiral" of a romance gone bad, and the postbreakup period (Cole 1971). Example 5.5 organizes Beach Boys girl songs in the nine early albums into these same four categories plus three others: anxiety/regret (e.g., "Don't Worry, Baby"), longing (e.g., "We'll Run Away"), and a final catchall. The diagram depicts the progression from songs about the crush ("Surfer Girl") or the breakup ("Lonely Sea") in the early albums, to songs involving more complex emotions such as anxiety ("Don't Worry, Baby") or longing ("Keep an Eye on Summer") or postbreakup heartbreak ("Wendy") in the craftsmen phase, to a more complete focus on mature emotions in the artist phase.

Lyrical Themes in the Artist Phase (1965–1966)

Some songs in the Beach Boys' repertoire are not just love songs, or songs about teenage experiences, but opportunities to explore deeper themes involving careful consideration and self-reflection. These "reflective" songs contrast sharply with their early songs about surf and cars, most of which take place in the present tense (see appendix 5.2). Often, the reflective songs look back on earlier days, and show a degree of deep thought or even analysis about situations that may have caused heartache or regret in circumstances of love and romance. Others, such as

Example 5.6: Wordle diagram for the Beach Boys' reflective songs

"In My Room" and "When I Grow Up (to Be a Man)," are personal and introspective in other ways. Reflective songs appear occasionally in 1963 ("In My Room") and 1964 (e.g., "The Warmth of the Sun"), but begin to dominate the songscape on side 2 of *Today* and on *Pet Sounds*.

Example 5.6 is a Wordle diagram of the lyrics of the Beach Boys' reflective songs. In comparison to the action words in the surfing Wordle (example 5.4), the most common words here are more related to feelings, especially in the realm of amour ("love," "heart," "kiss"). But as love gives way to heartbreak in the later songs of the group, words such as "sad" and "without" show their presence, alongside words of equivocation such as "think," "without," "guess," and "gone." Above all the words are personal and internal: "knows," "know," "wonder."

Some of these reflective songs approach more common Beach Boys' themes from a new angle. "In My Room," for example, relates strongly to the teenage experience, not extroverted activities like surfing or driving but the introverted experience of savoring solitude. As Kirk Curnutt explains, retreating to a private sanctuary doesn't actually resolve the singer's anxieties, but it does provide a "secure setting for contemplating them" (2012, 37). "Don't Worry, Baby" seeks comfort from the anxiety of a drag race in the words of a girl. Songs about relationships in this phase focus less on young love, more on mature complications. On side 2 of the *Today* album, for example, "Please Let Me Wonder" pleads for validation and reassurance ("Please let me wonder if I've been the one you love, if I'm who you're dreaming of"), while anxious questions arise in "Kiss Me, Baby" ("Were you still awake like me?") and "In the Back of My Mind" ("What will I do if I lose her?").

Reflection dominates *Pet Sounds*, in wistful songs about the past, enriched with a growing sense of self-awareness. The lyric of "That's Not Me," for example, concerns a young man finding out who he really is, reflecting on his past, and trying to change for the better: "I went through all kinds of changes, took a look at myself and said that's not me." Songs like "I Know There's an Answer" and "You Still Believe in Me" also touch on the positive aspects of entering adulthood. These lyrics, however, are offset by "I Just Wasn't Made for These Times" and "Caroline, No," which actively mourn the loss of youth. The easy, carefree friendships of "Chug-a-Lug" or "I Get Around" are gone, replaced by the desire for experiences that are fully resident in the adult world. Although *Pet Sounds* opens with "Happy time together we'll be spending" in "Wouldn't It Be Nice," by the time we get to "I Just Wasn't Made for These Times," the singer confesses, "Sometimes I feel very sad."

Example 5.7 is a Wordle diagram depicting word frequency in all of the Beach Boys' lyrics in this study. How to explain the prevalence of the word "now?" It's often used as a kind of placeholder in short phrases: "Well she got her Daddy's car and she cruised through the hamburger stand *now*" ("Fun, Fun, Fun"); "Let's go surfin' *now*, everybody's learning how" ("Surfin' Safari"); "Shut it off, shut it off, buddy *now* I'll shut you down" ("Shut Down"). Combined with the laid-back delivery of Mike Love's vocals, these *nows* often give the Beach Boys songs a conversational tone, as if the singer is addressing the audience members very personally.

Further, it reminds us that so many early Beach Boys songs (prior to the emergence of reflective songs mid-decade) are about events in the present, conveyed with an immediacy and energy, both lyrically and musically. They give listeners the sense that the California paradise they are singing about is happening *now*, and that there is no time to lose to get involved. They have the youthful attitude of living for the moment, without laments for the past or worries about the future. The California myth they helped create existed in a present world that seemed endless and filled with promise.

Vocals

Vocal harmonies are often the most identifiable aspect of the Beach Boys' sound: all but four songs recorded in the 1962–66 period feature

Example 5.7: Wordle diagram for all Beach Boys song lyrics, 1962–1966

at least some layered vocals, sometimes in as many as four or five parts.[3] "The harmonies that we are able to produce," explained Brian Wilson, "give us a uniqueness, which is really the only important thing you can put into records—some quality that no-one else has got. I love peaks in a song—and enhancing them on the control panel. Most of all, I love the human voice for its own sake" (Abbott 2001, 73). Their vocal harmonies have become the touchstone for more recent popular music that uses voices in similar ways (Fusilli 2008; Fricke 2011a). Commentators often cite the Beach Boys' influence on vocal-oriented groups such as the Fleet Foxes, Animal Collective, Grizzly Bear, Best Coast, and Bon Iver (among others reviewed on Pitchfork).[4]

The importance of vocal harmonies is evident in the way Brian Wilson recorded them. Most of the songs in this study were recorded at either Western Recorders or Gold Star in Los Angeles. The control rooms of these studios only had a three- or four-track recorder. Brian would mix down all of the instrumental backings onto one single track and then use the other three entirely for recording vocals and vocal overdubs (Abbott 2001, 72). By the time of *Pet Sounds*, he and studio engineers Chuck Britz and Larry Levine would connect two four-track recorders together, in order to transfer all the instrumental backings to one track, leaving *seven* tracks free for vocals and vocal overdubs (Abbott 2001, 72). As much as 88 percent of the available recording space was dedicated to vocals.

The importance of vocal harmonies has deep roots in the group's biography. At a very young age, Brian began teaching his younger brothers Dennis and Carl to sing in three-part harmony with him in their childhood bedroom. Their singing sometimes became the only means of soothing their father's explosive anger—not only an expression of brotherly closeness, but also personal safety. In Carl's words, "Recording [harmonies] had become a church to us" (Abbott 2001, 75).

This section will look at the development of three aspects of Beach Boys vocals in the albums being studied: "blow harmonies," nonsense syllables, and falsetto. Although examples of these types exist throughout the period, their peak usage supports the A-C-A paradigm. A concluding discussion will consider the evolving roles of Brian Wilson and Mike Love as lead singers during this time.

Vocals in the Apprentice Phase (1962–1963)

Blow harmonies. According to Gribin and Schiff, background vocals using breathy syllables such as "ha-oo" or "ah-hoo" are known as *blow harmonies.* They replaced humming as the predominant background style in the early 1950s, during the transition from rhythm and blues to doo-wop (Gribin and Schiff 1992, 17). They also became a key component in the Beach Boys' early sound. The group's first hit single, "Surfin' Safari," for example, features blow harmonies—long "ooh" sounds"—supporting Mike Love's lead vocal in the verse. We hear the same thing on the B-side, in the verse of "409."

In the background vocals of "409," however, we also hear the beginnings of a move toward diversity that would continue through the other developmental phases: a texted commentary filling in between phrases of the lead vocal ("Giddy up, giddy up, 409"). Near the beginning of the craftsmen phase, for example, "Little Deuce Coupe" includes such commentaries as well as other ideas. Supporting Mike Love's lead vocal are blow harmonies ("ooh"), alternative phrases ("deuce-coooupe"), block harmonies (in the refrain), and a textual echo ("Little deuce coupe, you don't know what I got"). By the time of the artist phase, blow harmonies were being layered and embellished in inventive ways.

Vocals in the Craftsmen Phase (1963–1964)

Nonsense syllables. The nonsense syllables that define doo-wop backgrounds—"doo doo," "bup bup," "dit, dit," and so forth—probably developed from vocal imitations of instruments (Gribin and Shiff 1992, 19). But they aren't always pure "nonsense": David Samuels (2004, 312) notes that doo-wop backgrounds can also be onomatopoeic ("Sh-Boom," "Buzz-Buzz-Buzz," "Mope-Itty-Mope," "Shimmy, Shimmy, Ko-Ko-Bop," "Rama Lama Ding Dong," "Ling, Ting, Tong," "Chop Chop Boom," "Ka-Ding Dong," "Rang Tang Ding Dong"). The absorption and, ultimately, reconception of doo-wop vocals became central to the development of the Beach Boys' sound, starting with Mike Love's doo-wop bass line in the group's first record, "Surfin'." In their music of the craftsmen phase we begin to hear background syllables that are less imitative and more thematically integrated.

The group's two "school-themed" songs, for example, "Be True to Your School" (*Little Deuce Coupe*, 1963) and "Pom Pom Play Girl" (*Shut Down, Volume 2*, 1964), use backing syllables to add to the lyrical narrative. The backing vocals in these songs mimic the kinds of cheerleader chants heard on the sidelines of a high-school football game. In the single version of "Be True to Your School" Brian even added actual spoken cheers by the girl group he was producing, the Honeys. "Pom Pom Play Girl" features a typical variety of backing styles, including blow harmonies, nonsense syllables ("chi chi nah"), block harmonies ("rah rah, pom pom play girl"), and a separate bass part ("She's a thinkin' 'bout the boy sittin' up in the stands"). Although only a few months separate the two recordings, the earlier one has more in common with actual doo-wop (and begins with the I–vi–ii–V doo-wop chord progression), while the latter is more distinctive and original.

Vocals in the Artist Phase (1965–1966)

Falsetto vocals. The employment of falsetto in popular music began, like blow harmonies and nonsense syllables, in classic doo-wop. It was used by white groups starting with Frankie Valli and the Four Seasons in 1962, and in Brian Wilson's upper line of Beach Boys vocals around the same time (Goosman 2005, 272). Perhaps the appeal of this vocal style is its sonic purity: Everett describes falsetto vocal sounds as "somewhat like a flute because it's almost a pure tone with few harmonics" (Everett 2009, 124). In Beach Boys songs, Brian's falsetto can symbolize the fragility and innocence of teenage life, by contrast with the confident, boyish bravado of Mike Love's earthier lead vocals.

Kirk Curnutt connects Brian's falsetto to broader themes, particularly the feminine element. In Brian's youth this was not always a good thing: Dennis Wilson recalled "seeing his big brother run home in tears after some schoolmates laughed about his girl-ish falsetto" (Carlin 2006, 19).

But Brian eventually grew to accept and embrace it. In a 1997 interview about a song from *Pet Sounds*, his comfort with feminine implications is readily apparent:

> "You Still Believe in Me" was more of what I would call a man who would not be afraid to take all of his clothes off and sing like a girl because he had feelings for people from that perspective. I was able to close my eyes and go into a world and sing a little more effeminately and more sweet—which allows a lot more love to come down through me, you know what I mean? . . . It's like Kenny Rogers. There's an example of a guy who has a fairly masculine sounding voice. "You Still Believe in Me" was quite the opposite. (Leaf 1997b, 9)

Well before *Pet Sounds*, we can hear him getting in touch with his feminine side in songs like "Surfer Girl" (*Surfer Girl*, 1963), "The Warmth of the Sun" (*Shut Down, Volume 2*, 1964), and "Don't Worry, Baby" (*Shut Down, Volume 2*, 1964). As Curnutt observes, the "sensitivity, vulnerability, even prettiness" that may be off-putting to fans of aggressive masculine rock are precisely what Brian's core audience finds appealing.[5]

Falsetto vocals are used in four main ways in Beach Boys songs. One distinctive usage characterizes wailing outro sections, in songs such as "Surfers Rule" (*Surfer Girl*, 1963) and "Fun, Fun, Fun" (*Shut Down, Volume 2*, 1964). Another helps reinforce a song's refrain, for example in "Little Deuce Coupe" (*Surfer Girl*, 1963) and "When I Grow Up (to Be a Man)" (*Today*, 1965). A third usage appears within the main melody itself, in songs such as "She Knows Me Too Well" (*Today*, 1965) and "Don't Talk (Put Your Head on My Shoulder)" (*Pet Sounds*, 1966). And in another *Pet Sounds* song, "Here Today," we hear a fourth usage, when the chorus features a falsetto atop the backing vocals, almost resembling a modest counter-melody.

The graph in example 5.8 demonstrates the increasing role of falsetto in Beach Boys songs through 1966. The peak in the *Today* album is a result of Brian's more frequent appearance as lead vocalist, and of the greater number of ballads in that album, better lending themselves to the emotive character of falsetto singing. Relating to the general rise in falsetto, of course, is a decline in simple blow harmonies in favor of greater thematic integration for background vocals in the craftsmen period, and a move toward more sophisticated techniques in the artist period, such as the contrapuntal layering of "God Only Knows" (*Pet Sounds*, 1966).

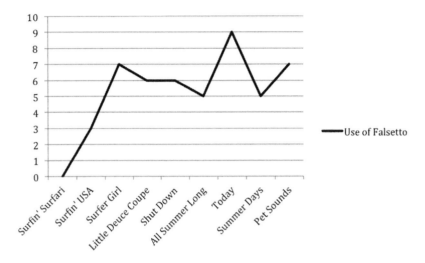

Example 5.8: Use of falsetto over time

Mike Love and Brian Wilson as Lead Vocalists

A frequent division of labor in Beach Boys songs has Mike Love singing lead in the verse, while Brian sings the chorus, refrain, or hook. Fifteen of the twenty-three songs featuring both vocalists follow this formula (e.g., "Surfin' USA," "Catch a Wave," "Little Deuce Coupe"). Musically, Mike's verses often span a smaller melodic range and are more rhythmically active. They carry the narrative of the story and have a more conversational feel, reinforced by conversational place-sitter words like "well" or "now" ("Well East Coast girls are hip"). These qualities are on display, for example, in the opening bars of Mike's verse for "Fun, Fun, Fun" shown in example 5.9a. In contrast, Brian's contributions tend to feature a wider melodic range and more held notes, as demonstrated in his falsetto wail at the end of that song, excerpted in example 5.9b.

As Walter Everett has observed, vocalists performing together on a single song each strive for an "independent texture," and may "oppose each other as if representing different parts of a singer's persona" (Everett 2009, 128). In the case of the Beach Boys, split vocals can portray not just the *singer's* persona, but the experience of teenage life in general, paradoxically filled with confidence and bravado, yet vulnerability and emotion. Or to borrow Allan F. Moore's framework, we as listeners try to identify what is real and fictional about Mike and Brian and

Well she got her dad- dy's car   and she cruised through the ham- bur- ger stand   now,

Example 5.9a: "Fun, Fun, Fun," first vocal phrase

Wee   oh   wee___   ooh___

Example 5.9b: "Fun, Fun, Fun," concluding falsetto wail

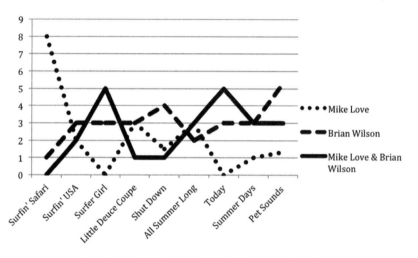

Example 5.10: Mike Love and Brian Wilson as lead vocalists

the lyrics they present (Moore 2012, 182). Their roles ring true: Mike the optimist versus Brian the melancholic. And the lifestyle they sing about also seems real, thanks to authentic-sounding slang and attitude. But in many cases, notably in the surfing songs, their lyrics were not grounded in personal experience. It was as much a fantasy to them as to many of their listeners. The Beach Boys' ability to simultaneously express reality and fantasy is one of their most enduring qualities, and this paradox is played out vividly in the vocal duets between Brian and Mike.

Example 5.10 charts Mike's and Brian's lead singing in the nine Beach Boys albums being studied. Supporting the A-C-A model, Mike Love's confident bravado defines the apprentice period, in up-tempo surf and car songs, while the craftsmen phase is evenly balanced between the two personae, and the artist phase sees a greater role for Brian, expressing themes of great depth and emotional complexity. As with form types or lyric themes, it's a pattern of development compellingly portrayed in a rich catalog of alluring songs. While the Beach Boys themselves were living out one of their own lyrics, growing up to be young men, so did their music evolve and mature.

NOTES FOR CHAPTER 5

1. The group also released *The Beach Boys' Christmas Album* (1964), *Beach Boys Concert* (1964), and *Beach Boys Party* (1965) during this period. I have decided to limit my study to the group's major releases of original material, as they are a clearer representation of their musical evolution.

2. Of course, the list also excludes instrumentals and album-filler novelties (e.g., "'Cassius' Love vs. 'Sonny' Wilson" on *Shut Down, Vol. 2* [1963]).

3. The only solo numbers are "Your Summer Dream" (on *Surfer Girl*, sung by Brian Wilson), "Girl Don't Tell Me" (*Summer Days*, Carl Wilson), and two Brian Wilson solos on *Pet Sounds*, "Don't Talk (Put Your Head on My Shoulder)" and "Caroline, No."

4. Pitchfork (www.pitchfork.com) is an influential website that reviews indie and alternative music. The vocal style of these groups, however, often has less in common with the Beach Boys' contrapuntal style and more resembles the block harmonies of a group such as Crosby, Stills, and Nash.

5. Curnutt 2012, 68; emphasis original. Nicola Diben 1999 addresses these issues as well.

Appendix 5.1. Songs Discussed Categorized by Form Type

A. Songs That Use Blues Forms, Including Variants

Surfin' Safari (1962)
409
Summertime Blues
Surfin' USA (1963)
Surfin' USA
Stoked
Shut Down
Honky Tonk
Surf Jam
Let's Go Trippin'
Surfer Girl (1963)
Catch a Wave
Boogie Woodie

Shut Down, Vol. 2 (1964)
  Shut Down, Part II
All Summer Long (1964)
  Carl's Big Chance

B. Songs that Use Surf-Rock (AB) Forms

Surfin' Safari (1962)
  Moon Dawg
Surfin' USA (1963)
  Misirlou
Surfer Girl (1963)
  The Rocking Surfer

C. Songs in AABA Form

Surfin' Safari (1962)
  The Shift
  County Fair
Surfin' USA (1963)
  Farmer's Daughter
Surfer Girl (1963)
  Surfer Girl
  The Surfer Moon
  South Bay Surfer
  Little Deuce Coupe
  In My Room
  Surfers Rule
  Our Car Club
  Your Summer Dream
Little Deuce Coupe (1963)
  Ballad of Ole' Betsy
  No-Go Showboat
  A Young Man Is Gone
Shut Down, Vol. 2 (1964)
  Fun, Fun, Fun
  Why Do Fools Fall in Love
  This Car of Mine
  Keep an Eye on Summer
All Summer Long (1964)
  All Summer Long
  Hushabye
  We'll Run Away
  Wendy
  Do You Remember?

Girls on the Beach
Drive-In
Today! (1965)
When I Grow Up (to Be a Man)
I'm So Young
In the Back of My Mind
Summer Days (1965)
Amusement Parks USA
Then I Kissed Her
Summer Means New Love
I'm Bugged at My Old Man
Pet Sounds (1966)
Wouldn't It Be Nice
God Only Knows
Caroline, No

D. Songs in Simple Verse Form

Surfin' Safari (1962)
Ten Little Indians
Surfin' USA (1963)
Lana
Surfer Girl (1963)
Catch a Wave
Shut Down, Volume 2 (1964)
In the Parkin' Lot
Warmth of the Sun
Pom Pom Play Girl
Summer Days (1965)
And Your Dream Comes True
Salt Lake City

E. Songs in Verse-Chorus Form

Surfin' Safari (1962)
Surfin' Safari
Little Girl (You're My Miss America)
409
Chug-a-Lug
Surfin'
Heads You Win, Tails I Lose
Cuckoo Clock
Surfin' USA (1963)
Noble Surfer
Finders Keepers

Surfer Girl (1963)
  Hawaii
Little Deuce Coupe (1963)
  Be True to Your School
  Car Crazy Cutie
  Cherry, Cherry Coupe
  Spirit of America
  Custom Machine
Shut Down, Volume 2 (1964)
  Don't Worry, Baby
  Louie Louie
All Summer Long (1964)
  I Get Around
  Little Honda
  Don't Back Down
Today! (1965)
  Do You Wanna Dance?
  Good to My Baby
  Don't Hurt My Little Sister
  Help Me, Ronda
  Dance, Dance, Dance
  Please Let Me Wonder
  Kiss Me, Baby
  She Knows Me Too Well
Summer Days (1965)
  The Girl from New York City
  Girl Don't Tell Me
  Help Me, Rhonda
  California Girls
  Let Him Run Wild
  You're So Good to Me
Pet Sounds (1966)
  Don't Talk (Put Your Head on My Shoulder)
  Sloop John B.
  I Know There's an Answer
  Here Today
  I Just Wasn't Made for These Times

F. Songs with Unconventional Structures

Surfin' USA (1963)
  Lonely Sea
Pet Sounds (1966)
  You Still Believe in Me
  That's Not Me

I'm Waiting for the Day
Let's Go Away for Awhile
Pet Sounds

Appendix 5.2. Songs Discussed in Chapter 5 Categorized by Lyrical Theme

	Surfing	Cars	Girls	Reflective
Surfin' *Safari* (1962):	Surfin' Safari Surfin'	409	County Fair Little Girl . . . Heads You Win . . . Cuckoo Clock The Shift	
Surfin' *USA* (1963):	Surfin' USA Noble Surfer Finders Keepers	Shut Down	Farmer's Daughter Lonely Sea Lana	
Surfer *Girl* (1963):	Surfer Girl Catch a Wave The Surfer Moon South Bay Surfer Hawaii Surfers Rule	Little Deuce Coupe Our Car Club	Surfer Girl Your Summer Dream	In My Room
Little Deuce *Coupe* (1963):		Little Deuce Coupe Ballad of Ole' Betsy Car Crazy Cutie Cherry, Cherry Coupe 409 Shut Down Spirit of America Our Car Club No-Go Showboat Custom Machine	Car Crazy Cutie	
Shut Down, *Vol. 2* (1964):		Fun, Fun, Fun Don't Worry, Baby In the Parkin' Lot This Car of Mine	Fun, Fun, Fun Don't Worry, Baby In the Parkin' Lot The Warmth of the Sun Why Do Fools . . . ? Pom Pom Playgirl Keep an Eye on Summer	Don't Worry, Baby The Warmth of the Sun
All Summer *Long* (1964):	Don't Back Down	I Get Around Little Honda Drive-In	All Summer Long Hushabye We'll Run Away Wendy Girls on the Beach	
Today! (1965):			In the Back of My Mind Please Let Me Wonder She Knows Me Too Well Kiss Me, Baby Do You Wanna Dance? Don't Hurt My . . . Sister Help Me, Ronda Good to My Baby I'm So Young	In the Back of My Mind Please Let Me Wonder She Knows Me Too Well Kiss Me, Baby When I Grow Up . . .

	Surfing	Cars	Girls	Reflective
Summer Days (1965):			Girl from New York City Then I Kissed Her Girl Don't Tell Me Help Me, Rhonda California Girls Let Him Run Wild You're So Good to Me And Your Dream Comes True	
Pet Sounds (1966):			Wouldn't It Be Nice That's Not Me I'm Waiting for the Day God Only Knows Here Today Caroline, No Don't Talk . . . You Still Believe in Me	Wouldn't It Be Nice That's Not Me I'm Waiting for the Day God Only Knows Here Today Caroline, No In Know . . . Answer I Just Wasn't Made . . . Times

Songs not categorized:

Surfin' Safari (1962):
    Ten Little Indians
    Chug-a-Lug
    Summertime Blues
Little Deuce Coupe (1963):
    Be True to Your School
    A Young Man Is Gone
Shut Down, Vol. 2 (1964):
    Louie, Louie
All Summer Long (1964):
    Do You Remember?
Today! (1965):
    Dance, Dance, Dance
Summer Days (1965):
    Amusement Parks USA
    Salt Lake City
    I'm Bugged at My Ol' Man
Pet Sounds (1966):
    Sloop John B.

Appendix 5.3. Surfing Slang in Beach Boys Songs

baggies	Loose-fitting trunks worn by surfers.
body whop	To be "dumped" by a large wave (Carlin 2006, 36). This is a term that only seems to be used in the Beach Boys' "Noble Surfer." It does not appear in any surfing dictionary, nor in other contemporaneous surfing songs.
hodad/hodaddy	[see discussion in main text]
honeys	Female surfers/girlfriends of surfers. (McParland 2006 [21] notes that this term may not have been used on the "beach" at that time.)
huarache sandals	Leather sandals worn by surfers, with soles made from the treads of tires.
meatball flag	A yellow flag with a black circle indicating "no surfing today" at the beach.
raise	To stand up on a surfboard.
shooting the pier	Riding a surfboard in between the pilings of a beachside pier.
twenty-footer	Short-hand for a twenty-foot-tall wave.
walking the nose	Moving forward on the board towards the front or the "nose."
wiped out	To fall off or be knocked off your board by a large wave.
woodie	A station wagon with wooded paneling along the sides, favored by surfers because it has room inside for their boards and gear.

SIX | Into the Mystic?

The Undergrounding of Brian Wilson, 1964–1967

DALE CARTER

DURING THE 1960S, Anglo-American popular music and the culture with which it was near-synonymous were transformed in many regards. Enabled in part by rising prosperity and in part by social, demographic, and technological change, the commercial record business burgeoned, both as an industry and as a cultural force.[1] Between 1965 and 1967 in particular, a wave of ambitious artists created innovative, commercially successful work. With the music of the Beatles and Bob Dylan catalyzing many of these transformations, the middle of the decade saw popular music modulate into what would soon be identified as rock, distinguished from its predecessor by its variety, structural innovation, textual depth, and diversity of influence—and by the credibility it was now able to command beyond its own aesthetic and demographic circuits (Gendron 2002, 170–205).

No homegrown American group experienced or advanced these transformations more than the Beach Boys. Following the group's formation in 1961, its early years had seen chief songwriter Brian Wilson, working alone and in association with various lyricists, addressing a limited set of concerns centered on Southern California's surfing subculture or conventional pop themes such as romance and cars. Even during this period, Wilson's melodic gift, arranging skills, and growing command of the recording studio were starting to shift some of the foundations upon which popular music in the United States had for many years stood. But from late 1964 onward, the thematic focus of his songs also began to change and diversify: on the one hand, deepening their introspective, emotional concerns (a move that in 1966 would culminate in the completion of *Pet Sounds*); on the other, following a wider trajectory to encompass major historical, social, and cultural matters (a move that in 1967 would lead to the noncompletion of *Smile*). In the space of only two to three years, Wilson—with his fellow group members holding on in varying states of anxiety to his seemingly runaway creative train—helped to transform the nature, ambition, and standing of popular music. In the process he also moved well beyond the world in which he had founded the Beach Boys just a few years earlier. Whether such departures saw Brian Wilson (to extend the railroad metaphor) going off the rails or opening up new territories; whether (to invoke surfing associations) they dragged him into deeper waters or bore him to greater heights, this chapter pursues the trip.

I: Underground Formations: Steps Toward a Counter-Cultural Los Angeles

Viewed retroactively, and with an eye on the currents that Wilson would follow in mid-decade, the Beach Boys were launched on fairly calm waters, musical and otherwise. Though hardly flat, the American popular music scene in the early 1960s was one in which the impetus provided by mid- to late 1950s rock 'n' roll had slowed; yet to register were the galvanizing effects of the Beatles-led "British Invasion," Motown's soul-pop fusions, and the folk revival and folk-rock forms associated with Bob Dylan and the Byrds. Among the white population, at least, economic growth and low inflation underwrote widespread satisfaction with and faith in the American way of life. In the White House, the Kennedy administration was combining rhetoric, symbolism, and Cold War nationalism to sustain allegiance in foreign policy and contain grassroots dissent (most obviously in relation to race relations) at home. Vietnam remained low on the public agenda. Outside the realms of government and party politics, meanwhile, the New Left had scarcely articulated itself; Rachel Carson's *Silent Spring* was yet to advance environmentalism beyond the margins of popular attention; juvenile delinquency (source of an earlier media panic) had been successfully restaged as *West Side Story*; and the Beat revolt readily commodified into so many beatnik styles. Such patterns were also evident in the Beach Boys' home environment. Its growth fueled by large-scale investments in aerospace, real estate, and private automobiles, early 1960s Los Angeles embodied (not least in its own self-representations) the nation's prosperous, secure, accommodating, and benevolent future.

Though well past its 1940s studio heyday, Hollywood was busy reconfiguring itself as a burgeoning television-based entertainment industry—with popular music its underdeveloped though promising revenue stream (Starr 2009, 3–28, 217–32, 245–66; Sanjek 1996, 345–50).

Yet even as the Beach Boys took their first steps into the latter, the countercultural tide upon which Brian Wilson would later ride was rising. Ironically, given its embodiment of the more hedonistic, consumerist aspects of the American way of life, the surfing craze that afforded Wilson's group its early profile was not solely, to use Herbert Marcuse's term, affirmative; if, like other subcultures, it helped sustain the dominant order, it also described, even pushed, some of its limits (Marcuse 1972, 59; Marcuse 1968, 95). It was not so much that surfers had initially received a mixed press, courtesy of associations with risk-taking, juvenile delinquency, and rock 'n' roll (May 2002, 96–98). Within their preoccupations with fun, escapism, and youth, as reported by Tom Wolfe in *The Pump House Gang* (1968), there also lay a cult of sensual pleasure, of rejuvenation through immersion in the Pacific's waves, which, as Wolfe showed in *The Electric Kool-Aid Acid Test* (1968), might lead into deeper waters of human experience (White 1994, 139–41; Phoenix 2001, 109; Wolfe 1989, 27–46; Wolfe 1968, 320–23). Even at the decade's outset, intersections between the bohemian dimensions of Southern Californian surf and West Coast Beat lifestyles were emblematic of the latter propensity (Chidester and Priore 2008, 48–49; Priore 2007, 35). Though North Beach in San Francisco quickly became synonymous with Beat literature and culture, Venice had its own Beat community, the subject of Lawrence Lipton's *The Holy Barbarians* (1959); and just as aspects of the North Beach ethos would help inspire Haight-Ashbury by mid-decade, so would Venice constitute a precursor to the alternative culture building around Sunset Strip during the same period (Lipton 1959; Maynard 1991; Puterbaugh 1999, 357–63; Chidester and Priore 2008, 229–37). Links between the Los Angeles surf and Beat scenes and the nascent counterculture would be exemplified by graphic artists and painters such as Rick Griffin and John Van Hamersveld, whose work lent all three a profile. Frank Holmes, later to provide the original cover art for the Beach Boys' *Smile*, first met the album's lyricist Van Dyke Parks when working at the Insomniac coffeehouse, a Beat hangout just south of Venice in Hermosa Beach (Chidester and Priore 2008, 48–49, 68–69).[2] Other musicians embodying the connection between Venice and the city's growing counterculture included David Crosby of the Byrds and Jim Morrison of the Doors, both of whom lived for a time in the coastal enclave.

One distinctive feature of the Beat scene in Venice—its radical politics—was emblematic of another subcurrent within the rising countercultural tide in Los Angeles. Official state-level investigations had deepened Cold War antiradicalism across California as a whole, and by the early 1960s the postwar red scare was not over. Yet the House Un-American Activities Committee hearings at San Francisco City Hall in early 1960 had triggered mass protests, and public fear of both communism and the anticommunist lobby was diminishing (Heale 1986, 17–29; McBride 2003, 116; Goodman 1969, 428–34). If the late 1950s saw a political New Left emerging across the country from (and beyond) the ashes of the Communist Party–associated Old Left, the conflation in Venice of political, social, and cultural radicalism—with the latter providing a good deal of the local impetus—provided a template for similar activity elsewhere in Los Angeles. This was in part because, even as long-established ideological leanings and the intensity of the red scare had kept the political Left relatively weak in the city, its status as a mass-media and mass-entertainment center ensured, as David McBride has noted, that the cultural sphere (and thus cultural radicalism) would be a "fundamental concern" (2003, 111, 116). The fact that Venice had a sizable black population (which the later countercultural scene around Sunset Strip would lack) no doubt underwrote the inclusion of civil rights on the local radical agenda.

But what both communities shared—a cultural dissidence that was also political and social—was scarcely restricted to these neighborhoods. Nor was it previously unknown. During the height of the postwar red scare, what durability progressivism had shown in the region owed more than a little to what Michael Denning later dubbed the "cultural front." Informal gatherings held by actor Will Geer and his wife, the actress Herta Ware, at their Topanga Canyon ranch, for example, provided an under-the-radar forum for the social networking of fellow radical theater activists and other cultural and political progressives, many of whom had been blacklisted for their Popular Front–era activities and associations. From the late 1950s onward their low-intensity but long-life pilot lights would ignite others (Denning 1998; Cray 2004, 354–55; Rossinow 2002, 104–5; Bell 2012, 64–65).

Playing a notable part within these communities of cultural radicals was a group of folk music collectors, enthusiasts, and artists whose activities constituted an additional indirect tributary of the Los Angeles counterculture. Active in the early postwar People's Songs group and inspired by the example (and periodic presence) of the Geers' friend

Woody Guthrie, figures such as Mario "Boots" Casetta and Earl Robinson not only carried the torch through the anticommunist era, particularly for topical songs; their efforts and those of others also provided the basis on which the folk music revival in Los Angeles would later build (Cohen 2002, 47–49, 75–77, 118–20; Cohen and Samuelson 1996, 132–34; Lieberman 1989, 60, 69, 117; Dunaway and Beer 2010, 70–73). In 1957 former union activist Herb Cohen opened the city's first folk music coffeehouse, the Unicorn, located on Sunset Strip. Over the next year two more folk venues opened in West Hollywood, a few blocks south of the Strip. The Ash Grove featured old-time, blues, and bluegrass artists, and became a focal point for the traditionalist wing of the folk revival. Sharing much of the Old Left's class-oriented outlook, club owner Ed Pearl supported a range of progressive causes emblematic of the long-standing association between folk music and radical politics, from labor unions via racial justice to nuclear disarmament (Lieberman 1989, 34–46; Sullivan 2009; Nolan 2008). The Troubadour, meanwhile, provided a gathering place for the revival's modernizing wing; more attuned to the politics of the personal, owner Doug Weston promoted what would later become the contemporary singer-songwriter genre, with its sensitivity to emotional and spiritual concerns (Hoskyns 1997, 74–75). Complementary in their activities and emblematic of its varied aspects, both the Ash Grove and the Troubadour would serve as seedbeds for the city's nascent underground as the 1960s progressed.

They did so in part by providing the physical venues for musicians—as well as counterculturalists more broadly—to gather. The Troubadour in particular served as a forum wherein the inheritance of traditional music and topical songs sustained at the Ash Grove interacted with the inspirations provided by the folk revivalism of Bob Dylan and the pop song innovations of the Beatles. From as early as 1962, the migration of a number of folk revivalists from New York City and elsewhere led to the coalescence around Los Angeles of a group of musicians—many of them also inspired by the Beats and then the Beatles—keen to create music that eroded the gulf between the supposed depth of acoustic folk-song and the assumed shallowness of amplified pop (Hoskyns 2005, 1–9; Hoskyns 1997, 74–77). The Troubadour became one early fulcrum of these activities. A regular at the venue from 1963, for example, Van Dyke Parks played piano in jam sessions there with a number of influential musicians, including Danny Hutton (later of Three Dog Night), whom he got to know at a Monday-night hootenanny in 1964, and Jim (subsequently Roger) McGuinn, whose meeting with Gene Clark at the club that March led to the formation of the Byrds. Others crossing the same circle included David Crosby (soon to become the Byrds' third recruit) and Steven Stills (later of Buffalo Springfield). Such figures would help provide bridges between the musical and cultural crucible of the folk and post-folk-revival club scene and the commercial pop world whose heights Brian Wilson and the Beach Boys had been successfully climbing over the preceding couple of years (Unterberger 2002, 75–80; Rogan 2012, 27–29, 35–36; Greenwald 2003).

Crucial in this connection were the debut performances of the Byrds at the Ciro's Le Disc club on Sunset Strip in March and April 1965. As Domenic Priore has shown, at precisely this time the area's club scene was undergoing rapid transformation, with demographic and cultural changes prompting the displacement of an older, more bourgeois, movie-oriented clientele by a younger, predominantly teenaged crowd attuned to pop music (Priore 2007, 16–25, 41–45; Hoskyns 1997, 71–74; Hoskyns 1994, 34–37; Adler 1967, 116–31; Bernhard and Friedenberg 1967, 8–13). The Byrds' shows were significant in part because they quickly attracted large numbers of teenagers, the group's appeal confirmed and further boosted by the rise of their recording of Bob Dylan's "Mr. Tambourine Man" to the top of the *Billboard* Hot 100 in June 1965. These events also mattered because that success demonstrated the commercial potential of the folk hybrids then being crafted at the Troubadour and elsewhere (Crosby 1989, 10, 64–66, 76–77, 79–84, 88–89, 98–99; Einarson 2005, 38–44; Priore 2007, 73–78; Hoskyns 1997, 76–79; Unterberger 2002, 113–17). It was not only subsequent record sales that made the shows important, however; grassroots word of mouth—lent strength by Bob Dylan's brief on-stage appearance with the Byrds on March 26—attracted fellow musicians and other creative types, entertainers and younger movie stars, talent scouts, bohemians, intellectuals, and journalists to Ciro's. Both the group's producer, Terry Melcher, and their financier, Eddie Tickner, subsequently described the residency there as a "catalyst," the latter dubbing it the start of a new "movement that was happening amongst the artists, the poets, and the freaky film people." While some of its "mythic dimensions" may have been ascribed in hindsight, the circumstances and participants' recollections suggest that such renderings were not simply hyperbole. Other groups would follow the Byrds onto Sunset Strip: the Mothers of Invention, Buffalo Springfield, the Doors, Love, and more. Insofar as they set the stage, the Byrds' appearances at Ciro's were emblematic of a new countercultural complex identifying itself and measuring its potential (Hjort 2008, 27–30; Robbins 1965, 6; Rogan 2012, 100–113).

These events were of particular significance vis-à-vis Brian Wilson because they helped bring together not only people who would make the Los Angeles counterculture a source of creative inspiration, but also those able to link it to the city's commercial music industry, such as producers, managers and A & R men. Some, like Columbia Records (later Elektra) talent scout and promoter Billy James, played important roles in this regard, but not in relation to Wilson. Others, however, would start to enter the head Beach Boy's circle over the next year or so. One such was David Anderle, a native Angelino once employed to prepare recorded music for in-car cartridge players, now applying his own Sunset Strip experience as an MGM Records talent scout, and subsequently to be introduced via a family member to Wilson and his group. A second was Massachusetts transplant Michael Vosse, onetime college friend of Anderle and television production assistant, then becoming active behind the scenes as what he called a "facilitator," liaising between record labels, musicians, other artists, and the burgeoning underground. A third was homegrown *Los Angeles Free Press* journalist Paul Jay Robbins, a former Ash Grove regular who had persuaded *Free Press* founder and editor Art Kunkin to publish his review of the Byrds' Ciro's shows (in spite of Kunkin's sense that such events were insignificant vis-à-vis his own Old Leftist concerns). Robbins's highly literate appreciation not only advised readers of the nation's second oldest alternative newspaper that these musical engagements were a manifestation of "a very important social and spiritual movement"; his attendance at the shows would also lead to friendships with David Crosby and (himself on the Ciro's dance floor watching the group) Van Dyke Parks. Looking back two years later, Robbins would write that from their Sunset Strip "launch pad" the Byrds had given voice to a "hymn [that] sounded from the total collective consciousness of a new breed of people" (Holzman 2000, 160, 164–65, 186; Williams 1997, 40–41; Vosse 1968; Hjort 2008, 30).

Particularly in its musical dimensions, such countercultivation could be traced back well before the Byrds' opening dates at Ciro's in the spring of 1965. Van Dyke Parks had first met David Crosby when both were performing on the West Coast folk revival circuit during 1963. He reconnected with Crosby, and as noted above, first met Danny Hutton at the Troubadour in 1964. Hutton initially crossed Brian Wilson's path at Gold Star studios in Hollywood late that year, and would move into his circle toward the end of 1965 after the two had been reintroduced by David Anderle, who had become Hutton's manager soon after the Byrds' debut performances at Ciro's. Though both Anderle and Parks had attended those shows, it was Hutton who introduced them to one another, with the result that the former—having by coincidence also heard Parks at work on an arrangement of the "Ode to Joy" from Beethoven's Ninth Symphony at Western studios—agreed to manage Parks, thereafter securing the MGM deal that would lead to the release of that arrangement as his debut single, "Number Nine," at the end of 1965. The single included the original German text translated into English by Paul Jay Robbins. Also in December 1965, David Crosby took Parks up to meet Brian Wilson at the latter's home in Beverly Hills following a session at the Troubadour; in February 1966 Parks and Wilson would meet again, this time at the home of Terry Melcher, recently deposed as producer of the Byrds.[3] Later in the year Parks would introduce Robbins, and reintroduce Michael Vosse, to Wilson.

From the Ash Grove via the Troubadour and the *Free Press* to Sunset Strip and Ciro's (and thereafter into Wilson's inner circle), Paul Jay Robbins's trajectory was illuminating. Both a reporter and a participant, he had picked up guitar tips from Woody Guthrie's protégé Jack Elliott, and prior to the Byrds' debut at Ciro's had taken part in the Selma-to-Montgomery civil rights march. In November 1966 he would witness the so-called "riot on Sunset Strip" and work in defense of its youthful partisans. He was therefore in a good position to register the modulations of the counterculture—not just musical—as it took shape. Such rearrangements were certainly generic in part, with blues and country-oriented traditional or topical music styles fading into early singer-songwriter experiments, and both then giving way to the varied innovations subsumed under the catchall label "folk-rock" (Unterberger 2002, 88–99). But they also had racial dimensions, the balance off- and onstage becoming whiter by degree as the catchment area and demographic profile of audiences evolved, while the stress on tradition that had given opportunities to older blues musicians yielded to an emphasis on youth and innovation.[4] The changes reflected new artistic values, too, as egalitarian, communitarian folk club norms became augmented (or supplanted) by the appeal to self-expression of the nightclub scene.

Insofar as he worked for a publication addressing a variety of interests, Robbins's journalistic role was similarly illuminating. With roots in the Old Left and an agenda at once New Leftist and countercultural, the *Free Press* had been founded in 1964 as (in Art Kunkin's words) "a community newspaper" run by "liberals" (Kunkin 1964, 1). Published at first from the basement of the Fifth Estate coffeehouse, directly opposite Ciro's on the Sunset Strip, it supported, at least metaphorically,

Beat, folk, and similar less market-oriented creative pursuits while also reflecting, more literally, on the underground's growing traffic with the higher-profile aspects of commercialized pop culture. It was here and hereabouts that Brian Wilson would tune in: one eye on popular youth trends and the other on musical and cultural innovations.

II: Establishing a Beachhead: Brian Wilson Tunes In

Biographies and memoirs offer various accounts of the role played by drugs—marijuana and LSD in particular—in the life and work of Brian Wilson, and in the development of the counterculture whose circuits he plugged into during the mid-1960s. Though politicians and others came to demonize it via scare tactics concerning drugs of which they disapproved, the counterculture was not simply an exercise in substance abuse, and the community finding itself on Ciro's dance floor was by no means in a narcotic haze. At the time, marijuana use was rare among younger audience members, and psychedelics were only starting to spread beyond their military and psychiatric test beds. Had drugs been "the primary motivation," the chronicler and firsthand witness Eve Babitz has noted, Ciro's would not have seen the energy levels it did (Hjort 2008, 30; Priore 2007, 75–76).

Nor was Brian Wilson initially attracted to the scene in order to gain access to narcotics, or necessarily drawn into it by malevolent individuals seeking personal gain by exposing him to them. It appears, rather, that the Beach Boys' leader first encountered this subculture as part of his quest for creative, intellectual inspiration among the musicians and their associates surrounding his work in the recording studio. He did so at a crucial time, for during the latter half of 1964 his expanding musical ambitions were starting to chafe against a relentless tour schedule, the demands of the Beach Boys' label Capitol Records for marketable (if not necessarily memorable) product, and his father's domineering attitude toward his work (all of which may have played a part in Brian's nervous breakdown at the end of the year). If he was (too) easily impressed by some of his new contacts, that experience also no doubt owed something to his own less-than-cosmopolitan upbringing, which had not exposed him to the sorts of ideas, lifestyles, and modes of artistic expression to be found within the Los Angeles counterculture. (As his first wife, Marilyn, remarked later, "Brian came from Inglewood: Squaresville.") In any event, Wilson was neither the first nor the only creative individual to cultivate novel ways of stimulating or tapping the imaginative wellsprings more deeply. To this extent his willingness to try drugs other than alcohol and nicotine was less than surprising (Carlin 2006, 53–59, 61–63; Lambert 2007, 151).

Identifying channels and timing is neither easy nor, in some regards, of prime importance. Wilson appears to have been introduced to marijuana in late 1964 by Loren Schwartz, an employee of the Beach Boys' representatives William Morris, not long after Wilson had moved into his own apartment in Hollywood. A few months later, most probably in April 1965, the same source gave Wilson access to LSD, supplied by Augustus Owsley Stanley III's newly established production facility. Schwartz's West Hollywood apartment served as a regular forum for those (musicians or otherwise) who shared an interest in creative expression and consciousness expansion beyond the mainstream. In addition to Wilson, guests included Byrds' members Jim McGuinn, David Crosby, and Chris Hillman, Schwartz's onetime high school friend Tony Asher, and former folk revivalist turned studio musician Van Dyke Parks. Schwartz's apartment was not unique: Parks's home on Melrose Avenue also provided a rendezvous point, particularly for writers, performers, producers, managers, and others then starting to reshape the Los Angeles music scene. Along with a number of local meeting-places (such as Ben Frank's restaurant, Canter's delicatessen, and Fred C. Dobbs's coffeehouse), such venues helped advance the city's countercultural network-building via social interactions, exchanges of texts and ideas, and more: "scores of people," as Robbins recalled, "clicking antennae together" (Carlin 2006, 64–65; Badman 2004, 73, 87; Gaines 1988, 145, 151–53; Wilson 1991, 103–5).

Perhaps more difficult to pin down precisely is the relationship between the new cultural climate that Brian Wilson encountered and cultivated at this time and his own creativity. Though influences are often asserted, they are not easy to identify and assess, at least in relation to marijuana and LSD; the varied, unpredictable, contingent nature of individual experiences with psychedelics in particular only complicates the task (de Rios and Janiger 2003, 76–87, 108–14; Letcher 2006, 186–91). In Wilson's case this is all the more so given the many developments in his life from late 1964 onward (the end of touring, married life, a pivotal confrontation with his father, a nervous breakdown) and the musical challenges—at once threatening and inspirational—being posed by the Beatles and others. For an artist whose work had been innovative from the outset, the extent to which any one "radical departure or dramatic advancement in composition elements" might be ascribed to consciousness expansion is thus debatable (Lambert 2007, 186–87, 190–91, 204–6;

Carlin 2006, 65). Yet, as Philip Lambert has shown, Wilson's experiments with marijuana and LSD can be associated with changes in his writing, arranging, and production work during the first half of 1965: vis-à-vis marijuana on "In the Back of My Mind" and (to a lesser degree) "Please Let Me Wonder"; in relation to LSD (as Wilson himself vividly recalled) on "California Girls." Such songs were emblematic of a new phase that would climax in the *Pet Sounds* album the following year and in the *Smile* project thereafter. Aspects of the change could be heard in the chord progressions, instrumental coloration, and melodic innovation of the songs. They were also discernible in their underlying design, becoming more complex and sophisticated, combining integration, fragmentation, and variation in forms that were subtle, graceful, and ingenious (Lambert 2007, 190–91, 204, 210, 212, 215–16, 221; Wilson 1991, 114–20). Though the Beach Boys can hardly be considered exemplars of acid rock, it is also possible—insofar as any such musical genre can be adequately defined—to identify in their mid-1960s work qualities and trends later associated with psychedelia: greater fluidity, elaboration, and formal complexity; a cultivation of sonic textures; the introduction of new (combinations of) instruments, multiple keys, and/or floating tonal centers; and at times the use of slower, more hypnotic tempos (Hicks 1999, 63–73; Whiteley 1992, 2–5).

Sound, in any event, was not the only means by which countercultural and psychedelic inspirations manifested themselves: innovation in Wilson's writing also took lyrical form, and any assessment of countercultural influences therefore invites attention to his songs' words. Firsthand and secondary accounts agree that the creative, inspirational bookshelf to which Wilson gained access from late 1964 included poetry and prose (by Kahlil Gibran, Hermann Hesse, Antoine de Saint-Exupéry, and others) as well as cultural criticism (Arthur Koestler's recently published *The Act of Creation* often being cited, not least by Wilson himself). It also featured diverse expressions of non-Christian religions and belief systems: Native American creeds; Hinduism, as embodied in the Bhagavad Gita; Confucianism, refracted via the *I Ching* or Book of Changes; various types of Buddhism, particularly Tibetan and Zen; Subud, a newer religious movement rooted in Islam; and other persuasions, from scientology via astrology to numerology (Carlin 2006, 65, 99; Gaines 1988, 152; Wilson 1991, 104). The countercultural bookshelf found room for the promotion of related practices, too, such as meditation and yoga, as well as disciplines like vegetarianism, in which Wilson evinced an interest. A number of these beliefs and activities were associated with the exploration of altered states of consciousness, Timothy Leary's widely read guide *The Psychedelic Experience* (1963), drawing on the *Bardo Thōdol* (or Tibetan Book of the Dead), for example (Leary, Metzner, and Alpert 1995, 11–15).

Testimony from close associates and his own statements at the time confirm that Wilson made himself familiar with various aspects of underground thought; and it is possible to discern links between compositional innovations noted by Lambert and countercultural aesthetic and psychological precepts (concerning representation, form, and identity, say). No more than experience, however, does reading necessarily shape creativity. Wilson was in any case less adept (perhaps less self-confident) in his use of words than of music, and during this period he continued to work with lyricists, as had been his custom since the Beach Boys' first recordings. If this complicates matters, the fact that the Los Angeles countercultural network included people who wrote song lyrics, rather than furnishing narcotic connections alone, also extended its value to him: during the two years following his introduction to marijuana and LSD, the innovations that marked his use of sounds would be matched lyrically, not only on individual tracks but on entire collections of songs.

III: From Flatlands to Highways: Sounding Out the Territory with Asher and Parks

Wilson's two main lyricists during these years, Tony Asher and Van Dyke Parks, brought to their collaborations distinctive experiences, interests, and skills. Born in England though raised in and around Hollywood, Asher had dabbled in jazz but by the time he met Wilson (at some point during 1965) was employed by the Carson-Scott advertising agency writing jingles for commercials.[5] A native of Mississippi later domiciled in Florida and Pennsylvania, Parks had exchanged a classical music education for the world of West Coast folk clubs and, latterly, work as a jobbing Hollywood studio musician. Asher's career trajectory was consistent with what he called his "pretty conservative" outlook; Parks, raised in a progressive family active in campaigns for social change, had taken risks. Though each played piano, perhaps the main thing the two men shared (in light of their self-ascribed lack of credentials) was surprise at the opportunity to work with Brian Wilson: both had met the Beach Boys' leader socially on occasion, but neither boasted a track record as a lyricist, nor did Wilson know all that much about their musical backgrounds (Abbott 2001, 39–40; Leaf 1996, 37; Gaines 1988, 173–74; *Endless Summer*

Quarterly 2010; Priore 2005, 39–40). Whether Wilson's invitations were more a function of instinct or of his assessment of their respective ways with words in conversation, they were emblematic of his own stance at the time, and of the leanings of youth-oriented American popular music: one foot in the entertainment industry's commercial, mass-market-oriented world; the other stepping into less familiar domains. Just as these domains tended to be less risk averse, so those entering them were more likely to draw on novel inspirations and unconventional resources, to speak to new communities, and to offer alternative types of musical expression.

The nature of Wilson's successive working relationships with Asher and Parks throws light on the trajectory of his songwriting between early 1965 and early 1967. Both men were familiar with the Los Angeles underground (thus Loren Schwartz's recommendation prompted Wilson to invite Asher's participation; see Leaf 1996, 17). Within that common context and their shared lyrical remit, however, what they brought to their work with Wilson, what he sought from them, and how their joint efforts took shape, differed in varying degrees. Asher's contributions were based on in-depth conversations with the Beach Boys' leader about either personal relationships and emotional states or spirituality and religious faith, in which he served as a sounding board-cum-amanuensis for what Wilson later called his "single-minded pursuit of a personal vision." While the two men also discussed a range of musical styles, Asher played a reactive part in that regard, at times having little idea of how songs to which he had contributed would sound until he heard the finished recordings (Abbott 2001, 41–44; Wilson 1991, 140; White 1994, 255–57). Parks, though also engaged for his facility with words, brought to his work with Wilson more diverse musical experience inside and outside the studio; he was invited both to observe and to take part in recording sessions. Perhaps more importantly, Parks was given greater scope not only in realizing their objectives lyrically but also in formulating them. (As he wrote in 2006, "Wilson asked me to take a free hand in the lyrics and the album's [*Smile*'s] thematic direction.") More precise assessments are rendered difficult by the varying emphases both men have placed on their collaboration over time. But if the primary themes of *Pet Sounds* ("autobiography: the gospel of Brian," in David Leaf's words) were compatible with—perhaps invited, even demanded—Asher's essentially interpretive role, such a reading is less persuasive vis-à-vis Parks's part in the making of *Smile*. Even taking Asher's own characterization into account ("autobiography, but . . . I wouldn't limit it to Brian's autobiography"), *Pet Sounds* had lyrical precursors in the Beach Boys' recordings; only to a much lesser degree could this be said of *Smile* (Leaf 1997a, 40; Jensen, n.d.; Staton 2005, 58–61; Parks 2006, 57; Priore 2005, 82–83; Leaf 1996, 39).

Most of *Pet Sounds* was written and recorded between July 1965 and April 1966 (with the lion's share of the studio work completed in the last four months of this period); if "Good Vibrations" is included, work on *Smile* began in February 1966 (if not, then May 1966) and was abandoned in May 1967. Regardless of precise dates, witnesses and participants have reported difficulties in separating the two projects. Insofar as both post-dated Wilson's introduction to marijuana *and* LSD, in any case, it makes little point to distinguish between the two albums in terms of their differential impact. (Wilson has explicitly acknowledged the influence of LSD on his writing of the earlier work; see Badman 2004, 96, 117, 126, 131–32, 187–88; Abbott 2001, 114–15; Holdship and Doggett 2007, 50.)

Timing should not be ignored altogether, however. For whereas both *Pet Sounds* and *Smile* may be characterized as countercultural to varying degrees, the former clearly carried the Beach Boys' previously well-established romantic themes into the psychedelic realm (witness the variant title of—and lyrics for—the *Pet Sounds* song "I Know There's an Answer": "Hang On to Your Ego"). If *Smile* had romantic dimensions too (which it did), these were aesthetic and political rather than personal in nature, and were informed by more than firsthand experience. By the time Wilson and Parks got to work during the early summer of 1966, in effect, the musical, psychological, and spiritual beachheads opened up via "In the Back of My Mind," "California Girls," and *Pet Sounds* had made room for (and were being extended by) an array of reinforcements, historical, social, political, and countercultural. While no single influence alone explains such advances, Wilson's choice of a new lyricist clearly played a part in the shift between the fields of vision of *Pet Sounds* and of *Smile*. Cosmopolitan, liberally educated, and well-read, Van Dyke Parks drew inspirations from the Beats, the folk revival, and more toward *Smile*.

In their occasional get-togethers, Wilson had no doubt recognized Parks's verbal dexterity; he may also have gleaned a sense of his interests, knowledge, and musical abilities (Carlin 2006, 92; Wilson 1991, 145–46; Priore 2005, 34–40). Yet whether it was anything more than his way with words that appealed is hard to say, not least because assessments have differed as to the breadth of Wilson's own horizons at this time. Abbott argues that in spite (or perhaps because) of his new countercultural leanings, career demands caused Wilson to be "isolated from . . . current affairs and world issues" during late 1965 and early 1966, and he displayed no interest in political concerns. Priore, however, refers to Wilson's intrinsic or nascent social conscience preceding his meet-

ings with Parks, and senses growing pacifist and environmental sensibilities between the early spring and summer of 1966. Reum credits the
Beach Boys' leader with similar feelings during the period in which he
and Parks worked on *Smile* (Abbott 2001, 41; Priore 2005, 39, 65, 79, 83,
89–91; Allen 2004, 16). Clearly Wilson was broadening his outlook and
knowledge: by the summer, for example, he was expressing fears about
urban pollution and an interest in healthy lifestyles (Carter 2013, 47–49).
Whatever latent concerns about American values, beliefs, and practices
he was beginning to harbor were, in any event, familiar territory to his
new cowriter. Parks, moreover, brought to the collaboration not only historical, social, and cultural knowledge but also an established interest in
creative writing that would enable him to articulate his and their ideas.
As a result, imagery and wordplay, allusions, quotations, and more would
make of *Smile* a complex palimpsest of songs whose vision was sustained
in words as well as sound.

Though witnesses suggest an understandable degree of struggle
to realize the composers' objectives, the work's close interlocking of
musical and lyrical motifs evinced a sharing of ideas, back and forth.
On the premise that its performance decades later completed, rather
than reconstructed, the original effort, *Smile* was certainly assuming
an overall form and direction. But its bearing was not only geographi-
cal, across the nation from east to west, as many observers have noted.
It was also social and political, ideological and cultural, across the varied contours of the so-called movement of the 1960s as it grew: from
New Left to counterculture. Even as Wilson recognized the concerns
Parks had voiced—about racial conflict at home, a militarized Cold
War strategy abroad, and the nation's conflicted self-definitions and
historical track record—so their exchanges yielded a work in progress in which current, more explicitly politicized radicalisms were effectively articulated via countercultural figurations of natives, nature,
and the naive. As important, in the course of this repositioning, *Smile*
also traversed complex landscapes of faith: from national allegiance
and ideological persuasion to religious belief and spiritual devotion, it drew listeners through history and experience into the mystic
(Priore 2005, 73, 77).

IV: Beyond Terra Firma: On *Smile's* Contested Ground

Articulating a journey that moves to and fro between realms of innocence and experience, *Smile* picks up where *Pet Sounds* leaves off. More

precisely, it describes a similar trajectory across congruent yet more varied terrains, in effect turning its predecessor's personal, intimate, introspective vision into an exploration of the nation's historical, social,
ideological, and cultural identity. This common trope is signified in a
variety of ways. At a superficial level, both albums announce departures
(on bicycle and train), literally making the right noises for travelers of
all ages; by sail and steam, shipping extends their metaphoric range.
More substantively, both rely on trusted countercultural lodestars: love,
self-knowledge, and personal commitment provide orientation throughout the bildungsroman of *Pet Sounds*, and are supported in *Smile* by native wisdom and natural piety, alternative religions, and altered states of
consciousness. Destinations in both journeys remain unclear, of course:
some routes are unmapped or lead nowhere; terrain can be broken or
choppy. Motivated and sanctioned by emotional, material, or spiritual
desire, moreover, protagonists on each album discover that the quest
for individual experience or collective wisdom brings neither security
nor clarity but only uncertainty and mystery. *Pet Sounds* begins and ends
with personal questions: yet as the hopeful speculations of "Wouldn't
It Be Nice?" give way to the mournful resignation of "Caroline, No," so
romantic disenchantment becomes the price of adolescent enlightenment. *Smile* carries a greater—not solely individual but also national—
burden, yet it describes a similar figure: the historical, social, ideological, and emotional promises of the American dream that are at stake
in "Heroes and Villains" (a west "lost and gone," "unknown" back east
on the city upon a hill) yield to the nightmare conflagrations of "Mrs.
O'Leary's Cow" in return for the briefest of tastes of the beloved community in "On a Holiday" and a mere hint of universal illumination, itself
dislocated and inexplicable, in "Good Vibrations" thereafter.

Whereas *Pet Sounds* concludes in a personal disillusion for which
any emotional maturity appears scant compensation, however, *Smile*
does conceive of a collective redemption and reenchantment for which
historical declension may serve as necessary precondition. The former
album moves from innocence to experience, describing a fall that, as
Lambert explains, is written musically into its fabric by way of recurring
melodic arches, minor-third key changes, and descending stepwise bass
lines (Abbott 2001, 88; Lambert 2007, 227–28, 230, 232–33, 234–35, 236,
238, 249; Lambert 2008). Metaphorically at least, *Smile* recapitulates
and combines, transposes and inverts those movements, both embedding and articulating personal, social, and historical trajectories via the
repeated figure—melodic, textual, and symbolic—of the wave, rising,

falling, and rising again. Waves of settlement, of wheat and of Indians; tidal waves, airwaves, and heat waves; sound waves and cosmic waves: all resonate across and beneath *Smile*'s surfaces, from "Heroes and Villains" and "Roll Plymouth Rock" via "Cabin Essence" and "Surf's Up" to "Mrs. O'Leary's Cow" and "Good Vibrations." On *Pet Sounds* the protagonist seeks security (to stay together, to retain the familiar, to go home) and tends to see change as loss; on *Smile*, no loss is final—indeed loss and gain are no more than parts of a whole—and the vibrations, if intangible, are ultimately good.

In keeping with Wilson and Parks's desire to write an avowedly, unashamedly American work (in part to show the Beatles and Rolling Stones raw materials that could *not* be misappropriated), *Smile*'s recoveries are distinctively New World—and more precisely star-spangled (Beard 2005, 3–4, 6–7; Carlin 2006, 97–98). Thus it enacts a captivity narrative in which the city upon a hill, fallen or at risk, is ultimately redeemed via an errand into the wilderness; it fixes nature's nation's broken heart by way of some Franklinite workshop tinkering; it rehearses the frontier experience to have the downtrodden, overridden, Jeffersonian yeoman reborn as a new wave-riding American Adam; and if it overturns Thanksgiving (or bids it farewell) in Plymouth, it does so only to see it restored in Hawaii. As these examples suggest, the exceptionalist myths that sustain its protagonists beyond the fall are in turn underwritten by faith. The latter is often Christian. *Smile* is thus a latter-day Puritan jeremiad—"just see what you've done!"—that enables atonement and recovery. Its errant subject's descent into the fiery pit leads to absolution and baptism; its children's *New-England Primer* prayer seeks mercy and salvation (Madsen 1998; Bercovitch 2012).

Yet insofar as *Smile*'s countercultural precepts include both an antiestablishment skepticism toward religious institutions and an interest in alternative belief structures, the album's exceptionalist leanings in no way constrain its spiritual strivings. Thus the ritual blessings it enacts may be Native American and the mysteries it alludes to pre-Christian; the elements it invokes appear classical, Egyptian, or Hindu; the mysticism toward which it gravitates, given its ultimate stress on vibrations, sounds at once psychedelic and Zen Buddhist. Whether guided by nationalist ideals or Christian precepts, romantic dreams or philosophical, alchemical, astrological, or spiritual inspirations, *Smile*'s recovery program brings together immortal girl and beloved community, common prayer and chosen land, enlightened vision and perfect wave: "their song is love / and the children know the way."

As realized on *Brian Wilson Presents Smile* in 2004, the ecstatic transcendence of "Good Vibrations" brings *Smile* to a more uplifting conclusion than does the grieving declension of "Caroline, No" at the end of
Pet Sounds. Yet even though the "Good Vibrations" single enjoyed critical
acclaim and commercial success in 1966, neither *Pet Sounds* nor *Smile*
took off as their principal creator desired. Based on melodic fragments
and what Wilson called "feels," which he "planned to fit . . . together
like a mosaic," each of these collections broke new but also untested
and demanding ground, musically and lyrically, thematically and vocally
(Umphred 1997, 31–32; Carlin 2006, 79, 90; Lambert 2007, 222; Badman
2004, 148; Wilson 1991, 131). They led Wilson, his cowriters, studio musicians, and the Beach Boys as a whole on demanding, hazardous journeys
into unfamiliar territories, much like their subjects and protagonists.
That in the process they prompted less confident travelers within their
orbit to advise Wilson that such trips were unnecessary and unappealing,
in light of the perceived risks, was less than wholly surprising. Accounts
of some of the Beach Boys' unhappiness with the overall tenor of *Pet
Sounds* ("Brian's ego music," as one described it) and with selected lyrics
on *Smile* have often been repeated; so too reports of Capitol Records'
halfhearted approach to promoting the former (Gaines 1988, 177–83;
Abbott 2001, 93–96; Carlin 2006, 83–85, 113–17).

Yet musical differences among group members and tensions born of
their label's devotion to its own short-term balance sheet were not the
only problems that hindered *Pet Sounds*' reception and helped prompt
Smile's abandonment. Again, most accounts suggest that if some of
Wilson's fellow Beach Boys harbored reservations about his new creative
directions, then their unease also applied to the external influences to
which they felt the new music was closely linked. At least in the eyes of his
established circle of family and group members, as Wilson began to plug
into the burgeoning Los Angeles counterculture during 1965 and 1966,
so a small coterie of its adepts did the same to him. Not only were established songwriting partnerships sidelined and long-standing social relationships displaced; those marginalized felt that in the process Wilson's
energies were drained, his talents squandered, and his faculties endan-
gered. In feeding and feeding off him, they believed, the underground—
with its radical ideas and avant-garde literature, its alternative religions
and mind-bending substances—was slowly burying the Beach Boys'
leader, at least metaphorically. By contrast, those who followed in Loren
Schwartz's wake, such as Vosse, Anderle, and Robbins, saw themselves as
catalysts, helping to broaden Wilson's personal experiences, expand his

cultural horizons, and encourage his artistic ambitions: enabling him in the process to realize his own creative needs instead of remaining tied to the self-serving agendas and financial interests of others (Carlin 2006, 99–103, 113; Gaines 1988, 214–17; Williams 1997, 54–58).

Not unlike the angelic bicycle rider negotiating *Smile*'s conceptual and lyrical contours, Wilson himself turned, back and forth, between the heavens and the earth: a hero fallen among villains or a hero-cum-villain balanced precariously (as he later described it) on a seesaw (Was 1995). In the wake of his breakdown and release from the rigors of touring in late 1964, and alongside his introduction to the burgeoning Los Angeles underground, countercultural inspirations had penetrated the back of his mind, encouraging and enabling him to wonder and wander, creatively, as he had wished. The consequences, in musical terms, were and are evident: recordings that in terms of ambition and innovation matched the new standards being set by the Beatles, Bob Dylan, and others.

Yet the social, physical, emotional and psychological costs were also considerable. Family and personal relations were clearly strained; commercial and legal disputes between the group and Capitol Records scarcely helped. Creatively, the principals were pushing their own limits and making enormous efforts to realize their artistic ambitions: in words and music, rhythm and arrangement, melody, myth, and symbol. Psychedelically, and for reasons unlikely to be resolved, Wilson was not prepared—at least not adequately or fully—to go with the flow. Though he showed a genuine interest in many things countercultural, he appears to have lacked the time or energy to pursue or maintain them all (while opting for rhetoric over practice when it came to healthy living and diet). Though his autobiography has him telling his wife that LSD had enabled him to see God, some in his new circle felt that his satori was not theirs. Though he had told one of them that laughter was "one of the highest forms of divinity," others felt his humor was less childlike than childish: whatever his reading of Arthur Koestler or the title of his latest work in progress, it was unlikely to enable the kind of enlightened smile displayed by the Buddha at the end of Hermann Hesse's *Siddhartha* (Wilson 1991, 116–18; Vosse 1968). Nor did his chief collaborator on *Smile* see all aspects of Wilson's lifestyle and behavior at this time as beneficial. Parks, of course, had himself contributed to the extension of Wilson's circle of countercultural friends, but he ultimately lamented the extent to which they and their concerns intruded on their songwriting: "It wasn't just Brian and me in a room," he later recalled, "it was . . . all kinds of self-interested people pulling him in various directions" (Priore 2005, 113, 117; Carlin 2006, 111).

One direction synonymous with both the counterculture and psyche-delia was posted on the destination board of the celebrated bus carry-ing author (and early LSD adept) Ken Kesey's merry pranksters in Tom Wolfe's *The Electric Kool-Aid Acid Test* (1968): *further* (or, as it was mis-spelled, "furthur"—see Wolfe 1968, 61; Torgoff 2004, 89–92, 113–18). Through *Pet Sounds* and on to *Smile*, Brian Wilson went further. The trip was, in many ways, an act of faith—an errand into the wilderness, or at least the Wild West—and his accounts have often emphasized how feel-ings of spirituality provided guidance en route; both Tony Asher and Van Dyke Parks have offered variations on this theme. *Pet Sounds* and *Smile* are each in their own way explorations of belief. One of Parks's lines in "Wonderful"—"farther down the path was a mystery"—is in this sense a description of a child's errand, an invitation to a nascent curiosity, and a punning appeal to the Almighty for guidance. But as the line and the song also imply, if the destination is unknown, the journey entails risk—a fall in which the harvest may be lost. Elsewhere, the corn being embraced (and allusively blessed) in "Cabin Essence" may wave and nourish, but the hovering crow suggests otherwise. If these songs invoke Greek myth rather than Christian authority or American poetic epic, moreover, the mysteries involved only provide for the corn maiden's return at great cost: woe betide those who take the seeds.

Wilson, it seems, himself appealed to yet another spiritual authority to gauge the changes involved, and the chances being taken, in their col-lective journey toward *Smile*. "All of us," the *I Ching* told him according to Michael Vosse, had been brought "together to . . . involve ourselves in a creative project" (of which *Smile* was the centerpiece) but "everything was going to collapse later." In Wilson's casting, however, "something else" lay beyond for all involved: that most distinctively American of ex-periences, the second chance to recoup one's bad luck or atone for one's failings (Carlin 2006, 80–81; Vosse 1968). Almost forty years further on, in his reflections on *Smile*'s pivotal "Surf's Up," songwriter Jimmy Webb felt the stakes had been higher, the voyage into the mystic more apoca-lyptic, and the happy ending less assured for one and all. Here, he told *Smile* documentary-maker David Leaf in 2005, was "a premonition of what was going to happen to our generation and . . . to our music—that some great tragedy that we could absolutely not imagine was about to befall our world." "Surf's Up," he went on, "seem[s] to say, watch out, this is not gonna last" (Leaf 2005).

NOTES FOR CHAPTER 6

1. In addition to the published sources cited, this chapter draws on a number of interviews with individuals involved in or witness to Brian Wilson's life and work during the period covered. Among others, I remain particularly indebted to David Anderle, Danny Hutton, Terry Melcher, Tom Nolan, Van Dyke Parks, Paul Jay Robbins, and Paul Williams for sharing their recollections. None of the interviewees, of course, are responsible for the readings advanced here, or for any factual errors.

2. Such links are considered tenuous by Walker 2006, xv–xvi.

3. In his ghosted memoir, Wilson implies that he may have met Parks (or at least heard of him) via a mutual friend as early as December 1964. See Wilson 1991, 104–5.

4. This is *not* to claim that by this time Sunset Strip clubs practiced racially exclusive or preferential policies vis-à-vis performers. As Domenic Priore has noted, the club scene was gradually desegregated during the 1950s, and by the 1960s any number of African American and Latino artists (as well as acts from other ethnic backgrounds) appeared, working in many musical genres, notably soul and jazz. The comparison being made here deals with tendencies and comparisons, and is restricted to the new generation of groups performing on Sunset Strip at this time. See Priore 2007, 31–34, 276–83.

5. Sources are inconsistent on the precise time at which Asher first met Wilson. Peter Carlin dates their initial get-together as early as the start of 1963, when both men happened to be working at the Western studios in Hollywood, not long after the Beach Boys had begun recording there. While the location is confirmed by Asher and other accounts, most date the first meeting to 1965, though more precise timings vary. It may be that prior to their studio meeting, Asher and Wilson both attended one or more get-togethers with Loren Schwartz at some point from late 1964 onward, but this is unclear. See Leaf 1996, 36–37; White 1994, 255–56; Abbott 2001, 39; Carlin 2006, 76; Gaines 1988, 173–74; Wilson 1991, 131; Badman 2004, 104.

SEVEN | Good Reverberations

PHILIP LAMBERT

THE STORY OF THE RECORDING and production of "Good Vibrations"—one of Brian Wilson's singular achievements, and the Beach Boys' most important and influential single—is by now a rock legend. The song began as a collaboration between Brian and lyricist Tony Asher in early 1966, when they were working on *Pet Sounds*, but was abandoned until after the album was finished in the spring. By the time the single was released in October, the lyrics had been revised by Mike Love, and the song had traveled an exploratory journey through at least twenty-five recording sessions in four different studios, amassing fifty thousand dollars of recording expenses (see Granata 2003, 112–14; Badman 2004, 117–48; Priore 2005, 53–56; Lambert 2007, 254–60). It had also evolved from a Motown-flavored rocker to a Brian Wilson signature, with shifting moods and tempos, varieties of instrumental colors and vocal textures, and a range of musical invention befitting the nickname bestowed on it by its primary creator, "pocket symphony."

But what happened to "Good Vibrations" after 1966? More than any other Beach Boys song, it continued to evolve, over decades of live performances, and in the hands of hundreds of cover artists. It also became, almost forty years later, the finale of Brian's resurrection of *Smile*, the legendary unfinished follow-up to *Pet Sounds*, featuring Asher's original lyric. This essay explores these various follow-up versions—by the Beach Boys, by the Brian Wilson band, and by others—as a means of learning more about the song itself. Arrangements for live performance highlighted its most distinctive and appealing features. At the same time, cover versions either paid tribute through imitation or brought out aspects of the original that were subtle, at best, possibly well-hidden beneath a veneer of vocal harmonies and sonic panoramas. The most interesting new renditions offer valuable insights into not only the essence of the original song—the road map of melody, lyric, and chords—but also the myriad ingenuities of Brian Wilson's 1966 arrangement and recording. The song seems to invite rehearings and reinterpretations, like a masterful painting that yields new secrets upon repeated viewings. It set off tremors across the cultural landscape when it was first released, and it has continued to reverberate ever since.

Elsewhere (Lambert 2007, 255–58) I have described the original version of the song as an interrupted verse-chorus form:[1]

verse 1	0:00	("I, I love the colorful clothes you wear . . .")
chorus 1	0:25	("I'm pickin' up good vibrations . . .")
verse 2	0:51	("Close my eyes . . .")
chorus 2	1:16	("I'm pickin' up good vibrations . . .")
"dream sequence"		
1. ascent	1:42	(instrumental vamp, then "I don't know where . . .")
2. meditation	2:14	(instrumental phrase, then "Gotta keep those lovin' good . . .")
chorus 3	2:57	("Good, good, good, good vibrations . . .")
fugato	3:13	("na-na-na-na-na, na na na . . .")
ending	3:27	(cello triplets, electro-theremin)

The opening verse-chorus pairs present a distinctive sound-world of ethereal instrumental sounds mashed together with bop-bop vocal harmonies and R & B–flavored backing rhythms, portraying the "vibrations" two people can share and experience but never really explain. After the second chorus we begin to be transported into that other world, through a "dream sequence" that begins with a vamp in tack piano and electro-theremin, as if in extraterrestrial "ascent." When a vocal phrase eventually enters, the lyric says it all: "I don't know where but she sends me there." That leads into the second part of the dream sequence, and the quietest part of the song, a simple "meditation" beginning with a slower organ phrase and followed by several vocal phrases repeating the lyric "Gotta keep those lovin' good, vibrations a-happenin' with her." At this point we're fully resident in the alternate universe, floating with the repeating vocal phrases and then a soaring, lazy tune in the harmonica. The reverie comes to an end, however, with a big vocal "ah" and a return to the chorus material and tempo. Soon we hear the iconic cello triplets, and then still another ethereal moment, a choral "fugato" offering a vision of angelic harmony. The song ends with a return of the cello triplets and electro-theremin, fading away but promising never to fade from memory.

It's easy to appreciate the impact of "Good Vibrations" on listeners in the mid-1960s who were actively seeking alternative experiences, artistic and otherwise. Despite tempo fluctuations likely to confound any attempts to dance along, at least in any traditional way, the song reached the top of the charts in America and Britain and became the Beach Boys' first million-selling single. And yet it is more than just a cultural phenomenon; it's also a resounding success as a work of art, a rich tapestry of masterfully crafted, interrelated musical ideas. After months of experimentation and tinkering, Brian found the perfect way to sequence and highlight the musical modules that he and his collaborators had finally developed. To string together such disparate threads—a verse and chorus in one style, a meditation and fugato in another, supported by sound colors ranging from cello to tack piano to electro-theremin—is a musical high-wire act, and Brian stays up and balanced for the entire three minutes and thirty-eight seconds, without the slightest stumble. In his words, "It was at Columbia [Studios]. I remember I had it right in the sack. I could just feel it when I dubbed it down, made the final mix down to mono. It was a feeling of power; it was a rush. A feeling of exaltation. Artistic beauty" (Leaf 1993, 38).

Of course, the first order of business after the recording was released was to get the song onto the stage, no easy task for such a pure studio creation. The Beach Boys' earliest concert version, which was officially released on the bonus disc of the 1993 *Good Vibrations* boxed set, was recorded in a concert at Michigan State University, just twelve days after the release of the single, before it had hit the charts. (Mike Love announces to the audience, "It's the second night we've tried it.") The Boys do manage to preserve the tone of the verses and choruses, but the vocal harmonies throughout are naturally thinner than they are in the studio recording, and the backing track is missing the cello, whose notes are played by guitars, and the harmonica, whose prominent melody at the

end of the meditation section is absent altogether. Another big difference is the ending—always a concern for live versions of studio recordings that fade out at the end—and in this instance they basically just stop
playing. The audience applauds appreciatively but seem a bit befuddled
by what they've heard, with no sense of an impending phenomenon.

In subsequent live versions, however, the Beach Boys do more than
just adapt a studio recording for live performance; they begin to develop and enhance the material in different and provocative ways. We
first hear this in August of the following year, in the recordings made in
Hawaii for an ill-fated live album provisionally known as *Lei'd in Hawaii*,
and in recordings made in December 1968 for the *Live in London* album
(released in the UK in 1970, in the United States in 1976). Live recordings of later years, such as those on the *In Concert* album of 1973, the *Good
Timin': Live at Knebworth* album recorded in 1980, and other more recent
recordings that have surfaced by audience members and in online post-
ings, offer still other perspectives on the original song. Appendix 7.1 at
the end of this chapter lists some prominent and generally accessible
Beach Boys recordings of "Good Vibrations" from the last five decades.
A chronological survey of these tracks offers an informative overview of
the song's evolution.

Many details are altered over the course of this history. The instrumentation naturally varies according to the available musicians and other circumstances, and the group ultimately does come up with a concert
ending worthy of the music that precedes it. But by far the most extensive changes occur in the meditation section, as the group gradually
begins to savor and flavor an exquisite moment in the song, and to call
upon the audience to join the transcendence. In the original recording
the meditation is six phrases:

1. An introductory phrase in the organ, establishing the main chord
   progression that will continue to repeat as vocal lines are added
   above. (2:14)
2. A unison vocal phrase ("Gotta keep . . .") in the low range (example 7.1a). (2:21)
3. The same vocal phrase again, enhanced by an upper octave dou-
   bling and harmonized in thirds and sixths (example 7.1ab). (2:29)
4. A phrase that begins like the previous one but quickly fades out
   while the hovering harmonica melody (example 7.2) emerges.
   (2:36)

5. A solo statement of the harmonica melody. (2:43)
6. A simple final chord supporting the final harmonica note, leading up to the big vocal "ah" preparing the return of the chorus. (2:50)

For the Hawaii rehearsal and performance in August 1967, however, Brian Wilson was on hand to add a new melody in thirds (example 7.1c), which enters in phrase 5 in place of the harmonica and expands the meditation section to seven phrases. The new line is essentially an embellishment of the harmonica melody (compare the lower notes in example 7.1c with example 7.2), evoking the doo-wop sensibility of some of the cuts on the *Smiley Smile* album that the group had been recording that summer (e.g., "With Me Tonight"). This new layer, and the seven-phrase meditation, remained part of the song in performances in Washington, D.C., in November 1967 (although not in Detroit two days earlier), and in the London performances in December 1968 that were recorded for the *Live in London* album (which includes additional, apparently improvised, vocal flourishes and an organ playing the harmonica melody in the background).

By the early 1970s the group had expanded the meditation to ten phrases by adding some extra vamping on the "Gotta keep" lines (example 7.1ab), before concluding with two passes through the doo-wop line (example 7.1c). On the 1973 *In Concert* album, for example, the "Gotta keep" vamp occupies phrases 3–7, followed by two phrases of doo-wop and then the usual retransitional phrase (equivalent to the original phrase 6). But by the early 1980s the meditation section had taken on the character of a revival meeting ("God Vibrations"?), with copious vamps and melodic combinations, and Mike asking various audience groupings to sing along ("Just the ladies!"), ballooning the overall length to seventeen phrases in the 1980 Knebworth performance (it was sixteen phrases in Long Beach in 1981, and in Seattle in 1983). The lead singer would promote a communal contrapuntal celebration, exhorting the audience to continue repeating the "Gotta keep" phrases while the Beach Boys added their doo-wop lines above ("You keep that up and we'll do some other stuff!").

Since the early 1980s the meditation has shrunk, first down to twelve or thirteen phrases (in 1984, 1985, 1990, 1991, and 1994), later to nine (1995), and eventually back to six, dropping the vamping and doo-wop lines altogether (2003, 2007). The Beach Boys' fiftieth anniversary tour in 2012, reuniting Brian Wilson, Mike Love, Al Jardine, David Marks, and

Example 7.1: Vocal parts (at pitch) in the "Meditation" section, with a new line (c) added in Hawaii in 1967 (*Hawthorne, CA*, 2001; *Good Vibrations* CD single, 2006)

Example 7.2: Harmonica melody in the "Meditation" section

Example 7.3: Vocal parts (at pitch) in the "Meditation" section, with a vocal strand (c) heard in session outtakes from 1966 and revived in *Brian Wilson Presents Smile* (2004)

Bruce Johnston, also kept it at the original six. Audience members were still encouraged to join in, but the earlier sense of communal reverie had been decidedly moderated.

In Brian Wilson's performances of "Good Vibrations" with his own band in recent years, his treatment of the meditation material has followed a similar trajectory. Appendix 7.2 lists some available highlights of performances of this song by the Brian Wilson Band since his return to the concert stage in the late 1990s. At first, through 2002, he simply preserved the six meditation phrases as in the original. But when the song became the finale of *Smile* in 2004, it acquired not only Tony Asher's original verse lyrics but also some additional material in the middle that expanded the meditation to ten phrases. This new meditation unfolds initially like the old one, with an introductory organ phrase followed by two vocal phrases and two harmonica phrases, but then at phrase 6 we hear a new vocal phrase, "hum-be-dum, hum-be-dum-(whoa)," resuscitated from the 1966 session tapes (example 7.3c).[2] Phrases 6 and 7 feature the "hum-be-dum" parts, and then phrases 8 and 9 combine "hum-be-dum" with the "gotta keep" melody in enchanting counterpoint (example 7.3abc). Finally phrase 10 brings the sequence to a close by just holding the final chord as in phrase 6 of the original. Except for time-constrained television performances, the Brian Wilson Band performed this ten-phrase version from 2004 until 2011. In 2013, however, apparently influenced by their experience with the reunited Beach Boys the previous year, the band dropped the "hum-be-dum" layer and returned to the original, less contrapuntal, six-phrase meditation.

The Brian Wilson version also has a unique concert ending, with additional vocals and big blasts of chord pairs leading to a sustained final chord. When "Good Vibrations" concludes a set (or the entire *Smile* suite) within a concert, providing the final sounds just before intermission or encores, the new spirited ending helps frame the whole event as much as the individual song. Although this new ending is inconsistent with the more subdued tone of the original recording, it nonetheless lends a celebratory tone to the occasion, welcomed by so many audience members who are there to pay homage to one of their longtime idols. During "Good Vibrations" and throughout an evening of expert musical re-creations by a superb band, they are amply rewarded.

Other acts of homage in the nearly fifty years since "Good Vibrations" was released have been of a more artistic variety, if no less personal.

Versions of the song by different artists began to appear in 1967 and have continued up to the present day, displaying a wide variety of stylistic imprints and artistic agendas. Appendix 7.3 lists some of the more prominent and accessible versions of "Good Vibrations" that have been released, on vinyl, on compact disc, and online. They reveal not only the vast shadow cast by the original song but also a wealth of opportunities to examine and explore the song's various essences.

In general usage, the concept of a "cover version" applies to anything from the most scrupulous copy to the most free-spirited deconstruction, including every tribute, enhancement, arrangement, send-up, and stylistic reimagining in between. Deena Weinstein (1998), Dai Griffiths (2002), Kurt Bailey (2003), George Plasketes (2005), and Kurt Mosser (no date) have attempted to bring order to this panoply, offering valuable perspectives that can be applied to the spectrum of "Good Vibrations" covers. Covers also raise questions about the nature of the original source, the primary text: is it the song itself—the road map of melody, lyric, and chords—or is it the original arrangement, as recorded in Los Angeles in 1966? This is not a question normally asked in studies of classic popular songs (e.g., Shirley 1997; Magee 2000; Kaskowitz 2013), but for a hit single in the era of rock auteurs, the circumstances are different. For the most part, it is difficult to separate "Good Vibrations" the *song* from "Good Vibrations" the *recording*.

On the literal end of the cover spectrum are simple *replicas* of the original song—attempts to preserve not only the song's original structure and sound, but also every detail of instrumentation and vocal nuance. A copycat's intentions may not be entirely honorable—as when white musicians copied blacks in the fifties, or when record companies release replicas by studio musicians as a way of circumventing artists' royalties (Weinstein 2003, 138–41; Bailey 2003, 152)—but tribute bands usually mean no harm. The recording of "Good Vibrations" by Papa Doo Run Run (1985) is an impressive act of reproduction, benefiting, no doubt, from the vocal contributions of Mike Love, Dean Torrence (of Jan and Dean), and Jeffrey Foskett (eventually a key member of the Brian Wilson Band). Likewise, the replicas by longtime Beach Boys band members Chris Farmer (2008) and Adrian Baker (2010) are understandably precise. Some of the other replica attempts listed in appendix 7.3 are also pretty close to the original, notably those by the Vanguards (1968), Frank Schöbel (1980), Studio 99 (1999), Landys and Chums

(2000), Phil Keaggy (2002), and Rangzen (2008). Perhaps the most notorious replica of "Good Vibrations" appeared alongside copies of songs
by Lennon and McCartney, Hendrix, and Dylan on Todd Rundgren's
Faithful album (1976). For puzzled listeners who wonder why a gifted
musician would expend so much effort to re-create sophisticated works
of other artists, Bailey explains:

> The irony here is that [Rundgren's] utilization of studio technol-
> ogy and personal virtuosity—normally tools for maximizing self-
> expression—produce a work free of personal commitment. . . . "Good
> Vibrations" by Rundgren becomes indistinguishable from "Good
> Vibrations" by the Beach Boys, and thus the technology that allowed
> Brian Wilson to create his pop masterpiece renders the achievement
> meaningless. (Bailey 2003, 153–54)

Well, Rundgren's version isn't exactly "indistinguishable" from the
original—only Beach Boys can sing like Beach Boys—but it is an impressive feat of mimicry. And yet it leaves listeners wondering why they would
choose to hear this version if the original is just as (probably more easily)
accessible.

Other covers of "Good Vibrations" differ only in small ways from the
original—"near replicas," perhaps. A live recording by Adrian Baker with
his group Gidea Park (1985) follows the standard live-performance format, including the Mike Love–style audience sing-alongs and a record-
setting twenty-five-phrase meditation. The live recording by Al Jardine,
Family, and Friends (1999) also mostly conforms. The version by the
Sunny Boys (2007), more influenced by the Brian Wilson Band, begins
with an expanding voice-leading wedge heard in some of the *Smile* recordings (and used in *Brian Wilson Presents Smile* at 4:17 of "Heroes and
Villains," beginning a transition), and includes the "Hum-be-dum" layer
(example 7.3c) in the meditation. Other attempted replicas, such as the
Finnish version by Ernos (1968), are sincere but substantially inaccurate.

As we move along the cover-version spectrum—as new recordings di-
verge from the original in ever greater degrees—female voices begin
to appear. If used only in the backing vocals, as in the versions by the
Cowsills (1969) and by Fred Mollin and the Blue Sea Band (2005), these
different vocal timbres just add a bit of richness to the backing track. But
when females sing the lead in a love song originally sung from a guy to a

girl, the result can take on other meanings (Griffiths 2002 explores this idea). Ann and Nancy Wilson of Heart don't change pronouns or any other words in their versions of "Good Vibrations" (2001, 2006), inviting questions about gender roles or homosexual implications. A women's quartet, the Lady Killers (2009), and Brian Wilson's daughters, singing with Chynna Phillips as Wilson Phillips (2012), do the same. Other female leads revise the lyric as a love song to a guy, requiring not only pronoun switches but also possibly a rethinking of various other words or phrases. For a woman singing about a man in the first verse, can the wind "lift *his* perfume through the air"? Apparently, the ladies of the Anita Kerr Singers (1973) and of Todos (2010) do have perfumed boyfriends. The Sugar Beats (1999) avoid the issue by removing the pronoun altogether, singing of a "wind that lifts *the* perfume through the air." Others invoke different airborne essences: for Jonna Gault (1968), the wind "lifts his whisper through the air"; for Nancy Dee (1987), the wind "lifts his after shave through the air." Kate Dimbleby (2000) avoids both the gender-specific pronoun and the gender-connoting fragrance, singing of a "wind that lifts your magic through the air."

Purely instrumental versions of "Good Vibrations"—or arrangements in which an instrument plays the lead melody over backing vocals—can be close to the literal end of the spectrum, if played in the same style, by roughly the same type of band. In the recordings by the Beach Boys Tribute Band (2005) and by Dan Rudin (2008), a guitar or saxophone simply stands in for the lead vocalist; otherwise, the music is a close imitation, including backing vocals. The lead guitar in the Shadows' (1974) version, however, is but one of a group of guitars (overdubs, presumably) who replace all the original vocal lines with guitar sounds. Saxophonist Steve Douglas, a member of the legendary "wrecking crew" of Los Angeles studio musicians and a frequent presence on Beach Boys records, takes the same approach in his arrangement of the song (1969), rendering vocal lines on various saxophones. And Charlie McCoy (1968) does this with a full complement of harmonicas over a standard backing band. The presence of the bass harmonica in this version may remind listeners of a distinctive timbre from *Pet Sounds* (e.g., in "I Know There's an Answer"). Meanwhile, the prominence of Charlie McCoy's lead harmonica connects to an important element of "Good Vibrations" itself: as if emboldened by its solo turn at the end of the meditation, the instrument has taken over.

Such connections between cover and source are exactly what lend distinction to the versions of "Good Vibrations" lying along the central part of the cover-song spectrum, where choices of instrumentation and style differ more substantially from the original recording. Ultimately, a cover version works best when it highlights and explores a particular feature of a song, perhaps realizing a potential that may not have been readily apparent in prior listenings. In his recording of "My Favorite Things," John Coltrane finds jazz elements of Richard Rodgers's melody that fans of *The Sound of Music* probably hadn't imagined. Jimi Hendrix's electrified take on Dylan's "All Along the Watchtower" exploits and sharpens a latent hard edge in the song. In the case of "Good Vibrations," the original recording is already multifarious enough to send an admiring artist in many different directions; perhaps that's one reason the song has been so frequently covered. Like Charlie McCoy's harmonica, a fixation on one element can inspire a complete arrangement.

So versions of "Good Vibrations" in a soft-rock style can be rationalized as exploring potentialities already inherent in the original arrangement (as it is in many Beach Boys songs). At the same time, however, there's no reasonable defense for the changes in the song's form heard in the extremely mellow recordings by Floyd Cramer (1967), Jonna Gault and Her Symphonopop Scene (1968), and Kenny Rogers and the First Edition (1974). At least the soft-core arrangement for an Elvis imitator, the King (2000), doesn't lop off a verse or the entire meditation section.

Adaptations into other popular idioms test the limits of what the original material can withstand. Silver Blue (1978) finds fertile disco riffs in the song's verse and chorus; Psychic TV (1986) and AntiProduct (2009) explore its punk potential; FM (1987) and the Johansson Brothers (1994) interpret it as a straight-ahead rocker; and Nancy Dee (1987), Nina Hagen (1991), and Aika Ohno (2002) see it as a vehicle for a synthpop groove, an aspect further explored in the electronica of Monkey's Uncle (2001) and Les Fradkin and Get Wet (2004). The original element most commonly highlighted in these versions is the hard-driving cello triplets in the chorus backing track, given special prominence in the final fade; they dominate the versions by Psychic TV and FM. But let's not forget that Brian described his original conception of the song as "something that was R and B but had a taste of modern, avant-garde R and B to it" (Preiss 1979, 57). This element is especially highlighted in the instrumental cover by the Electric Piano Playground (1967), which sounds like the backing track for an R & B version, and in both the vocals and instrumentals of the rendition by the Chambers Brothers (1973).

If these versions draw subtle or obscure elements from the original song, the arrangements of "Good Vibrations" for a cappella groups highlight its most conspicuous and alluring aspects. The A. Y. U. Quartet (2001) imagines the song as pure doo-wop—standing on a street corner in the Bronx on a moonlit summer evening. The singers in this group can't be bothered with the dissipated energy of the meditation or the artiness of the fugato. The Mighty Echoes (2005) and Bläck Fööss (2005) also bring out the doo-wop aspect but adapt the entire song, including six-phrase meditations. A mixed-voice octet, Voces8 (2010), aims for more of a "vocal jazz" style, reminiscent of the Swingle Singers. The Vocal Six (2006) even add some extra counterpoint in the fugato. Some of the other a cappella arrangements, however, aim for a more complete trans-lation of every aspect of the song into the vocal medium. Mouth noises imitate percussion sounds, and vocal imitations of the electro-theremin by members of the King's Singers (1993), 17th Avenue All-Stars (2006), and Vocal Spectrum (2008) sound remarkably close to the actual instru-ment. In these latter three renditions especially, the purely choral ren-dering of the organ part in the meditation, accompanying the original Beach Boys vocal parts and imitations of the harmonica melody by a vocalist (King's Singers, Vocal Spectrum) or a whistler (17th Avenue All-Stars), lend distinction and an almost reverential gravitas to the song's centerpiece. It's the only instance, among all the "Good Vibrations" cov-ers, of a reconception challenging the eminence of the original.

As vocal groups shift from doo-wop singing in the ascent to sounds that seem to belong in a house of worship in the meditation, they also accentuate a particularly artful moment in the song's structure. We get the same sense a short time later, in the fugato. The mere presence of the cello in the choruses, and with special prominence in the outro, also adds "classical" ambience. So an adaptation for symphony orches-tra isn't that much of a stretch. There are, of course, the unavoidable versions designed for doctor's offices or torture chambers (Hollyridge Strings [1967], 101 Strings [1990], New Symphonic Orchestra [1999], Alex Bollard and the London Starlight Orchestra [2009], Starborne Strings [2012]), but the arrangement for the Royal Philharmonic Orchestra (1998) probes the song's artfulness in compelling ways. Brass instruments take the place of voices throughout, with strings contributing chords and theremin countermelodies; the fugato sounds like it could have been originally conceived for brass choir. An arrangement for the International Pop Proms Orchestra and Singers (2010) also has its artful charms. The version by the Hampton String Quartet (1988), on the other hand, proves that the "classical" angle can only take you so far. Rather than finding common ground between the medium and the source—as in the Kronos Quartet's arrangements of Hendrix or Monk— this arrangement asks Brian Wilson melodies to do things they don't want to do. A mixed-voice a cappella group, Les voix animées (2013), has similar difficulties—or perhaps they're just too square, being forced by the music to do things they don't want to do. The adaptation for oboe, cello, and harp by Trio Rococo (1996) finds just the right balance of classic instrumental timbres with vernacular melodies and rhythms, as do the handbells of Music City Bronze (2010).

And a different arrangement of "Good Vibrations" by the Royal Philharmonic Orchestra (1993) brings out still another element of the original song: its eclecticism. A rendering of verse and chorus material with constantly changing instrumental combinations, including a slide whistle re-creating the electro-theremin part, and a meditation section that moves from a reverent brass choir to honky-tonk solos by clarinet and piano, somehow seems appropriate as an adaptation of an original recording that combines electro-theremin, tack piano, church organ, harmonica, and cello with the instruments of a standard rock band. Other oddball instrumentations yield similar revelations: the Four Bags (2005) adapt the song for accordion, trombone, guitar, and soprano saxophone; the Durham Ukulele Orchestra (2011) arranges it for three ukuleles, electric bass, celesta, and tambourine (plus vocals); and the Ian English Boodlum Band (2013) sends it up with ukulele, electric piano, "phonofiddle" (a bowed cello-like instrument with a flared metal bell sticking out the side), and Spike Jones–style percussion.

Of course, instrumental variety is just one aspect of the song's modularity—one reason that the ascent, for example, stands apart from the meditation. Some arrangements of "Good Vibrations" draw attention to modularity itself, by suggesting alternative orderings of modules. The version by Jonna Gault and Her Symphonopop Scene (1968) uses a brassy version of the fugato as an introduction, which returns, with added vocals, immediately after the meditation, skipping the chorus entirely. Lincoln Mayorga's arrangement (1968) returns to the verse after the fugato, fading on the final dominant harmony. A version for guitar and strings by the Freeway Philharmonic (1995) begins, after a breezy guitar vamp, with a rendering of the fugato and a chorus preceding the first verse. Colin Clary and the Magogs and Friends (2005) practice modularity in the extreme: after a few bars from the unrelated song "Oh, How I Hate to Get Up in the Morning" as an introduction, the modules of "Good Vibrations" are presented almost in reverse order, with the fugato and ending triplets near the beginning and the verses and choruses at the end.

Well, that's certainly overdoing it, but it's a point well taken. It's also an acknowledgment of the original song's debt to 1960s sensibilities and psychedelia. (Surely more than one listener has reacted to the reverse rendition with a comment something like, "What were they smokin'?") The cover by Fleshhouse (1993) evokes the era as well, with eerie sounds and general weirdness, as if the spirit of the theremin has infiltrated the entire song. Indeed, one of Brian Wilson's earliest ideas for "Good Vibrations" included an eerie atonal interlude, which is reincorporated in the generally spooky cover by the Secret Chiefs 3 (1998).[3] The heavily electronic cover by Xenovibes (2009) also has its moments of sonic waviness. And yet, how many other songs could accept full-on psychedelic assaults without losing their innocence? After listening to some of the harsher reinterpretations, listeners may want to cleanse their aural palates, if not their souls, with the arrangements for children's chorus by the Langley Schools Music Project (1976), for "music box" by Bernard Cade (2006), and for (synthesized) chiming percussion by Baby Deli Music (2010). Then later, after dark, perhaps they'll be open to appreciating the song's sensuality, as exploited by Reg Presley of the Troggs (1974), who revises the first line of the original lyric, "I, I love the colorful clothes she wears," as "I, I like the clothes she almost wears" and gets steamier from there.

What stylistic or interpretive reimaginings can the song *not* accommodate? Hugo Montenegro (1969) makes a weak case for an adaptation in Latin rhythms (with straight eighths), Little Joe Shaver and Devil Dog (1976) searches in vain for country-and-western possibilities, Legendary Acid Casualties (2000) makes a tepid attempt at a "Good Vibrations" rap, and the Bluegrass Tribute Band (2004) reminds us that Brian Wilson knew when to use a banjo, and when not to. But these shortfalls come as no surprise: nothing in the original recording suggested possibilities in any of these directions. On the other hand, the original "Good Vibrations" doesn't have overt jazz features either, and yet several artists have found in the song ample starting points for jazz reharmonizations and improvisations. The earliest jazz adaptations are the most free-form: the players of Young-Holt Unlimited (1967) mostly just improvise over the chorus chord progression, and the Gordon Beck Quartet (1968) uses the verse and chorus as the basis for a jazz fantasy, in the spirit the "free jazz" movement. Later jazz-flavored versions follow the original more closely, including an airy arrangement for jazz flute and band (including vocals) by Steve Kujala (1992), an up-tempo big-band version by Eric Winstone and His Orchestra (1997), and a harmonically enriched reinterpretation by a trio of two violas and Chapman stick calling themselves the Unbande (2008). The jazzy solo renderings by guitarist Michael Bristow (1999) and pianist Marius Nordal (2009) also find plenty to work with, even without the possibilities for extensive contrapuntal layering and timbral variety. The harmonic richness of Nordal's arrangement is particularly revelatory. It's easy to conclude from these adaptations that Brian Wilson's early self-study in jazz harmony, mostly from absorbing Four Freshmen records, left an indelible imprint that is likely to be found in many of his songs, whether above or just beneath the musical surface.

The free-form jazz of the Gordon Beck Quartet, or the radical reorganization of Colin Clary and the Magogs and Friends, or the stylistic implosion of Legendary Acid Casualties, takes us to the far end of the cover-song spectrum, where minimal elements of the original recording are preserved. To travel from one end to the other is to become more acutely aware of exactly what Brian Wilson's vibrations are, and exactly why they're "good." For the creator himself, they were good because of what they taught him about the development of a musical idea, and about modular composition, soon to be a principal aspect of his next project, *Smile.* For the rest of us, they're good because of the way they dazzle us and transfix us and lift us up off our seat, then reverberate far and wide, across decades and styles and artistic sensibilities.

NOTES FOR CHAPTER 7

1. A recording of this original version of the song and many of the other recordings discussed in this essay are collected together in the Spotify playlist "Good Reverberations," http://open.spotify.com/user/lambertessay/playlist/0 Iin5V28AerGeN9foQS98.

2. The original recordings of the "Hum-be-dum" material (example 3c)

can be heard at 6:23 of the "Sessions" track on the 1993 *Good Vibrations* boxed set bonus disc; the "Various Sessions" track of the CD single reissue of 2006; and the "Good Vibrations Session Highlights" track on the 2011 *Smile Sessions* compilation.

3. The atonal interlude can be heard at 2:31 of the "early take" of the song on a bonus track of the *Smiley Smile / Wild Honey* twofer CD.

Appendix 7.1. Selected Beach Boys performances of "Good Vibrations," 1966–2013

(*on Spotify playlist "Good Reverberations")

Year	Date	Album/source
1966	10/10	*single released, b/w "Let's Go Away For Awhile"
	10/22	live at Michigan State University (*Good Vibrations* boxed set bonus disc, 1993)
1967	8/25	*rehearsal in Hawaii (*Hawthorne* CD, 2001; *Good Vibrations* CD single, 2006)
	8/25	live in Hawaii (*Rarities* bootleg, vol. 12)
	9/18	*Smiley Smile* released: *"Good Vibrations" is the first cut on side B
	11/17	live in Detroit (http://www.youtube.com/watch?v=eMbI-SVtM3I [30:16])
	11/19	live in Washington, D. C. (*Rarities* bootleg, vol. 10)
1968	10/13	live on the Ed Sullivan Show (*Rarities* bootleg, vol. 9; *Video Hits* DVD)
	12/1	live in London (*Rarities* bootleg, vol. 11)
	12/8	*rehearsal in London (*Endless Harmony* soundtrack album, 1998)
	12/8	*live in London (*Rarities* bootleg, vol. 11; released with studio enhancements on *Live In London*, 1970)
1970	10/3	live at Big Sur, California (*Rarities* bootleg, vol. 12)
1972–73		*live performance released on *In Concert* album, 1973
1974	12/31	live performance on New Year's Rockin' Eve (television broadcast)
1976		live performance released on *Good Vibrations Tour* DVD, 2004
1979	4/27	live performance on Midnight Special (http://www.youtube.com/watch?v=ROebOHVIhZw)
1980	6/21	*live in Knebworth, England (released on CD and DVD, 2002)
1981		live in Long Beach, California (http://www.youtube.com/watch?v=-cTjUQ8NqKQ)
1983	5/22	live in Seattle (http://www.youtube.com/watch?v=i5uA58mO6to [1:16:51])
1984	7/4	live in Washington, D. C. (http://www.youtube.com/watch?v=ugjns5MFl-4 [36:56])
1985	7/13	live performance in Philadelphia for Live Aid 85 (http://www.youtube.com/watch?v=pf6vVtocLnM)
	9/22	live performance in Champaign, Ill. for Farm Aid (http://www.youtube.com/watch?v=VbwKIzqywlU)
1990	Sept.	live in Lake Tahoe, Nev. (http://www.youtube.com/watch?v=FB8nqS45n9E)
1991	Nov.	live in Japan (http://www.youtube.com/watch?v=SnstvDVpolY [34:41])
1994	5/12	live in Berlin (concert video)
1995	7/4	live in Philadelphia (http://www.youtube.com/watch?v=5UuohqFpFsA [48:32])
2003	July	live in Esher, England (audience recording)
2007		live in Gilford, New Hampshire (http://www.youtube.com/watch?v=HRb2BwMRorY)
2012		*The Beach Boys Live: 50th Anniversary Tour (released on CD and DVD)
2013	3/22	live in Macau (http://www.youtube.com/watch?v=VwZUKkZ633A)

Appendix 7.2. Selected performances of "Good Vibrations" by Brian Wilson, 1976–2013.

(*on Spotify playlist "Good Reverberations")

Year	Date	Album/source
1976	11/27	live on Saturday Night Live [just BW, accompanying himself on the piano] (*Rarities* bootleg, vol. 13; http://www.youtube.com/watch?v=Ydj86dfm-zA)
2000	April	live in Los Angeles (released on *Live At The Roxy* CD, 2000)
	9/24	live in Los Angeles (*Pet Sounds Symphonic Tour* bootleg)
2001		live performance released on *Brian Wilson On Tour* DVD, 2003
2002	Jan.	live in London (released on *Pet Sounds Live In London* DVD, 2002)
	6/3	live in London at the Queen's Jubilee concert (released on the *Party at the Palace* DVD, 2002)
2004	April	*Brian Wilson Presents Smile* released, with *"Good Vibrations" as the finale
	9/22	live on the Ellen show
2005	1/4	live on the Tonight Show
	2/11	live in Los Angeles at the MusiCares Person of the Year ceremony (released on DVD, 2007)
	6/26	live in Glastonbury (http://www.youtube.com/watch?v=YNqdrFf2EbA)
	7/2	live at Live8 in Germany (released on DVD, 2005)
	7/7	live in Spain (audience video)
2006	July	live in Australia (http://www.youtube.com/watch?v=t4uhdsDeosc)
	11/14	live in London for the UK Music Hall of Fame induction (http://www.youtube.com/watch?v=eHPWJIY_vko)
	11/22	live in New York (audience video)
2009	7/9	live in Bonn (http://www.youtube.com/watch?v=DsjXrXHT4hU)
2010	5/29	live in Scottsdale, Arizona (http://www.youtube.com/watch?v=GUIdvzwFQDs&list=PL9A59D55D1CE5656C)
2011	May	live on "Later... with Jools Holland," BBC (http://www.youtube.com/watch?v=BMPmxjFoxhc)
	6/17	live in Montreal (http://www.youtube.com/watch?v=_ETiJ4OKWbc)
	9/14	live in Birmingham, England (http://www.youtube.com/watch?v=m3lZgw5aP8Y)
2013	10/6	live in Bethlehem, Penn. (http://www.youtube.com/watch?v=xRnBZADbpbo)
	10/12	live in Westbury, N.Y. (http://www.youtube.com/watch?v=7T_KPWz2768)

Appendix 7.3. Selected versions of "Good Vibrations" by other artists.

(I = instrumental, I+ = instrumental with some background vocals, AC = *a cappella*; *on Spotify playlist "Good Reverberations")

Year	Artist(s)	Album/source
1967	*Electric Piano Playground (I)	Psychedelic Seeds
	Floyd Cramer (I+)	Here's What's Happening (http://www.youtube.com/watch?v=2hoU2W4idf4)
	*Hollyridge Strings (I)	Play the Beach Boys Song Book, Vol. 2
	*Young-Holt Unlimited (I)	The Beat Goes On
1968	Charlie McCoy (I)	The World Of Charlie McCoy
	Ernos [in Finnish as "Kaikki Hyvin"]	[single] (http://www.youtube.com/watch?v=QH8ouN3n23M)
	Gordon Beck Quartet (I)	Experiments With Pops
	*Jonna Gault and Her Symphonopop Scene	Watch Me
	*Lincoln Mayorga (I)	Sheffield S9
	*Vanguards	live recording
1969	Cowsills	The Cowsills In Concert
	*Hugo Montenegro	Good Vibrations
	Steve Douglas (I)	Reflections In a Golden Horn (http://www.youtube.com/watch?v=PLSpPvZqAsM)
1970	Gary Usher (I excerpt as part of medley)	Add Some Music to Your Day (released in 2001)
1973	*Anita Kerr Singers	My Colouring Book
	Chambers Brothers	Unbonded (http://www.youtube.com/watch?v=8x7e6ZctLaI)
1974	Kenny Rogers and the First Edition	Rollin' (http://www.youtube.com/watch?v=xpe2PdLdn5Y)
	*Shadows (I)	Rockin' With Curly Leads
	Troggs	[single] (http://www.youtube.com/watch?v=i_-3YmCaOdE)
1976	John Denver and Karen Carpenter	TV special (in medley + "Comin' Through The Rye") (http://www.youtube.com/watch?v=fJUIWYX8HlI)
	*Langley Schools Music Project	Innocence And Despair

Year	Artist(s)	Album/source
	Little Joe Shaver and Devil Dog	Sing the Hits of the Beach Boys
	*Todd Rundgren	Faithful
1977	*Glen Campbell	Rhinestone Cowboy In Concert [part of medley]
	P. K. and the Sound Explosion	The Beach Boys Songbook
1978	Silver Blue (I+)	[disco single] (http://www.youtube.com/watch?v=NlIEbIM2SEI)
1980	Frank Schöbel	Wir gehören zusammen
1985	*Adrian Baker with Gidea Park	Live in Concert
	Papa Doo Run Run	California Project (http://www.youtube.com/watch?v=ysUoiF8laY8)
1986	Psychic TV (Kundalini Mix)	The Magickal Mystery D Tour EP (http://www.youtube.com/watch?v=UOVAq-KSUqs)
1987	*FM	[single]
	Nancy Dee	[single]
1988	Hampton String Quartet (I)	What If Mozart Wrote "Born To Be Wild"
1989	*Oxygene (I)	16 Greatest Synthesizer Hits
1990	*101 Strings Orchestra	101 Strings Play Hits Made Famous by the Beach Boys
1991	Nina Hagen	Street (http://www.youtube.com/watch?v=1jdm9RaquCY)
1992	Steve Kujala (I+)	Arms Of Love (http://www.youtube.com/watch?v=LzSSJH9ny5U)
1993	Fleshhouse	Shut-Up Kitty: A Cyber-Based Covers Compilation (http://www.youtube.com/watch?v=U4MGJou7FZY)
	*King's Singers (AC)	Good Vibrations
	*Royal Philharmonic Orchestra (I)	Rock Dreams, Vol. 2
1994	*The Johansson Brothers	The Johansson Brothers
1995	*Freeway Philharmonic (I)	Sonic Detour
1996	*Jive Bunny and the Mastermixers	Beach Party
	Trio Rococo (I)	Friends (http://www.youtube.com/watch?v=7JTO9O1NL2Q)
1997	*Eric Winstone and His Orchestra (I)	Easy Going Sixties
1998	Royal Philharmonic Orchestra (I)	Symphonic Sounds: Music Of The Beach Boys [end of "Water Planet Suite"]

Year	Artist(s)	Album/source
	Secret Chiefs 3	Smiling Pets [covers compilation] (http://www.youtube.com/watch?v=I56Hmf7wKUY)
1999	Al Jardine, Family, and Friends	Live In Las Vegas
	Michael Bristow (I)	Ocean In A Box
	*New Symphonic Orchestra (I)	Plays the Beach Boys
	*Studio 99	The Beach Boys: A Tribute
	*Sugar Beats	Wild Thing
2000	Kate Dimbleby	Good Vibrations
	The King	Return To Splendor
	Landys And Chums	Net Sounds 3
	Legendary Acid Casualties	Net Sounds 3
2001	The A.Y.U. Quartet (AC)	Atomic Young Ultrasonics
	Heart, Jubilant Sykes, Boys Choir of Harlem	An All-Star Tribute To Brian Wilson (DVD)
	*Jim Horn (I+)	The Hit List
	Monkey's Uncle	In Bed With Brian Wilson (http://www.youtube.com/watch?v=_Kp4aECYLIQ)
2002	Aika Ohno	Hot Rod Beach Party (http://www.youtube.com/watch?v=KZXPyKzDckg)
	*Phil Keaggy	Making God Smile
2003	*Bläck Fööss (AC)	K-BF 33
	*Mike Hurst Orchestra (I)	Drivetime
2004	*Bluegrass Tribute Band (I)	Pickin' On the Beach Boys
	Les Fradkin and Get Wet (I)	A Day At The Beach
2005	A Cappella Pops (AC)	Happy Together
	Beach Boys Tribute Band (I+)	Guitar Tribute to the Beach Boys
	Colin Clary and the Magogs and Friends	You Already Have Way Too Many CDRs [compilation]
	*Four Bags (I)	The Four Bags
	Fred Mollin and the Blue Sea Band	Disney's Beach Party

Year	Artist(s)	Album/source
	*Mighty Echoes (AC)	A Cappella Cool
2006	17th Avenue All-Stars (AC)	Blend (http://www.youtube.com/watch?v=OkpQtNTOooU)
	*Bernard Cade (I)	Rock'N'Roll Baby Box
	*The Duke's Men (AC)	D.O.O.X.
	Heart	rhapsody.com exclusive
	*Vocal Six (AC)	International
2007	Delaytanten	But Leon Fell Then
	*The Sunny Boys	Back to the Beach
2008	*Chris Farmer	California Dreamin'
	*Dan Rudin (I+)	California Dreamin'
	*Rangzen	Rangzen Live
	*The Unbande (I)	Alto Logic
	*Vocal Spectrum (AC)	Vocal Spectrum II
2009	*Alex Bollard, London Starlight Orchestra	(I) Good Vibrations: Twenty Golden Guitar Oldies
	*AntiProduct	Please Take Your Cash
	*The Gentlemen of St. John's (AC)	Mix Well
	*The Lady Killers	Black is Black
	*Marius Nordal (I)	Boomer Jazz
	*Xenovibes (I)	Xing Paths
2010	*Adrian Baker	California Girls
	*Baby Deli Music (I)	Songs for Babies: Beach Boys
	*International Pop Proms Orch., Singers	Orchestra Conducted by Les Reed
	Music City Bronze [hand-bell choir] (I)	concert video (http://www.youtube.com/watch?v=fULoF3BJU6o)
	*Todos	Morangos com Açúcar – Escola de Talentos 2'
	*Voces8 (AC)	Aces High
2011	*The 12 Tenors	live recording
	Baby B Strings [string quar-tet] (I)	live video (http://www.youtube.com/watch?v=nCDF6dnY_N4)
	Durham Ukulele Orchestra	concert video (http://www.youtube.com/watch?v=w1Uv_vqQEsA)
	*Heavenly Music Group (I)	Heavenly Hits and More

Year	Artist(s)	Album/source
	*PR Project	Beacon Chilharmonic
2012	*Wilson Phillips (AC)	Dedicated
	*Starborne Strings (I)	Classical Gas
2013	Ian English Boodlum Band	music video (http://www.youtube.com/watch?v=5d045SF-QyY)
	*The O'Neill Brothers Group (I)	Good Vibrations: Acoustic Guitar Songs
	*Trance-Angels (I)	Best of Oldies Workout Mix
	United Kingdom Ukulele Orchestra	concert video (http://www.youtube.com/ watch?v=cuWTyEmmAC4)
	*Les voix animées (AC)	[Ré]créations A Cappella

PART 3 | *Smile*

EIGHT | Fandom and Ontology in *Smile*

ANDREW FLORY

IN 2011, Columbia Records released a new boxed set that chronicled the Beach Boys' 1967 *Smile* project. Rock critics uniformly praised the collection, which won a Grammy Award for "Best Historical Album" in February 2013.[1] After being known for nearly four decades as the most famous rock record never released, the musical content of *Smile* finally stood alongside the well-known legend surrounding the album's demise. The album's story had been the source of endless discussion in the rock community, and this set finally addressed the long-standing question of whether *Smile* had been a real musical masterpiece or a wisely abandoned flop.

The backstory of *Smile* was familiar to rock enthusiasts. In mid-1966 the Beach Boys had been among the most popular and important bands in the world after making the turn from a teen-oriented outfit that sang about surfing, cars, and girls, to the intellectual brainchild of leader Brian Wilson. The *Pet Sounds* album and following "Good Vibrations" single, recorded mostly between January and September 1966, led a larger movement by the group to embrace the new progressive rock of the psychedelic era, extending a nascent element of complexity in their earlier music. "Good Vibrations," in particular, was novel for its modular recording process, an accumulation of distinct song segments—which Wilson called "feels"—created individually and reassembled later in editing. The aural effect of Wilson's modular approach heightened a sense of musical seriousness and psychedelia in "Good Vibrations." Individual feels depicted vastly different sound worlds, and the juxtaposition of these sonic events was an important factor in the overall affect of the song.

As Wilson finished "Good Vibrations" in August and September 1966, he began work on *Smile*, which was to be the pinnacle of his modular recording approach. For the next ten months, he led more than eighty recording sessions with Los Angeles studio musicians, lyricist Van Dyke Parks, and sporadic vocal performances by the Beach Boys (between national and international touring engagements). Despite the energy and resources devoted to *Smile*, some combination of collaborative tension, psychosis related in part to heavy drug use, and the sheer weight of musical ambition led to the abandonment of the project. In the wake of *Smile* the group demurred by releasing *Smiley Smile* (1967), a hastily recorded album that underwhelmed both fan base and critics. Dribs and drabs of *Smile* material, some from original sessions and others rerecorded, trickled out during the next few years, on *Smiley Smile* and on later albums such as *20/20* (1969) and *Surf's Up* (1971). None of these releases was received enthusiastically, and we can now say, in hindsight, that *Smile* marked the creative decline of the Beach Boys in the eyes of the record-buying public. As lore would have it, while *Pet Sounds* became the easily available Beach Boys record that topped many best-of lists, *Smile* was the album we all *really* needed to hear.

This story was wonderful, of course, but prior to 2011, connecting it to actual music was a challenge because many original *Smile* recordings were available only as bootlegs. Listeners who explored them found that *Smile* lived up to its reputation, containing inventive audio production, pristine vocal performances, and adventurous writing—rising far above the artistic level of a typical bootleg. And yet there were major impediments to receiving the album alongside normal rock fare. *Smile* was consistently presented in wildly different forms, and the unpredictable running order and structure of individual songs found on nearly every bootlegged version prevented many listeners from thinking of the project as an "album." Instead, the project became known for the fact that it had been abandoned, better known for what it was not than for what it was.

The idea of a greatest unreleased album is paradoxical. How could *Smile* be "great" and an "album" if its final form was unclear, and if it had never been released to the public? From an official perspective, *Smile* was abandoned in 1967 and not revisited until the 1990s (with further consideration in 2004 and 2011). Many narrative accounts of *Smile* follow this sanctioned history, skipping the quarter-century after 1967 and only loosely mentioning the existence of bootlegs, focusing instead on the first official *Smile* material sanctioned by the Beach Boys, a half-hour trove released on the 1993 boxed set *Good Vibrations*.[2] Unofficially, however, the album had a much different history. During this time, when *Smile* was largely unclaimed by the Beach Boys and Capitol Records, Beach Boys fans maintained the vitality of the project. While the general public waited for official releases from the band, the Beach Boys audience engaged in a rare form of agency, slowly acquiring and verifying information about *Smile* and reveling in original sound sources. Eventually, this group was largely responsible for convincing Brian Wilson to revisit *Smile* in both live and recorded forms.

The Audience for *Smile*

The music of the Beach Boys during the 1960s equally represented two important and distinct aspects of rock history. The majority of the group's repertoire, from before 1965 and after 1967, conveyed simplistic stereotypes of a California lifestyle, while albums from 1965 to 1967, including *Pet Sounds* and *Smile*, encased musical and cultural tropes of beach life in an outer layer of musical and lyrical sophistication. This divide was magnified when Brian Wilson began to curtail his live performances with the Beach Boys in 1965, staying home as the intellectual studio mastermind while Mike Love led the more conservative live configuration of the group on the road. The reported antipathy between Wilson and Love after this point, whether real or sensationalized by the rock press, further highlighted different aesthetic approaches toward the group's repertoire.

In line with this musical divide, Beach Boys audiences were often segregated according to conservative and experimental aesthetics, which translated to different musical markets. One group of fans, who frequented the group's thousands of live shows, enjoyed being entertained by early hits such as "Surfin' USA" and "I Get Around."[3] This "oldies" audience viewed the Beach Boys as a wholesome pseudonationalistic representative of clean-cut popular culture as it existed before the political movements and societal changes of the mid-1960s (Simpson 2011, 65). A different group of Beach Boys fans valued more highly the group's psychedelic endeavors. These "classic rock" enthusiasts appreciated the energy and understated complexity of this dance-based surf music, but were fanatical about the ambition of Brian Wilson, his purported genius in the recording studio, and his position at the forefront of artistic attitudes toward rock during the dawn of psychedelia. These fans were more enthusiastic about Wilson's solo shows, especially concerts that focused on *Pet Sounds* between 2000 and 2003 and the introduction of *Smile* as a live performance piece in 2004.

The period when the Beach Boys turned toward more adventurous music coincided, not coincidentally, with the rise of the rock press in the United States. Today, the group's legacy in the rock press is contingent almost entirely on their experimental music. Albums such as *Pet Sounds* and *Today!* appear regularly on top album lists sponsored by publications such as *Rolling Stone*, while earlier surf-oriented albums receive little canonical attention.[4] Coverage of the Beach Boys in these new American publications, in addition to British weeklies that were less representative of alternative youth culture but older and more established in their reach, greatly aided the positive reception of *Pet Sounds* and "Good Vibrations" in the rock community.[5] Even though sales of *Pet Sounds* had been marginally disappointing in the United States, the album was wildly successful in Britain, and "Good Vibrations" was a runaway hit in both America and England. The Beach Boys launched a well-documented European tour in 1966, including eight stops in the British Isles, and were voted "Best World Vocal Group" by *New Musical Express* readers at the end of that year, with a vote count slightly higher than the Beatles. Following this success, the press anticipated *Smile* greatly, and developments on the album were known well in the rock community. Advertisements and articles depicting the recording process, many of which incorporated firsthand journalist accounts of Brian Wilson at work, appeared in a wide variety of music-oriented publications. Wilson even appeared in a prominent CBS television special hosted by Leonard Bernstein, called *The Rock Revolution*, in April 1967, performing "Surf's Up," giving fans tantalizing evidence of the experimental direction *Smile* was taking.[6] Put simply, had an unknown or unpopular group recorded *Smile*, it would have never become a legendary unreleased album. Instead, it was a well-publicized follow-up to some of the best-known music of 1966 by a group considered to be harbingers of future American pop, and the role of the rock press in promoting *Smile* during 1966 and 1967 was vital to the album's longevity.[7]

In both Europe and the United States, the distance between Brian Wilson as studio mastermind and the Brian-less configuration of the Beach Boys on stage was a regular topic in the press during those years.[8] A concerted campaign to highlight Wilson's creativity led to a series of long-form pieces in the American rock press beginning in 1966, with many articles explaining Wilson's split from the road band by focusing on his "genius" in the recording studio. Recalling his impression of a recording session from the fall of 1966, for example, Tom Nolan depicted Wilson as a potential radical and questioned his role in future musical developments. "And as you watch Brian Wilson up on [a] chair, with his head next to a speaker, you wonder if all that effort from this beardless, chubby prophet *will* cause a revolution of sorts," Nolan wrote in the *Los Angeles Times Magazine* (Nolan 1966). These depictions of Wilson only intensified after the *Smile* project was officially declared moribund by publicist Derek Taylor in May 1967. Jules Siegel's long profile in the first issue of the short-lived rock magazine *Cheetah* in October 1967 recalled the writer's perspective on *Smile* after the album's demise. Siegel had been one of the many journalists in Wilson's circle during the recording process, socializing at his house and trying to make sense of Wilson's status in the changing rock community.[9] References to Wilson as genius were so prevalent at the time that Siegel made a play on the word itself, asking if Wilson was "a genius, Genius, or GENIUS."[10] Even amid this critical perspective, Siegel greatly romanticized Wilson and *Smile*, echoing and fostering the pervasive audience view of Wilson as a *tortured* genius by writing that the album's demise was the result of "an obsessive cycle of creation and destruction that threatened not only his career and his fortune but also his marriage, his friendships, his relationships with the Beach Boys and, some of his closest friends worried, his mind" (Siegel 1967, 28–29). Throughout the piece, Siegel fixated on Wilson's relationship to the hip rock community, recalling Wilson's struggle with U.S. audiences to overcome a Beach Boys image of square surfers in matching candy-striped shirts. Depicting Wilson in decline, with the nonrelease of *Smile* as the most obvious by-product of mental and creative psychosis, achieved two important goals. First, Siegel gave rock fans a way to view Wilson as hip, helping countercultural audiences traverse the social chasm between "Fun, Fun, Fun" and "Good Vibrations." But more importantly, Siegel's article was one of many from the time that venerated *Smile* as a relic of this hipness, intensifying audience interest in the unavailable work.

Later Beach Boys albums such as *Smiley Smile* (1967), *Wild Honey* (1967), *Friends* (1968), and *20/20* (1969) were received coolly in the United States, and as the progressive music of the 1960s wore on and critics began to canonize the formative changes of the *Smile* era, the album took on greater significance in the rock press. Further investment in *Smile* as a rock masterpiece became increasingly apparent in articles on the Beach Boys, written ostensibly as promotional pieces for these subsequent albums but nearly always focusing on or significantly referencing the group's experimental music. An extended three-part conversation between David Anderle and Paul Williams printed in *Crawdaddy* in 1968 focused on *Smile* through the lens of the current *Wild Honey* (Williams and Anderle 1968a; 1968b; 1968c). Tom Nolan's 1971 two-part Beach Boys retrospective in *Rolling Stone*, the first in-depth treatment of the group by the magazine, also featured a lengthy profile of Anderle and gave considerable attention to *Smile*, despite the fact that the project had been abandoned more than four years earlier. "Remember 1967?" wrote Tom Smucker in a 1972 article about *Smile* in *Creem*, "When each new album was supposed to be an advance over the last?" And Nick Kent's three-part *New Musical Express* profile of Brian Wilson in the summer of 1975 included a lengthy section on the mysterious *Smile* sessions. Given the creative decline of the Beach Boys in the eyes of many critics during the 1970s, it is not surprising that *Pet Sounds*, "Good Vibrations," and *Smile* achieved exalted status during the decade after the project's abandonment. Moreover, the increasing instability of Brian Wilson seemed to indicate that there was merit to earlier claims that *Smile* marked a turning point in the mental and creative powers of this onetime genius. The increasingly positive reception of *Smile* in this period of the Beach Boys' career further solidified discerning rock listeners' interest in the group's psychedelic music, helping to forge an identity parallel to their earlier surf-music iteration.

Dominic Priore cites the release of *15 Big Ones* in 1976, the Beach Boys' first *Billboard* top-ten album after *Pet Sounds*, as a formative moment in the future of *Smile* (Priore 2005, 146–63). While the popularity of *15 Big Ones* was important in rekindling interest in the group, Priore focuses instead on a small advertisement for "Beach Boys Freaks United" on the back of the album that alerted listeners to a growing community of fans interested in corresponding outside of traditional channels (example 8.1). These Beach Boys fans became crucial in kindling interest in *Smile* during the next two decades, a period when little *Smile* music was officially available and the Beach Boys themselves provided scant discussion of the album in interviews. In her work on fandom, Joli Jensen writes extensively on the common impulse to overlook this type of fan agency, citing stereotypes of obsessed loners and frenzied and irrational loyalists. In the end, she writes, "Dark assumptions . . . haunt the literature on fans and fandom" (Jensen 1992, 15). It is a complicating factor that much of what we know about *Smile* derives from the work of devotees who were reluctant to write themselves into the story.

> **For more Beach Boy information, write to:**
> **BEACH BOY FREAKS UNITED**
> **1454 5th Street**
> **Santa Monica, California 90401**

Example 8.1: Fan club advertisement printed on the back cover of Beach Boys, *15 Big Ones*

At least a dozen people organized Beach Boys fan groups during the 1970s and early 1980s, including Alice Lillie, Paula Perrin, Peter Reum, David Leaf, Marty Taber, Don Cunningham, Dominic Priore, and Mike Grant.[11] While there were various conventions that facilitated face-to-face gatherings, Beach Boys fan groups communicated more often through postal correspondence. The galvanizing element of these fan clubs was the newsletter, which helped to distribute information, build community outside of official Beach Boys fan club aegis, and connect people who were interested in compiling information about Beach Boys music. The earliest fan club publication was the newsletter for the Beach Boys Freak United group, run by Lillie and Perrin. "It wasn't much of a publication, but it did include a 'Trading Post,'" recalls Priore, which "became an essential, pre-Internet contact source" (Priore 2005, 148). Grant formed a parallel group with a newsletter called *Beach Boys Stomp* during the late 1970s. Cunningham's *Add Some Music*, comprising sixteen issues published between 1978 and 1984, featured essays taking a more analytical approach to the music, seeking to understand both the history of the group and aspects of tonality and instrumentation in Beach Boys music.[12]

The range of approaches to these fan publications was considerable. David Leaf's *Pet Sounds*, for example, was an exquisitely organized, professional-looking bulletin, with original stories written about current Beach Boys music and events (example 8.2). In the inaugural February 1977 issue, Leaf announced a conservative and respectful approach to its content. "It won't be a scandal sheet," Leaf wrote in an introductory essay. "We will examine [the] personalities and private lives [of the Beach Boys] only to the extent that it affects the music" (Leaf 1977).[13] With access to the Beach Boys organization, Leaf's publication concentrated mostly on the present state of the Beach Boys. A discography column in each issue, written by collectors such as Peter Reum and Don Spears, lightly discussed bootlegs and *Smile* recordings, but the bulk of the material in *Pet Sounds* avoided rumors and unofficial bantering. Marty Tabor's contemporaneous *Friends of the Beach Boys* offered a stark contrast to

PET SOUNDS

© Leaf Publications 1977

Volume 1, Number 1 — February 1977 — 75¢

15th Anniversary Concert

Beach Boys Rock L.A. Forum

photo by Lester Cohen
Brian Wilson at the Forum, New Year's Eve, 1976. See pages 4 and 5 for more exclusive pictures of the concert and the party.

The Forum clock slowly ticked off the final minutes of 1976. Right in the middle of "Good Vibrations," Carl Wilson paused to count off the last five seconds of the old year. And with a loud whoop from Carl and the crowd hollering, the Beach Boys ushered in 1977 for nearly 20,000 adoring fans of all ages. The scoreboard had a simply message for everybody, "The Beach Boys Wish You A Happy New Year." On stage, the celebration wasn't quite so simple: Fireworks, a booming cannon and flashing explosions. Mike Love said, "Let's all start the New Year with some 'Good Vibrations' " and the Beach Boys went back into their most popular song, beginning their sixteenth year as they had ended their fifteenth.

For the huge Los Angeles throng, the show was perfect. The Beach Boys are the ultimate crowd-pleasers, and they never fail to perform all the old favorites that have somehow become the new favorites of a second generation of Beach Boys devotees.

But it wasn't just a night of nostalgia or a rehash of ancient material. First, there was the stage presence of Brian Wilson. Because it has been so long since Brian has regularly performed, he often exhibits a boyish enthusiasm that is refreshing. After all, the rest of the band has been doing this for a long time and they sometimes tend to get a little stale. But whether it was Brian's presence or the festive occasion, all the older songs sounded fresh.

A large measure of credit for this also has to go to the backup band. They are outstanding . . . a thumping rhythm section, the brassy Hornettes and guest star jazzman and group friend, Charles Lloyd, all combine to create a tremendous rocking sound.

The only negative factor evidenced is that the band is so good, the Beach Boys' harmonies occasionally get slightly ragged, almost as if they know they can rely on the horns to carry them through.

The structure of the show, however, is faultless. They have returned to the early 1970's concert format, a performance in two parts that gives the group a chance not only to rock, but to play some of the softer songs and newer material that keeps the older fans coming back for more.

The concert opened teasingly, with those powerfully slow chords that introduce "California Girls." They followed this with "Darlin'," and I have never heard Carl sound hotter. Brian was in the spotlight for the first time on "Sloop John B," and his lead vocal was fine. Two more classics were next, "Little Deuce Coupe" and "In My Room." Brian had sung the lead on "In My Room" in New York, but Al handled it nicely on this night.

Moving into the 1970's, two cuts from *Holland* were performed . . . "Sail on Sailor," sung well by Billy Hinsche (although not as soulful as Blondie's version), and "California," with Brian singing the opening line, as he did on the record.

Reaching back to the *Pet*

Sounds album, they came up with "God Only Knows," featuring an outstanding vocal from Carl.

The highlight of the evening was next. The group introduced a brand new Brian Wilson song, "Airplane." Although Brian had a little difficulty with his vocal in the early portion of the song, this number was definitely a Brian Wilson special. "Airplane" has great rhythm changes, a neat vocal arrangement and intriguing lyrics.

"Back Home" followed, and Brian stepped out on bass for the first time. His lead vocal was great and he had a lot of fun with it. Brian really rocked, kicking his leg and singing some great licks. The band, particularly Elmo Peeler's piano, was in high gear.

The first part of the concert ended with two older hits sandwiching a recent single as the band played spirited versions of "Catch A Wave," "Susie Cincinnati" and a crowd-rousing, "Be True To Your School."

After a lengthy intermission, the group returned with a solid performance of their recent Top 40 hit, "It's OK" and another song from *15 Big Ones*, "A Casual Look" which showed off the Beach Boys at

(Continued on Page 2)

Example 8.2: Cover page of David Leaf's *Pet Sounds* fan publication; reprinted by permission

Example 8.3: Cover of
Marty Taber's *Friends*
(issue 3); reprinted by
permission

Leaf's work (example 8.3). In spite of its departure from the style exemplified in the work of Leaf, many of the same names appear in issues
of both *Pet Sounds* and *Friends of the Beach Boys*, showing the closeness of
the community in the mid-1970s.[14] Set with a pedestrian typewriter, full
of offbeat humor, and probably more indicative of the liberal wing of
Beach Boys enthusiasts, Tabor's publication was chock full of contests,
polls, short reviews, and classified ads. The polls and audience feedback
in this publication indicate a continuing interest in older music by the
Beach Boys. Survey results published in the second issue of *Friends*, for
example, show readers' overwhelming interest in the release of *Smile*
and rare unreleased Beach Boys tracks among their "most desired Beach
Boys happenings." The next issue exhibited a similar predilection for
the psychedelic period of 1966 and 1967, when readers named "Good
Vibrations" their favorite Beach Boys song of all time, with nearly twice
as many votes as the next on the list ("I Get Around"), and *Pet Sounds* as
their favorite Beach Boys album by a similarly wide margin.
  Dominic Priore started a punkish, cut-and-paste zine called the *Dumb*

Angel Gazette in the late 1980s with collaborators such as Darian Sahanaja and Nick Walusco (who would become important musicians in Brian Wilson's band when he began solo touring in the late 1990s). The second issue of this series, published in 1988, was a tome dedicated to *Smile* called *Look! Listen! Vibrate! Smile!*, which is probably the most important of these unofficial fanzines (Priore 1995).[15] The stated goals of this publication grew out of, but were much different from, those of the first wave of fan-generated newsletters. In the spirit of *Friends*, Priore's group "didn't care what The Beach Boys Inc thought about anything," and "was no fan of the slick, middle-of-the-road sound that the Beach Boys had begun to pursue after the failure of the 'Brian is back' hype, and was not about to report on it" (Priore 2005, 152). The three hundred pages of the revised, widely available version of *Look! Listen! Vibrate! Smile!* tell the story of the album's genesis and demise through a trove of press clippings, reprints of extended articles, primary source documents such as handwritten notes and recording logs, and original writing about *Smile* and its music. While there had been a groundswell of support for the release of *Smile* during the late 1960s and throughout 1970s, Priore's work was the most focused effort to date that sought to understand and disseminate information about the actual music of this enigmatic work. The publication represented a new approach to *Smile*, a clarion call to assume the burden of the album within the fan community. "It's only the fault of bad business that we were not fortunate enough to hear this stuff at the time of its creation," wrote Priore in the introduction. But his call went further than extolling fans to exchange information about *Smile*. "I seriously doubt that any of you reading this don't have a homemade-cassette recorder," he wrote. "If you do, then try this suggestion on a blank homemade cassette: COMPILE A *smile* ALBUM BY YOURSELF AT HOME!!!" (Priore 1995, 2).

Bootlegging *Smile*

If the promulgation of history and lore surrounding *Smile* was the first stage in the album's regenesis, this tactile exploration of the album's content marked a new period in *Smile*'s history. Beginning in the 1980s, a growing fan base started to focus more squarely on musical aspects of the album through bootleg recordings. While rampant today, bootlegs of this type first emerged in the late 1960s, with famous fan-originated releases such as Bob Dylan's *The Great White Wonder* and the Rolling Stones' *LiveR Than You'll Ever Be* as the often-acknowledged exemplars (Marshall

2005, 110, 114–31; Kernfeld 2011, 174–79; Heylin 2003). As a form that defied industry involvement and regulation, bootleg releases required the agency of people who were not officially associated with the creative process. The manner in which the Stones' *LiveR* represented a live show, for example, was mediated by an audience member's process of recording multiple performances with specially chosen equipment (Heylin 2003, 47–48). Similarly, Dylan's *Great White Wonder* was curated from a variety of contextual sources, including early 1961 recordings from Minneapolis, upstate New York recordings with The Band from 1967, and additional studio outtakes and live performances. Even though the music of *Smile* was contemporaneous with the contents of these well-known illicit releases, audio bootlegs of *Smile* did not emerge in fan communities until the late 1970s. Furthermore, unlike these Stones and Dylan releases, most listeners conceived of *Smile* as an album, and each had their own conception of how it ought to be completed. Thus, compilers developed different track orderings and made selections from various material rumored to be associated with *Smile* in order to "complete" the project. In many cases these agents also edited individual pieces according to a modular construction in a manner similar to "Good Vibrations" or "Heroes and Villains," selected album art, and provided notes to explain their choices. All in all, a typical bootleggers' work with *Smile* was an interactive process, fully engaged with the creative elements of musical composition and album conception.

If fans could interact with the content of *Smile*, did the products of these interactions constitute an "authentic" work? Recorded commercial popular music is ontologically challenging in itself, because of its temporal and spatial distance from human performance, its sense of permanence as a form of aural notation, and its ability to incorporate aspects normally associated with the recording process into the musical work (Gracyk 1996, 1–36; Kania 2006). In the tradition of Western art music, we might consider the act of completing *Smile*, even by a fan with no connection the original recording process, as a type of performance. In this case, the modularity and differing outcomes of various versions of *Smile* call to mind the aleatoric, chance, or indeterminate music of composers such as John Cage, Karlheinz Stockhausen, and György Ligeti during the 1950s and early 1960s. Rather than a fixed ontological type, then, we need to consider *Smile* as a set of possibilities whose variable final form may be influenced by events, temporality, and individuation (Matheson and Caplan 2011). In spite of questions concerning the line between fandom and professionalism, legality, sound quality, or even appropriateness, bootlegs stubbornly represented *Smile* in the absence of an official release during the 1980s and early 1990s, and, for those who probed the world of these unauthorized recordings, these versions of *Smile* were the only releases available.

So what are the necessary criteria to consider a work an "album"? Bootlegs present problematic responses to this question, and in the same way that the myth of *Smile* made it an object of desire for many rock fans, most literature on the project reveals uneasiness with its illicit state of existence prior to 2011. Despite the fact that many collectors and authors owned bootleg versions of *Smile*, bootleg albums rarely appear in Beach Boys discographies, or are segregated into special sections (Badman 2004, 380–82). In a 1990 article published in *Wigwag*, Tim Page wrote eloquently about the music of *Smile*, which he experienced via a Japanese bootleg, but still called it "the most famous rock album never made," suggesting that authorial consent is perhaps the most important onto-logical criterion (Page 1992, 234). The bulk of Larry Starr's important article on *Smile* from 1994 also discarded bootlegs as "inevitably prob-lematic," showing a predilection for a definitive release from the Beach Boys or Wilson. Only after the sanctioned release of *Smile* material on the *Good Vibrations* boxed set in 1993 did Starr feel that we were able to "start coming to terms" with music that had otherwise been confused by the interaction of "cultists" (Starr 1994, 40). In a 2012 piece published in the *Journal on the Art of Record Production*, Marshall Heiser similarly rel-egated a discussion of bootlegs to his footnotes, claiming that *Smile* took on "a life of its own" when it was appropriated by the bootleg community (Heiser 2012, n. 10). Still, when Heiser asks in the body of his text, "What does *Smile* sound like[?]," he does not address the myriad issues raised by bootlegs, including the varying fidelity rising from *Smile* as a bootlegged work, and editorial decisions made by a host of bootleg compilers, which surely played a formative role in the listening and creative process for many fans during the 1980s and 1990s.[16]

Little is known about the process through which *Smile* material leaked into bootleggers' hands (Priore 2005, 150–54). Fans heard ac-counts of unreleased versions and fragments that had slipped out of the Capitol vaults via tape transfers or acetate discs made for band members to take home, but little of this material was available to bootleggers until the early 1980s. The strongest indication of *Smile*'s completed content was an album jacket that Columbia Records created in anticipation of a wide-selling release after the success of "Good Vibrations" in late 1966, which made its way into the fan community. The package printed a list of song titles, and an insert with drawings by Frank Holmes, color art, and photos of the band, all of which were incorporated into many later bootlegs.[17] Because of the unfinished nature of the album at the time of printing, the jacket bore the disclaimer "See label for correct playing order," fueling fan speculation about possibilities for variance. The repertoire list allowed fans to see that versions of some songs—including "Wind Chimes," "Surf's Up," "Cabin Essence," "Wonderful," "Vege-Tables," "Good Vibrations," and "Heroes and Villains"—appeared on Beach Boys albums during the late 1960s and early 1970s.[18] Listeners had no way of knowing, however, that each of these, save "Cabin Essence," had been rerecorded for these later releases. Some of the songs listed on the album verso were mysteriously absent from the Beach Boys catalog, however, and other works not listed on the original jacket were later linked to *Smile* by various fan-based investigative methods.

A major development in the availability of *Smile* material occurred in 1983, when a new cassette tape began to circulate among *Smile* enthusiasts.[19] In short order, an LP bootleg was pressed (see track listing in appendix 8.A). Known as the "Brother Records" version, it included about forty-eight minutes of *Smile* material. A manually typed set of liner notes accompanied the album bearing the headline, "you should read these notes before playing the record" (example 8.4). (Ironically, despite the fact that these notes accompanied an LP housed in a *Smile* cover, they bore the disclaimer "there was never an album called *SMILE*.") Far from a set of original *Smile*-era recordings, this set knowingly collected later versions of songs such as "Wonderful," "Wind Chimes," and "I Love to Say Da Da" (which came from "Cool, Cool Water" on *Sunflower*). Differing versions of "Can't Wait Too Long" were collected in sequential order, creating a six-minute medley that contrasted different approaches to the song. "Good Vibrations" appeared in an "alternate version," which was based on the same tracking sessions as the single but did not include vocal parts in some sections of the verse, used slightly different instrumentations in other sections, and incorporated different modules after the end of the standard verse-chorus song form (at 2:00). Drawing on interest in the innovative nature of Wilson's work, this set also contained expansive versions of both "George Fell into His French Horn," a raw studio experiment that rarely appeared on later bootlegs, and "Mrs. O'Leary's Cow," the well-known "fire" section of Wilson's "elements suite," which was presented in a shorter form on most later versions of the album. The version of "Vegetables" (the "earth" element) presented on this 1983 set was recorded by Dean Torrence of Jan and Dean, and

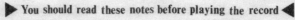

SMILE

▶ You should read these notes before playing the record ◀

Example 8.4: Opening selection of notes from Brother Records 1983 *Smile*

had been released previously in two forms (as a single in 1967 under the pseudonym Laughing Gravy, and in an edited version on an album collection in 1971). Collectors knew the origins of this recording, but rumors of Brian Wilson's involvement in the performance and production prompted its inclusion on this set. Unknown to the creators of the album, however, was the source of the song "Holidays," which was really an unrelated segment of Miles Davis's *Porgy and Bess* that had no place on a Beach Boys release and served as an example of the speculation often invoked in bootleg production. There was no attribution for the 1983 Brother Records Smile, but four organizational names and addresses appeared on the back of the album. These included Cunningham's *Add Some Music*, Taber's *Celebrate*, the Beach Boys Freaks United newsletter, and an Australian publication called *California Music*. In the tradition of fan club newsletters, this release seemed to be a work by fans for fans rather than the product of a profit-seeking entity looking to capitalize on unreleased music by a historically popular band.

A newer version of the Brother Records release appeared in 1985, seemingly organized by the same group but lacking the same list of names and addresses (see appendix 8.B). The most noticeable differences in this recording are a radically changed presentation order and the absence of "Holidays" and "George Fell into His French Horn." Deeper listening, however, reveals that this updated "Second Edition" showed considerable development in the assemblage and use of available *Smile* recordings. The 1985 recording of "Our Prayer" was simplified to include a *Smile*-era version that lacked many of the vocal doublings added to the track for release on *20/20*. "Wonderful" was also presented in an original version with Carl Wilson singing lead vocals, and "Child Is Father to the Man" was placed before "Surf's Up" and prefaced with a relaxed two-module introduction.

The changes in "Do You Like Worms" and "Cabin Essence" were more elaborate. "Worms" was slowed considerably from the 1983 version, lowering the pitch a full half step (from F♯ to F at the opening module), and a different module appeared in the first harpsichord-driven "Bicycle Rider" section of the newer version. Unlike the 1983 recording, which had included a dense vocal section during the second eight measures of this connective module, the 1985 version regressed to a simpler instrumentally based segment with no vocals.[20] The 1983 "Cabin Essence" had been taken directly from *20/20*, while the 1985 version was quite different. Both versions incorporated three main musical sections: an intimate verse around the lyrical theme of "cabin essence," an energetic module with the repeating text "who ran the iron horse," and an imitative vocal section asking about a "Grand Coulee Dam," leading into a farm scene with a crow flying over a cornfield. The 1985 version used instrumental passages for some sections, however, and eliminated the second verse while reordering the modules. Example 8.5 illustrates the formal and modular differences in these recordings, helping to convey how newly available material and differing attitudes toward track completion often prompted bootleggers to present modules in dramatically different configurations.

Not long after the release of the second Brother Records *Smile* in 1985, commercial bootleggers began to favor CDs over vinyl (Heylin 2003, 182–91). While fan-oriented cassettes of *Smile* material continued to flourish among tape traders, new sound sources for *Smile*-era material now appeared in digital form, and the possibilities seemed endless for fan-oriented versions and editions among a new CD-oriented bootleg community. There were two main approaches to *Smile* bootlegging during the 1990s. One was the creative completion of the album, often undertaken by ambitious fans who wanted to connect further with the material. The

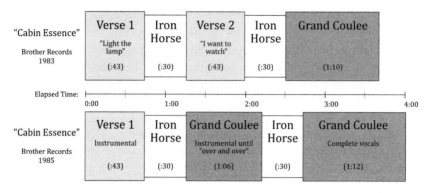

Example 8.5: Comparison of modules used in 1983 and 1985
"Brother Records" versions of "Cabin Essence."

second was a compiled repository of *Smile* material that documented sessions and allowed listeners to experience multiple versions of a single song with false starts and studio patter. These discs were traded but also sold commercially by mail order, through independent record stores, and at head shops. Like the Brother Records releases from the 1980s, CD versions of *Smile* often provided liner notes that explained the sources and decisions involved in the creative process behind each bootleg.

Of the dozens of bootleg *Smile* editions circulated during this time, the best-known were issued by Vigotone, an underground label started in 1990 and revived later in the decade, and Sea of Tunes, a European imprint that specialized in extensive Beach Boys issues (Heylin 2003, 277, 311–12).[21] These unofficial but semi-commercial compact-disc releases of *Smile* during the 1990s brought the recordings to listeners outside of the small Beach Boys fan community. Both Vigotone and Sea of Tunes released *Smile* sets that both completed and documented the album, and also compiled collections that documented sessions for a single song, with Vigotone's *Heroes and Vibrations* dedicated to "Heroes and Villains" (Vigotone 163), and a three-disc Sea of Tunes set chronicling session work for "Good Vibrations" (Unsurpassed Masters 15).[22] Unlike the "Brother Records" LPs from the mid-1980s, the Vigotone and Sea of Tunes discs were released after the Beach Boys' *Good Vibrations* boxed set, and freely used material from this official 1993 release (see appendix 8.C). In lieu of a definitively ordered version of *Smile* available through official channels, the wealth of new bootleg material that emerged in the 1990s further fueled fan interest in the musical challenges of the project.

The 1993 Vigotone release was probably the most heavily circulated version of *Smile* during the 1990s (appendix 8.D). This set included a lengthy version of "Good Vibrations" culled from session tapes, which mirrored the extended modular presentation of "Heroes and Villains" included in the official *Good Vibrations* box. Instrumental versions of songs such as "Wonderful" and "The Old Master Painter/You Are My Sunshine" allowed listeners to hear the intricacies of Brian Wilson's productions without the distraction of prominent vocal parts. This set was also interesting for the inclusion of studio outtakes, which allowed listeners to hear the process of working on the album through instrumental development and spoken dialogue. Sessions for "Surf's Up" and "Our Prayer" showed the process of Wilson meticulously crafting instrumental and vocal arrangements, giving directions to players and singers while creating tracks known well to *Smile* enthusiasts. The experimental nature of *Smile* was also apparent in this set through the inclusion of an extended version of "George Fell into His French Horn," which ran for more than nine minutes, and a twenty-four-minute track called "*Smile* Era Party," which was a lengthy conversation and improvised performance between Wilson and several people in and around Western Recorders on October 18, 1966, after a recording session for "Do You Like Worms" (Badman 2004, 151).

The single-disc *Smile* released on Sea of Tunes in 1999 was an effort to produce a completed version of the album, which differed only in small ways from the *Smile* versions discussed above (Unsurpassed Masters 16; see appendix 8.E). Perhaps the most interesting track on this release was an expanded version of "Surf's Up" that began with a full instrumental realization of two verses before presenting a complete version of the song with only vocals and piano. Sea of Tunes also released seven hours of *Smile* outtakes during this period. In addition to the triple-disc set devoted solely to "Good Vibrations," another three CDs explored the remainder of *Smile* (Unsurpassed Masters 17). The purpose of these collections was to lead listeners through the creative process by presenting instrumental sessions in sequential order, often revealing individual layers of multi-track recordings and overdub attempts. Like the short excerpts presented in the Vigotone set, these tracks showed Brian Wilson directing instrumental musicians and singers and finely crafting the arrangements that appear on modules used in most *Smile* bootlegs. Released more than thirty years after the original *Smile* recording sessions, collections by Vigotone and Sea of Tunes showed the amazing development in unofficial releases during the fifteen-year period after the first popular

Smile bootleg. By the late 1990s *Smile* had gone from being perhaps the most famous unreleased album in the history of popular music to one of the best-documented projects in the bootleg-trading community.

Official Release

Having been known for decades as one of rock's most acclaimed studio-oriented projects, it was ironic that the first official version of *Smile* led by Brian Wilson was a live performance. Many accounts of the album's history consider this 2004 London concert, and the release of *Brian Wilson Presents Smile* the same year, as the album's long-awaited emergence after nearly forty years (see appendix 8.F). Critics raved about the album, with nearly every review toeing the line that *Smile* was a masterpiece, finally finished, and presented to the world for the first time (Harrington 2004; Menconi 2004; Moon 2004).[23]

The bootleg community knew differently, of course. *Brian Wilson Presents Smile* was certainly ordered definitively, and contained some interesting new lyrics by Van Dyke Parks and vocal melodies by Wilson, but the album was rerecorded in a whirlwind stint in the spring of 2004 and sounded very different from the original sessions. The orchestration, instrumental arrangements, and vocal parts were uncannily identical, but the magical timbre of Wilson's productions before 1968 was gone, and his voice exerted only a fraction of its former power. While reviewers credited the impetus to complete the project mostly to Wilson's new-found health and stability, continuing interest in the project was actually a direct outgrowth of the efforts of members of the Beach Boys fan community, who wrote newsletters and traded bootlegs for more than two decades before the release of *Brian Wilson Presents Smile*. David Leaf, who once published the *Pet Sounds* newsletter and had since become an important Beach Boys historian, wrote the album notes. Mark Linett, whose unreleased *Smile* mixes were favored by tape-traders during the 1980s, served as engineer for the album. Darian Sahanaja, who had helped Dominic Priore construct *Look! Listen! Vibrate! Smile!*, served as musical director and secretary for the project, helping Wilson organize the modules for the live performance and album, and also creating several of the musical transitions between songs. Members of Sahanaja's power pop band the Wondermints also formed the nucleus of Wilson's backing band for both *Smile* and an earlier *Pet Sounds* live tour. In helping Wilson realize *Smile*, Leaf and Linett drew from decades of research and interest in the music and history of the project. Sahanaja worked much like a bootleg complier, loading all of the originally recorded modules into a digital audio-editing program to give Wilson the freedom to easily move and edit sections (Bell 2004).

The five-disc *Smile Sessions* boxed set, on Capitol Records in 2011, was the first official release of *Smile*. This set included both a single-volume realization of *Smile* as an album (appendix 8.G) and four additional discs of session outtakes. Like *Brian Wilson Presents Smile*, the Beach Boys fan community largely spurred the release of this set. Linett and longtime Beach Boys enthusiast Alan Boyd painstakingly edited and compiled the audio for the release, and Domenic Priore and Peter Reum contributed essays and consulted on the project. With new digital transfers, the audio quality on *Smile Sessions* was pristine.[24] Past the heightened audio clarity, however, the music included on *Smile Sessions* included no significant new musical material for the bootleg community. The "completed" album comprised modules known well to collectors and, much like Vigotone's approach, the tracks were arranged in order of recording and accumulating modular complexity, highlighting Wilson's direction through spoken instructions in the studio. Although fans had pieced together much of the factual information for *Smile* before the release of this set, extensive liner notes helped to complete and confirm knowledge about the sessions, including musicians' names derived from union sources.[25] The formal and modular construction of *Smile Sessions* matched nearly perfectly with Wilson's rerecorded 2004 album, showing that Linett and Boyd used the musical choices present on *Brian Wilson Presents Smile* as a playbook. On one hand, *Smile Sessions* was revelatory, as it released officially a comprehensive cache of *Smile* material for the first time. The set was immediately heralded by critics, won a Grammy Award, and appeared on the *Rolling Stone* "500 Greatest Albums of All Time" list in 2012, marking the emergence of *Smile* as a recognized entity by the music industry (Kot 2011; Richardson 2011; Petridis 2011; *Rolling Stone* 2012). In the reception of this "official" release, however, there was a gap of understanding in the history of the album. Virtually no reviews discussed in more than a cursory manner the significance of bootlegs in the album's history. Moreover, from a bootlegger's perspective, this set did little more than provide high-quality sound sources for material that had been available for years.

The appearances of *Brian Wilson Presents Smile* and *Smile Sessions* revealed a musical trove that was revelatory to those outside of the bootleg community. From a perspective of fixed ontology, these two official packages began a new, exciting history in which *Smile* was finally authenticated for those who sought official sanctioning. With such a rich history of fan involvement, however, it may be more interesting to consider how these releases changed the history of *Smile* within the bootleg community. The writings of a bootlegger known as Mok clearly illustrate the shift that occurred in bootleggers' views toward *Smile* after 2004. In the essay accompanying his 2001 compilation (before *Brian Wilson Presents Smile*), Mok reflected on the future of *Smile*, writing:

> Unfortunately, I don't feel that the *Smile* recordings will ever be released as a completed album. This is the main reason I attempted this project. I think for me, laboring through this project gave me enough of a sense of "completion" on the album, but Brian will always be a mystery. Ultimately, it's too long and overstuffed to be an "album," but there never was an album, and this is my way to feel totally complete with *Smile* (if ever one can).

And in a parallel essay accompanying a post-2004 packaging of the same compilation, Mok writes:

> It seems the more time goes by the more nostalgic I get about the time before [*Brian Wilson Presents Smile*]. That might not make sense, but there was a lot to dream of then, when *Smile* was a perfect figment in our imaginations, different each one. Although I was thrilled at Brian's finished album, this [bootleg] "version" will always have a spot in the rotation. It was quite a surprise to me that after Brian's was done, people would still want to hear what I did—maybe it is that nostalgic thing in others as well.

While mainstream record buyers cherished *Brian Wilson Presents Smile* and *Smile Sessions* for their revelatory nature, the bootleg community was more circumspect. On one hand, these releases legitimized much of the pre-2004 bootleg work, by mirroring and confirming many of their aspects. On the other, official sanction provided a sense of closure on the *Smile* saga that subjugated much of the *Smile* myth and extinguished the factors that drew the interest of the bootleg community in the first place. No longer was *Smile* a lost album with lingering questions. All of the available musical material was now fully fleshed-out and known to fans. No longer was it interesting to debate whether "Good Vibrations" should occur first or last on the album, or which modules to use in "Vegetables," or which version of "Wind Chimes" worked best.

Should the Beach Boys fan community be hailed or condemned for

their enthusiastic support of *Smile* during the 1970s and 1980s? The varying answers to this question are certainly shaded by views of authority in
popular music. There is a compelling argument that bootlegs might be
the most authentic manner in which to experience *Smile*. According to
this perspective, fans took the mantle of *Smile*, continued to develop it
through research and audio compilations, and fostered interest in the
project during a lengthy period when it was fallow in the minds of the
Beach Boys. Purists will probably accept only what they view as the unsul-
lied authentic vision of Brian Wilson, claiming that *Smile* bootlegs did
little more than usurp the authority of the artist. For those comfortable
with the album as a nonfixed, malleable artifact of a modular and communal compositional process, however, the history of *Smile* has a much
more nuanced past, one that reflects the peculiar shared agency of the
creative process in rock. In this manner of musical artistry, many hands
might influence a final product, including session musicians, audio engineers, and even a dedicated fan community. The story of *Smile* is unquestionably instructive for its lesson in the potential influence of fans and
the range of agency that might be considered in the creative process.
Despite common "dark assumptions" of rock's devotees, *Smile* shows us
that listeners can be integral to the creative process in rock, crossing the
line from passive recipient to active sponsor, or even creative partner.

NOTES FOR CHAPTER 8

1. Even though this boxed set was technically considered a "reissue," many
reviews were quick to point out that prior to this set, *Smile* had "never been officially released in anything resembling a completed form" (*Popmatters* 2011).

2. Many reviews also cite either Wilson's 2004 rerecorded *Brian Wilson Presents
Smile* or *Smile Sessions* as logical reentry points in the album's narrative. This was
especially evident in the popular press at the time of these later Beach Boys
releases, which were often viewed as "unearthing" *Smile* material. See *Vancouver
Sun* 1993; Weinraub 2004; Klinkenborg 2004; White 1994, 360; Stebbins 2011,
82–98. Brian Wilson's biographer Peter Ames Carlin begins the narrative in 1989
(Carlin 2006, 274).

3. I am reminded of a live Beach Boys performance I attended with members
of my family after a Cincinnati Reds baseball game in the 1990s, which held
virtually no connection to psychedelia and emphasized the group's all-American
image and music.

4. As a noncommercial album, *Smile* never appeared on these lists before
2012, for example, representing one of many distortions present in this best-of
genre (Levy 2005, 12–13, 175, 197; the Beach Boys' *Sunflower* [1970] also appears
on this list).

5. This is evident, for example, in the primary source content of Priore 1995,

which compiles many of the most prominent press pieces on the Beach Boys surrounding the group's work on *Smile*.

6. At time of writing this entire episode is widely available on the Internet.

7. *Rolling Stone* writers were wary of experimental Beach Boys music during the late 1960s, favoring instead the group's early repertoire. In January 1968, Ralph Gleason criticized the group's current music in light of reactions to British progressivism: "The Beach Boys, when they were a reflection of an actuality of American society (i.e., Southern California hot rod, surfing and beer-bust fraternity culture), made music that had vitality and interest. When they went past that, they were forced inexorably to go into electronics and this excursion, for them, is of limited scope, good as the vibrations were" (Gleason 1967, 10). This view changed during the 1970s.

8. For a contemporaneous view of the conflict between the Beach Boys experimental recording work and "totally disappointing" live performances, see Wenner 1967. See also Seidenbaum 1966 and Walsh 1966.

9. Siegel appears in a historic photo, known well to Beach Boys fans, of Brian Wilson with a cadre of his inner circle at Los Angeles International Airport in 1966 after Wilson returned from watching a Beach Boys show in Michigan. See Priore 2005, photo gallery page [3].

10. The source of "genius" rhetoric seems to be a promotional article written by publicist Derek Taylor called "Brian Wilson: Whizzkid behind the Beach Boys," which was released ca. 1966. For other "genius" references, see Traynor 1966; Walsh 1966; and Thomas 1967.

11. This roster represents some of the most active people who ran fan organizations and published fan-based materials relating to the Beach Boys.

12. Many of Cunningham's essays from *Add Some Music* have been edited and compiled in Cunningham and Bleiel 2000.

13. One reader (Molly Naples) questioned this hardline approach in the correspondence section of the next issue by writing, "I would be interested to know more about their personal lives. It does not necessarily have to be scandalous. The tone of your magazine is factual, not sensational."

14. For example, Leaf advertised for both *Pet Sounds* subscriptions and his own tape-trading interests in the second issue of *Friends*.

15. This has since been republished in a proper bound edition.

16. Likewise, accounting for and analyzing the multiplicity of popular "completed" *Smile* versions available to listeners would add greatly to Heiser's ideas of nonlinearity, mosaic structure, and dissipative structure.

17. A handwritten note by Brian Wilson that served as the source of this list has been reprinted in several publications, including Priore 1995, 15. A reproduction of the back album cover is included on the inside box lid of *Smile Sessions*. Many later bootlegs augmented this original list in a similar font and design.

18. The last two of these, of course, had been released as singles during the period surrounding the *Smile* recording sessions. "Cabin Essence" is spelled using two words on the original *Smile* album cover, while its later version on *20/20* was spelled using a single word. Similarly, "Child Is Father of the Man" was labeled "Child Is Father to the Man" in many early bootlegs.

19. Priore cites the date of this leak as 1984 (Priore 1995, 274–76). Yet a

Cunningham review dated February 1983 cited what seems to be this same cassette (Cunningham 2000, 133–34), and the original "Brother Records" liner notes are dated 1983. (A July 4 date and James Watt signature make this a questionable date, however.)

20. This section begins at about 0:35 in both recordings.

21. Some other fan versions include (but are no means limited to) *Smile (The Early Years)* (1989), *Smile (The Millennium Edition)* (2000), and Mok's *Smile* (2001).

22. Sea of Tunes "Unsurpassed Masters" volume 16 was a completed version, and volume 17 was a three-disc documentary collection. The first section of Vigotone 100/111 (on CD), and first disc of ST-9002 (on LP), represented a rendering of *Smile* songs listed on the album cover, with some editorial additions (substituting individual songs for "The Elements" and adding "Prayer"), while the remainder of these releases was documentary.

23. Tim Page wrote a more balanced review that considered the album in the larger context of historical sources (Page 2004).

24. The mastering of this set is much "hotter," however, raising issues within what many critics have dubbed a "loudness war" (Anderson 2007).

25. Inexplicably, the set does not include discographical information for disc 1, leaving listeners to wonder about the sources for some selections used in this "completed" version.

Chapter 8 Appendix: *Smile* Track Lists (Selected)

A. *Smile* (Brother Records, 1983)

A1	Good Vibrations	3:35
A2	Barnyard	1:08
A3	Do You Like Worms	3:26
A4	Old Master Painter / You Are My Sunshine	1:05
A5	Wonderful	2:20
A6	Bicycle Rider	0:23
A7	Can't Wait Too Long	6:14
A8	Tones	1:39
A9	Cabin Essence (incorporating Who Ran the Iron Horse and The Grand Coulee Dam)	3:37
A10	Our Prayer	1:07
B1	George Fell Into His French Horn	5:55
B2	Heroes and Villains	3:37
B3	Vega-Tables	2:21
B4	Wind Chimes	2:35
B5	Mrs. O'Leary's Cow	3:48
B6	I Love to Say Da Da	0:57
B7	Holidays	1:12
B8	Surf's Up	3:07
B9	Child Is Father to the Man	1:10

B. *Smile* (Brother Records, 1985)

A1	Good Vibrations	3:35
A2	Barnyard	1:10
A3	Do You Like Worms	3:36
A4	Old Master Painter / You Are My Sunshine	1:05
A5	Can't Wait Too Long	6:21
A6	Tones	1:39
A7	Cabin Essence (incorporating Who Ran the Iron Horse and The Grand Coulee Dam)	4:02
B1	Bicycle Rider	0:23
B2	Heroes and Villains	3:37
B3	Our Prayer	0:59
B4	Wonderful	2:04
B5	Vega-Tables	2:21
B6	Wind Chimes	2:35
B7	Mrs. O'Leary's Cow	3:48
B8	I Love to Say Da Da	0:57
B9	Child Is Father to the Man	1:40
B10	Surf's Up	3:13

C1. Relevant *Smile* material included in the *Good Vibrations* box CD2 (1993)

17	Good Vibrations (45 Version)	3:38
18	Our Prayer	1:07
19	Heroes and Villains (Alternate Version)	2:57
20	Heroes and Villains (Sections)	6:41
21	Wonderful	2:03
22	Cabinessence	3:34
23	Wind Chimes	2:33
24	Heroes and Villains (Intro)	0:35
25	Do You Like Worms	4:01
26	Vegetables	3:30
27	I Love to Say Da Da	1:35
28	Surf's Up	3:39
29	With Me Tonight	2:17

C2. Relevant *Smile* material included in the *Good Vibrations* box CD5 (1993)

8	Good Vibrations (Sessions)	15:18
9	Heroes and Villains (Track Only)	0:47
10	Cabinessence (Track Only)	4:00
11	Surf's Up (Track Only)	1:40

D. *Smile* (Vigotone, 1993)

1	Heroes and Villains	7:06
2	Do You Like Worms	3:56
3	Medley: The Old Master Painter / You Are My Sunshine	1:11
4	Wonderful	2:06
5	Child Is Father of the Man	1:56
6	Prayer	1:09
7	Cabin-Essence	2:34
8	Good Vibrations	3:33
9	Vege-Tables / I'm In Great Shape	3:34
10	Wind Chimes	2:23
11	Mrs. O'Leary's Cow	2:07
12	Cool, Cool Water	2:57
13	Surf's Up	5:18
14	Prayer	5:05
15	I Love to Say Dada	1:27

E. *Smile* (Sea of Tunes, Unsurpassed Masters 16, 1999)

1	Prayer	1:05
2	Heroes and Villains	2:55
3	Barnyard	0:54
4	Do You Like Worms	4:04
5	The Old Master Painter / You Are My Sunshine	1:10
6	He Gives Speeches	0:54
7	Wonderful	2:05
8	Child Is Father of the Man	1:45
9	Cabin Essence	3:30
10	Look	2:39
11	Good Vibrations	3:39
12	I Wanna Be Around / Friday Night	1:35
13	Vega-Tables	3:27
14	Wind Chimes	2:26
15	Mrs. O'Leary's Cow	2:34
16	I Love to Say Da Da	2:24
17	You're Welcome	1:05
18	Surf's Up	5:15

F. *Brian Wilson Presents Smile* (2004)

1	Our Prayer / Gee	2:08
2	Heroes and Villains	4:53
3	Roll Plymouth Rock	3:48
4	Barnyard	0:58
5	Old Master Painter / You Are My Sunshine	1:04
6	Cabin Essence	3:27
7	Wonderful	2:07
8	Song for Children (a.k.a. Look)	2:16
9	Child Is Father of the Man	2:18
10	Surf's Up	4:07
11	I'm In Great Shape / I Wanna Be Around/Workshop	1:56
12	Vega-Tables	2:19
13	Holidays	2:36
14	Wind Chimes	2:54
15	Mrs. O'Leary's Cow	2:27
16	In Blue Hawaii (a.k.a. I Love to Say Da Da)	3:00
17	Good Vibrations	4:36

G. *Smile Sessions,* disc 1 (2011)

1	Our Prayer	1:05
2	Gee	0:51
3	Heroes and Villains	4:52
4	Do You Like Worms (Roll Plymouth Rock)	3:35
5	I'm In Great Shape	0:28
6	Barnyard	0:48
7	My Only Sunshine (The Old Master Painter / You Are My Sunshine)	1:55
8	Cabin Essence	3:30
9	Wonderful	2:04
10	Look (Song for Children)	2:31
11	Child Is Father of the Man	2:10
12	Surf's Up	4:12
13	I Wanna Be Around / Workshop	1:23
14	Vega-Tables	3:49
15	Holidays	2:32
16	Wind Chimes	3:06
17	The Elements: Fire (Mrs. O'Leary's Cow)	2:35
18	Love to Say Dada	2:32
19	Good Vibrations	4:15

Chapter 8 Discography

Beach Boys, The. 1965. *Beach Boys Today!* Capitol, T2269 (LP).
Beach Boys, The. 1966. *Pet Sounds.* Capitol, T2458 (LP).
Beach Boys, The. 1967. *Smiley Smile.* Brother, 9001 (LP).
Beach Boys, The. 1967. *Wild Honey.* Capitol, T2859 (LP).
Beach Boys, The. 1968. *Friends.* Capitol, ST2895 (LP).
Beach Boys, The. 1969. *20/20.* Capitol, SKA0133 (LP).
Beach Boys, The. 1970. *Sunflower.* Brother/Reprise, 6382 (LP).
Beach Boys, The. 1971. *Surf's Up.* Brother/Reprise, 6453 (LP).
Beach Boys, The. 1976. *15 Big Ones.* Warner Brothers, MS-2251 (LP).
Beach Boys, The. 1983. *Smile.* Brother Records, ST-2580 (LP).
Beach Boys, The. 1985. *Smile.* Brother Records, ST-2580-RE-1 (LP).
Beach Boys, The. 1989. *Smile (The Early Years).* SPA, 3317 (CD).
Beach Boys, The. 1993. *Good Vibrations: 30 Years of the Beach Boys.* Capitol, C2–0777-7-81294-2-4 (5 CDs).
Beach Boys, The. 1993. *Smile.* Vigotone, 110–1 (2CDs).
Beach Boys, The. 1993. *Smile.* Vigotone, ST-9002 (3LPs).
Beach Boys, The. 1998. *Heroes and Vibrations.* Vigotone, 163 (CD).
Beach Boys, The. 1999. *Good Vibrations.* Unsurpassed Masters, vol. 15. Sea of Tunes, C-9946–8 (3 CDs).
Beach Boys, The. 1999. *Smile.* Unsurpassed Masters, vol. 16. Sea of Tunes, C-9949 (CD).
Beach Boys, The. 1999. *Smile Sessions.* Unsurpassed Masters, vol. 17. Sea of Tunes, C-9950–2 (3 CDs).
Beach Boys, The. 2000. *Smile (Millennium Edition).* Dumb Angel Records, 001 (CD).
Beach Boys, The. 2000. *Sunflower / Surf's Up.* Brother/Capitol, 72435–25692-2-9 (CD).
Beach Boys, The. 2001. *Friends / 20/20.* Brother/Capitol, 72435–31638-2-2 (CD).
Beach Boys, The. 2001. *Mok's Smile.* Self-published (Digital).
Beach Boys, The. 2001. *Smiley Smile / Wild Honey.* Brother/Capitol, 72435–31862-2-7 (CD).
Beach Boys, The. 2011. *Smile Sessions.* Capitol, 509990–27658–22 (5 CDs).
Dylan, Bob. 1969. *Great White Wonder.* [No publisher listed] GF 1–4 (2 LPs).
Jan and Dean. 1971. *Anthology Album.* United Artists. UAS-9961.
Laughing Gravy, The [Dean Torrence]. "Vegetables." White Whale 261.
Rolling Stones, The. 1969. *LiveR Than You'll Ever Be.* Various Publishers (LP).
Wilson, Brian. 2004. *Brian Wilson Presents Smile.* Nonesuch, 79846–2 (CD).

NINE | A Listener's *Smile*

LARRY STARR

THE STRANGE, CIRCUITOUS STORY of Brian Wilson's *Smile* is a familiar one. With good reason, the tale is generally told from the standpoint of the creators: Brian Wilson in particular, along with lyricist Van Dyke Parks, the other Beach Boys, and the many musicians and studio technicians who participated in extensive sessions for the ill-fated album in 1966 and 1967. The events subsequent to these sessions are well known, beginning with the extraordinary disappointment of the project's collapse by mid-1967. Brian Wilson's health and creativity declined rapidly thereafter, for a period extending over more than two decades. Meanwhile, as Andrew Flory has discussed in the preceding chapter, there was widespread circulation of bootleg recordings of the original *Smile* sessions, fueling the many mythologies that flourished surrounding the unfinished and unreleased album. This fire of rumor and speculation was fed further by the occasional appearance of *Smile* material—both original and re-created, and not specifically identified as such—on Beach Boys albums in the late 1960s and early 1970s. There came finally (or so it seemed) the official public release of a representative selection from the *Smile* session tapes, now fully identified, on the 1993 Beach Boys box set *Good Vibrations.*

Nothing up to this point could have led anyone to anticipate what followed early in the twenty-first century: a surprising and inspiring revival of Brian Wilson's interest in the *Smile* project. This culminated, of course, in the widely hailed 2004 release of *Brian Wilson Presents Smile*—essentially a re-creation of the original album's material with Wilson's new band. Equally unanticipated was the release in 2011 of *Smile Sessions,* a huge compilation that presented to the listening public all of the original session recordings from 1966–67 associated in any way with the *Smile* project. In effect, this returned *Smile* to its point(s) of origin. But for a listener such as myself, who had been following the recorded manifestations of the *Smile* saga chronologically over the decades, *Smile Sessions* created the bizarre sensation of having experienced history in reverse. It raised once again the questions: what, truly, is *Smile?* Is it any one thing at all?

Rather than attempting definitive answers to such questions, which threaten to turn metaphysical, the following chapter will offer a personal, sequential account of the *Smile* music as it was officially released to the public, in terms of the experience of a listener actively attuned to Brian Wilson's recordings during the entire period, beginning in 1966. This experience was naturally quite distinct from any "private" history of *Smile* as experienced by its principal creator, Brian Wilson.

The Stage Is Set (1966): *Pet Sounds* and "Good Vibrations"

The mid-1960s was a period of burgeoning creativity and excitement in popular music, and by 1966 it could seem to an avid radio listener and record buyer as if every week brought forth a striking new single, and every other week yielded a pathbreaking new album. Vocal groups were constantly expanding the complexity of their harmonies and vocal textures—a tendency embraced and led by the Beach Boys right from the beginning of their career as hit-makers, and one clearly demonstrated in successful 1966 recordings by newcomers such as the Mamas and the Papas ("California Dreamin'," "Monday, Monday") and the Association ("Cherish"). The Beatles' lyrics were revealing a new level of seriousness and introspection, exemplified by singles such as "Help!" and "We Can Work It Out" (from 1965), and "Nowhere Man" and "Eleanor Rigby" (from 1966), and just as strikingly by other songs from the albums *Rubber Soul* (1965) and *Revolver* (1966). The trend of according greater importance to lyrics doubtless received a fundamental push from Bob Dylan's new prominence as a singles artist during this same period, beginning with the enormous impact of his "Like a Rolling Stone" in 1965. Increasing sophistication in the instrumentation, arrangement, and production of recordings by rock groups was also in evidence, with the employment of bowed strings on the Beatles' "Yesterday" (1965) and "Eleanor Rigby" (1966) offering influential examples.

With the release of *Pet Sounds* in 1966, the Beach Boys at once positioned themselves in the vanguard of musicians who were exploring and exemplifying all of these progressive tendencies. *Pet Sounds* established itself immediately as a landmark album for serious listeners and for other musicians, by virtue of its admirably imaginative use of harmony and vocal textures, the remarkable variety in its instrumentation and arrangement from song to song, its touching and introspective lyrics, and the brilliant production values throughout. It even embraced formal experimentation in numbers such as "That's Not Me" and the instrumental "Let's Go Away for Awhile," selections that do not exemplify typical pop song forms. Above and beyond all this, *Pet Sounds* was also arguably a "concept album," presenting an orderly sequence of songs conveying the progress of a romance, beginning with joyful anticipation in "Wouldn't It Be Nice" and ending with the hopeless desolation of "Caroline, No." The album is often cited as the first concept album of the rock era.

The innovations of *Pet Sounds* have received ample attention in the critical literature—most particularly in the work of Philip Lambert (Lambert 2007, 222–52; Lambert 2008)—and do not require additional attention here. My purpose is simply to contextualize the album within the popular music culture of its time. This illuminates the album's significance for its contemporary audiences, and also helps explain why the Beach Boys albums that followed it occasioned disappointment on the part of so many listeners.

An analogous situation pertains to the Beach Boys singles released in 1966 and those that followed. Leaving aside the anomalous cover of "Barbara Ann" from early in the year, the top-ten singles "Sloop John B." and "Wouldn't It Be Nice," both cuts from *Pet Sounds*, served to showcase the group's new levels of ambition and achievement. Nothing, however, quite prepared anyone for "Good Vibrations." Released in October 1966, this celebrated number-one hit, with its gently psychedelic lyrics, unique instrumentation, remarkable vocal textures, outstanding production values, and unprecedented open-ended form, remains to this day one of the most innovative singles ever made.[1] The Beach Boys appeared to have finished the year at the head of the pack, under the direction of a Brian Wilson who seemingly could do no wrong. Anticipation for their already-announced forthcoming album, to be called *Smile*, approached feverish levels.

And then—a long, long silence.

The Bubble Bursts, and a Retreat (1967): "Heroes and Villains,"
Smiley Smile, and *Wild Honey*

About nine months elapsed between the release of "Good Vibrations" and that of the next Beach Boys single, "Heroes and Villains." An even longer period, about sixteen months, passed between the release of *Pet Sounds* and that of their next album of new material, *Smiley Smile.* It is important to understand that, according to standards previously established by the group itself, and by other groundbreaking artists of the 1960s such as the Beatles and Bob Dylan, these periods seemed little short of eternities. The Beach Boys' nine main albums leading up to *Pet Sounds,* for example, had been released over the course of less than three years, a rate of about one every four months. It didn't help that popular culture itself appeared to be moving at a breathless pace during 1967, pushed along in no small measure by the political unrest accompanying the Vietnam War and the civil rights movement. The nine months' pause between the release of the Beatles' *Revolver* and the June 1967 appearance of *Sgt. Pepper's Lonely Hearts Club Band* seemed long enough, and Dylan had been temporarily silenced since the summer of 1966 by a motorcycle accident. (Dylan would not release another album until *John Wesley Harding* came out in January 1968.) But of course *Sgt. Pepper* changed everything, and by the time the Beach Boys presented their first new material since "Good Vibrations" to the record-buying public, in the form of an odd-sounding single called "Heroes and Villains" in July 1967, any claim they might have had to a leadership role in popular music was hopelessly lost.[2]

"Heroes and Villains" was a minor hit, but its failure to make a major impact is not simply attributable to an altered cultural climate. The song's relatively limited appeal may be ascribed to two factors that remained problematic, or sometimes even disappointing, in the Beach Boys' output for the remaining years of the 1960s: the lyrics, and the production values. "Heroes and Villains" represented the first appearance of lyrics by Van Dyke Parks on a Beach Boys record. Parks is a remarkable lyricist, but both as a 1967 single and as the lead track on the *Smiley Smile* album, "Heroes and Villains" lacked a defining context in which its playful, nonsequential lyrics might be fully appreciated. (It was only in the larger context of the *Smile* album itself that the qualities and potential of these lyrics might have been appropriately understood, something that could well be said about most of the song lyrics originally intended for

Smile.) In fact, the lyrics for "Heroes and Villains," with their evocations of the American "Wild West," lacked any context whatsoever in the cultural environment of popular music in 1967, an environment immersed in the emerging counterculture and one that tended to prize lyrics with marked personal or social "relevance."[3]

In terms of production, the "Heroes and Villains" single was the last Beach Boys record for some time that would bear a production credit for Brian Wilson alone. But even here a significant difference from earlier Wilson productions is discernible, in both the sound and the sound quality. (I should emphasize that I am discussing the original analog recordings, not compact disc reissues, in all my descriptions of the Beach Boys' output through 1971, in order to characterize accurately the way in which the music was experienced by listeners at the time.) The minimal instrumentation employed in the 1967 version of "Heroes and Villains," dominated by the organ, produces a somewhat impoverished impression compared with the orchestral variety evident throughout *Pet Sounds*, or with the exotic-sounding ensemble (of flutes, cello, organ, percussion, and electro-theremin) that makes "Good Vibrations" so colorful. The source of biggest disappointment for listeners, however, may well have been the overall quality of the sound.

Brian Wilson mixed in monophonic sound, and it is no exaggeration to claim that the *Pet Sounds* mono LP stands as one of the richest and most beautiful monophonic productions in the history of recording. He mixed his singles to achieve maximum impact on the AM car radios and portable radios of the day, and "Good Vibrations" is one of his many triumphs in this arena, one that is particularly notable insofar as the vocal textures on the record, for all their complexity, always emerge clearly; the 45 has a bright and vivid sound quality throughout. In comparison, much of "Heroes and Villains" has a relatively muddy and dim quality. We now know that the "Heroes and Villains" single, and all of the new material on *Smiley Smile* (which also included a re-release of "Good Vibrations" at the beginning of side 2), was produced quickly in a rather makeshift home studio, representing a complete contrast to the way in which Wilson had worked previously—which involved multiple studios chosen for their individual sound characteristics, the employment of many skilled studio musicians executing often elaborate instrumental arrangements, and numerous takes and retakes in the course of a slow and painstaking creative process to achieve the desired results. It can be uncomfortable to compare the version of "Heroes and Villains" officially released in 1967 with the studio session material from 1966 and early

1967 that is included in *Smile Sessions* and that documents the extensive work Wilson did on the song while preparing it, he hoped, for a forthcoming *Smile* album. Even without the benefit of hindsight, however, the original "Heroes and Villains" single sounds thin in light of the Beach Boys recordings that immediately preceded it.[4]

The 1967 "Heroes and Villains" did not disappoint those who, in the wake of *Pet Sounds* and "Good Vibrations," were seeking novel vocal textures, unusual formal juxtapositions, and other elements of musical originality. The record even features varying tempos. After opening with a fast-moving verse, the song continues with a slower chorus, then proceeds to alternate the two tempos in an unpredictable pattern; a further surprise is the brief out-of-tempo a cappella section heard just before the final chorus and fade-out. Whether this all adds up to a satisfying entity is another matter. The song may come across as a somewhat arbitrary, non-integrated mosaic. Hindsight provides additional thrust for this argument, as it is now known that there was much material planned for possible inclusion in "Heroes and Villains" that was excluded from the 1967 version, most prominently a relatively extensive section of contrasting words and music that did finally find its way into the version of the song found on *Brian Wilson Presents Smile*. (This "In the cantina . . ." material functions in a manner somewhat analogous to that of the "Gotta keep those lovin' good vibrations happenin'" section in "Good Vibrations.") Hindsight aside, a simple comparison with "Good Vibrations" would not favor the "Heroes and Villains" single. "Good Vibrations" certainly possesses mosaic-like aspects, but the earlier song's most remarkable characteristic may well be its quality of formal integration and rightness.

Had the album *Smiley Smile*, which was finally released in September 1967, presented new material of significant substance, in addition to the already-released "Heroes and Villains" and the truly old news of "Good Vibrations," perhaps Brian Wilson and the Beach Boys could have recouped some momentum. But the new songs are all short in duration by comparison, and give the impression of being either slim efforts or strange experiments, or both. The three tracks on *Smiley Smile* that we know now as versions of *Smile* songs—"Vegetables," "Wind Chimes," and "Wonderful"—vie for the characterizations of odd, odder, and oddest. While unexpected juxtapositions of textures and formal elements, along with striking vocal effects, certainly occur in each of those songs, and in other new songs on the album, the effect is too often that of inadequately edited home movies rather than that of well-articulated musical conceptions. Writing in 1994, I rather uncharitably suggested that *Smiley Smile* might be regarded as "the sounds of a group undergoing a collective identity crisis," but I confess that the passage of years has not mitigated this assessment for me.[5] In any case, as of September 1967 it was difficult to say which seemed to have done more damage to the reputation of Brian Wilson and the Beach Boys: the nonrelease of *Smile*, or the actual release of its diminutive namesake.

The rapidly following release of *Wild Honey* just as the year 1967 ended seemed almost an act of compensation on the part of the Beach Boys, and the album represents an almost complete change in direction. It is an extremely modest album in terms of length and ambition, presenting eleven songs in well under half an hour of playing time—nothing like "Good Vibrations" or "Heroes and Villains" here. *Wild Honey* is also a much more conventional album, in terms of musical style, than those that had preceded it. On some cuts, especially the title song and "Darlin'," the Beach Boys seem to be reconceiving themselves as a kind of white soul group, a notion that is supported by the inclusion on *Wild Honey* of a cover version of Motown artist Stevie Wonder's "I Was Made to Love Her." Nevertheless, issues involving lyrics and production values continue to shadow the album as a whole. The love song lyrics are routine; a comparison with those for "God Only Knows" or "Caroline, No" from *Pet Sounds*, or even with those for the significantly earlier "The Warmth of the Sun" (1964) would prove painful. Much of the production has a throwaway quality, revealed most tellingly in the sometimes muddy textures and in careless, hastily abandoned fade-outs.

It could be argued that such observations and comparisons are beside the point, because *Wild Honey* was aiming for unpretentious simplicity. Surely a cut like "Country Air" radiates a kind of naive charm, while a number like "Darlin'" is compulsively danceable. Yet even these modest virtues have become evident only with the passage of years and decades. At the close of 1967 the vastly reduced ambition and achievement of *Wild Honey* was seen inevitably in light of the position held by the Beach Boys in the pop music pantheon at the close of the preceding year—when "Good Vibrations" was still emanating from radios and phonographs, with expectations for the *Smile* album running high. In this context *Wild Honey* added insult to the self-inflicted injury to the group's reputation represented by *Smiley Smile*. Calling attention to the quirky phrase structure of "Darlin'" or to the unusual chord progressions and waltz-like flow of "Let the Wind Blow" at that time would have seemed like grasping at straws, desperately seeking remaining evidence of the masterly innovations that were thought to be Brian Wilson's inexhaustible stock-in-trade.

The humorous one-minute-long "Mama Says," which serves as a kind of coda to *Wild Honey*, is an a cappella paean to healthy living that provides a distinctive conclusion to the album. It sounds unrelated to anything else on the record; its constantly repeated lyrics turn it into a type of vocal etude, more akin to *Smiley Smile* cuts like "With Me Tonight" or "Whistle In" than to the more conventionally shaped songs on the later album. In fact, "Mama Says" was pulled out of sessions for the *Smile* song "Vegetables," and this material eventually reappeared in an altered form as the middle section of "Vegetables" on *Brian Wilson Presents Smile*. On *Wild Honey*, it provided a pleasant, oddball conclusion to a very modest album, nothing more.

Treading Water: *Friends* (1968) and *20/20* (1969)

The Beach Boys' next album, *Friends*, represents something of a return to form for the group musically. Commercially, however, it made by far the poorest showing of any Beach Boys album in their career to date, failing even to make the Top 100 list during its brief stay on the charts, and revealing the extent of the group's fall from grace. The album's twelve songs are all short and do not demonstrate extensive ambitions in either their formal arrangements or in their lyrics. Still, musical aspects of many of the songs show that the group was attentive to the details of harmony, instrumentation, and vocal textures—much more consistently than on *Wild Honey*—and the production of *Friends*, while not brilliant, does yield a basically clear and pleasing sound. "Friends" and "Be Here in the Morning," along with "Let the Wind Blow" from *Wild Honey*, exemplify a brief interest in triple meter during this time, although this is not a common feature in most Beach Boys albums, or in rock-era music generally.

Friends broke no major new ground for the Beach Boys, but it is an agreeable album. Ironically, it was probably this very quality of amiability that made *Friends* seem so irrelevant and retrogressive in 1968. This was the year that brought the assassinations of the Reverend Martin Luther King, Jr. and Robert Kennedy, the riots and violence surrounding the Democratic Party convention in Chicago, and the heavily electrified musical intensity of number-one albums such as *Wheels of Fire* by Cream and *Cheap Thrills* by Big Brother and the Holding Company (featuring Janis Joplin). By the end of the year, the Beatles had released their "white album" *The Beatles*, a heterogeneous, disunited, and frequently disturbing response to the unsettled times.

The weakest aspect of *Friends* is its lyrics. Some are casually offhand in an unobtrusive way ("Wake the World"), but others push simplicity to the point of self-conscious naïveté ("When a Man Needs a Woman") or to an equally self-conscious dwelling in irrelevance ("Busy Doin' Nothin'"). Nevertheless, *Friends*, in its idyllic complacency, possesses an internal consistency not characteristic of either *Smiley Smile* or *Wild Honey*. Might this possibly be because, as we now know, there is no obvious *Smile* material in the album?[6] Had the band finally managed to free itself from the shadow of its unfinished "masterpiece"? Not at all, as it turns out.

The next album released by the Beach Boys, *20/20*, is as inconsistent in its content and tone as *Friends* is consistent. *20/20* appeared early in 1969, and it was the album that concluded the group's contract with Capitol Records, the label with which the Beach Boys had been associated virtually throughout their career thus far. The album comes across as a fairly random collection of songs, chosen and ordered with little thought given to creating any coherent overall impression. The production credits are similarly scattered, from cut to cut, among the individual Beach Boys and pairs; there are no fewer than eight distinct credits listed. On the album we find three vastly different cover versions (of the folk standard "Cotton Fields," of the 1958 rockabilly song "Bluebirds over the Mountain," and a particularly inspired cover of the Barry-Greenwich-Spector song "I Can Hear Music," first recorded by the Ronettes in 1966); one clever number in which the Beach Boys essentially parody their own earlier music and image ("Do It Again");[7] one sentimental-sounding instrumental ("The Nearest Faraway Place"); three Dennis Wilson songs of, at best, moderate interest; two new, gently charming waltzes, continuing the recent trend ("I Went to Sleep" and "Time to Get Alone"); and to conclude, out of the blue, two *Smile*-era selections that stand as previously unreleased finished songs ("Our Prayer" and "Cabinessence"). These two *Smile* songs were redone, without major alterations, on *Brian Wilson Presents Smile* in 2004, confirming ultimately their status both as completed numbers and as an integral part of Wilson's conception for *Smile*. The versions on *20/20* were culled directly from original sessions for *Smile* held several years earlier.

"Our Prayer" and "Cabinessence" represent the first time that material recorded for *Smile* was presented to the public in its original form. Why now? Why did the group use the original session recordings, instead of redoing and substantially altering the songs, as they did with the *Smile*-derived material on *Smiley Smile* and *Wild Honey*? Why these two songs? While "Our Prayer" and "Cabinessence" seem clearly to be finished songs, selections in an equivalent state of completion were also readily available from the *Smile* sessions, although admittedly most of these "finished" songs had already been released in altered form. Perhaps, in light of *20/20*, a different question arises: why hadn't the Beach Boys released original *Smile* session material earlier, instead of remaking the likes of "Vegetables," "Wind Chimes," and "Wonderful" on *Smiley Smile*?

In any case, "Our Prayer" and "Cabinessence" were obviously usable "leftovers" from the original *Smile* project that could simply be smacked onto an album as they were. It seems a thoughtless way to treat such outstanding material. Not only does the album provide no context for these two selections, which of course were not publicly identified as *Smile* songs in any way at the time, but they provide no context for each other. The brief and lovely a cappella "Our Prayer" was intended as an introduction to the *Smile* album as a whole; placing it after Dennis Wilson's reworking of a song by Charles Manson, "Never Learn Not to Love," did neither song any favor. And "Cabinessence," in the richness and complexity of its lyrics (by Parks) and music, has little obviously to do with "Our Prayer" and nothing whatsoever to do with anything else on *20/20*.[8]

An (All-Too-Brief) Renaissance: *Sunflower* (1970) and *Surf's Up* (1971)

An interval of a year and a half passed between the release of *20/20* and that of the next Beach Boys album, *Sunflower*, their first for Warner Brothers Records, serving as distributor of their own Brother Records label. During this same period, the Beach Boys also failed to score any hit singles, and they would continue to be a negligible presence on the singles charts for many years to come. Consequently, it does not seem surprising that little notice was taken of *Sunflower* at the time. Its songs were neither deeply probing nor topical, limitations that had become typical of the Beach Boys' output. Yet the album is now acknowledged as a significant accomplishment for the group. Certainly just the sound of the record is revelatory in comparison to that of the post–*Pet Sounds* albums that preceded it; from the opening moments of "Slip On Through," it is obvious that the production (credited to "the Beach Boys") is on an exceptionally high level, and the entire LP possesses a crisp, detailed, well-defined, and inviting sound. It is probably no accident that the back cover of the album offers extensive "technical notes" about the recording equipment that was used, a rather unusual feature to find on a pop recording from this period. Fortunately, the production is not the only memorable aspect of *Sunflower*, which presents a good number of fine, musically inventive songs with competent, if not innovative lyrics—the products of writing contributions from all the members of the group. The instrumentation is imaginative and varies engagingly from song to song.

By far the most unusual and arresting cut on *Sunflower* is the final one, "Cool, Cool Water." Any listener at the time who was even remotely aware of the legendary *Smile* album-that-never-was could have been excused for suspecting that "Cool, Cool Water" was actually a *Smile* song. The entire selection has an aura at once highly polished and experimental, a combination we can now appreciate as typical of Brian Wilson's *Smile*-period music. The extraordinary, overlapping vocal textures; the free, open-ended musical form (extending in this instance over a five-minute duration); the sections with minimal, repeated lyrics; the sound effects; the superior production values—I might be describing "Good Vibrations" as well as "Cool, Cool Water." In fact, "Cool, Cool Water" grew out of some *Smile*-era music recorded in December 1966 and May 1967 that was mysteriously labeled "I Love to Say Dada," but "Cool, Cool Water" expands and varies this material to an extent that renders it a truly independent, and significant, achievement. (Much later, on *Brian Wilson Presents Smile*, the "Love to Say Dada" music found its way into "In Blue Hawaii.")

In the case of *Sunflower*, as in that of *20/20* and *Wild Honey*, the ending of the album rather abruptly offers material taken from, or derived from, the music originally intended for *Smile*, and in all these instances the *Smile* material creates a marked contrast with everything else on the record. The anomaly is arguably less jarring on *Sunflower* in light of the album's high overall quality; still, "Cool, Cool Water" seems to transport us to some previously unforeseen, if delightful, place. The next Beach Boys album, *Surf's Up*, also concludes with *Smile* material—the song "Surf's Up"—that has been re-created in a similarly imaginative and respectful manner. But nothing in *Sunflower*, or any other album, could have prepared listeners for the remarkable concept underlying *Surf's Up*. Here, the song from *Smile* was not simply a final add-on, inspired or otherwise, to an album that had nothing really to do with it; instead, the song was employed as the source of inspiration and the point of departure for an entire album that bears its name. This concept was carried through with a thoroughness enabling one to claim that "Surf's Up" provides the basis for the mood, content, and ordering of all the other songs on the album. *Surf's Up*, then, is an integrated cycle of songs that is carefully structured to build toward its title song in a manner that makes "Surf's Up" its appropriate finale and culmination. This is a singular achievement, making *Surf's Up* both extraordinary and unique in the entire output of the Beach Boys. "Surf's Up" is arguably the greatest of the *Smile* songs, so the creation of an album worthy of it represented a huge challenge, and it is wonderful that the band was able to meet it. This is especially true because, of the nine new songs on the album, Brian Wilson was involved in the writing of only two.[9] *Surf's Up* may well represent the finest work the Beach Boys produced all together as a band.

To validate this praise, it is necessary to start with a brief look at "Surf's Up" itself, the song around which the album was constructed. Van Dyke Parks's poetic and allusive lyrics articulate the progression from a condition of disillusionment with a decadent and materialistic culture to the glimpse of a possibility for hope and renewal. This is all conveyed via an abundance of musical references and imagery. Finding himself at a fancy, formal concert led by "a handsome man and baton" in service to a "blind class aristocracy," the poem's narrator (or the song's singer) seeks instead "a song dissolved in the dawn." It remains nighttime, however, and a "carriage across the fog" arrives only at a scene of farewell (literal or metaphoric, or both) offering but a "cellar tune" and a somber "Auld Lang Syne" in which "the laughs come hard." Still, hidden in the rising surf accompanying a "tidal wave," the potential for a young spring of renewal exists, if only the "word" be heard and the song—a "children's song"—be joined. Particularly admirable is the way in which Parks embeds a hint of the "children's song" within the opening evocations of the overly formal concert, as the question "Are you sleeping?" develops in its second occurrence into "Are you sleeping, Brother John?" In the music, these words are accompanied by the appropriate melodic quotation, underlining the import of the lyrics; the quotation is introduced into Wilson's expressive and complex melody line with a seemingly spontaneous smoothness. (The poet/singer should not be sleeping, since he wants to be awakened to the "song dissolved in the dawn"—presumably the "children's song.")

Brian Wilson's music offers a sensitive setting for Parks's lyrics, illuminating and occasionally even illustrating the words. While retaining sufficient internal repetition to remain accessible, the song never returns to the music of its opening two stanzas, but changes and develops along with the words, and ends with previously unheard music to depict the "children's song." On the level of detail, the phrase "Columnated ruins domino" brings forth a melodic line that begins as a stepwise ascent, then leaps dramatically upward, and falls back; the "muted trumpeter's swan" is evoked by brass instruments on the backing instrumental track; and the children's "song" is heard as a long and ornate melisma at the top of the singer's range, the first such gesture in the entire piece.

"Surf's Up" existed as a complete song in the material originally prepared for *Smile*, in the form of a solo version by Brian Wilson accompanying himself at the piano. There were also takes for an elaborate instrumental track to be used for the first two stanzas of the song. For the *Surf's Up* album the Beach Boys created a beautifully produced composite that employed the existing instrumental track, with new vocals, for the song's opening section, followed by Brian's solo performance of the long second section, utilizing the tape from the *Smile* sessions. The profound inspiration of the entire enterprise was the adaptation of additional *Smile* material, the fragment called "Child Is Father of the Man," to overlay the coda of "Surf's Up" as it fades out. This enhances the impact of the "children's song" immeasurably. (The conception was almost certainly part of the original plan for *Smile*, since the version of "Surf's Up" on *Brian Wilson Presents Smile* ends in the identical fashion, albeit without the final fade.) The care evinced in the re-creation of the title song is clearly seen and heard in all other aspects of *Surf's Up*, from the production values throughout, to the selection and sequencing of songs, to the album cover, to the design of the lyrics insert.

"Surf's Up" is a very serious song, with an underlying somber tone for much of its duration that is leavened by wordplay, melodic beauty, and the near-miraculous turn toward hope as it ends. Its dark atmosphere is perhaps its greatest deviation, among many, from the features typical of the Beach Boys' work, and fashioning an album effectively around it obviously called for some strong measures.[10] The establishment of a radically new tone begins with the album cover itself, which tellingly transforms the image associated with Beach Boys' Brother Records logo; the picture of a proud Native American on horseback, with arms outstretched, fearlessly lifting his chest to the sky—which may be found on the record label—has here become that of a drooping, defeated-looking figure on an equally weary horse, hardly even holding his long spear as it points uselessly down to the ground. (Or is the man only sleeping, waiting to be awakened to the "song dissolved in the dawn"?) Accompanying the LP inside is a folded-over insert that opens up to reveal the lyrics and credits for all the songs. This is a first for the Beach Boys, and another indication of the album's serious intent. On the outside of this sheet, however, is a photograph of a dry, cracked beach.

There is a sense of bitter irony in these images, and that tone is taken up immediately by music and lyrics as soon as the tone arm hits the vinyl. What could be more perverse than a Beach Boys album opening with a song called "Don't Go Near the Water"—a song that commences with these same lyrics? Even during the first seconds of this joint effort between band members Al Jardine and Mike Love, before the lyrics are articulated, the music suggests something seriously amiss, with a dissonant keyboard part that produces a deliberately "out-of-tune" effect. "Don't Go Near the Water" decries the pollution of the waterways and urges the listener to help "avoid an ecological aftermath." The overt simplicity of its vocal tune sits disconcertingly atop the complex arrangement, the dissonant effects, and the frequent changes of musical texture; the impression created is something like a merciless parody of a "typical" Beach Boys song from their early, carefree days. "Don't Go Near the Water" sets the tenor of the album perfectly, and launches a musical journey that will end with a return to the water, when the surf is up, inviting us to hear once again the children's song of hope and spring.

"Don't Go Near the Water" ends with the suggestion that we might all try to "help the water." The immediately following song, however, muses on how difficult it is to "answer future's riddle" or to "plant the seed of reform." "Long Promised Road," credited to Carl Wilson and Jack Rieley, is as lyrically complex as "Don't Go Near the Water" is straightforward, and this second song on *Surf's Up* introduces a gently philosophical theme to the album as it ponders, without resolving, the challenges of living meaningfully in the world. The contrast between the direct depiction of specific concerns and the meditative consideration of life's meaning that is established in these first two songs continues to resonate throughout the album. Jardine and Winfrey's "Take a Load Off Your Feet," the third song, brings the issue of healthy living down to the purely physical level, and on the second side, Brian and Jack Rieley's "A Day in the Life of a Tree" reiterates ecological problems. "Feel Flows," another coeffort of Carl and Jack Rieley, and Brian Wilson's "'Til I Die," both on side 2, are contemplations of life's direction and purpose; the former seems at least open to hope, while the latter despairs of hope utterly. "Surf's Up" concludes the album by combining vividly specific imagery with a metaphoric evocation of the search for meaning. Acknowledging despair, it comes down finally, inspiringly, on the side of hope. The title song serves at once as the summary and the apotheosis of the album's themes.

The concept of musical parody, strongly suggested in "Don't Go Near the Water," resurfaces pointedly with the two songs that conclude side 1 of *Surf's Up*, Bruce Johnston's "Disney Girls (1957)" and "Student

Demonstration Time." The former offers a retreat from all serious problems, back into the culture in which the Beach Boys (and, presumably, most of their audience) grew up. The singer, fleeing from reality, seeks a "fantasy world," with "Disney girls," the songs of Patti Page, and a "local girl in a smaller town" who will be his "forever wife" in a "peaceful life." The setting of these words as a slow, sentimental waltz (like those often sung by Patti Page) is ideal for the purpose; the song accomplishes the neat trick of being simultaneously nostalgic and a commentary on nostalgia.[11]

The self-conscious sweetness of "Disney Girls (1957)" is shattered brutally by the onset of "Student Demonstration Time," a parody of a completely different sort. "Student Demonstration Time" directly borrows the music of a 1954 rhythm-and-blues classic by the Robins, "Riot in Cell Block #9" (composed and produced by the legendary team of Jerry Leiber and Mike Stoller), and provides the tune with new words written by Mike Love. "Riot in Cell Block #9" was a novelty number about a jail uprising; the deliberately exaggerated manner of the lead bass singer, an inspired synthesis of threat and swagger, prevented listeners from taking the record too seriously. Love's own lead vocal on "Student Demonstration Time" sounds as if it is being sung through the kind of megaphone that might have been used at the rallies described in his lyrics, and it may also represent his own parody of the bass singer's style on the Robins record. "Student Demonstration Time," however, with its recounting of contemporary protest movements, is anything but a novelty song or an indulgence in nostalgia for the age of 1950s rhythm and blues. It is, literally, dead serious, concluding with an account of the killing of four students by National Guardsmen at Kent State University in May 1970, and advising those "fed up with useless wars and racial strife" to "stay away when there's a riot going on." While "Disney Girls (1957)" appears to celebrate escapism into a fantasy world, "Student Demonstration Time" bluntly confronts the political realities of the early 1970s and then urges retreat. A sense of musical irony operates within both songs, as well as in their juxtaposition.

Side 2 of *Surf's Up* returns to the meditative mode with "Feel Flows," then dips briefly into sobering economic realities with Jardine and Winfrey's sketchy, barely hopeful "Looking at Tomorrow (a Welfare Song)." "A Day in the Life of a Tree" and "'Til I Die" follow, both very dark songs, the first bemoaning ecological catastrophe caused by pollution, and the second lamenting a loss of personal direction attributed to no specific cause other than "I lost my way." These two songs introduce the direct contemplation of death to the album's subject matter. Indeed, Brian Wilson's exceptionally poignant "'Til I Die" might have concluded *Surf's Up* powerfully by itself; it is one of his most moving songs, and only something quite stunning could succeed it appropriately. "Surf's Up," however, is up to that challenge, and more. Poetically and musically the most elaborate and sophisticated song on the album, it grapples directly with the despair of "'Til I Die," acknowledging the "broken man too tough to cry" while pointing him back toward life. The complex harmonic language of "'Til I Die" also prepares that of "Surf's Up" exceptionally well.

Much more could be said about *Surf's Up*, but let this brief exegesis serve as some indication of its many riches. The album has inconsistencies of quality both within individual songs and among the songs considered as a group. But a majority of the songs are satisfying, certain ones outstandingly so ("Long Promised Road," "Disney Girls (1957)," "'Til I Die," and of course "Surf's Up"); "Don't Go Near the Water" impresses especially with its imaginative arrangement and its variety of textures; and every song on the album contributes in some way to the striking effect achieved by the entire conception.

Like almost everyone else in the listening public, in 1971 I knew nothing about *Smile* (apart from vague rumor) and was given no confirmation that "Surf's Up" was a song originally written in 1966 and intended for an album that had never appeared. But when I first heard the album *Surf's Up* in 1971 I became convinced, as I hadn't been since 1966 (which had brought *Pet Sounds* and "Good Vibrations"), that the Beach Boys were still a very creative group that demanded to be taken seriously. This conviction was doomed to be short-lived. Unfortunately, for the Beach Boys *Surf's Up* marked an end as well as a beginning. The group had never done anything like it before. But they never produced new work that was anything like it again. Their next LP, *Carl and the Passions—So Tough* (1972), inaugurated a series of very spotty albums that lacked both the ambition and the achievement of *Surf's Up*. There were no further attempts to resurrect or rework *Smile* material. Meanwhile, the generous reissuing of the group's older work, often with spectacular success, both on Capitol and on Brother Records, only served to underline the limitations of their fresh material.

Two questions remain regarding *Surf's Up*. The first, probably unanswerable, is, What inspired the Beach Boys to come together for this one time around a resurrected *Smile* song and weave such an unprecedented album around it? The second is, Why has *Surf's Up* remained such an underappreciated work in the critical literature? Although the album performed reasonably well on the sales charts compared with other post–*Pet Sounds* albums by the Beach Boys, most commentators seem to single out *Sunflower* as the memorable effort from this period of the group's activity. Might it be the case that *Surf's Up* is so atypical of Beach Boys music that, despite its merits, it doesn't serve well as "representative" work? Representative or not, I was profoundly moved by this album the first time I heard it, and it has lost none of its power for me over my forty-plus years of listening to it.

And my "listener's *Smile*" now stops for a long hiatus. It is only with the dawning of the CD era that material from the original *Smile* sessions began at last to creep into public consciousness. Here was audible proof not only that *Smile* was more than a myth, but that there was music intended for *Smile* existing in listenable and nearly "finished" condition. First to arrive was an "alternate" version of "Heroes and Villains," released in 1990 as a "bonus track" on the CD reissue of *Smiley Smile / Wild Honey*. Then, in 1993, came something of a bonanza.

Yes, There Really Was (Supposed to Be) a *Smile*! And Now There *Is* a *Smile*—or Many *Smiles*! Where Do We Go from Here?

The five-CD box set *Good Vibrations*, released in 1993, included enough *Smile*-era music to construct a hypothetical version of the missing album, and many listeners, following the suggestion by David Leaf in his notes accompanying the box set, did just that—myself included. There was of course no one way and no obviously "correct" way to create this conceptual *Smile*. The CD format enabled one to experiment with various programming possibilities, including the omission of certain tracks, or the creation of a composite version of "Heroes and Villains" employing some or all of the extensive session material that was released for that particular song. Of particular importance was the now-explicit public acknowledgment that "Our Prayer" and "Cabinessence" from *20/20* were in fact *Smile* songs taken directly from the original sessions; that "Surf's Up" was a song that had been intended for *Smile*; that "Mama Says" from *Wild Honey* had had its origins as a section of the *Smile* song "Vegetables"; and that several of the songs on *Smiley Smile* were adaptations of *Smile* songs, adaptations that compared most unfavorably to the versions present on the original *Smile* tapes. *Good Vibrations* established that *Smile* had been an incipient masterpiece, and that much wonderful music had been created for it before the project was abandoned.

The importance of all this cannot be overstated, and yet it also served ultimately to underline how disappointing it was that Brian Wilson had never completed his *Smile* album.[12] Perhaps it was the very richness and fluidity of the material itself that had discouraged its arrangement into a final form? In any event, the surprise arrival of *Brian Wilson Presents Smile* in 2004 seemed to resolve any number of questions and conjectures. Ironically, it also opened up new issues.

Brian Wilson Presents Smile is an extraordinary achievement by any standards. It has been amply and appropriately celebrated by many, and its virtues need not be enumerated again here.[13] The album appears to fix a "definitive" version of *Smile*, the more so because it serves as a permanent record of the version of *Smile* that Brian Wilson and his band were presenting on tour during the period surrounding the album's release. This version is further documented in a DVD of a live performance, adding weight to the notion that it is indeed "definitive."[14] Yet even listeners who enthusiastically admire *Brian Wilson Presents Smile* might wonder: in the wake of this version, what happens to the previously released recreations of the *Smile* material? Are they superseded by the versions in *Brian Wilson Presents Smile?*—or even nullified, rendered "inauthentic"? Should *Smiley Smile* be officially withdrawn? Should *Surf's Up* be reissued with the substitution of Brian's "authentic" version for the one created for the album?—or even without its title song entirely, since *Brian Wilson Presents Smile* reveals the "authentic" placement of "Surf's Up" as the final number in a suite of three other songs (none of which are on the *Surf's Up* album)? And what about the session material released on *Good Vibrations* that never found its way into *Brian Wilson Presents Smile?* (I, for one, was always very taken with a harmonica melody and its accompanying vocalise that was recorded for "Heroes and Villains" but not used; I offer this only as one such example.)

History cannot be undone, of course. And in the age of digital technology, when "alternate" versions and "unreleased" takes proliferate everywhere, and any listener with standard sound-editing software can cut, copy, and paste existing music together in any fashion, regardless of the original intent of that music's creator, the kinds of questions being posed here may seem irrelevant, or perhaps silly. Those whimsically inclined might suggest that *Smile*'s apparent malleability could represent just one additional illustration of the extent to which it was ahead of its time. Nevertheless, at the time when the *Smile* music was originally being recorded, Brian Wilson obviously was intending it for an album with very specific content and ordering. Fans, music historians, and even the mildly curious may be forgiven for wondering—after all the years, rumors, myths, and false hopes—just what that content and ordering might have been. If *Brian Wilson Presents Smile* appeared at the time of its release to offer the closest thing to an answer that we were likely to get, the release in 2011 of *Smile Sessions* reopened the magic *Smile* box once again, and threw everything into glorious disarray.

With Brian Wilson's evident assent and cooperation, and with the help of an engineering and production team that demonstrated an archeologist's attention to detail, *Smile Sessions* presented every available scrap of music preserved on tape from the periods in 1966 and 1967 when the Beach Boys were actively working on *Smile*. These tapes themselves document aspects of the creative process in an often fascinating way, but they also enabled the producers of the project to do something else. *Smile Sessions* offers, both on CD and in "original" LP format, a version of a *Smile* album that employs the original session material, ordered essentially along the lines of *Brian Wilson Presents Smile*. Here is yet another *Smile*, fashioned from the period tapes, with the session musicians Wilson personally chose to play his music, and the voices of the Beach Boys from 1966–1967!

This "new" *Smile* album is not "complete." *Brian Wilson Presents Smile* does include some freshly created material, in "On a Holiday" and "In Blue Hawaii," that has no direct parallel on the original *Smile* session tapes. Was this material that existed on tape at one time but is now lost, or does it reflect plans for the original album that never reached tape? In addition, *Brian Wilson Presents Smile* incorporates transitional material between songs that was created by a member of his band, Darian Sahanaja. On the other hand, the version of *Smile* on *Smile Sessions* presents certain material in an order different from that found on *Brian Wilson Presents Smile*, for reasons that are not stated. Further, *Smile Sessions* is packaged with two 45s, supposedly representing projected single releases of *Smile* songs from the time when the original project was still developing, and one of these 45s is a double-sided "Heroes and Villains" that is different from *any* other version found anywhere of this song! (I am pleased to report, however, that this version does include the harmonica and vocalise music I so enjoy!) It is difficult to dismiss this studio-engineered *Smile* constructed from period tapes, and its accompanying singles, simply as what-might-have-been conjectures, and this is above all because of Brian Wilson's own statement in the book accompanying *Smile Sessions*: "Probably nothing I've ever done has topped the music I made with Van Dyke, my old crew in the studio and the voices of youth—me and the

Beach Boys." Certainly the reconstructed *Smile* on *Smile Sessions* sounds magnificent. Does this then mean that the version of *Smile* we can hear on *Smile Sessions* is the music that actually brings us closest to what Brian Wilson was imagining nearly five decades ago? In some way does this supersede even *Brian Wilson Presents Smile?*

I prefer to think that the idea there could be a "definitive" *Smile* decades after Brian Wilson abandoned the project was always chimerical, and that—intentionally or not—his agreement to issue *Smile Sessions* represents his acknowledgment of this. Why not let "Surf's Up" have multiple identities within the repertory of American popular song: as the title song and finale to a brilliant album that bears its name; as the concluding number of a breathtaking suite within *Brian Wilson Presents Smile*; and as a major event midway through the version of *Smile* on *Smile Sessions* (and as a single of the same version extracted from *Smile Sessions*)? Analogous questions could be posed about other *Smile* music. At last it may come to seem curiously appropriate that the music of *Smile* itself, considered as a whole, ultimately resists finalizing, especially when we consider that the music of some *Smile* songs recurs in varied form within other *Smile* songs (as is the case with "Heroes and Villains" returning in "Roll Plymouth Rock," "Child Is Father of the Man" returning in "Surf's Up," and "Our Prayer" returning to connect "In Blue Hawaii" with "Good Vibrations"), and that many songs in *Smile* elide directly into other songs without having conventional endings. How sweet it is that an album most people, including its composer, thought could never be born has ended up having multiple lives! For *Smile* is vibrant, life-affirming music, and it lives!

NOTES FOR CHAPTER 9

1. For an analysis of "Good Vibrations," see Starr and Waterman 2014, 313–15.

2. Another contributing factor, particularly for those closely following the work of Brian Wilson and the Beach Boys, was the fact that Brian's solo performance of the new song "Surf's Up" on the television special *Inside Pop: The Rock Revolution*, which aired in April 1967 and was hosted by Leonard Bernstein, heralded no forthcoming release on record of the obviously extraordinary song. (The performance had in fact been recorded the preceding December.) "Surf's Up" had been intended for *Smile* and remained unreleased in any form until a version of it was included on the 1971 Beach Boys album for which it served as the title song.

3. Among major hit singles of that year exemplifying these characteristics were Aretha Franklin's "Respect," Bobbie Gentry's "Ode to Billie Joe," the Beatles' "All You Need Is Love," Scott McKenzie's "San Francisco (Be Sure to Wear Flowers in Your Hair)," and even the Monkees' "Pleasant Valley Sunday."

4. In the unpaginated book accompanying *Smile Sessions*, Brian Wilson writes of this record: "I finished a version of 'Heroes and Villains,' but it sure wasn't what Van Dyke [Parks] and I originally had in mind."

5. See Starr 1994, 46. For a more sympathetic view of the *Smiley Smile* music, see Harrison 1997, 46–49.

6. In his article "Lost and Found: The Significance of *Smile*," found in the unpaginated book accompanying the *Smile Sessions* box, Peter Reum claims that "Little Bird" from *Friends* "quoted horn parts" from the projected *Smile* song "Child Is Father of the Man." I confess that I am unable to discern this connection. I can hear a slight resemblance between a horn line in "Wake the World" and one in "Song for Children" from *Brian Wilson Presents Smile*, but this relationship seems to me inconsequential, if it is not accidental.

7. The element of nostalgic parody would reappear to particularly strong effect on the 1971 album *Surf's Up*, to be discussed shortly.

8. On *Brian Wilson Presents Smile*, "Cabin Essence" (as it is titled on that album and in most other sources) comes as the concluding number of the first "suite"; six other selections separate it from the opening "Our Prayer," creating an aesthetic experience totally different from—and vastly superior to—that which results when the two songs are directly juxtaposed, as they are on *20/20*.

9. Doe and Tobler 2004, 78, and Lambert 2007, 296 credit Brian Wilson as a cowriter on "Take a Load Off Your Feet," but the original LP label and the lyrics insert for *Surf's Up* credit him only for "A Day in the Life of a Tree" and "'Til I Die," in addition to "Surf's Up."

10. "Caroline, No," the despairing finale of *Pet Sounds*, certainly comes to mind as another instance of a dark Beach Boys song, but the despondency in "Surf's Up" is related to cultural as well as personal matters.

11. This "neat trick" is carried out over the length of an entire album in *That's Why God Made the Radio*, the excellent 2012 release that marked the surprise reunion (and viability) of the living Beach Boys. At first, the band seems to be playing along with the expectation that they could only be a jolly nostalgia act, until the tide begins to turn on the song "Strange World." The concluding number, "Summer's Gone," which gently evokes "Caroline, No," is among the saddest songs Brian Wilson ever wrote. The Beach Boys' reunion marked yet a third unanticipated event in the twenty-first-century career of Wilson, following the appearance of *Brian Wilson Presents Smile* in 2004, and the release of *Smile Sessions* in 2011.

12. For one extensive account of how important the release of *Smile* material seemed at this time, see Starr 1994.

13. My own discussion of the album may be found in Starr 2007.

14. The DVD (Rhino Home Video R2 970415) offers no specific information about the live performance, other than "recorded in Los Angeles, CA."

General Bibliography

Books, Articles, Magazines, Newspapers

Abbott, Kingsley, ed. 1997. *Back to the Beach: A Brian Wilson and the Beach Boys Reader.* London: Helter Skelter.

Abbott, Kingsley. 2001. *The Beach Boys' "Pet Sounds": The Greatest Album of the Twentieth Century.* London: Helter Skelter.

Adler, Renata. 1967. "A Reporter at Large: Fly Trans-Love Airways." *New Yorker* 42/3 (February 25): 116–31.

Alencar, Aretha B., Maria Cristina F. de Oliveira, and Fernando V. Paulovich. 2012. "Seeing Beyond Reading: A Survey on Visual Text Analytics." *Data Mining and Knowledge Discovery* 2/6: 476–92.

Alexander, Shana. 1964. "Love Songs to the Carburetor." *Life,* November 6: 33.

Allen, Chris. 2004. "Light the Lamp: An Interview with Peter Reum." *Open Sky* 7: 3–32.

Anderson, Tim. 2007. "How CDs Are Remastering the Art of Noise." *Guardian,* January 17. http://www.theguardian.com/technology/2007/jan/18/pop.music.

Arkhonia. 2012. "*Smile*—My First 25 Years: Summer's Gone, It's Over Now." October 4. http://arkhonia.wordpress.com/2012/10/04/smile-my-first-25-years-summers-gone-its-over-now/.

Badman, Keith. 2004. *The Beach Boys: The Definitive Story of America's Greatest Band: On Stage and in the Studio.* San Francisco: Backbeat.

Bailey, Steve. 2003. "Faithful or Foolish: The Emergence of the 'Ironic Cover Album' and Rock Culture." *Popular Music and Society* 26/2: 141–59.

"The Beach Boys Hang 15; That's Years, and Better Still, Brian Wilson's Back from His Crack-Up." 1976. *People Weekly* 6/8 (August 23): 31–35.

Beard, David. 2005. "Van Dyke Parks: Have You Seen the Grand Coulee Dam?" *Endless Summer Quarterly* 68: 3–9.

Becker, Howard S. 1978. "Arts and Crafts." *American Journal of Sociology* 83/4: 862–89.

Bell, Jonathan. 2012. "Building a Left Coast: The Legacy of the California Popular Front and the Challenge to Cold War Liberalism in the Post–World War II Era." *Journal of American Studies* 46/1: 51–71.

Bell, Matt. 2004. "*Smile.*" *Sound on Sound*, October. http://www.soundonsound.com/sos/Oct04/articles/smile.htm.

Bercovitch, Sacvan. 2012. *The American Jeremiad*. Anniversary edition. Madison: University of Wisconsin Press.

Bernhard, Anthony, and Edgar Z. Friedenberg. 1967. "The Sunset Strip." *New York Review of Books* 8/4 (March 9): 8–13.

Bielen, Kenneth G. 1999. *The Lyrics of Civility: Biblical Images and Popular Music Lyrics in American Culture*. New York: Garland.

Bourdieu, Pierre. 1984. *Distinction: A Social Critique of the Judgment of Taste*. Translated by Richard Nice. Cambridge: Harvard University Press.

Bourdieu, Pierre. 1993. *The Field of Cultural Production: Essays on Art and Literature*. Edited by Randal Johnson. New York: Columbia University Press.

"Brian Births a New Song." 1964. *Teen Set*, [circa] Fall: 9–12, 27.

Burford, Mark. 2012. "Sam Cooke as Pop Album Artist: A Reinvention in Three Songs." *Journal of the American Musicological Society* 65/1: 113–78.

Buxton, David. 1983. "Rock Music, the Star System, and the Rise of Consumerism." *Telos* 57: 93–106. Reprinted in Frith and Goodwin 1990, 427–40.

Carlin, Peter Ames. 2006. *Catch a Wave: The Rise, Fall, and Redemption of the Beach Boys' Brian Wilson*. Emmaus, Penn.: Rodale.

Carter, Dale. 2004. "What's Still Left of My Memory: Recovery and Reorientation in the Songs of Van Dyke Parks." *Popular Music and Society* 27/4: 387–405.

Carter, Dale. 2013. "Surf Aces Resurfaced: The Beach Boys and the Greening of the American Counterculture, 1963–1973." *Ecozon@: European Journal of Literature, Culture and Environment* 4/1: 44–60.

Cashmore, Ellis. 2006. *Celebrity Culture*. London: Routledge.

Chidester, Brian, and Domenic Priore. 2008. *Pop Surf Culture: Music, Design, Film and Fashion From the Bohemian Surf Boom*. Santa Monica, Calif.: Santa Monica Press.

Christgau, Robert. 1970. "Rock Is Obsolescent, but So Are You." *Village Voice*, November.

Christgau, Robert. 1988. "Nothing to Say, but as Far as He Could Go: John Lennon." In *Grown Up All Wrong: 75 Great Rock and Pop Artists from Vaudeville to Techno*. Cambridge: Harvard University Press, 104–24.

Coates, Norma. 1997. "Rock and the Political Potential of Gender." In *Sexing the Groove: Popular Music and Gender*, ed. Sheila Whiteley. New York: Routledge, 50–64.

Coates, Norma. 2013. "Excitement is Made, Not Born: Jack Good, Television, and Rock and Roll." *Journal of Popular Music Studies* 25/3: 301–25.

Cohen, Ronald D. 2002. *Rainbow Quest: The Folk Music Revival and American Society, 1940–1970*. Amherst: University of Massachusetts Press.

Cohen, Ronald D., and Dave Samuelson. 1996. *Songs for Political Action: Folk Music, Topical Songs and the American Left, 1926–1953*. Hamburg: Bear Family Records.

Cole, Richard R. 1971. "Top Songs in the Sixties: A Content Analysis of Popular Lyrics." *American Behavioral Scientist* 14: 389–400.

Covach, John. 2006. "From 'Craft' to 'Art': Formal Structure in the Music of the Beatles." In *Reading the Beatles: Cultural Studies, Literary Criticism, and the Fab*

Four, ed. Kenneth Womack and Todd F. Davis. New York: State University of New York Press, 37–53.

Cralle, Trevor. 2001. *The Surfin'ary: A Dictionary of Surfing Terms and Surfspeak.* 2nd edition. Berkeley, Calif.: Ten Speed Press.

Cray, Ed. 2004. *Ramblin' Man: The Life and Times of Woody Guthrie.* New York: Norton.

Crosby, David, with Carl Gottlieb. 1989. *Long Time Gone: The Autobiography of David Crosby.* London: Heinemann.

Crowley, Kent. 2011. *Surf Beat: Rock 'n' Roll's Forgotten Revolution.* New York: Backbeat.

Cunningham, Don, and Jeff Bleiel. 2000. *Add Some Music to Your Day: Analyzing and Enjoying the Music of the Beach Boys.* Cranberry Township, Penn.: Tiny Ripple.

Curnutt, Kirk. 2012. *Brian Wilson.* Bristol, Conn.: Equinox.

de Clercq, Trevor, and David Temperley. 2011. "A Corpus Analysis of Rock Harmony." *Popular Music* 30/1: 47–70.

de Rios, Marlene Dobkin, and Oscar Janiger. 2003. *LSD, Spirituality and the Creative Process.* Rochester, Vt.: Park Street.

Denning, Michael. 1998. *The Cultural Front: The Laboring of American Culture in the Twentieth Century.* London: Verso.

Diben, Nicola. 1999. "Representations of Femininity in Popular Music." *Popular Music* 18/3: 331–355.

Dillon, Mark. 2012. *Fifty Sides of the Beach Boys: The Songs That Tell Their Story.* Toronto: ECW.

Doe, Andrew G., and John Tobler. 2004. *Brian Wilson and the Beach Boys: The Complete Guide to Their Music.* London: Omnibus.

Doggett, Peter. 2007. "The Last Waltz: Brian Wilson Bids Farewell to *Pet Sounds*." *Mojo* 158 (January): 54.

Doherty, Thomas. 1988. *Teenagers and Teen Pics: The Juvenilization of Movies in the 1950s.* Boston: Unwin Hyman.

Doll, Christopher. 2011. "Rockin' Out: Expressive Modulation in Verse-Chorus Form." *Music Theory Online* 17/3.

Doyle, Patrick. 2012. "Mike Love Books Beach Boys Shows without Brian Wilson." *Rolling Stone*, June 26. http://www.rollingstone.com/music/news/mike-love-books-beach-boys-shows-without-brian-wilson-20120626.

Dunaway, David King, and Molly Beer. 2010. *Singing Out: An Oral History of America's Folk Music Revivals.* New York: Oxford University Press.

Einarson, John. 2005. *Mr. Tambourine Man: The Life and Legacy of The Byrds' Gene Clark.* San Francisco: Backbeat.

Everett, Walter. 2000. "The Learned vs. the Vernacular in the Songs of Billy Joel." *Contemporary Music Review* 8/4: 105–29.

Everett, Walter. 2004. "Making Sense of Rock's Tonal Systems." *Music Theory Online* 10.

Everett, Walter. 2008. "Pitch Down the Middle." In *Expression in Pop-Rock Music: Critical and Analytical Essays*, 2nd edition, ed. Walter Everett. New York: Routledge, 148–234.

Everett, Walter. 2009. *The Foundations of Rock: From "Blue Suede Shoes" to "Suite: Judy Blue Eyes."* New York: Oxford University Press.

Fitzgerald, Jon. 1999. "Musical Form and the Early 1960s Pop Song." In *Musical Visions*, ed. Gerry Bloustein. Kent Town, South Australia: Wakefield, 35–42.

Fricke, David. 2011a. "Fleet Foxes: Helplessness Blues." *Rolling Stone*, April 28. http://www.rollingstone.com/music/albumreviews/helplessness-blues-20110428.

Fricke, David. 2011b. "The Greatest Pop Album Never Made." *Rolling Stone*, November 10.

Frith, Simon. 1983. *Sound Effects: Youth, Leisure, and the Politics of Rock 'n' Roll.* London: Constable.

Frith, Simon. 2007. *Taking Popular Music Seriously: Selected Essays.* London: Ashgate.

Frith, Simon, and Andrew Goodwin, eds. 1990. *On Record: Rock, Pop, and the Written Word.* New York: Pantheon.

Frith, Simon, and Angela McRobbie. 1978. "Rock and Sexuality." *Screen Education* 29: 3–19. Reprinted Frith and Goodwin 1990, 371–89.

Fusilli, Jim. 2005. *Pet Sounds.* New York: Continuum.

Fusilli, Jim. 2008. "The Sum of the Vocal Parts." *Wall Street Journal*, September 6. http://online.wsj.com/article/SB122064389510804655.html.

Gaines, Steven. 1988. *Heroes and Villains: The True Story of the Beach Boys.* London: Grafton.

Gendron, Bernard. 2002. *Between Montmartre and the Mudd Club: Popular Music and the Avant-Garde.* Chicago: University of Chicago Press.

Gleason, Ralph. 1967. "Perspectives: The British Group Syndrome." *Rolling Stone*, January 20.

Goodman, Fred. 1997. *The Mansion on the Hill: Dylan, Young, Geffen, Springsteen, and the Head-On Collision of Rock and Commerce.* New York: Random House.

Goldstein, Richard. 1966. "Pop Eye: Evaluating Media." *Village Voice*, July 14: 6–7.

Goodman, Walter. 1969. *The Committee: The Extraordinary Career of the House Committee on Un-American Activities.* London: History Book Club.

Goosman, Stuart L. 2005. *Group Harmony: The Black Urban Roots of Rhythm and Blues.* Philadelphia: University of Pennsylvania Press.

Gracyk, Theodore. 1996. *Rhythm and Noise: An Aesthetics of Rock.* Durham, N.C.: Duke University Press.

Granata, Charles L. 2003. *Wouldn't It Be Nice: Brian Wilson and the Making of the Beach Boys' "Pet Sounds".* Chicago: A Cappella.

Greco, Nicholas P. 2011. *"Only If You Are Really Interested": Celebrity, Gender, Desire, and the World of Morrissey.* Jefferson, N.C.: McFarland.

Greenwald, Matthew. 2003. "The *MusicAngle* Interview: Van Dyke Parks: Song Cyclist and Brian Wilson Collaborator Speaks." *MusicAngle*. http://www.analogplanet.com/content/musicangle-interview-song-cyclist-and-brian-wilson-collaborator-speaks-0.

Gribin, Anthony J., and Matthew M. Schiff. 1992. *Doo-Wop: The Forgotten Third of Rock 'n' Roll.* Iola, Wisc.: Krause.

Griffiths, Dai. 2002. "Cover Versions and the Sound of Identity in Motion." In *Popular Music Studies*, ed. David Hesmondhalgh and Neith Negus. London: Arnold, 51–64.

Harrington, Michael. 1962. *The Other America.* Simon and Schuster, 1997.

Harrington, Richard. 2004. "Brian Wilson's Grin." *Washington Post*, October 8.

Harrison, Daniel. 1997. "After Sundown: The Beach Boys' Experimental Music." In *Understanding Rock: Essays in Musical Analysis*, ed. John Covach and Graeme M. Boone. New York: Oxford University Press, 33–57.

Heale, M. J. 1986. "Red Scare Politics: California's Campaign against Un-American Activities, 1940–1970." *Journal of American Studies* 20/1: 5–32.

Heiser, Marshall. 2012. "SMiLE: Brian Wilson's Musical Mosaic." *Journal on the Art of Record Production* 7 (November). http://arpjournal.com/2161/smile-brian-wilson's-musical-mosaic.

Heylin, Clinton. 2003. *Bootleg: The Rise and Fall of the Secret Recording History*. London: Omnibus.

Hicks, Michael. 1999. *Sixties Rock: Garage, Psychedelic, and Other Satisfactions*. Urbana: University of Illinois Press.

Hill, Richard A. 1994. "You've Come a Long Way, Dude: A History." *American Speech* 69/3: 321–27.

Hine, Thomas. 1986. *Populuxe*. New York: Knopf.

Hjort, Christopher. 2008. *So You Want to Be a Rock 'n' Roll Star: The Byrds Day-by-Day, 1965–1973*. London: Jawbone.

Holdship, Bill, and Peter Doggett. 2007. "Summer's Almost Gone." *Mojo* 158 (January): 48–53.

Holmes, Tim. 2007. "US and Them: American Rock's Reconquista." *Popular Music and Society* 30/3: 343–53.

Holzman, Jac, and Gavan Daws. 2000. *Follow the Music: The Life and High Times of Elektra Records in the Great Years of American Pop Culture*. Santa Monica, Calif.: First Media.

Horton, D., and R. R. Wohl. 1956. "Mass Communication and Para-Social Interaction: Observations on Intimacy at a Distance." *Psychiatry* 19/3: 215–29.

Hoskyns, Barney. 1994. "The Strip." *Mojo* 3 (January–February): 32–44.

Hoskyns, Barney. 1997. *Waiting for the Sun: Strange Days, Weird Scenes and the Sound of Los Angeles*. London: Bloomsbury.

Hoskyns, Barney. 2005. *Hotel California: Singer-Songwriters and Cocaine Cowboys in the LA Canyons, 1967–1976*. London: Fourth Estate.

Huisman, Rhonda, Willie Miller, and Jessica Trinoskey. 2011. "We've Wordled, Have You? Digital Images in the Library Classroom." *College Research Library News* 72/9: 522–26.

Huyssen, Andreas. 1986. *After the Great Divide*. Bloomington: Indiana University Press.

Jensen, Jan. N.d. "The Brian Wilson Interview." http://www.songcycler.de/misc-files/bwinterview.html.

Jenson, Joli. 1992. "Fandom as Pathology: The Consequences of Characterization." In *The Adoring Audience: Fan Culture and Popular Media*, ed. Lisa A. Lewis. London: Routledge, 9–29.

Kania, Andrew. 2006. "Making Tracks: The Ontology of Rock Music." *Journal of Aesthetics and Art Criticism* 64 (Fall 2006): 402–14.

Kaskowitz, Sheryl. 2013. *God Bless America: The Surprising History of an Iconic Song*. New York: Oxford University Press.

Keightley, Keir. 2001. "Reconsidering Rock." In *The Cambridge Companion to Pop and Rock*, ed. Simon Frith, Will Straw, and John Street. Cambridge: Cambridge University Press, 109–42.

Keightley, Keir. 2003. "Low Television, High Fidelity: Taste and the Gendering of Home Entertainment Technologies." *Journal of Broadcasting and Electronic Media* 47/2: 236–59.

Keightley, Keir. 2004. "Long Play: Adult-Oriented Popular Music and the Temporal Logics of the Post-war Sound Recording Industry in the U. S. A." *Media, Culture, and Society* 26/3: 375–91.

Keightley, Keir. 2008. "Music for Middlebrows: Defining the Easy Listening Era, 1946–1966." *American Music* 26/3: 309–35.

Keightley, Keir. 2011. "The Historical Consciousness of Sunshine Pop." *Journal of Popular Music Studies* 23/3: 343–61.

Keightley, Keir. 2015. "The Pantophonographic Patsy." *The Cine-Files* 8. http://www.thecine-files.com/dossier-on-film-sound/.

Kent, Nick. 1975a. "The Last Beach Movie: Brian Wilson, 1942–." *New Musical Express*, June 21.

Kent, Nick. 1975b. "The Last Beach Movie, Part 2." *New Musical Express*, June 28.

Kent, Nick. 1975c. "The Last Beach Movie, Part 3." *New Musical Express*, July 12.

Kernfeld, Barry. 2011. *Pop Song Piracy*. Chicago: University of Chicago Press.

Klinkenborg, Verlyn. 2004. "Brian Wilson and the Significance of an Abandoned Masterpiece." *New York Times*, September 18.

Kot, Greg. 2011. "Brian Wilson's Lost *Smile* Album Finally Unearthed, with All the Trimmings." *Chicago Tribune*, November 2.

Kunkin, Arthur. 1964. "Why We Appear." *Los Angeles Free Press* 1/2 (July 30): 1.

Laing, Dave. 2015. *One Chord Wonders: Power and Meaning in Punk Rock*. London: PM Press.

Lambert, Philip. 2007. *Inside the Music of Brian Wilson: The Songs, Sounds, and Influences of the Beach Boys' Founding Genius*. New York: Continuum.

Lambert, Philip. 2008. "Brian Wilson's Pet Sounds." *Twentieth-Century Music* 5/1: 109–33.

Lavin, Maud. 1992. "Photomontage, Mass Culture, and Modernity." In *Montage and Modern Life, 1919–1942*. Cambridge: MIT Press, 37–59.

Leaf, David. 1977. "Hello." *Pet Sounds*, February 2.

Leaf, David. 1985. *The Beach Boys and the California Myth*. Philadelphia: Courage.

Leaf, David. 1993. Liner notes to *Good Vibrations: Thirty Years of the Beach Boys* (Capitol D-207100).

Leaf, David. 1996. *The Making of Pet Sounds*. In Beach Boys, *The Pet Sounds Sessions* (Capitol Records CDP 7243 8 37662 2 2).

Leaf, David. 1997a. "Landmark Albums: *Pet Sounds*." In Abbott 1997, 40–42.

Leaf, David. 1997b. Liner notes to *Pet Sounds Sessions* (Capitol 7243-8-37662-2-2).

Leary, Timothy, Ralph Metzner, and Richard Alpert. 1995. *The Psychedelic Experience: A Manual Based on the Tibetan Book of the Dead*. New York: Citadel.

Lennon, John. 2000. *Lennon Remembers*. New ed. New York: Verso.

Letcher, Andy. 2006. *Shroom: A Cultural History of the Magic Mushroom*. London: Faber and Faber.

Levine, Lawrence W. 1988. *Highbrow/Lowbrow*. Cambridge: Harvard University Press.

Levy, Joe. 2005. *Rolling Stone: The 500 Greatest Albums of All Time*. New York: Wenner.

Lieberman, Robbie. 1989. *"My Song Is My Weapon": People's Songs, American Communism, and the Politics of Culture, 1930–50*. Urbana: University of Illinois Press.

Lipton, Lawrence. 1959. *The Holy Barbarians*. New York: Julian Messner.

Madsen, Deborah L. 1998. *American Exceptionalism*. Edinburgh: University of Edinburgh Press.

Magee, Jeffrey. 2000. "Irving Berlin's 'Blue Skies': Ethnic Affiliations and Musical Transformations." *Musical Quarterly* 84/4: 537–80.

Marcuse, Herbert. 1968. *Negations: Essays in Critical Theory*. Harmondsworth: Penguin.

Marcuse, Herbert. 1972. *One-Dimensional Man*. London: Abacus.

Marshall, Lee. 2005. *Bootlegging: Romanticism and Copyright in the Music Industry*. London: Sage.

Marshall, Lee. 2007. *Bob Dylan: The Never Ending Star*. London: Polity.

Matheson, Carl, and Ben Caplan. "Ontology." In *The Routledge Companion to Philosophy and Music*, ed. Theodore Gracyk and Andrew Kania. New York: Routledge, 38–47.

Matthews, Scott A. 2004. *Riptionary: Surf Lingo Lexicon*. iUniverse.

May, Kirse Granat. 2002. *Golden State, Golden Youth: The California Image in Popular Culture*. Chapel Hill: University of North Carolina Press.

Maynard, John Arthur. 1991. *Venice West: The Beat Generation in Southern California*. New Brunswick, N.J.: Rutgers University Press.

McBride, David. 2003. "Death City Radicals: The Counterculture in Los Angeles." In *The New Left Revisited*, ed. John McMillian and Paul Buhle. Philadelphia: Temple University Press, 110–36.

McLean, Albert F. 1965. *American Vaudeville as Ritual*. Lexington: University of Kentucky Press.

McNaught, Carmel, and Paul Lam. 2010. "Using Wordle as a Supplementary Research Tool." *Qualitative Report* 15/3: 630–43.

McParland, Stephen J. 2006. *Surf Music USA: All the Surf, Hot-Rod, Motorcycle, and Skateboard Hits 1960–1965*. Sydney: CMusic.

Menconi, David. 2004. "Best Music." *News and Observer*, December 26.

Miller, Jim. 1992. "The Beach Boys." In *The Rolling Stone Illustrated History of Rock & Roll*. New edition. New York: Random House.

Mills, C. Wright. 1959. *The Sociological Imagination*. New York: Oxford University Press.

Minow, Newton. 1961. "Address to the National Association of Broadcasters Convention." Washington, D.C., May 9.

Moon, Tom. 2004. "Lost and Now Found, Wilson's *Smile* Beams." *Philadelphia Inquirer*, September 26.

Moore, Allan F. 1992. "Patterns of Harmony." *Popular Music* 11/1: 73–106.

Moore, Allan F. 2001. *Rock: The Primary Text; Developing a Musicology of Rock*. 2nd edition. Burlington, Vt.: Ashgate.

Moore, Allan F. 2012. *Song Means: Analysing and Interpreting Recorded Popular Song*. Burlington, Vt.: Ashgate.

Mosser, Kurt. N.d. "'Cover Songs': Ambiguity, Multivalence, Polysemy." *Popular*

Musicology Online 2. http://www.popular-musicology-online.com/issues/02/mosser.html.

Murphy, James B. 2015. *Becoming the Beach Boys, 1961–1963.* Jefferson, N.C.: McFarland.

"Needling the Wax." 1964. *Teen Set,* [circa] Fall: 5–7.

Negus, Keith. 1996. *Popular Music in Theory: An Introduction.* Cambridge: Polity.

Nolan, Tom. 1966. "The Frenzied Frontier of Pop Music." *Los Angeles Times Magazine,* November 27.

Nolan, Tom. 1971. "The Beach Boys: A California Saga, Part 1." *Rolling Stone,* October 28: 32–39.

Nolan, Tom. 2008. "Ash Grove: The Other Side of Melrose." *LA Weekly,* April 16. http://www.laweekly.com/2008–04–17/music/the-other-side-of-melrose/

Nugent, Stephen. 1986. "Critical Response." *Critical Studies in Mass Communication* 3: 82–85.

O'Brien, Geoffrey. 2004. *Sonata for Jukebox: Pop Music, Memory, and the Imagined Life.* New York: Counterpoint.

Orton, James K. 1902. *Beach Boy Joe; or, Among the Life Savers.* New York: Street & Smith.

Page, Tim. 1992. *Music from the Road: Views and Reviews, 1978–1992.* New York: Oxford University Press.

Page, Tim. 2004. "Brian Wilson Finally Cracks a *Smile.*" *Washington Post,* September 29.

Parks, Van Dyke. 2006. Letter to the Editor. *New York Review of Books* 53/1 (January 12): 57.

Petridis, Alex. 2011. "The Beach Boys: *Smile* Sessions—Review." *Guardian,* October 27. http://www.theguardian.com/music/2011/oct/27/beach-boys-Smile-sessions-review.

Phoenix, Charles. 2001. *Southern California in the '50s: Sun, Fun, Fantasy.* Santa Monica, Calif.: Angel City Press.

Pinto, Aaron. 2012. "It's So Sad to Watch a Sweet Thing Die: The Beach Boys 50th Anniversary Tour, PNC Bank Arts Center, Homdel, NJ, 6/27/12." *Manik Music.* http://www.manikmusic.net/features/its-so-sad-to-watch-a-sweet-thing-die-the-beach-boys-50th-anniversary-tour-pnc-bank-arts-center-homdel-nj-62712/

Plasketes, George. 2005. "Re-flections on the Cover Age: A Collage of Continuous Coverage in Popular Music." *Popular Music and Society* 28/2: 137–61.

Ponce de Leon, Charles L. 2002. *Self-Exposure: Human Interest Journalism and the Emergence of Celebrity in America, 1890–1940.* Chapel Hill: University of North Carolina Press.

Popmatters. 2011. "The 25 Best Reissues of 2011." November 30. http://www.popmatters.com/feature/151768-the-25-best-re-issues-of-2011.

Preiss, Byron. 1979. *The Beach Boys: The Authorized Biography of America's Greatest Rock and Roll Band!* New York: Ballantine.

Price, Jeff. 2008. "Andy Lippincott: 1945–1990." *The Dead That Never Lived,* February 18. http://thedeadthatneverlived.blogspot.com/2008/02/andy-lippincott-1945–1990.html.

Priore, Dominic. 1995. *Look! Listen! Vibrate! Smile!* San Francisco: Last Gasp.

Priore, Dominic. 2005. *"Smile": The Story of Brian Wilson's Lost Masterpiece*. London: Sanctuary.

Priore, Domenic. 2007. *Riot on Sunset Strip: Rock 'n' Roll's Last Stand in Hollywood*. London: Jawbone.

Puterbaugh, Parke. 1999. "The Beats and the Birth of the Counterculture." In *The Rolling Stone Book of the Beats: The Beat Generation and the Counterculture*, ed. Holly George-Warren. London: Bloomsbury, 357–63.

"Radio Pictures Parade Today." 1931. *Los Angeles Times*, September 5.

Reynolds, Simon. 1989. "Against Health and Efficiency: Independent Music in the 1980s." In *Zoot Suits and Second Hand Dresses: An Anthology of Fashion and Music*, ed. Angela McRobbie. Basingstoke: Macmillan, 245–55.

Richardson, Mark. 2011. "The Beach Boys: The *Smile* Sessions." *Pitchfork*, November 2. http://pitchfork.com/reviews/albums/16000-the-Smile-sessions.

Riesman, David. 1950. "Listening to Popular Music." *American Quarterly* 2/4: 359–71. Reprinted Frith and Goodwin 1990, 5–13.

Riley, Tim. 1988. *Tell Me Why: The Beatles Album by Album, Song by Song, the Sixties and After*. New York: Knopf.

Robbins, Paul Jay. 1965. "Byrds Live." *Los Angeles Free Press* 2/17 (April 23): 6.

Rogan, Johnny. 2012. *Byrds: Requiem for the Timeless, Volume 1*. New York: Random House.

Rolling Stone. 2012. *500 Greatest Albums of All Time* (special collectors issue).

Romano, Andrew. 2012a. "The Beach Boys' Crazy Summer." *Daily Beast*, May 27. http://www.thedailybeast.com/newsweek/2012/05/27/the-beach-boys-crazy-summer.html.

Romano, Andrew. 2012b. "The Joe Thomas Interview: On Brian Wilson, the Beach Boys Reunion, and *That's Why God Made the Radio*." http://andrewromano.tumblr.com/joethomasbeachboys.

Rossinow, Doug. 2002. ""The Revolution Is about Our Lives": The New Left's Counterculture." In *Imagine Nation: The American Counterculture of the 1960s and '70s*, ed. Peter Braunstein and Michael William Doyle. New York: Routledge, 99–124.

Rusten, Ian, and Jon Stebbins. 2013. *The Beach Boys in Concert: The Ultimate History of America's Band on Tour and Onstage*. Milwaukee, Wisc.: Backbeat.

Samuels, David. 2004. "Language, Meaning, Modernity, and Doowop." *Semiotica* 149: 297–323.

Sanchez, Luis. 2011. "To Catch a Wave: The Beach Boys and Rock Historiography." Ph.D. diss., University of Edinburgh.

Sanjek, Russell, with David Sanjek. 1996. *Pennies from Heaven: The American Popular Music Business in the Twentieth Century*. New York: Da Capo.

Schinder, Scott. 2008. "The Beach Boys." In *Icons of Rock: An Encyclopedia of the Legends Who Changed Music Forever*, ed. Scott Schinder and Andy Schwartz. Westport, Conn.: Greenwood Press / ABC-CLIO, 101–30.

Scobie, Stephen. 2003. *Alias Bob Dylan Revisited*. Calgary: Red Deer Press.

Seidenbaum, Art. 1966. "Beach Boys Riding the Crest of Pop-Rock Wave." *Los Angeles Times*, March 20.

Sharp, Ken. 1992. "Love among the Ruins." *Goldmine*, September 18: 12–22, 146.

Shield, David S. 2013. *Still: American Silent Motion Picture Photography*. Chicago: University of Chicago Press.

Shirley, Wayne. 1997. "The Coming of 'Deep River.'" *American Music* 15/4: 493–534.

Siegel, Jules. 1967. "Goodbye Surfing, Hello God! The Religious Conversion of the Beach Boys." *Cheetah*, October: 27. Reprinted Priore 1995, 82–91; and in *The Rock History Reader*, ed. Theo Cafetonis, 2nd edition (New York: Routledge, 2012), 83–94.

Simpson, Kim. 2011. *Early 70s Radio: The American Format Revolution*. New York: Continuum.

"Singles Hit Makers Crash LP Charts Often, Fade Fast." 1963. *Billboard*, September 7: 3.

Snow, Mat. 2008 "Endless Summer." *Mojo* 178 (September): 99.

Sorapure, Madeleine. 2010. "Information Visualization, Web 2.0, and the Teaching of Writing." *Computers and Composition* 27/1: 59–70.

Starr, Kevin. 2009. *Golden Dreams: California in an Age of Abundance, 1950–1963*. New York: Oxford University Press.

Starr, Larry. 1994. "The Shadow of a Smile: The Beach Boys Album That Refused to Die." *Journal of Popular Music Studies* 6: 38–59.

Starr, Larry. 2007. Review of *Brian Wilson Presents Smile*. *Journal of the Society for American Music* 1/2 (May): 285–89.

Starr, Larry, and Christopher Waterman. 2014. *American Popular Music: From Minstrelsy to MP3*. 4th edition. New York: Oxford University Press.

Staton, Scott. 2005. "A Lost Pop Symphony." *New York Review of Books* 52/14 (September 22): 58–61.

Stebbins, Jon, with David Marks. 2007. *The Lost Beach Boy*. London: Virgin.

Stebbins, Jon. 2011. *The Beach Boys FAQ: All That's Left to Know about America's Band*. Milwaukee: Backbeat.

Sten, Mark. 1978. "The In-Between Years (1958–63)." In *Rock Almanac*, ed. Stephen Nugent and Charlie Gillett. Garden City, N.Y.: Anchor, 55–76.

Stephenson, Ken. 2002. *What to Listen for in Rock: A Stylistic Analysis*. New Haven: Yale University Press.

Sullivan, Denise. 2009. "Ed Pearl: Back to the Ash Grove." *Crawdaddy*, March 4. http://www.crawdaddy.com/index.php/2009/03/04/ed-pearl-back-to-the-ash-grove.

Summach, Jason. 2011. "The Structure, Function, and Genesis of the Prechorus." *Music Theory Online* 17.3.

"Teen-Beat Soars on LP Chart." 1964. *Billboard*, September 26: 1, 8.

Templeton, Ty. 2010. "The Seven Best Gay Characters in Comics." Comments section. Ty Templeton's ART LAND!! September 12. http://tytempletonart.wordpress.com/2010/09/12/the-seven-best-gay-characters-in-comics/

Thomas, Tracy. 1967. "Brian: Loved or Loathed Genius." *New Music Express*, January 28.

"Tiger Beat Salutes Chuck Berry: To Many, Including the Beatles, His Talent Is the Greatest in the Rock World." 1965. *Tiger Beat*, September: 4.

Torgoff, Martin. 2004. *Can't Find My Way Home: America in the Great Stoned Age, 1945–2000*. New York: Simon and Schuster.

Traynor, Don. 1966. "Brian, Pop Genius!" *Melody Maker*, May 21.

Trudeau, Gary. 2010. *40: A Doonesbury Retrospective.* New York: Andrews McNeel.

Umphred, Neal. 1997. "Let's Go Away for a While: The Continuing Saga of Brian Wilson's *Pet Sounds.*" In Abbott 1997, 28–39.

Unterberger, Richie. 2002. *Turn! Turn! Turn! The '60s Folk-Rock Revolution.* San Francisco: Backbeat.

Van der Merwe, Peter. 1992. *Origins of the Popular Style: The Antecedents of Twentieth-Century Popular Music.* New York: Clarendon.

Vancouver Sun. 1993. "Beach Boys: After Three Decades the Kings of Surfin' Music Are Still Going Strong with the Release of Deluxe Discs." June 29.

Vosse, Michael. 1969. "Our Exagmination Round His Factification for Incamination of Work in Progress: Michael Vosse talks about *Smile.*" *Fusion* [Boston] 8 (April 14): n.p.

Walker, Michael. 2006. *Laurel Canyon: The Inside Story of Rock 'n' Roll's Legendary Neighborhood.* New York: Faber and Faber.

Walsh, Alan. 1966. "Brian Wilson's Puppets?" *Melody Maker*, November 12.

"WB-Reprise Target: Teen Mart." 1964. *Billboard*, October 17: 8.

Weinraub, Bernard. 2004. "Rebuilding Brian Wilson's *Smile.*" *New York Times*, September 12.

Weinstein, Deena. 1998. "The History of Rock's Pasts through Rock Covers." In *Mapping the Beat: Popular Music and Contemporary Theory*, ed. Thomas Swiss, John Sloop, and Andrew Herman. London: Blackwell, 137–51.

Wenner, Jann. 1967. "Rock and Roll Music." *Rolling Stone*, December 14.

Whitburn, Joel. 2004. *The Billboard Book of Top 40 Hits.* 8th edition. New York: Billboard.

White, Timothy. 1994. *The Nearest Faraway Place: Brian Wilson, the Beach Boys, and the Southern California Experience.* New York: Henry Holt.

Whiteley, Sheila. 1992. *The Space between the Notes: Rock and the Counter-culture.* London: Routledge.

Whyte, William, Jr. 1957. *The Organization Man.* Garden City, N.Y.: Doubleday Anchor.

Williams, Paul. 1967. "What Goes On." *Crawdaddy*, March: 19–23.

Williams, Paul. 1968. "Outlaw Blues." *Crawdaddy*, February: 5–18.

Williams, Paul. 1997. *Brian Wilson and the Beach Boys: How Deep Is the Ocean?* London: Omnibus.

Williams, Paul, and David Anderle. 1968a. "Brian: Part One." *Crawdaddy*, March-April: 18–23.

Williams, Paul, and David Anderle. 1968b. "Brian: Part Two." *Crawdaddy*, May: 33–41.

Williams, Paul, and David Anderle. 1968c. "Brian: Part Three." *Crawdaddy*, June: 16–22.

Wilson, Brian, with Todd Gold. 1991. *Wouldn't It Be Nice: My Own Story.* New York: HarperCollins.

Wolfe, Tom. 1968. *The Electric Kool-Aid Acid Test.* New York: Bantam.

Wolfe, Tom. 1989. *The Pump House Gang.* London: Black Swan.

Zappa, Frank, with Peter Occhiogrosso. 1989. *The Real Frank Zappa Book.* New York: Poseidon.

Videos

Blackburn, Ida B. 1964. Interview with the Beach Boys. Springlake Park, Oklahoma City, August 28 or 29. http://www.youtube.com/watch?v=6Z4N4BSs4Ic.

Coelenbrander, Kees, dir. 2002. *Van Dyke Parks: Een Obsessie Voor Muzick*. Amsterdam: Palantine Pictures.

Endless Summer Quarterly. 2010. *Endless Sky, Vol. IV: Tony Asher and Alan Boyd*, ed. Chris Allen. Charlotte, N.C.: Endless Sky Video.

"Far Away Places." 2012. *Mad Men*. AMC-TV (April 22).

Ghomeshi, Jian. 2011. Interview with Brian Wilson. CBC Radio, May 24. http://www.youtube.com/watch?v=_m1va4JjgfY.

Godley, Kevin, Bob Smeaton, and Geoff Wonfor, dirs. 1995. *The Beatles Anthology*. United Kingdom: Capitol Video.

Leaf, David, dir. 2005. *Beautiful Dreamer: Brian Wilson and the Story of Smile*. Los Angeles: LSL Productions.

Was, Don, dir. 1995. *I Just Wasn't Made for These Times*. Los Angeles: Cro Magnon Productions / Palomar Pictures.

Contributors

Dale Carter is an associate professor of American studies in the Department of English, School of Communication and Culture, Aarhus University (Denmark), and director of the university's American Studies Center. He is author and editor of a number of books dealing mainly with aspects of twentieth-century American history, society, and culture, and has published a variety of scholarly articles on Brian Wilson, Van Dyke Parks, and the Beach Boys.

Kirk Curnutt is professor and chair of English at Troy University's Montgomery, Alabama, campus. He is the author of *Brian Wilson*, an entry in Equinox Publishing's Icons of Pop Music series (2012). Among his other works are three novels, *Breathing Out the Ghost* (River City, 2008), *Dixie Noir* (Five Star, 2009), and *Raising Aphrodite* (River City, 2015), plus studies of Gertrude Stein (Greenwood, 2000), Ernest Hemingway (Gale, 2000), and F. Scott Fitzgerald (Oxford, 2004; Cambridge, 2007).

Andrew Flory is an assistant professor of music at Carleton College, where he teaches courses in American music, rock, rhythm and blues, and jazz. His book, *I Hear a Symphony: Motown and Crossover R&B*, is forthcoming from the University of Michigan Press. He is also coauthor of the history of rock textbook *What's That Sound?* (Norton).

Daniel Harrison is the Allen Forte Professor of Music Theory at Yale University. He has also taught at the University of Rochester and the Eastman School of Music. He specializes in tonal theory, especially at historical margins of the common-practice era, and is the author of *Harmonic Function in Chromatic Music* (Chicago, 1994) and *Pieces of Tradition*

(Oxford, 2015). Previous work on the Beach Boys has appeared in *Understanding Rock* (ed. Covach and Boone, Oxford) and in the film *I Just Wasn't Made for These Times.*

Keir Keightley is associate professor of media studies at the University of Western Ontario and teaches in the Popular Music and Culture Master's program offered jointly with the Faculty of Music. His work has appeared in *Musical Quarterly, American Music, Media Culture and Society, Popular Music,* and *Modernism/Modernity,* and in edited collections including *The Cambridge Companion to Pop and Rock, Movie Music: The Film Reader, Migrating Music,* and *The Sage Handbook of Popular Music.* He is currently working on a book about early critiques of mass culture entitled *Tin Pan Allegory: Music, Media, Modernity.*

Philip Lambert is a professor of music at Baruch College and the Graduate Center of the City University of New York. He has written books about the music of Charles Ives (Yale, 1997), Brian Wilson (Continuum, 2007), Jerry Bock and Sheldon Harnick (Oxford, 2011), and Alec Wilder (Illinois, 2013), and a music fundamentals textbook, *Principles of Music* (Oxford, 2014). He also served as editor of a book of essays on Charles Ives (Cambridge, 1997) and of the journals *Theory & Practice* (1994–1996) and *Music Theory Spectrum* (1998–2000).

Jadey O'Regan is a lecturer in popular music and performance at the Sydney Conservatorium of Music, Australia. She completed her doctorate at the Queensland Conservatorium (Griffith University) with a dissertation on the early music of the Beach Boys and the construction of the group's unique sound. Her research interests include contemporary music history, popular music analysis, and power-pop music of the 1990s. She also has a degree in audio production and is an active songwriter and performing musician.

Larry Starr holds a Ruth Sutton Waters endowed professorship at the University of Washington, Seattle, where he heads the new program in American Music Studies. He has written books on the music of Ives (Schirmer, 1992), Copland (Pendragon, 2002), and Gershwin (Yale, 2011), and is coauthor of *American Popular Music: From Minstrelsy to MP3* (Oxford, 4th edition, 2013) and *Rock: Music, Culture, and Business* (Oxford, 2012).

Index